Vanuatu

a Lonely Planet travel survival kit

David Harcombe
Denis O'Byrne

World view resoirse

Vanuatu

2nd edition

Published by
Lonely Planet Publications
Head Office: PO Box 617, Hawthorn, Vic 3122, Australia
Branches: 155 Filbert St, Suite 251, Oakland, CA 94607, USA
               10a Spring Place, London NW5 3BH, UK
               71 bis rue du Cardinal Lemoine, 75005 Paris, France

Printed by
Colorcraft Ltd, Hong Kong

Photographs by
Denis O'Byrne (DO)
Air Vanuatu, Melbourne (AV)
Michael Czarny (MC)
Mark Spencer (MS)
David Harcombe (DH)

Front cover: Scuba diving off Bokissa Island (Michael Cufer, Aquamarine Ltd)

First Published
August 1991

This Edition
August 1995

National Library of Australia Cataloguing in Publication Data

Harcombe, David.
    Vanuatu: a travel survival kit.

    2nd ed.
    Includes index.
    ISBN 0 86442 293 8.

    1. Vanuatu – Description and travel – Guidebooks.
    I. O'Byrne, Denis, 1947- . II. Title. (Series: Lonely
    Planet travel survival kit).

919.59504

text & maps © Lonely Planet 1995
photos © photographers as indicated 1995
climate charts compiled from information supplied by Patrick J Tyson, © Patrick J Tyson, 1995

David Harcombe

Born in England, David spent much of his early years reading about faraway places and peoples. This led him, after an Oxford politics and economics degree, to work as a fundraiser for Oxfam, a large British-based overseas aid charity. After brief visits to Eastern Europe and West Africa, he was lured eastwards through Asia to Australia. By now an avid fan of freedom and travel, he returned to Australia after a spell in the Caribbean, Latin America and southern Africa, to live in its remote north-western bush, working among Aboriginal Australians. While there he became a sometime gold prospector and amateur disc jockey on a community radio station.

David is the author of Lonely Planet's *Solomon Islands – a travel survival kit.* When he's not writing, his interests include scuba diving and the underwater world, soccer, squash, jogging, exotic food, reading comic strips, lazing around on sandy beaches and just going places.

Denis O'Byrne

Denis was born and bred in country South Australia and received his first taste of overseas travel as an army surveyor in the 1960s. Since then he's earned a living at various pursuits including mine surveyor, national park ranger, plant operator, builder's labourer and travel writer. He has travelled in Europe, southern Africa, New Guinea and New Zealand and lived in Zimbabwe for a time. Currently a freelance writer and building consultant, Denis lives in Alice Springs in the centre of Australia. He contributed a major share of Lonely Planet's *Outback Australia* before heading to Vanuatu to update this book.

From the Authors

Many people provided expert advice and much assistance during this update and Denis is grateful to them all. In particular, thanks go to Luca and Steve for their kind hospitality. Special thanks also go to Max Stephen Aru, Stan Barnett, Ann Devine, Caroline Goodall, Kevin & Mayumi Green, Mike van Hessing, Fred Kleckham, Eileen Ligo, Denise Parent, Ralph Regenvanu and Karl Waldeback. Denis would also like to mention Rob van Driesum, publisher at Lonely Planet, whose idea it was in the first place.

This Book

The 1st edition of this book was researched

and written by David Harcombe. It was revised and completely updated for this 2nd edition by Denis O'Byrne. Thanks to the following readers whose letters helped with this update (apologies if we've misspelt your name):

Alain Avreault (F), John Burton, Alison Cavill (AUS), Ronald Corlette-Theuil (F), Ian Diddams (UK), Robert Franz (AUS), Norma Glanfielsd (AUS), Harriet Loeffler (UK), James McIntyre (USA), Jim McKay (AUS), Bronwyn Meyrick (AUS), Christian Michel (F), Eugenie Ombler (NZ), Wendy Ostgaard (USA), Alain Portier (F), Julie Reeves (AUS), Elsie Richards (NZ), Guenther Schaefer (D), David Sharland

AUS – Australia, D – Germany, F – France, J – Japan

From the Publisher

This second edition of *Vanuatu – a travel survival kit* was edited by Jane Fitzpatrick. The incomparable Jacqui Saunders was responsible for maps, design, artwork and layout. Stephen Townshend pummelled the book into shape and put it through production. Thanks to Louise Callan for her work on the language section, Kay Dancey for additional help with maps, Rob van Driesum for editorial advice, Simon Bracken for cover design, Margaret Jung and Ann Jeffree for extra illustrations, and Sharan Kaur, Brigitte Barta, Mary Neighbour and Chris Wyness for proofing. Special thanks go to Katie Purvis who helped proof and organise the book and to Sharon Wertheim who put together another marvellous index.

Warning & Request

Things change – prices go up, schedules alter, good places go bad, and bad places go bankrupt – nothing stays the same. So if you find things better or worse, recently opened or long since closed, please write and tell us, so we can make the next edition that much better!

Your letters will be used to help update future editions, and where possible, important changes will also be included as a Stop Press section in reprints.

We greatly appreciate all information that is sent to us by travellers. Back at Lonely Planet we employ a hard-working, though cheerful, readers' letters team to sort through the many letters we receive. The best letters will be rewarded with a free copy of the next edition or another Lonely Planet guide if you prefer. We give away lots of books at Lonely Planet, but, unfortunately, not every letter or postcard receives one.

Contents

Map Legend

BOUNDARIES

.... International Boundary
.... Internal Boundary
.... Regional Boundary
.... Disputed Boundary
.... Equator
.... Tropics
.... Latitudes & Longitudes

ROUTES

.... Highway
.... Unsealed Road or Track
.... Four Wheel Drive Track
.... City Street
.... Walking Track
.... Ferry Route
.... Fence with Gate
.... Bridge

AREA FEATURES

.... Park, Gardens
.... National Park
.... Built-Up Area
.... Pedestrian Mall
.... Market
.... Cemetery
.... Reef
.... Beach or Desert
.... Rocks

HYDROGRAPHIC FEATURES

.... Coastline
.... River, Creek
.... Intermittent River or Creek
.... Lake, Intermittent Lake
.... Canal
.... Swamp

SYMBOLS

✪ CAPITAL		National Capital
◉ Capital		Regional Capital
◍ CITY		Major City
● City		City
● Town		Town
● Village		Village
■		Place to Stay
▼		Place to Eat
▼		Pub, Bar
✉	☎	Post Office, Telephone
❶	⦵	Tourist Information, Bank
⬤	℗	Transport, Parking
🏛	⌂	Museum, Youth Hostel
⚏	⚐	Caravan Park, Camping Ground
⚑	⚓	Golf Course, Diving Site
† ◼ †		Church, Cathedral
⚚	✿	Mosque, Synagogue

✪	★	Hospital, Police Station
✈	✝	Airport, Airfield
◳	✿	Swimming Pool, Gardens
❖	🐘	Shopping Centre, Zoo
⚘	⊓	Winery or Vineyard, Picnic Site
←	A25	One Way Street, Route Number
	∴	Archaeological Site or Ruins
🏛	⚲	Stately Home, Monument
♖	◼	Castle, Tomb
⌒	⌂	Cave, Hut or Chalet
▲	☀	Mountain or Hill, Lookout
⚔	⚓	Lighthouse, Shipwreck
)(	⌐	Pass, Spring
		Ancient or City Wall
		Rapids, Waterfalls
		Cliff or Escarpment, Tunnel
		Railway Station

Note: not all symbols displayed above appear in this book

Introduction

Vanuatu (pronounced 'Van-WAH-too') is generally taken to mean 'our land'. Its people are called ni-Vanuatu, or 'of Vanuatu'.

Prior to independence from the UK and France in 1980, this long, Y-shaped archipelago of mainly very small islands was known as the New Hebrides. Captain James Cook gave the country this name during his explorations in 1774 – the archipelago's dark, rugged islands reminded him of the Hebrides group, off Scotland's western coast.

Vanuatu has three official languages: Bislama, English and French. Bislama – a type of pidgin English – is spoken by about 60% of the population, making it the most widely understood of the three. English is next. Otherwise, Vanuatu is a veritable Tower of Babel with at least 105 distinct traditional languages still in use.

The national capital, Port Vila, or Vila as it is more commonly called, is the attractive and charming hub of the country's tourist trade. Most visitors get so wrapped up in its many attractions that they forget to look elsewhere. This is a shame, because there are numerous other outstanding highlights including the volcanoes on Tanna and Ambrym, the land-diving ceremonies of Pentecost, and Santo's scuba-diving sites. There are also plenty of excellent walking opportunities, regardless of whether you're a masochistic enthusiast or just out for a stroll.

Until recently it was official government policy to restrict tourism to just a few areas of the country. This has now changed. Village-based enterprises such as tours and guest houses have sprung up in many places

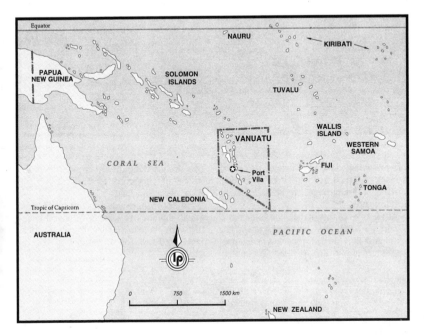

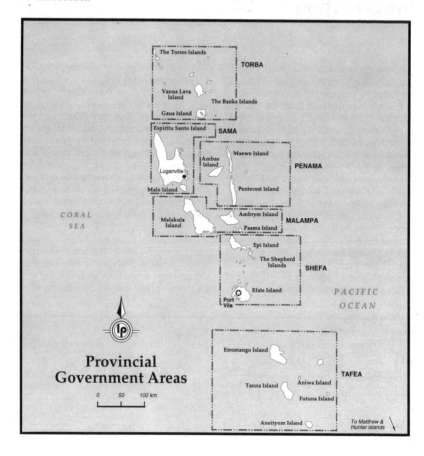

The Torres Islands

TORBA

Vanua Lava
Island

The Banks Islands

Gaua Island

Espiritu Santo Island   SAMA

Maewo Island

Ambae
Island

PENAMA

Luganville

Malo Island

Pentecost Island

Ambrym Island   MALAMPA

Malakula
Island

Paama Island

CORAL
SEA

Epi Island

The Shepherd
Islands   SHEFA

Efate Island

PACIFIC
OCEAN

Port
Vila

Provincial Government Areas

0   50   100 km

Erromango Island

TAFEA

Tanna Island   Aniwa Island

Futuna Island

Aneityum Island   To Matthew &
Hunter islands

that previously saw few visitors. However, the lack of infrastructure, particularly transport, is a great handicap to these new developments.

At the time of this update, the Luganville airport on Santo was being upgraded. On completion it will be promoted as an alternative international gateway to the country.

This will no doubt bring an increase in the number of tours and other services operating in the northern islands.

Further changes came in November 1994, when Vanuatu's 11 local government councils were abolished and replaced by a less centralised form of six provincial governments.

Facts about the Country

HISTORY

Vanuatu emerged from the sea about 22 million years ago, when a series of earth movements on the ocean floor forced huge underwater mountains to the surface. This event created the northern islands of Santo, Malakula and the Torres group. Next to appear were Maewo and Pentecost, between five and 11 million years ago. All the remaining islands resulted from two separate phases of earth movement that took place less than five million years ago.

Until about two million years ago these islands covered only a fraction of their present area. The dramatic increase during this geological blink of an eye has largely resulted from continual slow uplift, together with the formation of fringing coral reefs. On some islands, ancient reefs have been raised several hundred metres above sea level. As well, new land is continuously being created as a result of volcanic activity.

First Arrivals

Most historians believe that the peoples of the western Pacific originated in South-East Asia. From there, at least 40,000 years ago, they began moving through Indonesia and the islands of the New Guinea chain towards Australia and the South Pacific. These proto-Melanesians colonised the many islands further south, including the Solomons and Vanuatu archipelagoes, beginning about 3000 BC.

The earliest evidence of human occupation discovered so far in Vanuatu comes from a site on Malo Island, in the northern part of the country. Archaeologists claim this was first settled in about 1400 BC. The islanders who left these remains were people of the Lapita culture, named after an archaeological site at Lapita in New Caledonia. In the course of a remarkable millennium of long-range exploratory canoe voyages, they left their highly distinctive, pinhole-incised pottery at a string of island and coastal sites,

from north-eastern Papua New Guinea all the way to Samoa.

The Lapita people, possibly finding the larger islands already occupied, chose small islands or coastal areas as their new homes. They brought with them yams, taro, domesticated animals such as pigs, poultry and dogs, and a considerable appetite for shellfish.

By 500 BC the more intrepid members of the Lapita culture had reached the eastern Pacific. Meanwhile, other Melanesian peoples were spreading slowly southwards through the archipelago and intermarrying with those already there.

Between the 11th and 15th centuries AD, a new wave of settlers arrived but this time from the east. These were Polynesian people from the central Pacific who, spurred by population pressures on their home islands, made long-distance migratory journeys in sailing canoes holding up to 50 people. A number of Vanuatu's traditions tell of cultural heroes arriving around this time from islands to the east, bringing with them new skills and customs.

Pre-European Times

Island communities were separated by forest and broad stretches of sea. People lived in small clans on land which their ancestors had occupied since their arrival many generations before.

Everyone lived in the shadow of their ancestral spirits. Some ghosts were usually benevolent, others were believed to be always hostile, quick to harass the living with famines, natural disasters or unsuccessful wars. Such spirits had to be placated, so magic was widespread. When anyone suffered a serious misfortune, sorcery was automatically assumed to be the culprit.

In the northern part of Vanuatu, status within the clan was earned by males through grade-taking ceremonies, known as the *nimangki* system. Lavish pig-killing rituals and feasts were held to promote each adult male's rise up his village's social ladder. Each grade meant a step closer to achieving chiefly status. On a supernatural plane, the more grades a man had earned, the more powerful would be his defences against sorcery while alive, and the more potent would be his spirit after death.

Deep suspicion was shown towards anyone from another island, tribe or settlement, especially if they spoke a different language. In some areas, coastal and inland people were hostile towards each other until the mid-20th century. Any journey away from the safety of one's own clan was fraught with danger.

War was a regular activity for men. Although large-scale raids did occur, minor skirmishes and ambushes were the more usual form of combat. Usually these conflicts arose over such matters as the theft of coconuts or other crops, intrusion into another group's land, or through suspected sorcery.

Often, however, the attackers' aim was to kill or capture one or two males, whom they would carry off to eat. Only men of certain rank were allowed to consume the victims. It was considered a friendly gesture to present a neighbouring settlement with an arm or leg ready for cooking!

Naturally the injured village would prepare its own form of reprisal. Such hostilities, once started, often continued indefinitely.

Meanwhile, the women were busy attending to less exciting but more necessary chores such as gardening, cooking and child-minding. Despite working much harder than men, women were generally considered as having inferior social status. In fact, many husbands thought their pigs were more important than their wives – a situation that still exists.

Spaniards on the Scene

Meanwhile in early 17th-century Europe, there was a strong belief that a great southern continent, or Terra Australis as it was called, must exist to balance the northern

Pedro Fernandez de Quiros

hemisphere's huge landmasses. Two Spanish expeditions had already left Peru in the previous century to search for it. Although they visited the Solomon Islands, the fabled continent remained elusive.

The chief pilot of the second Solomons expedition in 1595 was Pedro Fernandez de Quiros, a Portuguese in the service of the Spanish crown. For 10 years, Quiros petitioned first the Spanish king, then Pope Clement VIII and finally the Viceroy of Peru to finance another expedition to the long-sought land. Finally in 1605, he was given command of an expedition to find the missing continent, colonise it for Spain and convert its people to Roman Catholicism.

On 21 December 1605 Quiros left Callao in Peru with three small ships. Aboard them were 130 adventurers serving as soldiers and sailors, plus 10 monks. Quiros' indecision over which course to sail, his injunctions against swearing and gambling, and his insistence on daily prayers soon brought his rough-and-ready crew close to mutiny.

Fortunately, on 25 April 1606 the lookout spied land. It was the tall peak of Mere Lava, one of the Banks Islands in northern

Vanuatu. After a brief, and initially well-received, stopover at nearby Gaua, Quiros pressed on.

On 3 May 1606, the small Spanish fleet sailed into Big Bay in northern Santo. Quiros believed he had at last found the great southern continent and named it 'Austrialia del Espirito Santo'.

Quiros claimed Santo and all lands south of it to be under Spain's rule, and attempted to make a permanent settlement at Big Bay. The fledgling colony lasted a mere 54 days before it was abandoned following the desertion of Quiros' mutinous crew.

Later Explorers

In 1766 the French nobleman Louis Antoine de Bougainville left France with two ships on a voyage of exploration. On 21 May 1768 he sighted Maewo and Pentecost in eastern Vanuatu. He landed at Ambae and Malo, sailed between Malakula and Santo (proving Vanuatu's largest island was not the fabled Terra Australis after all) and rediscovered Big Bay in northern Santo. Displaying his classical education, Bougainville named Vanuatu's northern islands Les Grandes

Captain James Cook

Cyclades, or 'The Great Cyclades', after the Greek islands of the same name.

On 16 July 1774, in his second Pacific expedition, Captain James Cook in his ship HMS *Resolution* also spotted Bougainville's Grandes Cyclades. Sailing southwards from Maewo to Tanna and Futuna, he then turned northwards towards northern Santo, leaving the island group 46 days later.

As with Quiros and Bougainville, Cook gave his own names to the islands he visited. Many are still in use today, including Tanna, Erromango, Ambrym and the Shepherds group. He renamed the archipelago the New Hebrides, by which it was known up to the country's independence in 1980.

Several other explorers followed over the next 20 years. In 1788 the Frenchman La Pérouse and his two ships, the *Boussole* and *Astrolabe*, may well have passed through the archipelago. However, no records of their route exist as both ships were lost in the south-eastern Solomons.

The next explorer on the scene was William Bligh in 1789, shortly after the famous mutiny on HMS *Bounty* in Tongan waters. While on his epic longboat journey to safety in Timor in the East Indies, he sighted several previously unrecorded islands in the northern Banks group. He returned in 1792 to confirm these discoveries.

Two more Frenchmen then came by searching for their missing compatriot, La Pérouse. D'Entrecasteaux was the first in 1793, followed by Dumont d'Urville in 1828. Although whalers occasionally made landfall on isolated islands in the archipelago around this time, they seldom reported their discoveries. Instead, they kept them secret to preserve their commercial advantage.

The Sandalwood Trade

Traditionally, the Chinese have always been major consumers of sweet-smelling sandalwood, which they burn as incense. By the 1820s most sandalwood supplies in the northern Pacific were exhausted and traders were searching for new sources.

In 1825 the Irish explorer-trader Peter

Dillon reported seeing huge numbers of sandalwood trees on Erromango in southern Vanuatu. Other traders, keen to satisfy the demands of the Chinese market, soon found smaller quantities on several other islands, particularly Efate, Aneityum, Tanna and Santo.

Initially, a token payment such as a small piece of metal, a goat, a cat or a dog was sufficient to buy a boatload of the aromatic wood. But as the supply of slow-growing sandalwood dwindled, islanders began demanding weapons, ammunition and tobacco as payment. Sometimes the payment required was men from enemy villages, who were eaten. Sandalwood negotiations were always delicate. Not only did the crews have to contend with the ferocity of the islanders, but also with the lack of widely influential chiefs in ni-Vanuatu society, the constant interclan warfare, and the many different dialects and languages. Sometimes villagers would try to persuade crews to join them in their wars against their neighbours, pleading for the ships' guns to be used to lay waste their enemies' huts.

There were many attacks on ships' crews, often in return for a previous White atrocity. While the Europeans usually only wished to punish guilty individuals, the Melanesians would consider a whole tribe guilty of a misdemeanour committed by one of its members. In islanders' eyes, all White men were from the one tribe. So, if one ship cheated some villagers or fired its cannon at them, the next vessel, or group of Europeans, could expect an automatic and violent reprisal.

The sandalwood trade virtually ceased in 1868 with the removal of the archipelago's last accessible stands.

Blackbirding

As the sandalwood trade declined, an even more insidious one developed on the islands of Vanuatu and elsewhere in the western Pacific. This was blackbirding, or 'labour recruiting'. Increasingly, cheap labour was in demand for the sugar cane industries of Fiji and Queensland, the nickel mines of New Caledonia, and the coconut plantations of Western Samoa. Satisfying this demand became a major commercial activity from 1863 onwards.

It's true that many ni-Vanuatu were keen to work abroad. They wanted to savour the European way of life at first hand, and to acquire a broader selection of modern goods than was available on trading ships.

Others, however, were reluctant to go and unscrupulous blackbirders, or 'agents', devised various means to secure their services. Often people were simply captured ashore, taken aboard and chained below deck. On other occasions whole villages were enticed aboard ship by the promise of trade, then seized. A blackbirder might dress up in priestly garments, hold a shoreside service and then kidnap the worshippers.

Recruits were shown three raised fingers by the ship's crew, and encouraged to believe they would only be away for three months, not three years as this gesture really meant. Often this initial three-year term was arbitrarily extended, sometimes up to as long as 12 years once the islander was safely overseas. When they reached Queensland or Fiji, it was common practice for the unfortunate victims to be lined up on the beach and sold to the highest bidder.

The profits made by blackbirders were such that a ship's purchase price could be paid out in less than two voyages. Many vessels made several round trips a year, earning huge sums for their owners.

Blackbirding ships were often extremely overcrowded and unhygienic. In addition, the limited supply of food served was usually quite different from an islander's normal diet. Consequently many recruits died while still at sea, or from overwork once they reached their destination.

Frequently, all a blackbirded islander would be able to show from three years' overseas labour was about 30 items of personal property. These usually included a musket, a hatchet, some knives and ammunition, a simple musical instrument such as a jew's-harp, and an outfit of European clothes.

Some returned labour recruits were carelessly dropped off at the wrong island. Such unfortunates would be promptly robbed of their hard-earned wealth, and perhaps killed and eaten into the bargain.

Islanders soon realised how treacherous the blackbirders were. Labour ships were targets for reprisals in some areas as late as the 1900s. Some returned labourers, incensed by their mistreatment on overseas plantations, deliberately enticed crew from blackbirding ships to row their longboats close inshore, then opened fire once they were in range.

British and Australian colonial officials initially only attempted to regulate the traffic, not to ban it. When sailors from the *Carl* in 1872, and the *Hopeful* in 1884, were tried in Sydney for committing multiple murders while blackbirding, Australian public opinion was strongly on the sailors' side.

The blackbirders' most persistent and effective enemies were Presbyterian missionaries, who rightly argued that blackbirding was often no more than abduction into slavery. They campaigned relentlessly in Britain and Australia against the trade. Finally – and aided by the White Australia Policy legislation of 1901 – the churches were able to secure the banning of overseas labour recruitment to Queensland (in 1904), Fiji (in 1911) and Western Samoa (in 1913).

The Missionaries

The first missionaries arrived in Vanuatu in 1839. However, after two of their number were killed and eaten almost immediately after setting foot on Erromango, the churches decided to move carefully. For the next nine years, missionary teaching was largely dependent on the dedication and persistence of Polynesian teachers. These people seem to have been regarded as a form of cannon fodder: it was felt that if they survived, Europeans could safely follow.

The churches hoped their Polynesian representatives would be more acceptable to the islanders than Europeans. However, they had no status in Melanesian society, often could not speak the local language, and were devastated by malaria. Several were killed and eaten.

Presbyterianism soon became the dominant Christian denomination in Vanuatu. The missionaries immediately took an uncompromising stand against many time-honoured Melanesian customs such as cannibalism, grade-taking, ancestor worship and polygamy. Some even barred their converts from smoking, drinking kava and dancing.

Other denominations followed. In 1860 the less dogmatic Anglican Diocese of Melanesia (DOM) arrived, whilst the Roman Catholics settled permanently in 1887. Unlike the missionaries from the more fundamentalist Protestant churches, the Catholics proved to be tolerant towards Vanuatu's ancient traditions.

Although a steady stream of converts emerged, the ni-Vanuatu often mingled their new belief with their traditional customs. At the same time, the churches often made their work more difficult by treating other denominations as rivals rather than allies, an attitude that newly converted islanders naturally found hard to understand.

Epidemics & Catastrophe

The infection-ridden vessels of the sandalwooders and blackbirders brought new diseases to which the peoples of the Pacific had little resistance. Often the missionaries' new converts succumbed first. They were more exposed to European germs than custom-oriented islanders, who tended to keep their distance.

Cholera, measles, smallpox, influenza, pneumonia, scarlet fever, mumps, chickenpox, whooping cough and dysentery all took a terrible toll. Even the common cold proved capable of wiping out whole populations.

Custom medicine had no effect on these epidemics. Some non-Christian islanders regarded the high body count among converts as proof that the new religion was equally impotent. Others contended that all illnesses came from sorcery anyway, so Christianity must be a particularly malevolent form to attack its own supporters so violently. Because of this belief, several missionaries were killed by vengeful islanders following epidemics.

Some estimates put Vanuatu's population at about one million in the early 1800s. By 1870 the number was down one-third to 650,000, and in the next 20 years it fell to around 100,000. This gloomy trend continued until 1935 when the indigenous population was down to a mere 41,000. The worst affected islands were Aneityum and Erromango, both of which had lost all but 5% of their original population.

European Settlement

Although there was a sandalwood station on Aneityum as early as 1843, and missionaries were active there from 1848 onwards, the first true European settler was a cattle rancher who arrived on the scene in 1854. Others followed, and this trend accelerated when the high price of cotton during the US Civil War in the early 1860s lured settlers from Australia. However, cotton gave way to coconuts and cocoa when peace in the USA brought a slump in prices.

France annexed New Caledonia in 1853 and the Presbyterian Church immediately petitioned Britain to proclaim Aneityum a protectorate. Six years later they tried again, this time extending their appeal to cover all Vanuatu. But the British government could see itself faced with a costly no-win situation, and refused to act.

Neglected by their government, most British settlers (including the Australians) were near bankruptcy by the early 1880s. Meanwhile, large numbers of French people had settled and prospered. Thanks to their administration's official support they now dominated Vanuatu's fledgling economy.

In 1882 a French land speculator, the Irish-born John Higginson, founded the Compagnie Calédonienne des Nouvelles-Hébrides (CCNH). That same year, in a concerted effort over six weeks, he purchased more than 20% of the country's agricultural land from disillusioned and bankrupt British settlers as well as local chiefs. In the case of the latter the signatory was often not the true custom owner but simply the first islander who happened to come along. Obviously these people had no authority to dispose of the block of land in question. However, the marks they made on documents they couldn't comprehend were considered legally binding. Eventually by 1905 the CCNH owned 55% of Vanuatu's cultivable land. In 1894 the CCNH was renamed Société Française des Nouvelles-Hébrides (SFNH).

Meanwhile, intense rivalry existed between the British and the French settlers (who now outnumbered the former three to one). Brawls were common as settlers on both sides took advantage of the absence of law and order. At the same time, thanks largely to the sale of alcohol and firearms to islanders, native attacks on settlers were a continuing problem.

To curb this disorder, the Anglo-French Joint Naval Commission was established in 1887 and began operating the following year. This required British and French warships to act in concert, except when the situation was one of extreme urgency. As their commanders were not permitted to intervene in land disputes between settlers and islanders, nor evict any Europeans from land they had occupied, the Joint Naval Commission was a failure overall.

The Condominium

By the early 1900s the archipelago was moving rapidly towards joint British and French rule. In 1906 the Anglo-French Condominium of the New Hebrides was created as a response to German expansionism in the region. (At the time there were only about 2000 French, 1000 British and 65,000 islander subjects for the Condominium to worry about.) Its authority over the archipelago was further extended in the Anglo-French Protocol of 1914, although this document remained unratified until 1922.

These agreements established the island chain as an area of equal influence for the two colonial powers, with neither having exclusive sovereignty. British and French nationals had equal rights, and retained their home country's citizenship. Ni-Vanuatu islanders were left officially stateless. If they wished to travel abroad, they had to carry an identifying document signed by both the British and French resident commissioners.

The Condominium's senior organ of government was the Joint Court. While both British and French courts existed to pronounce judgements in cases involving their nationals, the Joint Court decided disputes between British and French, Europeans and ni-Vanuatu. There was another court for the islanders themselves.

Cynics renamed the Condominium the Pandemonium, as the dual administration produced an amazing duplication of authorities which were seldom effective. Although a handful of government services were unified, there were two police forces, two health services, two education systems, two currencies and two prison systems.

Overseas visitors who were citizens of neither British Commonwealth nor French Union countries had to opt on arrival to accept either British or French authority. British law was stricter, but British prisons were considered more humane. French jails were very uncomfortable, but the cooking was superior!

Towards the end of the Condominium's life, Vanuatu was ruled by the British queen and French president as joint heads of state. Some islanders believed the pair were married, and suspected the relationship had its good and bad moments like any other. This was frequently confirmed. Whenever the French president was replaced, the queen obtained a new 'husband' in addition to Prince Philip!

WW II

The archipelago's French population were France's first overseas subjects to declare their support for General de Gaulle's Free French forces in 1940. But Japan's lightning advance through the Pacific, which reached as far as the nearby Solomons by early 1942, convinced settlers that Vanuatu would be the next Allied territory to fall.

In May that year a large US fleet arrived and quickly began constructing bases, first at Efate and then a much larger one in southeastern Santo. Vanuatu's population tripled overnight as over 100,000 US servicemen were garrisoned around Luganville. In all, half a million Allied soldiers passed through the area.

Many islanders either joined the small local regiment, the New Hebrides Defence Force, or went to work at the US base on Santo. All were astounded by the apparent equality between White and Black military personnel. Also, no islander had ever been paid such a generous wage before.

With Japan's defeat in 1945, the Americans began withdrawing as quickly as they had arrived three years before. Impatient to leave, they abandoned huge quantities of equipment. Some of this was sold at bargain-basement prices, the rest was dumped into the sea near Luganville.

Cargo cults appeared on several islands as villagers sought to secure the kind of wealth they'd seen being so wantonly discarded – they believed that if they acted like Europeans then 'cargo' would automatically come their way. But these movements generally waned when the cargo failed to materialise as expected. Most durable was the Jon Frum cult of Tanna which has remained a potent force to this day.

Postwar

The enormous stimulus that the US wartime presence had given to Vanuatu's economic development was soon dissipated. The postwar Condominium authorities had neither the funds nor the energy to maintain the standard of facilities that had operated during WW II.

The economic boom in other parts of the world did begin to filter through in the late 1950s, although official apathy remained the order of the day for another decade. By then, education and medical services, previously left entirely to the missions, had begun to expand as government efforts to bring services to the people increased. The economy was still precariously dependent on copra, but beef cattle and tourism were showing promise as significant sources of income.

Towards Self-Rule

Land became Vanuatu's central political concern in the mid-1960s. It was the spark that finally spurred the country to take the path to independence.

Europeans viewed land as a commodity just like any other item. But to the ni-Vanuatu this was contrary to ancient customs, in which land is held by the present generation in trust for future ones. They found the European concept of land ownership impossible to accept.

At this time White settlers owned about 30% of the country's land area, and about half of that had been cleared and developed, mainly for coconuts. When the planters began clearing their undeveloped land to take up cattle ranching, it led to immediate ni-Vanuatu protests in Santo and Malakula. Villagers argued that the settlers had no right to extend the existing coastal strip any deeper into the bush than had been done already. This land, in the villagers' opinion, was exclusively theirs.

Consequently, a custom-oriented movement called Nagriamel sprang up under the leadership of the charismatic Jimmy Stevens. Operating from Santo, its aims were to protect Melanesians' claims to their traditional land. By the late 1960s, and spurred on by reports of the acquisition of large blocks of land by US developers, Nagriamel had expanded to other islands in northern Vanuatu.

In 1971 Stevens petitioned the United Nations (UN) for Vanuatu's early independence. In the same year, the New Hebrides National Party, later called the Vanua'aku Party, was formed by an Anglican minister, Father Walter Lini. It drew its support from English-speaking (Anglophone) Protestants, whereas Nagriamel became clearly identified with French interests.

While the Anglophones joined the Vanua'aku Party, the Francophones supported several political groupings often at odds with each other. They ranged from custom-oriented movements like Nagriamel to small conventional political parties. The latter represented both French-educated islanders and mixed-race people, who considered themselves more French than Melanesian.

The Francophones were strongly opposed to the UK's declared aim of an early independence for the archipelago. They also objected to the Vanua'aku Party's petition to the UN in 1974 supporting this. The Francophones became known as the Modérés or 'Moderates', because most wanted the Condominium either to remain as it was or be replaced by France ruling alone. However, they did support greater autonomy for individual islands.

As Vanuatu became more politicised the Condominium authorities agreed to hold the country's first general election. The presence of a number of nominated, nonelected members in a newly created assembly allowed minority parties to govern until an election in November 1979 produced a clear winner. This was the Vanua'aku Party, with Lini as the chief minister.

But the victors were extremely unpopular in some areas, particularly on Santo and Tanna. Nagriamel had been beating the secessionist drum since 1976 and most of Santo's French community now joined in.

Meanwhile, independence for Vanuatu was fixed for mid-1980. The French government, seeing the Anglophones sweeping all before them and their own influence visibly declining, began supporting the Modérés.

Independence

Specific threats of secession were frequently heard on Santo and Tanna in early 1980, but the UK and France could not agree on how to react. The UK wanted to respond militarily. France said 'non'.

Late in May matters came to a head. An insurrection on Tanna split the island between government supporters and rebel Modérés. On Santo, secessionists seized Luganville and hoisted the flag of the independent republic of Vemarana. The Lini government blockaded Santo in retaliation.

Modéré supporters on several other northern islands, including Malakula, Ambae, Maewo and Ambrym, proclaimed their own secessions during June. These then merged and announced a Provisional Government of the Northern Islands, under Jimmy Stevens. However, the Vanuatu government was able to secure Papua New Guinea's support, and the promise of troops if need be to quell the rebellion. But that could only come after independence, due on 30 July 1980.

Desperate to retain some semblance of control over the situation, France asked the UK to consider postponing the now imminent independence. When this was vigorously rejected by the UK, which enjoyed the backing of Australia and New Zealand, the two colonial powers despatched a small joint military force to restore order in Luganville.

But the Anglo-French troops had no power of arrest and so failed even to prevent the rebels from looting Luganville's shops. Once it attained power, the Vanuatu government replaced them with soldiers from Papua New Guinea, who quickly restored order and arrested the secessionist ringleaders.

Following Stevens' arrest, many documents came to light suggesting that the French administration had played a double game throughout the whole episode. Officially backing the Lini government as the duly elected representatives of the people of Vanuatu, France had all along secretly supported its secessionist citizens.

The New Nation

The Vanuatu government's desire since independence has been for development to benefit everyone equally, while preserving the new nation's age-old customs and traditions. It has established diplomatic relations with over 70 countries, and taken an activist stand in foreign affairs by declaring the archipelago a nuclear-free zone.

But land ownership has remained the principal political issue. Differences of view over the matter have produced factionalism within the Vanua'aku Party, with several major figures either leaving to form breakaway movements or making dramatic challenges for leadership. Indeed, a constitutional crisis in 1988 led to the dismissal and temporary detention of Vanuatu's first president, Ati George Sokomanu.

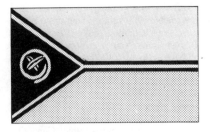

The flag of Vanuatu

As a result of all this, in 1991 the Vanua'aku Party finally lost power to a coalition of a newly formed offshoot (lead by Lini), the National United Party (NUP), and the mainly Francophone 'Union of Moderate Parties'. Since taking office the new government has reversed the drift towards Anglophony. As well, it has softened the country's previous hard line on independence for New Caledonia. Also see the later section on Government.

GEOGRAPHY

Vanuatu is a Y-shaped chain of Pacific islands, extending 1176 km in a north-south direction between the equator and the tropic of Capricorn. Its nearest neighbour is the Solomon Islands, just over 170 km to the north. New Caledonia lies 230 km to the south-west, while Fiji is 800 km to the east. The capital, Vila, is about 1900 km northeast of Brisbane, Australia.

The total area of Vanuatu is about 860,000 sq km, of which only 12,336 sq km is land. This comprises about 80 islands – if you count every tiny islet and isolated rock you'll find over 300 – most of which are formed by the summits of mountain ranges that rise from the deep ocean floor.

Only 12 islands can be called significant in terms of economy and population. The largest are Santo (4010 sq km), Malak

(2069 sq km), Efate (980 sq km) and Erromango (900 sq km). Santo also boasts the country's highest peak: 1879-metre Mt Tabwemasana. Ambae, Ambrym and Tanna all have peaks over 1000 metres high.

Most islands are either mountainous or steeply undulating, with 35% of the country being above 300 metres and 55% having slopes greater than 20 degrees. Some areas are so deeply and heavily dissected that they're virtually impenetrable. Generally, the steeper country is covered with lush forest and secondary growth, while coconut plantations and gardens dominate the narrow coastal plains.

Volcanoes & Earthquakes

Vanuatu lies squarely on top of the Pacific Ring of Fire. In fact, the archipelago is on the edge of the Pacific tectonic plate, which is being forced up and over the Indo-Australian plate. This enormous and relentless pressure causes constant seismic activity in the form of earthquakes and volcanic eruptions.

Some areas of Vanuatu are being uplifted at a rate of two cm a year, while others are subsiding. Seismographs record numerous earth tremors each day, though only a small number are strong enough to be noticed by the general population. An earthquake in 1994 rated over seven on the Richter scale and caused considerable damage. Earlier ones in 1875 and 1948 created tsunamis that destroyed villages.

Vanuatu has nine active volcanoes, with seven being on land and two under the sea. The most menacing of all is Lopevi, about 130 km north of the capital, although Yasur, on Tanna, has become increasingly more hostile since the 1994 quake. Mt Garet, on Gaua, is considered potentially the most dangerous. This is because of the rather thin layer of rock that separates its large crater lake from the magma underneath.

Early in 1995, an increase in seismic activity on Ambae created fears that its long-dormant volcano was about to erupt. At the time of publication it seemed that the island may have to be evacuated.

Ambrym's two volcanoes are a tempting target for fit bushwalkers, while Yasur's spectacular fireworks are easily accessible to all. In recent times the ash fallout from these three volcanoes has caused serious damage to gardens and cash crops. Far to the south, the tiny islands of Matthew and Hunter belch out smoke from time to time. Several other islands have active fumaroles and thermal springs, some of which are hot enough to be used for cooking food.

CLIMATE

Vanuatu's climate varies from wet tropical in the north to subtropical in the south, with much drier rain-shadow areas in between. From May to September, fresh south-easterly breezes produce fine sunny days and pleasantly cool nights. This is the country's dry season and is the best time to visit. November to April is the wet season, when higher temperatures, heavy rains and occasional cyclones are experienced. In Vila, the average daily hours of sunshine range from 4.9 in June to 6.7 in October.

The prevailing winds throughout the year are from the south-east (the famous southeast trade winds of sailing ship days). However, in the wet season the winds are more variable in speed and direction. Squalls can blow up in the space of a few minutes, reaching 90 km/h and presenting a real danger to yachts and other small shipping.

Temperature & Humidity

Mean maximum temperatures in Luganville, in northern Vanuatu, range from 27.2°C in July to 30.2°C in January. Vila's are almost identical, whilst Tanna (in the south) is a degree or two cooler. Mean minimums are eight or nine degrees below the mean maximums in all three areas.

Throughout the year humidity is highest in the early morning. In Vila, from December to February (the hottest part of the year) the average daily reading is around 83%. In the cooler months, daily humidity averages a much more acceptable 70% to 74%.

Even during the height of the wet season, cool sea breezes along the coast generally keep the temperature at a comfortable level.

Lenakel

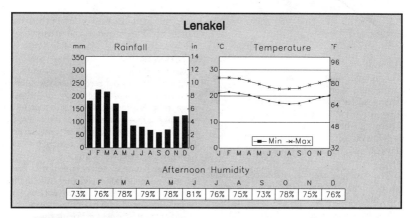

J	F	M	A	M	J	J	A	S	O	N	D
73%	76%	78%	79%	78%	81%	76%	75%	73%	78%	75%	76%

Luganville

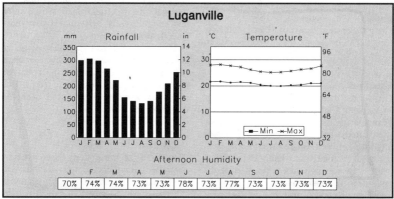

J	F	M	A	M	J	J	A	S	O	N	D
70%	74%	74%	73%	73%	78%	73%	77%	73%	73%	73%	73%

Port Vila

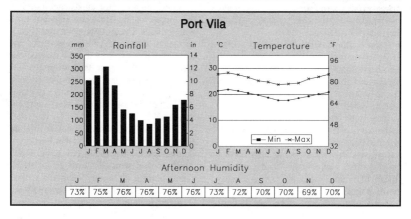

J	F	M	A	M	J	J	A	S	O	N	D
73%	75%	76%	76%	76%	76%	73%	72%	70%	70%	69%	70%

But once you go inland, you really start to feel the heat.

Rainfall

Throughout Vanuatu, January to March are the months with the heaviest rains. March averages 21 days with rain, contrasting with 13 in August at the height of the dry season. There can be long periods of calm, dry weather during the wet, just as there can be days of low cloud and intermittent rain in the dry.

The north-easternmost islands of Vanuatu get more than 4000 mm of rainfall per year, but those in the south receive just over half that amount. Luganville is deluged by 2300 mm per year on average, with Vila only slightly drier. Vanuatu's wettest places lie along the eastern coasts of Maewo and Pentecost. The driest are on the north-western slopes of the central mountains.

Cyclones

On average, there are 2.5 cyclones every year in Vanuatu. Called hurricanes in the Caribbean and typhoons in the South China Sea, these intense tropical depressions can occur any time between November and May, with the usual cyclone season being December to March. On average, any given part of the country is devastated by a cyclone every 30 years, and receives some damage each year from either wind or rain. This makes cyclones by far the country's worst natural hazard.

Most cyclones develop over the Coral Sea west of Vanuatu and tend to move initially south or south-east. The most destructive advance at about 12 to 20 km/h, speeding up as they lose strength over either land or cooler water.

Any small inter-island vessel caught in the open sea is in grave danger. Indeed, Cyclone Uma in February 1987 sank or damaged over 30 vessels in Vila alone. It also flattened shops, offices and hotels, and cost many lives. In urban situations, flying sheets of roofing iron present the greatest danger to anyone unwise enough to be outside during a cyclone. In rural areas you have to be more careful of falling coconuts and trees.

FLORA & FAUNA

Apart from malaria-carrying mosquitoes, Vanuatu is free of dangerous land creatures. Nastiest of its plants is the *nanggalat*, whose large, purple-veined leaf produces a painful nettlelike rash – your skin goes red where it has been stung and can itch for a week. Islanders use the sap from the plant's roots, or below the bark, as an antidote.

Vanuatu has rather fewer bird species than its northern neighbours and very little in the way of native mammals. Invertebrates are better represented – for example, there are 64 species of butterfly, 73 land snails (including the giant East African land snail, which arrived in the early 1970s and is now widespread) and 124 insects.

Most visitors (or at least those who go snorkelling) will be enthralled by the exuberance of marine life around the country's numerous fringing reefs. Here you'll find about 300 species of coral and over 450 species of reef fish.

Vegetation

About 75% of the country is covered by natural vegetation including grasslands, secondary growth and rainforest. While most of the forest has been heavily disturbed by cyclones, logging and subsistence farming, the more pristine areas are like botanical wonderlands. These contain as many as 1500 species of flowers, ferns, shrubs, vines and trees. Equally inspiring are the damp cloud forests with their large trees dripping with moss. They are called 'cloud forests' because they are usually in cloud and are very damp. The best of these are in south-west Santo and Ambae.

Lord of the forest is the huge banyan tree, whose crown can be 70 metres or more across. There are some beauties within Vila itself, so you won't have to go far to see them. Forests of mighty kauri trees up to three metres in diameter once covered much of Erromango and Aneityum, but these have been almost entirely logged out. Fortunately, there are still some good-sized forests left on Erromango, although the logging companies are keen to get at them.

Orchids festoon the trees in many areas, such as along the beaches in north-eastern Santo. Vanuatu has 158 species of orchid, of which about 40 are endemic. The best place to see them is Aneityum, where you'll find over 50% of the total species. Also of interest are the ferns – all 250 species of them.

Less enchanting are the introduced weeds, of which lantana and the widespread American vine are most noticeable. The latter was brought from the southern states of the USA as a camouflage plant during WW II, but did its job too well. It has gone mad and now covers large areas to the detriment of native vegetation.

Animals

Rats, cats, dogs, cattle, horses, pigs and goats were all introduced to Vanuatu and have now gone wild. Thanks largely to the relative youth and isolation of the islands, the only native land mammals are four species of flying fox and eight bats. Only one of these – the white flying fox – is endemic.

Rats are the bane of village life throughout the Pacific. The first type to reach Vanuatu was the small Polynesian rat, with others being brought in by Europeans. They cause much damage to the copra industry as well as to nesting birds. You may even find one nibbling your toes if you stay overnight in a village leaf house.

The country's largest resident mammal is the dugong, or sea cow, which is at the easternmost limit of its range in Vanuatu.

Coral

Coral is usually stationary and often looks decidedly flowery but it's an animal, and a hungry carnivorous animal at that. Although a 3rd century AD Greek philosopher surmised that coral was really an animal it was still generally considered to be a plant until only 250 years ago.

Corals are Coelenterates, a class of animals which also includes sea anemones and jellyfish. The true reef-building corals or Scleractinia are distinguished by their lime skeletons. It is this relatively indestructible skeleton which actually forms the coral reef, as new coral continually builds on old dead coral and the reef gradually builds up.

Coral takes a vast number of forms but all are distinguished by polyps, the tiny tube-like fleshy cylinders which look very like their close relation, the anemone. The top of the cylinder is open and ringed by waving tentacles which sting and draw into the polyp's stomach (the open space within the cylinder) any passing prey. Each polyp is an individual creature but each can reproduce by splitting to form a coral colony of separate but closely related polyps. Although each polyp catches and digests its own food, the nutrition passes between the polyps to the whole colony. Most coral polyps only feed at night: during the daytime they withdraw into their hard limestone skeleton, so it is only at night that a coral reef can be seen in its full colourful glory.

Hard corals may take many forms. One of the most common and easiest to recognise is the staghorn coral, which grows by budding off new branches from the tips. Brain corals are huge and round with a surface looking very much like a human brain. They grow by adding new base levels of skeletal matter and expanding outwards. Flat or sheet corals, like plate coral, expand at their outer edges. Many corals can take different shapes depending on their environment. Staghorn coral can branch out in all directions in deeper water or form flat tables when they grow in shallow water.

Like their reef-building relatives, soft coral is made up of individual polyps, but does not form a hard limestone skeleton. Without the skeleton which protects hard coral, it would seem likely that soft coral would fall prey to fish but it seems to remain relatively immune either due to toxic substances in its tissues or due to the presence of sharp limestone needles which protect the polyps. Soft corals can move around and will sometimes engulf and kill off hard coral.

Corals catch their prey by means of stinging nematocysts (a specialised type of cell). Some corals can give humans a painful sting and the fern-like stinging hydroid should be given a wide berth.

Tony Wheeler

Growing to two metres long and weighing up to 400 kg, they spend most of their time feeding on seagrass in calm, shallow water. Although not common, dugong occur in small groups throughout the archipelago. A couple of groups have even become tourist attractions.

Several species of sea turtle also live and breed around the islands. However, turtle meat and eggs are considered a delicacy by the ni-Vanuatu, and populations are dwindling as a result of increased exploitation both here and elsewhere in the Pacific. Several chiefs have created small sanctuaries in an effort to conserve them, but the outlook is not good.

Birds

Vanuatu boasts 121 bird species, of which 32 are seabirds, 15 are shorebirds and 74 live on land or freshwater. Santo has the richest bird fauna, with 55 species including all seven of the country's endemics. Of these the Santo mountain starling is rarest, being found only in the higher mountains of that island. In contrast, the endemic white-eye is widespread and common throughout Vanuatu.

Perhaps the most interesting of the country's birds is the megapode, or 'incubator bird'. Also known in Bislama as *namalao*, or *skrab dak* (scrub duck), it often lives close to active volcanic areas, where it lays its eggs in the hot soil. A large, dark bird with a small head and short tail, the megapode grows to just over 30 cm in length. Its young, which emerge fully feathered, can run immediately after hatching and can fly within 24 hours. Megapodes spend much of their time on the ground scratching around like fowls.

Less interesting, but extremely common around populated areas, is the introduced Indian mynah, which was introduced to control insects. You'll easily identify it by its cheeky attitude and the large white patch on the upper surface of each wing.

Reptiles

Vanuatu has 19 lizard species, of which 13 are skinks and five are geckoes. The remaining one is the banded iguana, which has been introduced from Fiji and is found only on Efate. Ironically, Vanuatu is now the stronghold of this species as the Fijian populations have been almost wiped out by the introduced mongoose. It grows to a metre long and has an emerald-green body with black bands, so there's no mistaking it.

Snakes Vanuatu's two types of land snake are perfectly harmless. These are an introduced burrowing snake and the native Pacific boa – the latter is often known as the 'sleeping snake' from its habit of lying absolutely still when threatened. Growing to about 2.5 metres long, this mainly arboreal species shows great variety in appearance – it ranges from silver to orange-brown. Being fond of rats, mice and chickens, Pacific boas often live close to villages where meals are easy to find.

Vanuatu's only venomous snakes are the yellow-bellied and banded sea snakes. These graceful creatures are often curious, but rarely aggressive unless provoked. In fact, they only have small mouths and teeth, which aren't at all suitable for savaging humans. If you really want to get bitten you'll probably have to stick a finger down one's throat!

Crocodiles Over the years saltwater (or estuarine) crocodiles have appeared from time to time around Vanuatu's northern islands. It's generally accepted that they have come down from the Solomons, having lost their way in cyclones. Currently the 'salty' population stands at two, both of which are on Vanua Lava. The larger is estimated at six metres in length.

Frogs & Toads

Another introduced animal to do well in Vanuatu is the green and golden bell-frog. It was brought in from Australia during the 1920s to control mosquitoes. Now they're thriving and widespread, while their fellows in Australia are becoming rare.

Fortunately, cane toads haven't reached

the country in numbers: two specimens were found on Santo recently, but it's thought that they'd just come ashore. Let's hope so!

Marine life

Vanuatu's waters contain a massive variety of fish. You'll find huge swarms of small, attractively coloured species, especially around coral gardens and reefs.

Line fishers will quickly find the archipelago extremely rewarding. Routine catches include bonito, yellowfin tuna, sailfish, barracuda and swordfish.

Turtles often come close inshore in the cooler months of the year, mating on the surface. They then lay their eggs deep in the sand along the coasts of some of the country's smaller, quieter islands, returning night after night to complete the process.

In deeper waters beyond the reefs, or in the open ocean, roam dolphins, porpoises, sharks and flying fish (locally called *naika*). Further out, there are whales occasionally.

Sharks There have been a number of shark attacks in the waters of Vanuatu, and particularly around Ambae, Ambrym, Paama, Pentecost and Malakula. Efate is generally considered to be safe, except for Teouma Bay. Always ask locals if there are any sharks

---

Poisonous Reef-Dwellers

Probably the most dangerous thing you'll have to worry about when snorkelling or reef walking is sunburn. However, there are several nasty creatures worth mentioning because there's always the chance that you'll meet one.

The worst of these is the stonefish, which is found in both rocky and sandy areas. This ugly looking thing spends much of its time on the bottom pretending to be a weed-covered rock, which is how it catches its prey. It has sharp, extremely venomous dorsal spines. If you tread on one you'll find that the pain is immediate and incapacitating.

Another is the lionfish, which is a relative of the stonefish. This strikingly banded, brown and white species has large, graceful dorsal fins containing venomous spines. Lionfish are obvious when they're swimming around, but they can also hide under ledges.

Then there's the cone shell, several species of which have highly toxic venom. The bad ones have a venomous proboscis – a rapidly extendible, dart-like stinging device which can reach any part of the shell's outer surface. Cone shell venom can be fatal.

Generally speaking, the best way to avoid contact with any of the above while you're in the water is to look but don't touch. In most cases reef walking should be discouraged as it can permanently damage the reef. ■

Stonefish   Lionfish

around before swimming, and take their advice!

Coconut Crabs

Closely related to lobsters, and called *krab kokonas* in Bislama, the coconut crab is a speciality of most of Vanuatu's more up-market restaurants. Inevitably, this has led to a serious decline in crab numbers and strict conservation measures are required to save the crab. The species matures very slowly, taking 15 years to reach harvesting size. It can live for 50 years and grows to have a leg span of one metre. This makes it the world's largest land crab.

The crab is so named because it eats coconut flesh, among other things – it's mainly a scavenger. However, a nut first has to be damaged, perhaps by a rat gnawing through the shell, before the crab can begin nibbling through to the meat. It's said that they'll climb palms and break off the nuts, some of which will split when they hit the ground.

Coconut crabs live in forested areas within about one km of the sea. Villagers catch them quite easily by fixing split-open coconuts to the ground, then checking the baits with a torch at night. Being skilful they can pick the crabs up without being crunched by their nippers, but you shouldn't try it as an adult crab will have no difficulty taking your finger off.

GOVERNMENT

The Republic of Vanuatu achieved its independence from the UK and France on 30 July 1980. Since then, it has remained in the South Pacific Commission, and joined 28 other international organisations including the UN, the Commonwealth and the South Pacific Forum.

Vanuatu has a Westminster-style constitution. The country's single legislative chamber, or parliament, sits in Vila. Its 46 members are elected for a four-year term.

The prime minister and the eight or nine co-members of the council of ministers (the number of ministers is at the prime minister's discretion) comprise the executive, or cabinet. All ministers must be members of parliament.

Vanuatu's head of state is the president. He/she is elected by an electoral college composed of members of parliament, and the presidents of the 11 regional (ie local government) councils.

There's also a national council of chiefs called the Malfatu Mauri. This body advises parliament on all constitutional matters relating to Vanuatu's traditional customs.

Justice

The judicial system is based on British law. Most routine legal matters appear before magistrates' courts, though there is a Supreme Court which exists for serious matters. Above them both is an Appeal Court with three judges, two of which are appointed by the president and chosen from Supreme Court judges in South Pacific as and when required.

At a lower level, there are six island courts presided over by chiefs. These deal with minor breaches of the law, disagreements over the interpretation of local customs and traditions, and land ownership disputes.

Civil Administration

Vanuatu has 10 government ministries, as well as a further 38 government agencies under ministerial control. Unlike many new nations, which have an excess of government officials, only a very small percentage of the population is in public employment.

Out with the Old, In with the New!
The previous system of 11 local government councils was abolished in November 1994 and replaced by a system of six provincial governments. Islands that had local government council headquarters (such as Pentecost Island) that have not become provincial government headquarters are now operated as island administration centres (branch offices of the provincial government, if you like).

Confused? Don't be. The changeover will have little or no effect on the visitor. ■

National Coat of Arms of Vanuatu

Political Parties

Politics in Vanuatu is largely polarised by language – the major parties are either French or English speaking – and are still dominated by the old guard from pre-independence days. However, there is a growing number of young, educated ni-Vanuatu who are the face of the country's political future.

The first decade of independence was reasonably stable as far as Vanuatu's political groupings were concerned: the major players remained the Vanua'aku Party (VP) and the Union of Moderate Parties, with the former consistently winning government.

In 1991, however, charges of nepotism and other politician-type crimes led to the VP ousting its leader, Father Walter Lini. He and several supporters then left the VP and formed the National United Party (NUP). Elections in September 1991 saw a coalition of the UMP and NUP take office, under the leadership of Maxime Carlot, with 29 of the 46 seats.

Since then the situation can best be described as fluid, if not chaotic. In 1993 the NUP split into two halves, with the defectors

– the People's Democratic Party (PDP) – going to the cross-benches. Then a VP member joined the UMP and was rewarded with the rank of minister.

In early 1995 the coalition had a majority of one, but the PDP was talking of deserting to the opposition. This, of course, would bring down the government. Tune in for the next exciting episode! There are to be elections in late 1995.

ECONOMY

Vanuatu's economy is essentially agricultural, with about 80% of the population primarily engaged in subsistence farming of food crops such as taro and yams. Most villagers also produce cash crops of, in particular, coconuts (copra), cocoa, kava and vegetables. As well, there are several large plantation enterprises mainly involved in supplying the copra market. Other significant income is derived from tourism, beef production, logging and the country's role as a tax haven. Mining and fishing are negligible in terms of export dollars.

The gross domestic product (GDP) in 1990 was US$152 million, of which agriculture accounted for US$31 million and services for US$102 million. The GDP per capita that same year was US$1030. In 1994, the minimum wage was 8500VT (about US$73) per month.

Vanuatu's imports exceed exports by a factor of at least four. The principal imports are consumer goods, in particular rice, clothing, processed food, electrical goods and vehicles. Also important are medical supplies, fuel, oil, lubricants, machinery and industrial materials. The principal suppliers are (in order) Australia, New Zealand, Japan, France and New Caledonia.

Agriculture

Vanuatu's fertile volcanic soil is among its greatest assets – so much so, in fact, that agriculture earns over 90% of the country's export income. In 1993 domestic exports totalled US$19 million, an increase of 5% on the preceding year.

Subsistence farming takes place on small

plots usually hacked out of the rainforest. Most family plots cover about three hectares, but only a very small part of this is used at any one time. Crops are usually only grown on the one spot for a year, after which the soil is exhausted. The next year another spot is cleared and burnt, while the previous one is left to replenish its nutrients. These fallow periods generally last for about 15 years, although on heavily populated islands, such as Paama, one to three years is the norm.

About 40% of the country is considered to have at least reasonable agricultural potential. However, only about half of this is currently in use, the bulk of it for subsistence farming. Copra, cocoa and beef are the major export earners, with copra being by far the most important – 28,000 tonnes worth US\$6.3 million in 1993. Apart from world price fluctuations, the major factor affecting the value of production of all crops is cyclones.

Copra Although the production of dried coconut meat is the country's major export earner, it has declined as a percentage of the total – from 47% in 1986 to 33% in 1993 – thanks to the increase in other sectors. (Beef increased from 15% to 21% over the same period.) More than half the copra is produced by large plantations and small holdings on Santo and Malakula. The main overseas markets are Holland, Belgium and France, where copra is processed into soap, margarine and industrial products.

Unfortunately, the world market price for copra has crashed in recent times thanks to massive competition from Asian palm oil. This has had a devastating effect on many village economies. In 1994 the situation in some areas was so bad that parents couldn't even afford the modest fees required to send their children to school.

Travelling around Vanuatu you'll soon notice that the coastal plains of most islands are mainly devoted to coconuts. The palms are generally planted eight or nine metres apart, with 100 to 160 trees per hectare. The average tree bears 50 to 80 nuts or more each

year. As at least eight nuts are needed to make one kg of dry copra, each hectare ideally yields eight tonnes. In practice, however, the yield is usually much less.

Producing copra is hard physical work, yet for their pains the villagers can count themselves lucky to receive US\$250 per tonne. Having been dried and bagged, the copra is transported to either Vila or Luganville by the small trading boats that ply the coast from beach to beach.

The metal bands you'll notice encircling the trunks of many trees are to stop rats climbing up and damaging the nuts.

Cattle The beef industry is Vanuatu's next largest agricultural export, having earned US\$4 million in 1994. The national herd numbers about 120,000, over half of which are on Santo and another fifth in Efate. Cattle can be grazed in coconut plantations without affecting copra production, so the more affluent growers have tended to diversify. Most beef exports go to Japan while about 20% of the annual production is locally canned.

Kava The huge domestic demand for kava – the country's traditional intoxicating beverage – has made it the fastest growing agricultural commodity. Drinkers in Vila and Luganville consumed 500 tonnes of kava root in 1993, and there always seems to be a shortage. Kava dominates garden production on Pentecost, Epi and Tanna. In fact, the majority of households in northern Pentecost no longer grow their own food, instead purchasing it with the money earned from kava crops. This is a new trend in rural Vanuatu.

Mining

Few minerals have yet been found in sufficient quantities to justify the expense of full-scale mining. So far, only manganese and pozzolana – a component of hydraulic cement – have attracted significant attention. Deposits of both minerals were mined on Efate in the 1960s and 1970s. At the time of writing the Australian government was funding a geological survey of the country as part of its aid programme.

Manufacturing

The sole manufacturing industry of any real importance is meat canning. Small-scale industries include the production of soft drinks, beer, dairy foods, clothing, building materials, furniture and souvenirs (including so-called artefacts).

Fishing

You'd imagine that Vanuatu's vast ocean area would be a rich resource in terms of fish. Yet although there is a thriving domestic fishing industry, export earnings are negligible. What earnings there are come from the re-export of deep-sea species to Asian canneries. At present, the country's single patrol boat spends most of its sea time chasing Taiwanese trawlers that illegally fish inside the territorial limit!

Forestry

There is very little forestry as such. The term forestry implies management, and this can hardly be applied to the way in which Vanuatu's dwindling timber resources are being exploited. Although rainforest covers about 35% of the country, its value in economic terms is limited by steep terrain, lack of commercial species, small tree sizes and the damage caused by cyclones and shifting agriculture. A number of plantations have been established in recent years in an effort to create a sustainable timber industry.

Tourism

Tourism is the country's largest foreign exchange earner after agriculture. In 1992, 42,700 visitors arrived by aircraft and stayed an average of nine days. In the same year there were visits from 59,300 cruise ship passengers, most of whom spend only a day or two on land. About 1000 visitors arrived by yacht.

Over 50% of the country's tourists come from Australia, with another 14% from New

Zealand and 12% from New Caledonia. The busiest period is the southern winter.

Formerly it was official policy to discourage tourism beyond certain areas of Efate, Santo and Tanna, the aim being to protect isolated island cultures from the negative effects of mass tourism.

In more recent times the policy has changed to allow the industry's economic benefits to be spread more widely. This has resulted in a mushrooming of village-based tourism enterprises – mainly guest houses and so-called resorts – throughout the archipelago. However, transport and other services are still very inadequate to meet any surge in demand.

The Financial Centre

Vanuatu's third-largest source of overseas income is its financial centre, or tax haven. Since 1971, foreign businesses and individuals have been able to operate shell companies and/or make deposits in Vila's banks free of local income, company, capital gains, gift or withholding taxes, exchange controls and estate duties. As well, despite external efforts to minimise tax avoidance, Vanuatu has avoided entering into any double taxation treaties with foreign countries.

Over 1500 overseas businesses are registered with the financial centre, generating about 16% of the country's annual foreign exchange income.

The Shipping Register

In 1981 Vanuatu created an open register for ships requiring a flag of convenience. Currently about 550 vessels are registered. However, they are required to meet the safety standards described in the nonstatutory maritime rules of the USA.

Overseas Aid

With its recurrent trade deficit, Vanuatu has been unable to finance all the developments necessary for an emerging nation. As a result the country is forced to rely on aid donations from other countries, although increasingly these contributions are in the form of expertise rather than cash. Vanuatu's most generous aid donors have been the UK, France, Australia and the European Development Fund.

POPULATION

Vanuatu's population in 1993 was estimated at 160,000, of which all but 3500 were ni-Vanuatu. The 'others' included about 1500 Europeans, with the remainder being mainly Asians and other Pacific Islanders.

Two-thirds of the population live on Efate, Santo, Malakula and Tanna, and 82% live in rural areas. The 1989 census identified a total of 69 inhabited islands, with 3233 inhabited rural localities varying from a single family to large villages of over 200 residents. It showed that 52% of the rural population lived in localities containing 10 to 49 people, while 26% lived in smaller ones.

On most islands the population is concen-

Ecotourism

'Ecotourism' is on the lips of every concerned traveller these days, but what does it really mean?

Generally, ecotourism is ecologically sustainable, nature-based tourism with an emphasis on educating people about the natural environment. This includes cultural components. 'Ecologically sustainable' means achieving an appropriate income for the local community while ensuring the long-term conservation of the resource.

The philosophy behind Vanuatu's first Tourism Master Plan, which was completed in 1994, is that the natural environment is the foundation on which the industry should be developed. This recognises that the country's tremendous natural beauty and diverse cultures set it apart from all others, and that these things should be conserved.

From an internal point of view, tourism is seen as just another form of economic activity that brings in foreign capital. The fact that a particular species, for example, occurs nowhere else in the world has little meaning in isolation. However, visitor interest puts such an attraction in context and provides an impetus for conservation and long-term management. This is one of the very positive aspects of ecotourism.

The other major benefit of ecotourism is that it provides for sustainable development. Like other Melanesian countries, Vanuatu is under threat of losing its forests through rampant exploitation. Some international logging companies are offering ridiculously low prices for standing timber. In this way such companies earn massive profits, while the forests' owners receive a pittance. At the same time, the resources that sustain their lifestyle are often ruined or seriously degraded in the process.

The landowners desire economic development and in many cases the sea and the forest are their only hope. They do not necessarily want these resources to be damaged beyond repair, but they do want to earn a living. For these people, ecotourism provides a very real alternative. Instead of selling their forests for a small one-off return, they can 'rent' them to tourists to walk through, photograph and generally enjoy. Visitors pay the landowner a sum for this rental. When they leave, the forest is still in its pristine state ready to be rented to those who follow.

In the past, tourism in Vanuatu has generally been run by expatriates with ni-Vanuatu merely servants to the industry. Now ni-Vanuatu wish to become more involved, and one area in which they have developed a strong interest is ecotourism. Guest houses are being built in rural villages, the creation of national parks and reserves is on the agenda, and local people are keen to improve their guiding skills. In some places, customs and traditions that were in danger of being forgotten have been restored as a means of earning income.

If you're at all interested in giving ni-Vanuatu the opportunity to develop a tourism industry, and at the same time want to help conserve their environment and culture, then support these local enterprises. Most times you'll find they provide truly memorable experiences of this fascinating corner of the globe. Don't begrudge paying modest entry fees and guide fees – 1000VT sounds a lot, but it's only about US$9. If landowners find they can't earn sufficient income from ecotourism, they'll inevitably turn to more destructive forms of land use.

Remember also that tourism is new in rural Vanuatu, and its concepts are often not well understood. If you encounter problems let the people know as well as the National Tourism Office. They'll appreciate the feedback.

Jeremy Challacombe

trated along a narrow coastal strip, or on tiny offshore islands, whilst the mountainous forested interiors are uninhabited. However, the interior plateaus are often relatively densely populated.

Population densities vary from island to island depending on size, topography and agricultural capacity. A number of the offshore islets have the nation's densest population figures. For example Atchin, off Malakula, and Ifira, off Efate, are bursting at the seams with about 1000 people per sq km. This is in striking contrast to the national average of 11.7 per sq km.

A recent disturbing trend is the drift into towns, particularly Vila, by young ni-Vanuatu in search of jobs and the bright lights. As elsewhere, young people tend to find the opportunities of town life an exciting change from the relatively mundane world of their home village. However, jobs are hard to find and survival often depends on family generosity. This drift saw Vila's population double to 26,000 in the 10 years to 1993; Luganville's was nearly 9000 in the same year, but increasing at a much slower rate.

Population Growth

Vanuatu's population has more than doubled since the 1967 census, which recorded 77,988 persons. There are now nearly four times as many people in the country as there were in the darkest years of depopulation, when only 41,000 ni-Vanuatu remained. A reflection of this explosion is the fact that, in 1989, 31% of the population were under 10 years of age while only 5% were over 60 years. Fortunately the growth rate is slowing, but the population is still expected to double again by 2010.

PEOPLE
Melanesians

The term Melanesia comes from the Greek words *melas* and *nesos* meaning 'black' and 'island' respectively. Melanesians are Black people who live on the islands of western Oceania.

Most Melanesians in Vanuatu are of medium height and strong in stature. Their skin pigmentation is usually mid to darkish brown. Thick, black, curly hair is commonplace, though some people from western Santo have gingerish locks.

Anthropologists have identified genetic links among Melanesians with Papuans, Polynesians and Australian Aborigines. However, cultural values, traditional ceremonies, and rules about hierarchy differ considerably between individual groups of islanders, and even between neighbouring villages within the tight confines of certain small islands.

Polynesians

The term Polynesia comes from the Greek word *poly* meaning 'many'. Polynesians are the people from the many islands (in the eastern Pacific).

Most of the Polynesians you'll see around Vila are settlers who came from France's Pacific territories prior to independence. However, others are descended from those who arrived centuries ago, so are considered indigenous. Among the latter are the residents of Ifira Island and the village of Mele, both near Vila, and of Aniwa to the south, and Emae in the Shepherds group. These people speak a Polynesian dialect, yet are often as dark as Melanesians.

Malakulan man

Futuna in the Tafea group has a significant proportion of pure Polynesians in its population. Here you'll find tall, stocky people with yellow-brown to fair skin and straight, light-brown hair.

Other ni-Vanuatu with Polynesian roots have thick, curly, black hair, especially on Maewo, Ambae, northern Pentecost and the Banks group. Although by now thoroughly intermixed with Melanesians, the people of these four areas are still often paler-skinned, taller and have rounder faces than people from the purely Melanesian islands.

Albinos

As in the Solomons and parts of Papua New Guinea, some ni-Vanuatu have thick, sandy, curly hair and Melanesian features, with white skin. In neighbouring countries, albinism occurs in families where people inherit a recessive gene from each parent. This happens occasionally in those islands where there has been intermarriage between Melanesians and Polynesians.

Albinos themselves seldom marry thanks to a general knowledge of the inherited aspects of albinism. When an albino marries a non-albino who carries the recessive gene, at least some of the offspring are also likely to exhibit a recessive gene.

Europeans

The vast majority of Europeans live in Vila and Luganville. A few missionaries, doctors, overseas aid volunteers, hoteliers and planters are spread elsewhere around the archipelago, though distinctly fewer than before independence.

Up to 1980, there were many more French than British people in the country. However, since then there has been a noticeable departure of French nationals. Australians have been the principal new arrivals, mainly working in Vila in tourism.

Asians

The small Asian community, which is largely made up of the descendants of Chinese and Vietnamese immigrants, contains many of the country's entrepreneurs. Looking at the startling number of Chinese stores in Luganville and, to a lesser extent, Vila, you'll wonder if it's not the Chinese rather than the English who are a nation of shopkeepers.

EDUCATION

Vanuatu has inherited a dual education system from its former colonial masters. Every one of the 272 primary schools follows the same curriculum, but the medium of instruction is either English or French. Whichever of the two languages a pupil does not learn in primary school is taught as a second subject at secondary school.

In English-language schools, English is spoken in class while Bislama is spoken outside in the playground. A parallel situation exists in French-medium schools. About 55% of pupils receive an Anglophone education, while the remainder study in French-language schools.

In some areas, education is provided in both English and French. In these schools, English-speaking children sit next to Francophone pupils of the same age and ability, yet they can only understand each other in Bislama. So the teacher asks one child a question in French, and the next pupil one in English.

Although 90% of ni-Vanuatu children have primary education, only about 9% go on to the country's 27 secondary schools. As a result, the national literacy level is only around 60%.

Vanuatu has three tertiary institutions, all of which are in the Vila area. These are the Malapoa Teachers College, the Tagabe Agricultural School and an annexe of the University of the South Pacific (USP).

ARTS

Villagers in rural Vanuatu are basically farmers, with art as their second string. Their usual subjects are the human form, and ancestral figures based on traditional interpretations of what they may have looked like.

The most important artefacts are made for nimangki grade-taking ceremonies. The best examples nowadays come from areas where this is still an integral part of traditional village life.

Many ritual objects are destroyed as soon as the ceremony for which they were made is completed. This is because islanders believe the artefacts are taken over by malevolent spirits during or after the ceremony.

Carvings

While wood is the main carved material in the archipelago, objects are also made from tree fern, stone and coral. The majority of carvings are decorated with a stylised human face or a representation of an ancestral spirit. Serious carving is almost entirely created for ceremonies, while items for sale to tourists are usually small copies of the real thing. In terms of the tourist trade, the best carvings come from north Ambrym.

Bowls Large platters and bowls are used to pound yams and kava in, or to serve *laplap* (see the Food section in the Facts for the Visitor chapter). Some are carved like birds or fish, such as those from the Shepherds group.

Poles & Walking Sticks Some chiefs use carved wooden staffs as badges of office. On Tanna, the host village's chief carries a feather-decorated pole while dancing during an important part of the annual Toka ceremony. On some islands walking sticks are made, complete with figurines in place of handles.

Clubs & Weapons Bows and arrows, and ceremonial spears, are still carved, as are clubs for war and pig killing. The most accessible places to find traditionally designed spears are Mele and Ifira islands, both near Vila. The artistic style clearly shows Polynesian influences.

War clubs are made to traditional designs which seldom vary from generation to generation, let alone carver to carver. To alter a basic shape is considered a breach of custom,

especially as the design is often attributed to a cultural hero of the distant past.

Another type of club is used for pig killing. These are shaped like mattocks, with two stylised faces carved on either side.

Canoes Full-size paddle canoes, equipped with outriggers, are in daily use throughout the archipelago. The best miniature model canoes, from Makura in the Shepherds, come fitted with sails fashioned from dried pandanus leaves. Atchin Islanders from north-eastern Malakula carve their miniature canoes complete with figureheads.

Fern Figures Tall statues made from tree ferns, or black palms as they are called locally, were once widespread. Nowadays they are only made in Ambrym and Malakula. They represent both male and female ancestral figures and are carved for nimangki ceremonies by men of middle rank.

Tree fern statues are often painted in several different colours. These tints are extracted from vegetable dyes and crushed shells; the choice of colours depending on the grade being taken.

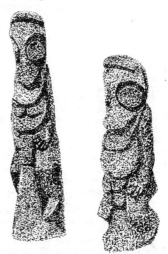

Tree fern figures

Stone Carvings Small ancestral figurines made from volcanic pumice stone come from Ambrym. In addition, in both Malakula and Vanuatu's northernmost islands, small statues in spirit or human form are sometimes carved out of coral.

Magic Stones These basic items of equipment for all sorcerers are made from pumice. Most magic stones are oval shaped and small enough to hold in your hand. As they are regarded as valuable examples of Vanuatu's history, their sale is prohibited to non-nationals, though replicas are sometimes available.

Traditional Dress

Urban ni-Vanuatu usually exchange their European clothing for traditional dress whenever they attend clan ceremonies on their home islands.

In custom-oriented parts of Tanna, Malakula, Pentecost and Ambrym, men still wear *nambas* (penis wrappers) every day, while women dress in grass skirts. Some women from the Big Nambas tribe of Malakula wear nothing more than a long purple headdress, woven from dried pandanus leaves.

Grass Skirts In southern Malakula, the Small Nambas women wear raffia skirts woven from banana tree fibres. This soft material is first soaked in water, then dried and rolled into lengths.

In other parts of Vanuatu, grass skirts are fashioned from the bark of the younger branches of the *burao* or wild hibiscus tree. Once it's stripped, the bark is placed in seawater, dried and measured into lengths. The material is then made into soft skirts and, if necessary, dyed.

Men on Futuna traditionally wear long kilts made from tapa, which is fashioned from breadfruit bark. It's the only part of Vanuatu where this typically Polynesian practice prevails.

Tamtams

Tamtams – also known as slit-gongs and slit-drums – essentially are carved logs with large, hollowed-out slits that enable them to be used as drums. They're usually stood at an angle to make playing easier. They were originally used to send coded messages as well as forming drum orchestras for festivities and celebrations of all kinds. The largest could transmit a message 30 km downwind – the original 'bush telegraph'. Today, these instruments rarely exceed three metres tall, although in earlier times they were much larger.

The typical tamtam has a representation of a human face carved above the drum part. Faces on Malakulan drums are generally very simple and crude, but those from Ambrym can be extremely ornate. The latter have up to five faces, with bulging 'full moon' eyes and exaggerated noses being common features. Each face has a hole cut through its nasal septum to allow two cycad leaves to be passed through and draped on either side. Around the heads are lines of indents that look like dogs' teeth but represent hair.

Tamtams are made from very hard wood, so you can imagine the awesome amount of work that goes into creating their hollowed centres. In the old days, stones were heated and placed in the slit so that the wood became charred. The burnt layers were then scraped away with adzes of stone or shell. The tools used today are more efficient, of course, but creating a tamtam is still a slow task requiring much patience and skill.

On Ambrym, specific tamtam designs belong to particular families. If a carver from outside that family wants to use its design he must pay a fee. A design can be recognised by such characteristics as the number of heads, the way they're facing, and the shape of eyes and other features. The lines of carved 'dog's teeth' indicate the owner's social status. The more lines, the greater the status.

In the past, only men who had achieved a certain grade were allowed to make tamtams. The local chief used to rigorously check each new carver's work, the slightest error being treated as carelessness and disrespect for custom. Serious infractions were sometimes punished with death.

Ambrym tamtams are used as decorative objects around Vila; the Royal Palms Resort has some particularly fine examples, including a monster six metres high. ■

Masks The wearing of elaborate headgear is a major aspect of traditional ceremonies, especially on Ambrym, Ambae, Maewo and Malakula. Only men who have advanced far up the ceremonial ladder may wear such items.

Masks are usually made from tree fern material and represent the faces of demons and ancestral spirits. Others are constructed out of clay reinforced with coconut fibres and layered onto a wickerwork frame. On Pentecost and Vao, masks are made from hard, dark-brown, unpainted wood.

Highly painted fern face masks in southern Malakula are decorated with feathers and carved pigs' tusks. From the same area come hand-held puppets. These are assembled out of clay and represent ancestral figures.

Musical Instruments

Tamtams Vanuatu's most striking musical devices are the huge, carved wooden tamtams, also called slit-gongs or slit-drums, that come from Malakula and Ambrym (see p 34).

Flutes & Conch Shells Panpipes, usually complete with seven small bamboo flutes, are found all over Vanuatu. Ambrym people play a long, geometrically carved musical pipe, while in Santo a simple three-holed flute is used.

On many islands, large triton shells are blown as a means of communication. Unlike Polynesians further east, ni-Vanuatu make a hole in the side of the shell and use that to blow through.

Visual Arts

Sand Drawing On several northern islands, villagers do sand drawings to illustrate local legends or leave messages. The most elaborate and picturesque versions of this artform come from Ambrym, though you can see it done as far north as the Banks.

The artist first draws the foundation design, usually a sequence of squares or rectangles in the sand. Then he or she begins to circle with a finger, making many delicate loops and circles without raising the finger until the design is finally finished. It may just be a message, or may recount a legend, a song or a ceremony.

Modern education has made sand drawing almost redundant, and most sand artists are at least middle-aged.

Tattooing Although tattooing was widely used in the past it's rarely practised these days. Women on Tanna are still marked on the back and arms to indicate marital status, and you'll often see women from other areas with their faces decorated by small tattoos.

Painting Painting styles include bark art in the Banks Islands. Body painting is popular throughout the country as part of various traditional ceremonies.

Traditionally, there were only five colours. White came from burnt coral, mauve from the tree fern, ochre from clay, yellow from the ginger plant, and black from charcoal. Blue was added after European settlement, when traders brought 'washing blue' to the country. Petroglyphs and rock paintings are the country's most ancient forms of pictorial art. The former is common and widespread, though the carvings' meanings and traditions have been lost and their main significance these days is to archaeologists. Several islands have caves whose walls are decorated with hand stencils and simple paintings of animals.

Pottery

Pottery was once a widespread industry and large finds of ceramics dating back to around 500 AD

Tamtam

Man doing a sand drawing

and northern Pentecost. Large numbers of these items are presented at weddings, grade-taking ceremonies, births, funerals and for the payment of customary debts. The mats are coloured by first printing them with a banana-bark block, then immersing them in a dye made from a local bush plant. In the past they were used as everyday clothing, but nowadays are only worn during ceremonies.

Plain sleeping mats are made throughout the country.

CULTURE

The immense variety of Vanuatu's culture and customs reflects the existence of 105 indigenous languages among a small population.

Dances, ceremonies, funerals, weddings, initiations, status and systems of authority, artistic styles, and animal and crop husbandry all differ from island to island, and often from one district to another within the larger islands. Yet there are common themes, particularly the acceptance of the obligation to pay for all services rendered.

Some chiefs bemoan the apparent passing of custom, or *kastom* as villagers call it in Bislama, especially when so many young people are leaving for Vila. However, others say custom will live forever, and they may be right. Despite more than 100 years of missionary teaching, small groups on several islands still follow ancient ancestral religions and customs.

have been made. Others unearthed are from the prehistoric Lapita period. Today, the only remaining traditional potters live in two isolated villages in south-western Santo (see Santo's West Coast in the Espiritu Santo Island chapter).

Weaving

Baskets and mats are made according to local design throughout the country. Fish, bird and shellfish traps are also manufactured, as are items such as furniture and Panama-style hats.

Weaving is always done by hand, and mostly by women, with pandanus leaves and burao stalks being the most favoured materials. Wicker, coconut leaves and rattan are used for the more robust items.

Bags & Baskets Pandanus shopping baskets are made on a number of islands, with the artisans of Mataso (in the Shepherds) and Futuna being noted for their intricate basketware.

Mats Locally made red pandanus mats are traditionally used as money in the Polynesian-influenced islands of Ambae, Maewo

Land Ownership

Traditional View Melanesians believe that they are nurtured by their land in the same way that plants and trees are. It feeds them as a mother nourishes her child.

Families only have the right in customary law to occupy specific sections of land, not to sell them. These rights go back to the first ancestors who settled each particular piece of ground.

Land can only be transferred to those who are related to the clan which originally occupied it. The simplest method for a ni-Vanuatu man to acquire territorial rights outside his own clan area is to marry into another group.

Rights to reefs and boat landing places are similarly inherited. Islanders acknowledge boundaries on reefs according to where their ancestors first came ashore. Fishing rights extend out from the beach or rocks as far and as deep as shoreside angling and free diving for seashells are possible.

Noncustom Ownership When Europeans arrived all the ancient concepts of traditional ownership were put in jeopardy. To the Anglo-French mind, land was a saleable commodity.

Much of the impetus for national independence resulted from ni-Vanuatu concern over foreign land purchases. Since independence, only custom owners and the government are permitted to own land. Noncustom-owning islanders and foreigners may lease land for a maximum of 75 years, which is the productive life of a coconut tree. One of the main stumbling blocks to leasing land is the difficulty that's often experienced in identifying the true custom owner.

Village Life

While townspeople's lives in Vanuatu have altered considerably in recent times, village life is much as it has always been. Virtually the entire rural population is engaged in subsistence farming of food crops. This is supplemented by hunting, gathering and fishing, with cash cropping also of importance. The forests are a major resource, providing medicine, food, building materials and timber for boat building and artefacts. Freshwater is often in short supply and must sometimes be collected from other islands.

Women do most of the hard work. Typically they spend up to 10 hours a day away from home in the family garden, while men spend about the same in such activities as cash cropping, fishing, hunting, boat building, artefact carving and discussing council matters. While the women prepare the evening meal, the men sit around in the *nakamal* drinking kava and talking about the day's events. Generally, it's the woman's responsibility to attend to the gardening,

cooking, cleaning, child care and water collection.

Usually more food is grown than is needed. This is to ensure that there will be enough to entertain friends and relatives, and to put away for use during shortages (such as usually occurs after droughts and cyclones). In Melanesian custom it's also important to be able to give away any surplus as a gesture of public hospitality.

Tabus

You'll frequently hear the word *tabu*, from which comes the English 'taboo'. In Pacific island terms, the expression means 'sacred' or 'holy', as well as 'forbidden'. In its simplest form, it can mean 'no entry' when written across a doorway or gate.

Traditionally, certain places are tabu and can only be approached with the utmost respect. In the past, failure to observe the correct rules would require the payment of pigs as a penalty, or even the death of the transgressor.

Many tabus relate to traditional ceremonies. Women, and uninitiated men, are barred from seeing parts of certain ceremonies in the country's more custom-oriented areas. At the same time, other functions are limited to women, with men being excluded.

Women in particular must endure some rather unusual restrictions. For example, in some areas they may not stand higher than a male. Nor may they step over a fire as its smoke – while she's standing in it – may rise higher than a man.

At the same time, men may not deliberately place themselves below a woman. So walking under a woman's clothes line or swimming under her canoe is forbidden, even for male tourists. If you do this, everything involved may have to be destroyed, in which case you'll be expected to pay compensation.

Menstruation and birth are surrounded by all sorts of tabus. Most traditional villages have an area set aside both for childbirth and for women to go to during menstruation. For a woman living in a custom-oriented area to fail to do so, to continue gardening and cooking, or even to go fishing while pregnant, is a serious breach of custom. The penalty for this is a hefty fine to the chief in pigs, or else departure from the village. In the past the transgressor would have been killed.

Just as women may not go to those places which are reserved for men, it's forbidden for men to visit the part of the village reserved for women's use during menstruation. This also applies if a woman is having her child there, rather than in hospital. Ablutions are the same. Each sex has its own area. If you're staying in a village, you should check which is your section as soon as possible after arrival.

Magic

Custom-oriented ni-Vanuatu believe that, in addition to ordinary humans, their world is populated by ancestral spirits and demons. The ghosts of the recently dead are considered especially potent as well as being potentially malicious, even towards their own family.

The practice of magic is generally tabu for women, but most grown men in the tradi-

---

Avoiding Offence

While village people will usually make allowances for the ignorance of tourists, the observance of a few simple rules will help you avoid giving offence. You'll also earn points by being seen to be trying to do the right thing.

Make sure you stick to the road when passing through a village. As a rule, if you want to enter a small village to buy food or enquire about accommodation etc, wait at the outskirts until someone comes up. There are always children about, so you won't be standing around unnoticed for long. It's bad manners to simply walk in and knock on someone's door as you would in Australia or Europe.

If you leave the road and walk on a bush path, always ask the first person you meet for permission to use it. Either approval will be given straight away, or you will be introduced to the chief for his ruling. Be prepared to hire a guide for longer walks.

Land ownership and food growing are extremely delicate matters, so you should resist the temptation to pick fruit growing by the wayside. It may look untended, but it still belongs to someone. The same applies to reefs, all of which are owned in customary law by individual islanders or their families.

Melanesians always assess a foreigner's reaction to them by seeing whether he or she will share food with them. In response, they will often offer some treat, usually a coconut or banana, on your arrival. They won't expect you to respond with any more than thanks if you're only with them a short time. But if you stay longer, they will expect you to pay them back. In the Melanesian world, nothing comes for free. At the same time, generosity with food is considered a great virtue.

If you want to repay your hosts' kindness with a gift, present them with items such as cans of tinned meat of fish, matches, candles, tea or sugar. Tobacco sticks are often appreciated in remote areas, plus a few pages from a school exercise book to use as cigarette paper. Send them a postcard when you get back home and they'll be delighted.

Islanders seldom wear scant or revealing clothing, though plenty of foreigners do. Male visitors to a traditional village should always be fully dressed, regardless of how little clothing the local men may be wearing.

The same applies to female tourists. They should wear longish dresses, slacks or jeans, even if the local women are wearing nothing but grass skirts. Bathing suits, shorts and skimpy clothes are considered suggestive, and therefore disrespectful. However, you may certainly wear these in Vila and other tourist-oriented areas. Dresses or full-length black slips are the most appropriate swimsuits in rural areas.

Generally, Vanuatu is a stronghold of male chauvinism, and women are often regarded as second-class citizens. For a female visitor to address or treat a chief as an equal is unthinkable. Thus you should be extremely respectful, if not servile, until you've at least had a chance to gauge the chief's reaction to you.

Finally, always observe local tabus. If an area is off-limits to your sex (eg *natsaros* - dancing grounds - are generally tabu to females) stay away from it. As in most things, all you have to do to avoid embarrassment or offence is to ask first. ■

tional parts of Vanuatu know a few useful spells. These may be used to further love affairs or to produce good crops. An actual magician is employed for more specialised tasks such as raising or calming storms, healing the sick, banishing spirits or controlling volcanoes.

Sorcery can also be used to harm rivals. Indeed, magic is usually suspected if someone dies suddenly.

Because of their specialised knowledge, magicians generally feel they are superior to the average person. If a middle-aged or elderly man from a traditional village refuses to shake your hand when everyone else does, it could be because he's the local sorcerer.

Dances & Ceremonies

Traditional dances in Vanuatu involve either impersonation or participation. Impersonation dances require more rehearsal as each dancer pretends to be an ancestor or legendary figure. Because the character being represented is not human, the dancer's actions and dress are similarly nonhuman. This allows the participants to wear elaborate masks or headdresses, such as in the Rom dances of Ambrym.

In participatory dances, several people usually take part to enact traditional themes such as hunting, war or death. These events serve to bring villagers together as team rehearsals are often needed, as in the extraordinary Toka celebrations of Tanna.

Male dancers in most custom-oriented parts of Vanuatu perform wearing either nambas or *mal mal* (a piece of cotton or tapa cloth) only, while women wear grass skirts. On islands where Polynesian influences apply, both sexes may dance wearing small mats around their hips.

Chiefs

All of Vanuatu's chiefs are men. A ni-Vanuatu chief acts as a justice of the peace and as a delegate to speak for the people of the village. Each chief achieves this status in most northern areas by holding a series of lavish feasts which allow him/her to pass through many ceremonial grades. During

these rites he/she ensures the support of ancestral spirits by making sacrifices to them.

In contrast, chiefs in the lower part of the archipelago, from the Shepherds southwards, either inherit their titles or are elected. Inheritance is particularly significant on Futuna, Ifira Island and the village of Mele near Vila, all of which have a strong Polynesian influence.

A chief puts fellow villagers in his debt when they consume his food at a feast. In this way he creates a party of supporters who look to him for leadership and guidance when their interests are threatened. On the other hand, he faces the sack if he fails in his responsibilities as spokesperson and arbiter of disputes.

The Nimangki

From Epi northwards, and particularly on Malakula, Ambae and Ambrym, status and power are earned by taking grades through the nimangki system. Prestige flows to those aspirants who have publicly given away their wealth by holding a series of spectacular ceremonies, which are always accompanied by traditional dancing and feasting.

Each step up the village social ladder is accompanied by the ritual killing of pigs. Because a boar takes between six and seven years to grow a good set of tusks, which are the prized article, only those men wealthy enough to own a large number of pigs can hope to reach society's highest levels.

The nimangki system allows even those men who can only afford to hold a few pig-killing ceremonies to take their place on the social ladder. It also provides a man with status in the afterlife. A villager who has risen far in his clan hierarchy believes that his spirit, once he is dead, will command considerable respect from those who are still alive.

To rise a grade, a man holds a feast with sometimes scores of pigs lined up for slaughter. Then, in front of his fellow villagers, he walks along the line killing selected animals with blows to the head. Others he will simply touch to show that although he considers them suitable food, they'll be slaughtered later.

In addition, the aspirant will present a number of woven mats as well as sufficient yams and taro for a lavish meal. By means of this conspicuous destruction of his assets, the villager moves up a nimangki grade, earning new respect from his fellows for his wealth and generosity. South-western Malakulan males can take up to 35 grades, while on Ambae only four are required.

Not all grade-taking is restricted to men. Women from the Small Nambas tribe in southern central Malakula take grades, though they have much fewer levels than their menfolk.

Beginning Grade-Taking Although the nimangki process can begin early in a boy's life, few take any grades until they've passed their teens. Usually a youth begins by borrowing five to 10 boars to pay his bride-price. As soon as he can he buys some sows, which become the source of his future wealth and status.

In time, to clear his debts for his wife's bride price and his sows, the young man starts lending out male piglets. Even so, it often takes him several years to pay off his initial debt. Once his liabilities are discharged, and he has lent out enough pigs, he celebrates with a special yam feast. This is usually followed two years later by a nimangki ceremony.

Pig Kills The higher a man rises in his grades, the greater must be the number and value of the pigs he kills. The more curved and sizeable its tusks, the more valuable is the pig. Boars with large, fully developed tusks forming at least one circle – and preferably more – are worth up to 40,000VT each.

A boar is first castrated, then, when the lower pair of tusks are well grown, its upper teeth are removed. The tusks take between six and seven years to complete a circle. At this stage, the teeth begin to penetrate the animal's jaw, causing it considerable discomfort when eating. The pig is then handfed

and kept tied up to prevent it foraging and fighting, either of which could damage its tusks.

A double-circling tooth takes about 14 years to grow, and is extremely valuable. Should the animal's tusks grow a third circle, which happens very occasionally, it costs a pig just for the privilege of looking at it. Once the boar has been killed, the owner wears the curved teeth around his neck as a sign to others of his great wealth.

The Nakamal

In most custom-oriented parts of north and central Vanuatu, the nakamal corresponds to a men's club house, or clan hut. When built in traditional style, a nakamal is a long enclosed building with two rooms. The front one is where men meet at the end of the day, while the rear room is the clan's trophy store or museum. This section often contains ancestral skulls and other sacred objects.

In other parts of Vanuatu, such as Tanna, the nakamal is the place where men meet their chief daily at sunset to talk and drink kava. In these areas, a nakamal may simply be an open-ended hut, or a shelter beneath a large tree. In Christian parts of the country, the nakamal may be no more than a special section in someone's garden. It can even be a rough shed where men come after work to drink kava.

As a rule you should never enter a traditional nakamal without the permission of one of its members. Indeed, such nakamals are usually strictly tabu to women, especially in strongly custom-oriented parts of the country. On the other hand, most of the so-called nakamals of Vila (in reality these are just kava bars) allow women.

Initiations

In the traditional parts of Vanuatu, teenage initiation conveys a child straight into adulthood. Boys, usually aged from 10 to 12, are either taken into the bush or kept secluded in a special hut for several weeks, during which circumcision takes place. When their wounds have healed, they return to their families amid much feasting. In southern

Malakula, special puppets and masks are made to record each boy's progression to maturity.

Once a boy has been initiated, he is considered to have the status and duties of a man. He can no longer be chastised by his mother because his rank is now greater than hers. He goes to live in either his father's or the young men's house, where he learns adult responsibilities and his clan's traditions. He can now wear a namba, and begin taking nimangki grades once he has acquired some pigs.

In some areas, particularly inland Malakula, girls are initiated by having a front tooth ceremonially removed. This painful process takes several hours.

Marriage

In the past a man might have paid up to 100 pigs, as well as scores of mats and shells, for a wife. Nowadays the bride-price is usually between five and 10 pigs, or their value in modern currency.

A new version of this has recently evolved in southern Efate, where young unmarried women are often light-heartedly called 'Toyotas'. This is what Vila's bride-price among wealthier families is roughly equivalent to.

Funerals

In most parts of the country, ceremonies and feasts are held at regular intervals after an important man's death, sometimes continuing intermittently for more than a year. The frequency varies from place to place, but the aim is to appease the man's spirit.

In south-central Malakula, when a chief who has advanced especially far up his nimangki grades dies, his relatives make a full-size replica of him eight to 12 months later. Clay is layered over his skull and an attached bamboo frame, which represents the body. After the replica has been displayed, and a secondary brief period of mourning has passed, the effigy is allowed to decompose. This is the final laying to rest of the spirit.

Women's Lives

The average ni-Vanuatu female can expect to live a shorter, and usually harder working, life than her male compatriots. In clear contrast to trends in most other countries, where females usually outlive males, ni-Vanuatu women over 60 are outnumbered by local men of the same age four to three. This is considered to be largely because of the high birth rate – an average of six children per family – and resulting workload that prevailed until very recently.

An attractive daughter, who may command a dowry of several hundred thousand vatu, is considered an excellent means by which a family can enrich itself. However, other than earning her parents a sizeable bride-price, a woman's life is still considered to be one of helping her husband increase his assets and social position. This usually involves working in his gardens, cooking his meals, looking after the children and tending his pigs. Naturally, increasing numbers of educated women are rejecting such a limited lot in life.

RELIGION
Background

The early Christian missionaries, who were mainly Presbyterians, were very strict in their beliefs. Their eventual successes in Vanuatu were partly due to Christianity having some distinct similarities to certain local legends.

Southern island mythologies had a snake god who was associated with death. Other parts of the country had similar stories to those of Adam and Eve, including one about the first ni-Vanuatu man and woman being tempted to eat the forbidden fruit of a sacred rose apple tree. Tagaro, the genial creator of the heavens, was sometimes called Tahara, a name which islanders felt sounded remarkably like Jehovah. Likewise Sem-Sem, also called Saratau, a name reminiscent of Satan, was a legendary pre-Christian demon who traditionally hindered local people from enjoying a rewarding life after death.

During the early period of the Condominium, medicine and education were left in the hands of the missions. By the late 1950s, this financial burden had become clearly too much for them.

While they had helped by providing medical services, missions often created divisions between differing Christian denominations. In addition, many missionaries – particularly the Presbyterians – took the pleasure and spontaneity out of people's lives by refusing to allow participation in many of their age-old traditions.

The Current Situation

About 90% of the population is Christian, with nearly half these being Presbyterian. Roman Catholics and Anglicans are also significant. Non Christians are largely made up of John Frum worshippers and adherents to traditional religions.

While the Presbyterians are spread reasonably evenly throughout the archipelago, the Anglicans are mainly found in the Banks group, Ambae, Maewo and Pentecost.

The Roman Catholics are widespread, being strongest in the areas where French is widely spoken. Their main islands are Santo, Malakula and Efate.

Most of the Church of Christ's members live on Ambae, Maewo and Pentecost. The Apostolic Church is also present in western Ambae, and in Luganville and Vila. The Seventh Day Adventists are evenly spread in Santo, Efate, Ambae, Malakula and Tanna. Other recent arrivals include the Assemblies of God, the Free Evangelical Church, Mormons, Jehovah's Witnesses and Bahais.

Most people are extremely devout in their belief with virtually every village having a church. The general pattern is for a mission to have come to a village, and almost all the people there to follow that particular denomination.

On the other hand, a village may be more-or-less equally divided between two or more Christian denominations, or with some residents being Christian and others following traditional religions. In these cases it's usual for the village to be physically divided – either by space or some barrier – such that the particular groups live in separate areas.

LANGUAGE

Vanuatu claims the highest concentration of different languages per head of population of any country in the world. There are at least 105 local languages as well as the more widely spoken English, French and Bislama. The latter, which is a form of pidgin (or 'business') English, is the national lingua franca.

Vanuatu's many indigenous tongues are a reflection of the fact that its people have always lived in small, isolated communities in island and forest environments.

Bislama

Also called Bislaman by elderly islanders, and *bichlamar* or *bichelamar* by French speakers, Bislama is the English-based pidgin used throughout the archipelago. Both Papua New Guinea and the Solomon Islands have similar languages, though Bislama has acquired a number of French terms as well.

Bislama enables a person from one part of the country to converse with someone from a totally different area. It also allows the approximately 40% of the population who have been educated in French-language schools to communicate with the remaining 60% who have studied in English-language institutions.

Bislama evolved from the 'business' English, or pidgin, that was used by the Europeans who traded throughout the Pacific from the 1830s onwards. Their main interests were sandalwood and trepang (sea cucumbers), the latter being called *bêche-de-mer* in French. Indeed, trepang is called *bislama* by ni-Vanuatu in their new language.

By the 1930s, Bislama was being used by missionaries all over the country, which helped to spread it even further. Nowadays, most ni-Vanuatu speak this language with varying degrees of fluency, while the more educated also speak either English or French at least reasonably well.

Because it functions as a link language between indigenous vernaculars and both English and French, Bislama is now

Vanuatu's most important official national language. While most commerce and government correspondence are conducted in English or French, parliamentary debates are held in Bislama.

Pronunciation

There are a number of differences in pronunciation between English and Vanuatu's indigenous languages. For example, 'Vanafo', a village in Santo, is spelt and pronounced 'Tanafo' and 'Fanafo' as well as plain 'Vanafo'.

Consonants As well as **v**, **t** and **f** sometimes being interchanged, **b** and **p** are also sometimes confused with each other. **B** and **d** are often pronounced by Melanesians as **mb** and **nd** respectively. Similarly, **g** is frequently enunciated as **ng**, while **ch** comes out as **s**. This linguistic phenomenon, widespread in Melanesia, is called prenasalisation. However, it's not uniform throughout Vanuatu, so pronunciation errors can easily occur.

Vowels In Bislama, there are two special rules relating to vowels. Firstly, where two such letters are used together, they are usually sounded jointly as diphthong except with the letter **i**, and occasionally **e**. When these letters are juxtaposed with another vowel, as in *ia* and *wea,* meaning 'here' and 'where' respectively, both vowels are pronounced separately. In addition, no word begins with a **u**. Instead the letters **yu**, as in *yumi,* are used.

Grammar

Bislama is free of redundant features such as gendered nouns and pronouns. There are also no verb endings identifying time, such as present, past or future tenses. However, Bislama distinguishes between activities which have begun, and those which have not.

Verbs Tenses can be identified by using time words such as *nekis wik,* ie 'next week', or *las yia,* ie 'last year'. Alternatively the expression *stap* or *nao* reveals the action to be in the present, whilst *bambae* at the beginning of the phrase identifies the future tense.

Bin and *finis* are used to show the action was in the past. *Bin* is placed before the relevant verb, while *finis* appears at the end of the phrase.

Nouns If a noun's gender is unclear, a word can be added to clarify it – eg *man puskat* is a 'tom cat'. Where plurals are concerned, English has a number of irregularities – eg, 'children'. In Bislama, this is *olgeta pikinini. Olgeta* is used here before *pikinini* to signify the plural.

Many nouns have the expression *samting blong* preceding them. This means 'the thing which is used for...' For example, *samting blong katem fis* is a 'fish knife'.

An interesting permutation involves items which originated overseas. In these cases, the words *blong waetman* are often used whenever some new device first appears in the country. For example, a piano often used to be described as *samting blong waetman wetem blak mo waet tut, sipos yu kilim, hem i save krae aot.* This translates as 'a whiteman's thing with black and white teeth; if you strike it, it cries out'.

Pronouns Plural pronouns in Bislama have grammatical features which are absent in English. There are five ni-Vanuatu terms for 'we' or 'us', and three for the plural 'you'. Bislama has no specific gender words for the third person singular (ie he, she or it), as is the case for English. In Bislama, the third person is *hem,* or *em,* followed by *i* and the word or verb – eg *hem i stap ia* means 'he/she is here'. Depending on the context, this statement can also mean 'he/she lives here'.

Bislama Pronouns

I/me	*mi*
you (singular)	*yu*
he/him, she/her, it	*hem, em*
we, us (including the person/people spoken to)	*yumi*
we, us two (excluding the person/people spoken to)	*mifala*

| you (plural) | *yufala* |
| they, them | *olgeta* |

In Bislama, *tu* and *tri* are incorporated into the pronouns 'we', 'us' and 'you', when the speaker is with two or three other people. Its purpose is to include or exclude the person/people spoken to:

we, us two/three (ie you and I)	*yumitufala/yumitrifala*
we, us two/three (ie not you)	*mitufala/mitrifala*
you two	*yutufala*
you three	*yutrifala*

Vocabulary

While many of Bislama's words are based on English vernacular, there are many differences of meaning in the new language. For example *swim* in Bislama can mean swim, bathe, bath or shower.

A particularly versatile word is *long*. This can mean to, at, from, in, among, along, during, or about, depending on the situation. Increasingly, long is pronounced *low*.

Colourful Expressions English has about 35,000 words, while Bislama and other similar contact languages have only about 2500. It requires a considerable degree of ingenuity to fill this gap, with some very colourful expressions resulting. For example, Frenchmen, now known as *man Franis*, in the last century were commonly called *man wiwi*, which literally means the 'men who say *oui, oui*' ('yes, yes').

A commonly used word is *blong*, meaning 'of' or 'for'. The expression *glas blong* produces *glas blong lukluk big*, ie 'magnifying glass' or *glas blong sip* which translates as 'porthole'. *Gras blong faol* means 'a chicken's feather', though *gras blong man* does not mean 'beard' or 'moustache' as is commonly thought by expatriates, but 'pubic hair'.

Warning! Some words are perfectly polite in Bislama but not in English – and vice versa. If you wanted to say something was 'broken', you'd say *bagarap* in Bislama. Likewise a tool for repairing damaged machinery is a *bagarap tul*.

Once avoided in polite English-speaking circles but gaining acceptability in these worrying days of AIDS, is the word 'condom'. Bislama has come to the rescue over this delicate matter with the expression *rubba blong fak-fak*.

Care should always be taken whenever *puspus, hambag, plei, mekem trabol, mekem no gud, stil, krangke*, or *blong rod* are used. Whilst *puspus* is sexual intercourse, *hambag* usually refers to extra-marital sex, as does *mekem no gud*. *Krangke* usually means 'mad', but can refer to 'being adulterous' in a woman's case. *Mekem trabol long yang gel* means 'getting a young woman pregnant', whilst *stil* ('steal') in *hem i woman Ostrelya stap stil long man ples*, means 'the Australian woman is having an affair with a married ni-Vanuatu man'. Lastly, *plei* can refer to playing a game, or to sexual play, depending on the context.

Dictionaries & Phrasebooks

A Descriptive Dictionary: Bislama to English by Pastor Bill Camden (Maropa Bookshop, Vila 1977) is the most informative guide to the ni-Vanuatu language. An entertaining and amusingly illustrated work is Darrell Tryon's *Let's Talk Bislama* (Media Masters South Pacific Pidgin Post, Vila 1986).

Also useful are the *Jacaranda Dictionary & Grammar of Melanesian Pidgin* by F Mihalic (Jacaranda Press, Australia 1971) and J B M Guy's *Handbook of Bichelamar* (School of Pacific Studies, Australian National University, Canberra 1974).

An Illustrated Bislama-English & English-Bislama Dictionary by Terry Crowley (University of the South Pacific, Vila 1990) is extremely comprehensive. It's an essential reference if you're serious about learning the language.

There's only one conversation and language guide to Bislama available in Vila for French speakers. This is *Apprenons le Bichlamar* (edited by Socom SA of Vila). It has about 700 words and phrases in the two languages.

Whatever time you can devote to learning this unusual but interesting new language will be well spent, particularly if you're going to be spending time in rural Vanuatu.

While you'll usually get by speaking simple English or French, depending where you are, at least a basic understanding of Bislama will improve your communication skills no end.

Greetings & Civilities

English	Bislama	French
Hello.	*Alo.*	*Bonjour.*
Goodbye.	*Tata.*	*Au revoir.*
Good morning.	*Gudmorning.*	*Bonjour.*
Good afternoon.	*Gudaftenun.*	*Bonjour.*
Good night.	*Gudnaet.*	*Bonsoir/Bonne Nuit.*
Please.	*Plis.*	*S'il vous plait.*
Thank you (very much).	*Tank yu (tumas).*	*Merci (beaucoup).*
You're welcome.	*I oraet nomo.*	*C'est de rien.*
Yes.	*Yes.*	*Oui.*
No.	*No.*	*Non.*
Maybe.	*Ating/Maet/Mebi.*	*Peut-être.*
Excuse me.	*Skiusmi.*	*Excusez-moi/Pardon.*
I'm sorry.	*Mi sori tomas.*	*Pardon/Je suis désolé/ée.*
How are you?	*Olsem wanem/Yu oraet?*	*Comment ça va?*
I'm fine, thanks.	*I oraet, tank yu/ I gud nomo.*	*Ça va bien, merci.*

Useful Phrases

I understand.	*Mi save. (pronounced 'savvy')*	*Je comprends.*
I don't understand.	*Mi no save.*	*Je ne comprends pas.*
I don't speak ...	*Mi no toktok ...*	*Je ne parle pas ...*
Do you speak ...?	*Yu toktok ...?*	*Parlez-vous ...?*
English	*Engglis*	*anglais*
Bislama	*Bislama*	*bichlamar*
Franis	*French*	*français*
I want to talk to the chief/pastor	*Mi wantem toktok long jif/pasta.*	*Je voudrais parler au chef/ pasteur.*
Help!	*Help!*	*Au secours!*
Go away!	*Gowe!*	*Allez-vous-en!*
Call a doctor/the police!	*Singaot doctor/polis!*	*Appelez un médecin/ la police!*

Small Talk

What's your name?	*Wanem nem blong yu?*	*Comment vous appelez-vous?*
My name is ...	*Nem blong mi ...*	*Je m'appelle ...*
Where do you live?	*Yu blong/Stap wea?*	*Où habitez-vous?*

I'm from ...	*Mi blong ...*	*Je viens de/d' ...*
How old are you?	*Hamas yia blong yu?*	*Quel âge avez-vous?*
I'm ... years old.	*Mi kat ... yia.*	*J'ai ... ans.*
Do you like ...?	*Yu ting you likim ...?*	*... vous plaît?*
I like it very much.	*Mi likim tumas.*	*Ça me plaît beaucoup.*
I don't like ...	*Mi no likim ...*	*... ne me plaît pas.*
Wait a moment.	*Weit smol.*	*Attendez un moment.*
It's all right/No problem.	*I olraet/I no problem.*	*Ça va/Pas de problème.*

Getting Around

Can I go to ... ?	*Mi save go long ...?*	*Je peux aller à ... ?*
That place is a prohibited area.	*Ples ia i tabu.*	*C'est interdit d'y aller.*
I want to go to ...	*Mi wantem go long ...*	*Je veux aller à ...*
What time does ... leave/arrive?	*Wanem time ... i leave/i kasem long ples ia?*	*A quelle heure départ/arrive ...?*
the boat	*bot*	*le bateau*
the aeroplane	*plen*	*l'avion*
How long does the trip take?	*Bae i longfela alsam wanem?*	*Combien de temps prend ce voyage?*
I'd like to hire ...	*Mi wantem rentem ...*	*Je voudrais louer ...*
a speedboat	*spidbot/bot*	*une vedette*
a guide	*tour guide*	*un guide*
a taxi	*taksi*	*un taxi*
a canoe	*kanu/kenu*	*un canoë*

Directions

How do I get to ...?	*Bi mi go kasem ... olsem wanem?*	*Comment fair pour aller à ...?*
Where is ...?	*Wea ples ...?*	*Où est ...?*
Is it far from here?	*Hamas farawe long ia?*	*C'est loin d'ici?*
What ... is this?	*Wanem ... ia?*	*C'est quoi ... là?*
street/road	*rod*	*cette rue*
village	*vilej*	*ce village*
up/down	*an tap/daon*	*en haut/en bas*
behind/opposite	*bihaen/narasaed long*	*derrière/en face de*
here/there/everywhere	*long ples ia, long hia/ longwe/olbaot*	*ice/là/partout*
east/west	*is/wes*	*à l'est/à l'ouest*
north/south	*not/saot*	*au nord/au sud*

Around Town

Where is the ...?	*Wea ples i ...?*	*Où est ...?*
bank	*bang*	*la banque*

entrance/exit	*rod blong go insaed/ aosaed*	*l'entrée/la sortie*
hospital/clinic	*hospitel/klinik/haos meresin*	*l'hôpital/le centre médical*
market	*maket*	*le marché*
post office	*post ofis*	*la poste*
store	*stoa*	*le magasin*
telephone	*pablik telefon*	*le téléphone*

| Where are the public toilets? | *Wea ples i pablik tolet/ klosis/smolhaous* | *Où sont les toilettes?* |

| I want to make a telephone call. | *Mi wantem telefon.* | *Je voudrais faire un coup de fil.* |

beach	*sanbij*	*la plage*
bridge	*brij*	*le pont*
church	*joj*	*l'église*
coral reef	*korel rif*	*le récif de corail*
island	*aelan*	*l'île*
lake	*lek*	*le lac*
plantation	*platesen*	*la plantation*
river	*reva*	*la rivière*
school	*skul*	*l'école*
sea	*solwota*	*la mer*
volcano	*volkeno*	*le volcan*

Accommodation

I'm looking for ...	*Mi stop lukaot ...*	*Je cherche ...*
a hotel	*hotel*	*un hôtel*
a guest house	*reshaos*	*une pension de famille*
the manager	*managa/bos blong ...*	*le gérant*

Do you have a ... available?	*Yu kat ... long ples ia?*	*Avez-vous ...?*
bed	*bed*	*un lit*
single/double room	*rum blong wan/tu*	*une chambre à un lit/une chambre à deux*

| for one/two nights | *blong wan/tu naet* | *pour une/deux nuit(s)* |

| How much is it per night/per person? | *Hamas i blong wan naet/ wan man?* | *C'est combien la nuit par personne?* |
| Is breakfast included? | *Hemia i blong brekfas tu?* | *Est-ce que le petit déjeuner est compris?* |

| Can I see the room? | *Mi save luk rum?* | *Je peux voir la chambre?* |

This room is very ...	*Rum emi ...*	*Cette chambre est très ...*
dirty	*toti*	*sale*
noisy	*tumas nois*	*bruyante*
expensive	*sas*	*chère*

Do you have ...?   *Yu gat ...?*   *Avez-vous ...?*
  a clean sheet   *klin kaliko blong bed*   *un drap net*
  · hot water   *hot wota*   *l'eau chaud*
  a key   *wan kei*   *un clef*
  a shower   *ples blong swim/rum*   *une douche*
                     blong swim

Food & Drink

I'm hungry/thirsty.   *Mi wantem samting long*   *J'ai faim/soif.*
                   kakae/dring.

I would like ...   *Mi wantem .../*   *Je voudrais ...*
                   Mi laekem ...

Another ..., please.   *Wan mo ..., plis.*   *Encore un(e) ... s'il vous*
                                      plaît.

Do you have a kava bar   *Mi save dring kava long* *Est-ce qu'il ya un kava bar*
  here?   *ples ia?*   *ici?*
Can I buy some young   *Mi save pem kokonas*   *Est-ce que je peux acheter*
  coconuts?   *blong dring?*   *des nouvelles noix de*
                                        coco?

I'm a vegetarian.   *Mi no kakae mit.*   *Je suis vegetarien/ienne*
I don't eat ...   *Mi no kakae ...*   *Je ne mange pas de/d' ...*

breakfast   *brekfas*   *le petit déjeuner*
lunch   *dina*   *le déjeuner*
dinner   *kakae long sapa*   *le dîner*
food stall   *stol blong salem kakae*   *le kiosque d'alimentaire*
market   *maket*   *le marché*
restaurant   *restoron*   *le restaurant*
roadside stall   *rod maket*   *l'éventaire*
supermarket/store   *supamaket/sto*   *le supermarché*

beef   *mit blong buluk*   *boeuf*
beer   *bia*   *biere*
bread   *bred*   *pain*
chicken   *jikin*   *poulet*
coconut   *koknat*   *noix*
coffee   *kofe*   *café*
eggs   *egs*   *œfs*
fish   *fis*   *poisson*
food   *kakae*   *nourriture*
fruit   *frut*   *fruit*
green vegetables   *kabis*   *légumes verts*
meat   *mit*   *viande*
milk   *melek/milk*   *lait*
pepper   *pepa*   *poivre*
pork   *mit blong pig*   *porc*
salt   *sol*   *sel*
soup   *sup/lasup/supsup*   *soupe/potage*
sugar   *suga*   *sucre*
tea   *ti/lifti*   *thé*
wine   *waen*   *vin*

A: Tannese boy in ceremonial dress (AV)
B: Woman from Tanna Island (AV)
C: Man from custom village, Tanna Island (MC)
D: Children from Port Vila (AV)

All photographs courtesy of Air Vanuatu, Melbourne

Shopping

How much is this?	*Hamas long hemia nao?*	*C'est combien?*
I would like to buy ...	*Mi wantem pem ...*	*Je voudrais acheter ...*
It's too expensive for me.	*I sas tumas long mi.*	*C'est trop cher (m)/chère(f).*
Can I look at it?	*Mi save luk?*	*Je peux le/la regarder?*
I'm just looking.	*Mi stap lukluk nomo.*	*Je ne fais que regarder.*
I'm looking for ...	*Mi stap lukaot ...*	*Je cherche ...*
candles	*kandel*	*des bougies*
clothing	*klos*	*des vêtements*
matches	*boks masis*	*des allumettes*
a mosquito net	*moskito net*	*une moustiquaire*
Do you have another colour/size?	*Yu nogat kalar/saes ia?*	*Avez-vous un autre couleur/ une autre taille?*
big/bigger	*Yu gat big wan mo?*	*grand(e)/plus grand(e)*
small/smaller	*Yu gat smol wan mo?*	*petit(e)/plus petit(e)*
cheap/cheaper	*I no saes tumas?*	*bon marché(ée)/plus bon marché(ée)*
No shoes, no shirt, no service!	*No gat but, no gat sat, no gat sevis!*	*Pas de chaussures, pas de chemise, pas de service!*

Times & Dates

When?	*Wanem taem/Wataem?*	*Quand?*
today	*tude/tede*	*aujourd'hui*
tonight	*tede naet/tunaet*	*ce soir*
tomorrow	*tumoro*	*demain*
the day after tomorrow	*afta tumoro*	*après-demain*
yesterday	*yestede*	*hier*
all day/everyday	*fulde/evri dei*	*toute la journée/tous les jours*
Monday	*Mande*	*Lundi*
Tuesday	*Tuste*	*Mardi*
Wednesday	*Wenste*	*Mercredi*
Thursday	*Toste*	*Jeudi*
Friday	*Fraede*	*Vendredi*
Saturday	*Satede*	*Samedi*
Sunday	*Sande*	*Dimanche*
January	*Januari*	*Janvier*
February	*Febuari*	*Février*
March	*Maj*	*Mars*
April	*Epril*	*Avril*
May	*Me*	*Mai*
June	*Jun*	*Juin*
July	*Julae*	*Juillet*
August	*Ogis/Oks*	*Août*

September	*Septemba*	*Septembre*
October	*Oktoba*	*Octobre*
November	*Novemba*	*Novembre*
December	*Disemba*	*Décembre*
What time is it?	*Yu save wanem taem naoia?*	*Quelle heure est-il?*
It's ... o'clock	*... oklok*	*Il est ... heure(s)*
in the morning	*long moning*	*du matin*
in the evening	*long aftenun*	*du soir*
1.15	*kwotapas wan*	*une heure et quart*
1.30	*hapas wan*	*une heure et demi*
1.45	*kwota tu tu*	*deux heures moins le quart*

Numbers

1	*wan*	*un*
2	*tu*	*deux*
3	*tri*	*trois*
4	*fo*	*quatre*
5	*faef*	*cinq*
6	*sikis*	*six*
7	*seven*	*sept*
8	*eit*	*huit*
9	*naen*	*neuf*
10	*ten*	*dix*
11	*leven*	*onze*
12	*twelef*	*douze*
13	*tatin*	*treize*
14	*fotin*	*quatorze*
15	*feftin*	*quinze*
16	*sikistin*	*seize*
17	*seventin*	*dix-sept*
18	*eitin*	*dix-huit*
19	*naentin*	*dix-neuf*
20	*twante*	*vingt*
30	*tate*	*trente*
40	*fote*	*quarante*
50	*fefte*	*cinquante*
60	*sikiste*	*soixante*
70	*sevente*	*soixante-dix*
80	*eite*	*quatre-vingts*
90	*naente*	*quatre-vingt-dix*
100	*handred*	*cent*
1000	*taosin*	*mille*
1,000,000	*milian*	*million*

Health

I'm allergic to antibiotics.	*Mi no save dring antibiotics.*	*Je suis allergique aux antibiotiques.*

I'm ...	*Mi sik blong ...*	*Je suis ...*
diabetic	*suga*	*diabétique*
epileptic	*sik blong foldaon*	*épileptique*
asthmatic	*gat sotwin*	*asthmatique*

antiseptic	*meresin we i klinim so blong/mekem se i no save solap*	*l'antiseptique*

aspirin	*asprin*	*l'aspirine*
condoms	*kondoms*	*les préservatifs*
contraceptive	*meresin blong blokem pikinini*	*le contraceptif*

diarrhoea	*sitsit wota*	*la diarrhée*
medicine	*meresin*	*la médecine*
nausea	*harem trot*	*la nausée*
sunblock cream	*meresin blong skin mo sun*	*le lait de solaire*
tampons	*koteks*	*les tampons*

Facts for the Visitor

VISAS & EMBASSIES

Every visitor must have a passport which is valid for at least four months from the date of arrival in Vanuatu. On arrival, you must also show your return or onward ticket out of Vanuatu. If you cannot satisfy these conditions you will probably not be allowed to enter.

Immigration staff sometimes ask visitors to show proof that they have sufficient money to support themselves while in the country. The authorities reserve the right to refuse admission to anyone who may have 'insufficient funds', without specifying how much is deemed sufficient.

Entry visas are not required for nationals of Commonwealth countries, nor for nationals of most Western European nations. Also exempt are holders of passports issued by Cuba, China, Japan, South Korea, the Philippines, Taiwan, Thailand and the USA. Most other nationalities require visas. The visa requirement is waived for those in transit.

Visitors from nonexempt countries are permitted to stay the same length of time as those who don't need a visa. Permission to stay is initially for 30 days, but can be extended one month at a time for up to four months within the same 12-month period.

The Getting There & Away chapter contains visa information for countries that you might visit on the way to Vanuatu.

Vanuatuan Diplomatic Representatives

Vanuatu does not have embassies or consulates overseas. Its honorary consuls include:

Australia
    Princes Hill Gallery, 213 Canning St, Carlton,
    Vic 3053 (☎ (03) 9347 7455)
France 9
    Rue Dary, 75008 Paris (☎ (1) 40 53 82 25)
Japan
    The Forum 4-1, K101-cho Chioda-ku, Tokyo
    (☎ (3) 3238 5535)

Honorary consuls are to be established in the future in New Zealand, the UK and Sydney, Australia.

Visas

Vanuatu's handful of honorary consulates abroad do not process visa applications. Nonexempt visitors can obtain entry visas either from UK consulates, local prefectures in France, or the Principal Immigration Officer (☎ 22354), PMB 0092, Port Vila. The appropriate forms can be obtained from the overseas offices of Air Vanuatu (for their addresses see the section on Tourist Offices in this chapter).

Applications for residency permits must be completed prior to arrival in the country.

Visa Extensions You can only apply for visa extensions at the immigration department's offices in Vila and Luganville.

Foreign Embassies & Consulates in Vanuatu

All the diplomatic representations to Vanuatu are in Port Vila. High commissions or embassies are maintained by Australia, France, New Zealand, the People's Republic of China and the UK. Papua New Guinea and Sweden are represented by honorary consuls.

Australia
    Australian High Commission, Melitco House,
    Avenue du General de Gaulle (PO Box 111)
    (☎ 22777)
France
    Ambassade de France, Kumul Hwy, BP 60
    (☎ 22353)
New Zealand
    New Zealand High Commission, Prouds Build-
    ing, Kumul Hwy, Port Vila, PO Box 161
    (☎ 22933)
Papua New Guinea
    PO Box 594 (☎ 23930)
People's Republic of China
    Rue d'Auvergne, PMB 071 (☎ 23598)

Sweden

> Moore Stevens House, Kumul Hwy, PO Box 169
> (☎ 22944)

UK

> British High Commission, Melitco House,
> Avenue du General de Gaulle, PO Box 567
> (☎ 23100)

DOCUMENTS

No vaccination certificate is needed for entry into Vanuatu. However, if you plan to travel from an infected area make sure to check with your travel agent that there have been no changes to Vanuatu's health regulations. An International Driver's Licence is not needed to drive in Vanuatu. For information on work permits, see the section on Work later in this chapter.

CUSTOMS
Concessions

As long as you are over 15, you may bring in 200 cigarettes, or either 100 cigarillos, 50 cigars or 250 grams of tobacco. You may also have two litres of wine and two bottles of spirits (maximum 1.5 litres), a quarter litre of toilet water, 100 ml of perfume, and other items up to a value of 20,000VT. There are no restrictions on personal effects, including cameras and film, whether already used or not, as long as they are not intended either for gift or sale.

Regulations

All plants, fruit, seeds, meat, fish, shellfish, dairy and poultry products must be declared on arrival. Failure to do so can lead to prosecution and fines.

In regard to pets, tourists may apply to bring only cats and dogs into Vanuatu. To avoid disappointment, ring the Department of Agriculture in Vila (☎ 22525), at least four months before your intended arrival and ask them to send you the necessary form, or write to PMB 40, Port Vila.

No firearms or ammunition may be brought into the country. If you have any in your possession you must hand them over to the authorities on arrival – they will return them to you when you leave. You'll find the Customs Department in the large, two-storey building across from the town market in central Vila (☎ 24544) and at the main wharf in Luganville (☎ 36225).

There are also restrictions on what you can take out of Vanuatu. (See Things to Buy later in this chapter.)

MONEY
Currency

Vanuatu's currency is the vatu, abbreviated to 'VT' although airlines often use 'VUV' instead. Vatu means 'stone' in some of the country's traditional languages. In the distant past large stones symbolised permanence, while certain smaller ones were regarded as having a variety of magical properties.

Vanuatu uses 500, 1000 and 5000VT banknotes. There are seven coins, worth 1, 2, 5, 10, 20, 50 and 100VT.

There are no limits on the amount of money you may bring in to or take out of the country. However, the vatu isn't a frequently seen currency elsewhere, so any vatu may be heavily discounted when you come to change it at your local bank.

Exchange Rates

The vatu has been reasonably steady against most international currencies in recent years, with the following approximate exchange rates at the time of going to print:

Australia	A$1	=	80.5VT
Fiji	F$1	=	79.7VT
France	FFr 1	=	22.6VT
Germany	DM1	=	78.9VT
Japan	¥100	=	131VT
New Zealand	NZ$1	=	67.8VT
Papua New Guinea	PNG K1	=	91.8VT
Solomons	S$1	=	33.3VT
UK	UK£1	=	175VT
USA	US$1	=	109VT

Banks & Money Exchange

Major commercial banks include: Australian-owned ANZ Bank and Westpac Bank; the American-owned Banque d'Hawaii; and the locally owned National Bank of Vanuatu (NBV). The main offices of all four banks are in the central part of Vila. All banks have branches in Luganville. Westpac has an agency in Lenakel (on Tanna) while the NBV has numerous agencies around the country. The NBV handles savings accounts only.

The best exchange rates in Vila are given by Goodies Money Exchange, opposite the Cultural Centre on Kumul Hwy. Its rates are invariably two or three vatu per A$1 above what the banks will give you and at least 5VT better than most hotels. As well, unlike the banks, it doesn't charge a fee for any transaction involving travellers' cheques. Goodies is open seven days, but in the morning only on Sunday and public holidays.

Banks, duty-free shops, restaurants and hotels in Vila should have no difficulties with cash and travellers cheques in major international currencies. However, the few hotels outside the capital may only be willing to accept Australian or US dollars. Make sure to ask before it's too late.

Always take plenty of vatu when travelling in rural Vanuatu as you will almost certainly be unable to change foreign currencies in village situations. In the remoter areas it's best to carry a good reserve of 500 and 1000VT notes and 10, 20, 50 and 100VT coins for such things as taxi fares and small purchases. This will help avoid embarrassment when it comes to getting change.

Banking Hours ANZ opens at 8 am and closes at 3 pm, while Westpac operates between 8.30 am and 3 pm. Both the NBV and the Banque d'Hawaii take a siesta, being open from 8 to 11 am and 1.30 to 3 pm.

Credit Cards
Major credit cards such as American Express and Diners Club are accepted by hotels, car rental agencies, airline offices, and most of the tourist-minded shops and restaurants in Vila and Luganville. Both ANZ and Westpac are agents for Visa and MasterCard, while Westpac also acknowledges American Express. The Banque d'Hawaii is the local agent for Diners Club. Don't expect to be able to use your plastic card outside Vila and

Luganville, and the resorts on Tanna and Santo.

Costs
Vila is not a cheap place to visit, particularly if you're eating out all the time and staying in a reasonable hotel. Even if you're lucky enough to find self-catering budget accommodation, it's easy to spend 4000VT a day without doing very much at all; take a day tour or enjoy a three-course meal at a good restaurant and you can expect that amount to double. Air fares within the archipelago are high, but living costs outside Vila are more reasonable, particularly in village situations.

You'll get a good idea of the styles and costs of meals and accommodation in Port Vila and Luganville by looking under the Places to Stay and Eat sections of the chapters on Efate and Santo.

Most of the food that visitors eat in Vila and Luganville is imported and thus expensive – apart from freight costs it carries a hefty import tax. (There is no income tax in Vanuatu, so indirect taxes are high to compensate.) However, locally produced beef and fish are surprisingly cheap, as are fruit and vegetables if you buy them from local markets. Fresh vegetables are usually available in the supermarkets, but tend to be dearer as they are mostly imported.

In Vila's major supermarkets, you can expect to pay: 520VT for a one-kg bag of toasted muesli, 320VT for a 300-gram tin of powdered milk, 40VT for a stick of French bread, 120VT for a 250-gram container of margarine, and 340VT for a 12-slice pack of plastic cheddar. White rice costs 90VT a kg, while eggs are 280VT a dozen. The cheapest local beer is 110VT for a 330-ml bottle or can. The price per kg for grilling steak is 520VT, for fish fillets 900VT and for chicken breasts 720VT.

Tipping
There is no tipping in Vanuatu. In customary terms, tipping creates an obligation which the receiver has to return. Naturally a person can't do this if they're passing through, so to

avoid embarrassment keep your 'tip' to a smile of thanks.

Bargaining

There is no bargaining in Vanuatu. In fact, village people will invariably take their produce back home from market rather than accept a lower price than that asked.

Occasionally people in isolated areas will quote you grossly inflated prices for artefacts or accommodation, mainly because they have no idea what the current price would be in Vila or Luganville. When this happens, explain that you can't afford that much and then tell them what it would cost in the big city. Hopefully, they will accept it. Otherwise you'll have to either pay the first price or try elsewhere.

Consumer Tax

There's a 10% government tax on all hotel and licensed restaurant bills, but not on private or local government council rest houses, church hostels or snack bars.

WHEN TO GO

The most pleasant time to visit Vanuatu is during the dry season from May and October. If you intend walking, the months June to August are best. Visitor numbers peak during school holiday periods in June/July and September, so travel tickets and accommodation should be booked well in advance.

If you're interested in culture, time your visit to coincide with one of the major events, such as land diving (see Cultural Events, later in this chapter).

WHAT TO BRING

People wear light cotton summer clothes all year round except on the islands south of Efate; it has cool nights during winter, especially in July. A light pullover is handy after diving or for sea travel. Wet-weather gear and warm clothing are a must for most mountain treks, particularly if staying overnight.

Clothing styles are quite casual. In general, ties are worn at weddings or going to court; socks are worn with shorts at the 'better' establishments after dark. The stan-

dard footwear for most locals is rubber 'thongs', otherwise known as flip-flops.

You will need to bring special shoes for reef walking. An old pair of sneakers will do, though you can expect the razor-sharp coral to tear through them in a short time. Diving boots give the best protection.

You'll also need stout footwear if you plan to climb volcanoes or go bushwalking. Bring loose-fitting cotton trousers and long-sleeved shirts to protect yourself from scrapes, scratches and stinging plants. Light-coloured clothing will also help protect you from mosquitoes.

A light sleeping bag, inner sheet, inflatable pillow and closed-cell sleeping mat will be useful if you're planning to spend time in village rest houses. Other items to bring with you for rest houses and some of the so-called village resorts include a mosquito net and a good torch; water canteens and some means of purifying water are another good idea. A tent will also be necessary for treks in unpopulated areas.

TOURIST OFFICES
Local Tourist Offices
The National Tourism Office (NTO) (☎ 22685, fax 23889), PO Box 209, Port Vila is the logical place to start for information about accommodation and tours throughout the archipelago. It's above the Nissan dealership on Kumul Hwy in the centre of town. It's best to ring (or write/fax well in advance of your booking date) if you want to be sent information.

The major hotels in the Vila area and Luganville carry a wide range of promotional material.

Other useful sources are the larger tour operators, particularly Frank King Tours (☎ 22808) and Tour Vanuatu (☎ 22733), both of which are in central Vila in the vicinity of the GPO. Although their literature concentrates on their own products, it will give you an idea of available activities and prices. Frank puts out a very entertaining guide which is worth getting hold of. His address is PO Box 635, Port Vila; Tour Vanuatu's is PO Box 409.

The best source of general information on the northern islands is Espiritu Santo Tours & Travel (☎ 36391), next to the Asia Motel in Main St, Luganville. Eileen Ligo, the manager, is a native of Pentecost and has been involved in the Vanuatu travel industry for many years. Her address is PO Box 222, Luganville, Santo.

Overseas Representatives
The National Tourism Office of Vanuatu is represented by the country's national airline, Air Vanuatu, which has offices in:

Australia
> Level 5, Bloomberg Corporation Building, 293 Queen St, Brisbane, Qld 4000 (☎ (07) 3221 2566)
> 126 Wellington Pde, East Melbourne, Vic 3002 (☎ (03) 9417 3977)
> 17 Castlereagh St, Sydney, NSW 2000 (☎ (02) 9223 8333)

New Caledonia
> 20 Rue du Général Mangin, Noumea (☎ 28 6677)

New Zealand
> Cnr Customs and Albert Sts, Auckland (☎ (09) 373 3435)

USEFUL ORGANISATIONS
Cultural Centre
If the NTO can't help you, the Cultural Centre (☎ 22129), on Kumul Hwy directly opposite the NTO, is an excellent alternative source of information on the remoter parts of Vanuatu. Either telephone or write to the curator at PO Box 184, Port Vila, who'll be happy to advise you on access, styles of accommodation available and other general matters on the island you may be interested in. He can also arrange for guides. You're unlikely to be charged a fee for any advice given, although a small donation to the Cultural Centre would be appropriate.

Island Fisheries
The Department of Fisheries has outer-island extension centres at Lakatoro on Malakula, Lolowai on Ambae, Sola in the Banks group, and Laman Bay on Epi. These are good places to hire speedboats.

For up-to-date information on these areas,

go to the department's offices on the waterfront in Vila (☎ 23119) or Luganville (☎ 36218). The staff will be happy to make enquiries on your behalf over their HF-radio network. Both offices are about 150VT by taxi from the respective town centres.

Vanuatu National Council of Women

The Vanuatu National Council of Women (☎ 23018) on Rue Bougainville in central Vila is an excellent source of useful information for both male and female travellers. The staff can advise you on all cultural matters relating to women in Vanuatu. They can also help you by providing names of contact persons and information on accommodation and transport in remote areas.

Women intending to travel by themselves to the outer islands should definitely contact the VNCW first and discuss likely problems. Likewise, male visitors would benefit from learning a thing or two about correct behaviour towards ni-Vanuatu women.

Council Offices

You should also try the local government council and local council offices scattered around the country, as the staff will certainly be able to advise you on all travel matters in their area or region. All such offices are connected into the telephone or radio telephone networks. Unfortunately, however, such places can be notoriously difficult to contact directly – you'll often find that either the phone isn't working or either constantly engaged. This is an instance where a 'service message' over Radio Vanuatu can be very useful (see Post & Telecommunications in this chapter).

Just to make life even more interesting, the current local government system is about to change to a less centralised form of provincial government, with six regions instead of the present 11. However, the telephone numbers for most offices are unlikely to change.

Missions

Vanuatu has a large number of Christian mission stations scattered about the various islands. These sometimes have beds for guests, while the denominational women's groups in the villages can often put you up either in a proper guest house or in their clubhouse.

If you want to visit Catholic missions, ring the Mission Catholique Cathédrale Paroisse (☎ 22640) in Vila. Ask for advice on their locations and how to contact them.

For information on Presbyterian missions contact the Presbyterian Church of Vanuatu, also in Vila, on ☎ 22722. Ask about the location of Presbyterian Women's Missionary Union clubs, which invariably have places you can stay.

The Seventh-Day Adventists are also active, particularly in the northern islands. For information on their missions contact the SDA Mission in Vila on ☎ 22157. The Anglican Church (☎ 22411) in Vila may be able to give you details on the few Anglican missions.

Tourist Publications

The free, magazine-style publication *Hapi Tumas Long Vanuatu* provides a fairly good overview of what's available to visitors throughout the country. You should be able to get hold of a copy from the National Tourism Office and major tourism businesses. If not, ring the publishers, Pacific Publishing & Advertising, in Vila on ☎ 23642 and ask if they'll send you one. Their address is PO Box 1292, Port Villa. You will probably need to forward a self-addressed envelope complete with international reply coupons.

BUSINESS HOURS & HOLIDAYS

Government offices open Monday to Friday from 7.30 to 11.30 am, and 1.30 to 4.30 pm. Most businesses operate during the same hours, but will generally stay open until 5 pm. They are also active on Saturday mornings.

Shops normally begin trading at 7.30 am, but, in true Gallic style, most close between 11.30 am and 1.30 or 2 pm. Fortunately, all the shops continue trading after the midday siesta until around 6 or 7 pm. Saturday shopping generally ceases between 11.30 am and midday, although Chinese stores and supermarkets throughout the country tend to remain open all weekend. Regardless of what day it is, Vila's duty-free shops will stay open until late whenever a cruise ship is in port. Luganville's Chinese stores are usually open from dawn to dusk.

Village trade stores will generally open whenever there's a customer. This includes the Sabbath (Friday for Jon Frum worshippers, Saturday for Seventh-Day Adventists, and Sunday for the rest), provided the manager isn't too strict in his or her religious beliefs.

Vanuatu has several official national holidays including:

1 January
  New Year's Day
5 March
  Custom Chiefs' Day
March/April
  Easter – Good Friday and Easter Monday
1 May
  Labour Day
May/June
  Ascension Day – 40 days after Easter Sunday, and always a Thursday
24 July
  Children's Day
30 July
  Independence Day
15 August
  Assumption Day
5 October
  Constitution Day
29 November
  National Unity Day
25 December
  Christmas Day
26 December
  Family Day

When a national holiday falls on a weekend, the accompanying public holiday is usually taken on the following Monday.

CULTURAL EVENTS

Independence Day festivities in July are Vanuatu's most important annual event. There are celebrations in every provincial centre, with Vila naturally having the widest range of activities. These include a number of sporting events, a grand military parade at Independence Park, fiercely competitive canoe and yacht races in the harbour, a string band competition and custom dancing by groups from different islands.

A number of notable events of interest that occur around the country during the year include:

February
  Jon Frum Day – Sulphur Bay, Tanna; includes much festivities, dancing and a number of parades
April/May/June
  Land Diving – this exciting form of bungee jumping occurs in several villages in southern Pentecost
July
  Horse Racing – annual race meeting in Port Vila
August to November
  The Toka – clan alliance dance, held in Tanna over a period of three days every year

POST & TELECOMMUNICATIONS
Post
Vanuatu has no street postal delivery service, so you must either write to a PO Box or use the poste restante service. All important centres have either post offices or agencies.

There are regular and frequent internal postal deliveries to all main islands. However, some outlying areas are served solely by ships, in which case mail days can be a week or more apart.

Stamps Vanuatu issues an average of 25 to 40 stamps annually. These are usually colourful, with designs varying from traditional dances and ceremonies to local marine life, birds, butterflies and flowers. The philatelic sales counter is on the ground floor of Vila's post office.

Telephone & Fax
Vanuatu boasts a national microwave telephone network that connects all major islands. In addition, HF and VHF teleradio (ie radio telephone, or 'radphone') services are provided to over 200 isolated island communities. Public telephones are available only in Vila, Luganville, Isangel and Norsup.

Calls within Vanuatu To use the HF teleradio network, dial ☎ 22759 in Vila and ☎ 36710 in Luganville; for the VHF network, dial ☎ 22221 in Vila and ☎ 36248 in Luganville. You don't need to know the call sign of the other party – just tell the operator who you want. You have to speak in turns, so you should signal to the other party for them to reply by saying 'Over!'

As the chances of getting through to a subscriber who speaks only Bislama are quite high, it's a good idea to have someone available who is fluent in this language to help you out if need be.

The most convenient (and sometimes the only) way to pay for local calls from public telephones is to advance-purchase a phone card from Telecom Vanuatu and its licensed sales centres. These are available in 30 units for 560VT, 60 units for 1120VT and 120 units for 2240VT. The cheapest rates are between 6 pm and 6 am Monday to Friday and all weekend; at these times you get six minutes for one unit regardless of where you're calling. At other times, costs vary from one unit for three minutes for calls within the same area to a maximum charge of one unit for 30 seconds to other areas.

When using coins, the minimum charge for a local telephone call is 20VT; for a teleradio call it's 40VT.

There are no area codes in Vanuatu.

Service Messages Villages that are not yet connected to either the telephone or teleradio systems can usually be contacted by sending a service message over Radio Vanuatu. The station has daily broadcasts of such messages and villagers listen in case there is one for them. Often this is the only way you can let them know that you're coming.

To send a service message in Vila, go along to Radio Vanuatu's office on Bligh St at the northern end of the city centre, or call ☎ 22999. In Luganville, call the Telecom Vanuatu office (☎ 36000), near the Hotel Santo.

International Calls If you want to make an international call from Vanuatu, the code is ☎ 00 from Vila, and ☎ 000 from Luganville. Phone calls into Vanuatu require the international direct dialling code of the country you're ringing from followed by ☎ 678 (the code for Vanuatu), and then the subscriber's number.

Public international telephone, telex, telegraph and fax facilities are available at the Vila GPO and the Telecom Vanuatu office in Luganville. At Vila the booths are open from 7.30 am to 8 pm Monday to Friday, and 7.30 am to noon on Saturday. In Luganville they're open from 7 am to 7 pm Monday to Friday, and 7.30 to 11.30 am Saturday.

These services are also available at most hotels, but you can expect to pay a surcharge of up to 50%.

TIME
Vanuatu time is GMT/UMT plus 11 hours, which is one hour ahead of Australian Eastern Standard Time. Noon in Vila is 1 am in London, 8 pm in New York and 11 am in Sydney. Local time is the same as in New Caledonia, but one hour behind Fiji and New Zealand.

Usually it's only tourists who get excited about the passage of time, so don't be surprised if you find things rather more laid-back than you're accustomed to. It can take a while to settle into the unhurried pace of life in Vanuatu, but you'll eventually get used to it.

ELECTRICITY
Town power is provided in the main urban centres of Vila and Luganville, and in a few other towns such as Norsup and Lakatoro. Rural hospitals have their own generators as do some of the larger missions.

The current in Vanuatu is 220 to 240 V, 50 cycles AC, using flat two or three-pin plugs of the Australian type. Most electrical goods shops in Vila and Luganville sell adaptors which are usually compatible with foreign designs.

LAUNDRY
Your accommodation house will either have its own laundry facilities or it will be able to

arrange to have your washing done. If you're in a village with no commercial-style accommodation, the women will normally be pleased to help if you can't do your own, though some of their methods tend to be a little rough on the clothes. Vila and Luganville both offer commercial laundry services. Vila has the country's only dry-cleaning facility.

WEIGHTS & MEASURES

Vanuatu uses the metric system. Petrol and milk are sold by the litre, fish and fruit by the kg. Distance is measured in metres or km, and speed limits are in km per hour (km/h). Temperatures are measured in degrees Celsius. If you need help with metric conversions, turn to the tables on the inside back cover of this book.

BOOKS & MAPS

History

An exceptionally good history of Vanuatu is *To Kill a Bird with Two Stones* (Vanuatu Cultural Centre Publications, Vila, 1980) by Jeremy MacClancy. Its lucid prose takes the country from its earliest beginnings through the Condominium period (the 'two stones' of the title) right up to independence.

A remarkably interesting work about the archipelago's early trading days is Dorothy Shinberg's *They Came for Sandalwood* (Melbourne University Press, 1967). This book is a study of the 19th-century sandalwood trade, and the best account of those turbulent times.

Fragments of Empire (Australian National University, Canberra, 1967) by Deryck Scarr is an informative history of early British imperial policies concerning the archipelago.

A colourful collection of letters written in the 1920s is R J Fletcher's *Isles of Illusion: Letters from the South Seas* (London, 1925; reissued by Century Hutchinson, 1986). Fletcher was a thoughtful Englishman, who found his fellow Anglo-Saxons in the area anything but sensitive.

Achieving Independence *Beyond Pandemonium: From New Hebrides to Vanuatu* (Asia Pacific Books, Wellington, 1980) is by the former prime minister, Father Walter Lini. In it he tells of his early life and the role he played in the lead-up to his country's independence.

New Hebrides: the Road to Independence (USP & South Pacific Social Sciences Association, Suva, 1977) was written by Kalkot Matas Kele-Kele and others, and edited by Chris Plant. This book has contributions from a number of young ni-Vanuatu writers about their contrasting hopes for national self-determination prior to independence.

An extremely illuminating account of the 1980 rebellion in Luganville is *The Santo Rebellion: An Imperial Reckoning* (University of Hawaii Press & Heinemann, Melbourne, 1984) by John Beasant. The author records the sometimes underhand roles played by Vanuatu's former imperial rulers during the Santo uprising.

A very readable version of the Santo rebellion is Richard Shears' *The Coconut War: The Crisis on Espiritu Santo* (Cassell Australia, Sydney, 1980).

Anthropology

A remarkable and highly recommended study of traditional cultural activities which were still intact in the archipelago in the early 1930s is Tom Harrisson's *Savage Civilization* (Victor Gollancz, London, 1937). It gives a fascinating picture of many of Vanuatu's now-lost customs, especially Malakula's.

One of the most delightful books I've ever read is *Charlene Gourguechon's Journey to the End of the World* (Charles Scribner's Sons, New York, 1977). It was originally published as *L'Archipel des Tabous* (Éditions Robert Laffont, Paris, 1974). Charlene Gourgechon's tells of daily life with traditional tribes in Malakula, Pentecost and Ambrym, as well as the inward-looking, artificial world of the pre-independence European community in Luganville.

Margaret Gardiner's *Footprints on Malakula* (Salamander, Edinburgh & Free

Association Press, London, 1988) is a tribute to Bernard Deacon, a young British anthropologist active in southern Malakula in the late 1920s. Many of his notes were published posthumously as *Malakula: A Vanishing Race in the New Hebrides* (edited by Camilla Wedgewood, Routledge, London, 1934). This book is considered to be the most informative study yet written about the Small Nambas tribe of south-central Malakula.

Arts & Customs

Vanuatu (Les Éditions du Pacifique, Papeete, 1975 & 1980), written by Joel Bonnemaison and illustrated by Bernard Hermann, has some interesting pictures of those aspects of ni-Vanuatu traditional life which still survive. Another attractively illustrated work is Ronald van der Plaat's *This is Vanuatu* (Braynart, Sydney, 1984), with features about Ambrym, Tanna, Malakula and Pentecost – particularly the Pentecost land divers.

Art in the New Pacific (Institute of Pacific Studies, Suva, 1979) by Vilsoni Tausie is an informative study of Melanesian art, dance, sculpture and oral traditions, including those of Vanuatu. Also on the same subject is Angus McBean's *Handicrafts of the South Seas* (South Pacific Commission Publications, Noumea, 1964 & 1976).

The *Handikraf Blong Vanuatu* (USP Centre, Vila, 1985) catalogue, prepared by Marcelle Saint-Pierre on behalf of Vila's principal handicrafts shop, displays in a most informative way the full range of the country's currently produced traditional-style art objects.

Novels

James Michener's novel *Tales of the South Pacific* (Macmillan, New York, 1947) gives a very good picture of life in Santo when US forces were garrisoned there during WW II. His *Return to Paradise* (Secker & Warburg, London, 1951) ranges all over the Pacific, but also contains some stories set in Vanuatu.

Two novels about island life in the archipelago are written in French. These are Pierre Benoit's *Erromango* (Albin Michel,

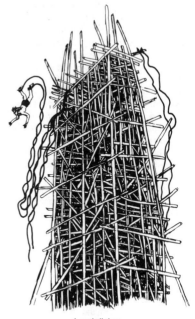

Land diving

Paris, 1967), and Daniel Gray's *L'Île Aurore* (Flammarion, France, 1962). Benoit's story is built around French colonial life on Erromango, while Gray has some interesting descriptions of Maewo. Unfortunately English translations are hard to get hold of.

The story of *Beachmasters* (Penguin, Melbourne, 1987) by Thea Astley has many interesting parallels to the events of the 1980 Santo rebellion. Gwendoline Page's very readable *Coconuts and Coral* (George R Reeve, Norfolk, UK, 1993) is a detailed and often amusing account of life in the New Hebrides during the 1960s as seen by a young English family.

Religion

There have been several biographies published about missionaries who were active in late 19th-century Vanuatu. *Peter Milne of Nguna* (Foreign Missions Committee, New

Zealand, 1927) by Alexander Don gives an insight into attitudes of the time. Milne was active on Nguna between 1870 and 1924.

Islands Won by Blood (Covenanter Press, Strathpine, Queensland, 1922) by A K Langridge vividly records the exceptional courage displayed by missionary couples on Erromango in the mid-19th century.

Two other, similar books have also been published. These are *John G Paton, Missionary to the New Hebrides* (London, 1889), a very self-justifying autobiography by John Paton, and *Misi Gete: John Geddie, Pioneer Missionary to the New Hebrides* (Hobart, Tasmania, 1975) by R S Miller.

Edward Rice's *Jon Frum, He Come* (New York, 1974) is the only full-length work about the Jon Frum movement of southeastern Tanna.

Flora & Fauna

For bird-watchers, Heinrich Bregulla's detailed *Birds of Vanuatu* (Anthony Nelson, Oswestry, UK, 1992) is required reading. The book contains good general information as well as specifics on the country's 121 bird species. Unfortunately, it's too large to be carried in the field.

Orchids of Vanuatu (Royal Botanic Gardens, London, UK, 1989) by B Lewis & P Cribb covers the country's 158 species of orchids. It's the only available reference on this topic.

J I Wheatley's *A Guide to the Common Trees of Vanuatu* (Dept of Forestry, Vila, 1992) includes a field key and illustrated descriptions of 100 species. It also contains information on traditional uses, but like the bird guide is a little too large to carry around comfortably.

Travel Guides

Two alternative guidebooks to Vanuatu are Norman & Ngaire Douglas' *Vanuatu: A Guide* (Pacific Publications, Sydney, 1990) and Stuart Bevan's *Vanuatu* (Other People Publications, Rozelle, NSW, 1990). Both make useful reading.

An earlier work, which is very well illustrated in B&W, is *Vanuatu* (Club Publications/Lycée Professionelle, Port Vila, 1978), by P Prudhomme, revised by Claudine Ellis in 1984.

Yachting

Alan Lucas' *Cruising New Caledonia & Vanuatu* (Universal, Melbourne, 1981) is a very useful guide for yachties. Giving details of many tiny harbours and anchorages, it demonstrates how a yacht can be a very good means of getting round Vanuatu, as so many of the country's attractions are coastal.

Bookshops & Libraries

There are several bookshops in Vila, but only one small outlet in Luganville. Vila also has a number of libraries. For details see the relevant Information sections in the Efate and Espiritu Santo chapters.

Research

If you can't find what you are after at the Cultural Centre in Vila, try the Pacific Manuscripts Bureau, Research School of Pacific Studies, Australian National University, Canberra, ACT 2601, Australia. It has an extensive range of publications and microfilms about Oceania, including Vanuatu.

Maps

The best place to buy quality ordnance survey maps is the Department of Lands Survey (☎ 22427) in the Georges Pompidou Building on Montfort St in central Vila. To get there, walk up Rue Bougainville from Kumul Hwy, then turn left at the Sacré-Cœur Roman Catholic Cathedral. The Georges Pompidou Building is about 300 metres away and facing you at the T-intersection.

At the far end of the building, and down the stairs, the topographic survey office sells a complete stock of detailed maps covering all Vanuatu's islands at a scale of either 1:50,000 or 1:100,000, depending on the size of the island. Unfortunately, they're only available in B&W and are many years out of date.

The department also has a Luganville branch (☎ 36330), which mainly stocks maps of the country's northern islands.

MEDIA
Newspapers & Magazines

The major newspaper available is a government publication called *Vanuatu Weekly Hebdomadaire*. It costs 70VT, and has a few pages of local news in Bislama, English and French. For local gossip, coverage of sporting and cultural events and society happenings, there's the weekly English-language *Trading Post*, for 50VT. It's the only privately published newspaper in Vanuatu.

The quarterly magazine *Pacific Paradise*, published by the House of Nania, Port Vila, contains useful visitor information and interesting feature stories on various aspects of the country. It costs 450VT.

As well, the *Pacific Islands Monthly*, which is published by The Fiji Times Ltd in Suva, often has features on Vanuatu. It's available from newsagents in Australia and throughout the Pacific.

Radio & TV

The country's only radio station, Radio Vanuatu, provides trilingual FM, AM and SW services throughout the country. All services operate continuously from 6 am to 10 pm and offer international and local news bulletins on the hour.

TV has recently come to Vanuatu and is available on a single channel from 6 to 10 pm daily. The lifestyles it portrays are considered a significant reason for the recent increase in petty crime!

International satellite coverage of news and major sporting events (eg the Australian Football League grand final) is available at the Club Vanuatu in Vila.

FILM & PHOTOGRAPHY

You'll have no difficulty buying the more common types of 35 mm slide and print film in Vila, but it's a different story elsewhere. In Luganville you'll probably only be able to find colour print film. If your film requirements are of a more specialised nature, the smart thing to do is to bring your own.

Print film can be developed at several outlets in Vila, but E6 slide film is processed only by Top Shots in the Rue Bougainville, next door to the Iririki Centre Ville Hotel.

Several of the capital's duty-free shops sell 35 mm cameras and accessories. Fung Kei has the best range, including video and super 8 cameras, and its prices are said to be as cheap as anywhere in the world.

Photography

Film in the tropics needs to be protected from both heat and humidity. Sachets of silica crystals will protect your equipment from moisture, but it's more important is to keep your camera and film in a cool place.

Automatic cameras and light meters are often fooled by Vanuatu's strong light, and as a result your photos may be too dark. This can be a real problem if you're photographing subjects against a bright background such as a white beach. In these situations it's often best to deliberately overexpose by 1.5 stops (eg use f11 instead of f16/22). Conversely, it's a good idea to underexpose by the same amount if taking close-ups of ni-Vanuatu faces and other dark subjects. If you're taking slides, the best idea is to bracket exposures as some guarantee of success.

A flash is useful for a range of situations, such as interiors, rainforests and evening cultural dances. (Remember that kava makes the drinker's eyes sensitive to light, so go easy in these situations.) A telephoto lens – 100 mm is recommended – is invaluable for people shots. Use a polarising filter for dramatic effects and maximum colour saturation, particularly if shooting over the sea.

Always ask before photographing anyone, including children. Most people will be very happy to be your subject, though of course there are always exceptions. Some adults, particularly those from the more traditional villages, may prefer not to pose. Instead they'll just go on with their business, apparently indifferent to your clicking camera. Elderly women in rural areas may be reluctant to be photographed by foreign men.

Remember, too, that you'll often be

charged a fee to take photographs of people, villages and ceremonies. Sometimes these can be very high, as with the land diving on Pentecost. Generally, videos and movie cameras attract the highest fees.

HEALTH

Travel health in Vanuatu largely depends on your predeparture preparations, your day-to-day health care while travelling and how you handle any medical problem or emergency that does develop. Generally speaking, Vanuatu is a safe place to visit although malaria is a significant health risk in most areas. The only other significant danger for visitors is gastric-related problems.

Vanuatu's major medical facilities are in Port Vila and Luganville, both of which also have well-stocked pharmacies and dental facilities. There are five hospitals as well as numerous clinics, dispensaries and aid posts scattered throughout the archipelago. Facilities in rural areas may be rudimentary or non-existent. At last count the country had 370 hospital beds, 15 doctors and 342 registered nurses.

Self-diagnosis and treatment can be risky, so wherever possible seek qualified help. Although we do give treatment dosages in this section, they are for emergency use only. Medical advice should always be sought where possible before administering any drugs.

There are a number of books on travel health:

Staying Healthy in Asia, Africa & Latin America, Moon Publications. Probably the best all-round guide to carry, as it's compact but very detailed and well organised.

Travellers' Health, Dr Richard Dawood, Oxford University Press. Comprehensive, easy to read, authoritative and also highly recommended, although it's rather large to lug around.

Travel with Children, Maureen Wheeler, Lonely Planet Publications. Includes basic advice on travel health for children.

Predeparture Preparations

Health Insurance A travel insurance policy

Underwater Photography

The urge to take underwater photographs eventually comes upon those who enjoy snorkelling and diving. Underwater photography is much easier than it used to be. At one time it required complex and expensive equipment whereas now there is a variety of reasonably priced and easy-to-use underwater cameras available.

As with basic cameras out of the water, the best photos taken with the simplest underwater cameras are likely to be straightforward snaps. You are not going to get superb photographs of fish and marine life with a small, cheap camera but, on the other hand, photos of your fellow underwater enthusiasts can often be terrific.

More than with other types of photography, the results can improve dramatically if you spend more on equipment, particularly on lighting. As you descend, natural colours are quickly absorbed, starting with the red end of the spectrum. You can see the same result with a picture or postcard that has been left in bright sunlight: soon the colours fade until everything looks blue. It's the same underwater: the deeper you go the bluer things look. Red has virtually disappeared by the time you're 10 meters down. the human brain fools us to some extent by automatically compensating for this colour change, but the camera doesn't lie. If you are at any depth, your photos will look blue and cold.

To put the colour back in you need a flash, and to work effectively it has to be a much more powerful and complicated flash than you'd use above water. Thus, newcomers to serious underwater photography soon find that having bought a Nikonos camera they have to lay out as much money again for flash equipment to go with it. With the right experience and equipment the results can be superb. Generally the Nikonos cameras work best with 28- or 35-mm lenses; longer lenses do not work so well underwater. Although objects appear closer underwater, with these short focal lengths you have to get close to achieve good results.

Patience and practice will eventually enable you to move in close to otherwise wary fish. Underwater photography opens up a whole new field of interest to divers and the result can often be startling. Flash photography can reveal colours which simply aren't there for the naked eye. ■

to cover theft, loss and medical problems is a must. There is a wide variety of policies and your travel agent will have recommendations. You may not want to insure that grotty old army surplus backpack – but everyone should be covered for the worst possible case: an accident, for example, that will require hospital treatment and a flight home. An emergency evacuation to Australia by chartered jet is hugely expensive, and you'll be the one paying for it.

The international student travel policies handled by STA Travel or other student travel organisations are usually good value. Some policies offer lower and higher medical expenses options but the higher one is chiefly for countries like the USA which have extremely high medical costs. Check the small print:

1. Some policies specifically exclude 'dangerous activities' which can include scuba diving, motorcycling, even trekking. If such activities are on your agenda you don't want that sort of policy. A locally acquired motorcycle licence may not be valid under your policy.
2. You may prefer a policy which pays doctors or hospitals direct rather than you having to pay on the spot and claim later. If you have to claim later make sure you keep all documentation. Some policies ask you to call back (reverse charges) to a centre in your home country where an immediate assessment of your problem is made.
3. Check if the policy covers ambulances or an emergency flight home. If you have to stretch out you will need two seats and somebody has to pay for them! Even worse, a charter jet flight to get you to Australia for emergency treatment will cost around A$30,000.

It's a good idea to make a copy of your policy, in case the original is lost. If you are planning to travel for a long time, the insurance may seem very expensive – but if you can't afford it, you certainly won't be able to afford to deal with a medical emergency overseas.

Medical Kit A small, straightforward medical kit is a wise thing to carry. A possible kit list includes:

- Aspirin or Panadol – for pain or fever.
- Antihistamine (such as Benadryl) – useful in easing the itch from insect bites or stings or to help prevent motion sickness. Antihistamines may cause sedation and interact with alcohol so care should be taken when using them.
- Decongestant (such as Sudafed) – can be useful for colds and in the oral treatment of blocked ears and noses.
- Antibiotics – useful if you're travelling well off the beaten track, but they must be prescribed and you should carry the prescription with you. Some individuals are allergic to commonly prescribed antibiotics such as penicillin or sulfa drugs. It would be sensible to always carry this information when travelling.
- Kaolin preparation (Imodium or Lomotil) – for stomach upsets.
- Rehydration mixture – for treatment of severe diarrhoea. This is particularly important if travelling with children, but is recommended for everyone.
- Antiseptic such as Betadine, which comes as impregnated swabs or ointment, and an antibiotic powder or similar 'dry' spray – for cuts and grazes.
- Calamine lotion – to ease irritation from bites or stings.
- Bandages and Band-aids – for minor injuries.
- Scissors, tweezers and a thermometer (note that mercury thermometers are prohibited by airlines).
- Insect repellent, sunscreen, suntan lotion, chap stick and water purification tablets.
- A couple of syringes, in case you need injections in a country with medical hygiene problems. Ask your doctor for a note explaining why they have been prescribed.

All the above items are available from chemists in Port Vila.

Ideally antibiotics should be administered only under medical supervision and should never be taken indiscriminately. Take only the recommended dose at the prescribed intervals and continue using the antibiotic for the prescribed period, even if the illness seems to be cured earlier. Antibiotics are quite specific to the infections they can treat. Stop immediately if there are any serious reactions and don't use the antibiotic at all if you are unsure that you have the correct one.

Health Preparations Make sure you're healthy before you start travelling, and that your teeth are OK; being in desperate need of a dentist when you're in the remoter parts of Vanuatu is one of the last things you'd want.

There's only one optician in Vanuatu – in Port Vila – so if you wear glasses take a spare pair as well as your prescription.

If you require a particular medication take an adequate supply, as it may not be available locally. Take the prescription or, better still, part of the packaging showing the generic rather than the brand name (which may not be locally available), as it will make getting replacements easier. It's a wise idea to have a legible prescription with you to show you legally use the medication.

Immunisations Vaccinations provide protection against diseases you might meet along the way. It is important to understand the distinction between vaccines recommended for travel in certain areas and those required by law. Essentially the number of vaccines subject to international health regulations has been dramatically reduced over the last 10 years. Currently yellow fever is the only vaccine subject to international health regulations. Vaccination as an entry requirement is usually only enforced when coming from an infected area.

On the other hand, a number of vaccines are recommended for different areas of travel. These may not be required by law but are recommended for your own personal protection.

Although Vanuatu has no requirement for vaccination certificates on entry, it is worth having all vaccinations recorded on an International Health Certificate (available from your physician or government health department).

Plan ahead for getting your vaccinations: some of them require an initial shot followed by a booster, while some vaccinations should not be given together. It is recommended you seek medical advice at least six weeks prior to travel.

As a common-sense precaution you should at least immunise yourself against hepatitis A, and measles, polio and tetanus (all booster shots) if you're planning to visit

the country's remoter areas. The period of protection offered by vaccinations differs widely and some are contraindicated if you are pregnant.

The possible list of vaccinations includes:

Tetanus Boosters are necessary every 10 years and protection is highly recommended as a general precaution.

Hepatitis A This is the most common travel-acquired illness which can be prevented by vaccination. Protection can be provided in two ways – either with the antibody gammaglobulin or with a new vaccine called Havrix.

Havrix This provides long-term immunity (possibly more than 10 years) after an initial course of two injections and a booster at one year. It may be more expensive than gammaglobulin but certainly has many advantages, including length of protection and ease of administration. It is important to know that (being a vaccine) it will take about three weeks to provide satisfactory protection – hence the need for careful planning prior to travel.

Gammaglobulin This is not a vaccination but a ready-made antibody which has proven very successful in reducing the chances of hepatitis infection. Because it may interfere with the development of immunity, it should not be given until at least 10 days after administration of the last vaccine needed; it should also be given as close as possible to departure because it is at its most effective in the first few weeks after administration and the effectiveness tapers off gradually between three and six months later.

Basic Rules

Care in what you eat and drink is the most important health rule; stomach upsets are the most likely travel health problem but the majority of these upsets will be relatively minor. Don't become paranoid; trying the local food is part of the experience of travel, after all.

Water The water in Vanuatu's major urban centres is normally quite safe for drinking, although in some areas (eg Luganville) it should be boiled towards the end of a long dry season. If in doubt, check the situation with local health authorities or hospitality staff.

In rural areas, drinking water is usually

obtained from rainwater catchment tanks, wells, bores, springs or small creeks. Springs are generally OK, but water from other sources should be boiled or otherwise treated to make it safe.

Unless you know for certain that it's safe, the number one rule is *don't drink the water* – without treating it. If you don't know for certain, always assume the worst. Reputable brands of bottled water or soft drinks are generally fine. Only use water from containers with a serrated seal – not tops or corks. Milk should be treated with suspicion, as it is often unpasteurised. Boiled milk is fine if it is kept hygienically and yoghurt is always good. Tea or coffee should also be OK, since the water should have been boiled.

Water Purification The simplest way of purifying water is to boil it – vigorous boiling for five minutes should be satisfactory.

Simple filtering will not remove all dangerous organisms, so if you cannot boil water it should be treated chemically. Chlorine tablets (Puritabs, Steritabs or other brand names) will kill many but not all pathogens, including giardia and amoebic cysts.

Tincture of iodine (2%) or iodine crystals can also be used. Four drops of tincture of iodine per litre or quart of clear water is the recommended dosage; the treated water should be left to stand for 20 to 30 minutes before drinking. Iodine crystals can also be used to purify water but this is a more complicated process, as you have to first prepare a saturated iodine solution. Iodine loses its effectiveness if exposed to air or damp so keep it in a tightly sealed container. Flavoured powder will disguise the taste of treated water and is a good idea if you are travelling with children.

Food There is an old colonial adage which says: 'If you can cook it, boil it or peel it you can eat it...otherwise forget it'. Salads and fruit should be washed with purified water or peeled where possible. Ice cream is usually OK if it is a reputable brand name, but beware if it has melted and been refrozen.

Thoroughly cooked food is safest but not if it has been left to cool or if it has been reheated. Shellfish such as mussels, oysters and clams should be avoided as well as undercooked meat, particularly in the form of mince. Steaming does not make shellfish safe for eating.

Nutrition If you are planning to travel in remote parts of Vanuatu and carry your own food, make sure your diet is well balanced. Eggs, tofu, beans, lentils and nuts are all safe ways to get protein. Fruit you can peel (bananas or oranges for example) is always safe and a good source of vitamins. Try to eat plenty of grains (rice) and bread. Remember that although food is generally safer if it is cooked well, overcooked food loses much of its nutritional value. If your diet isn't well balanced or if your food intake is insufficient, it's a good idea to take vitamin and iron pills.

Make sure you drink enough, particularly if you are exercising – don't rely on feeling thirsty to indicate when you should drink. Not needing to urinate or very dark yellow urine is a danger sign. Always carry a water bottle with you on long trips. Excessive sweating can lead to loss of salt and therefore muscle cramping. Salt tablets are not a good idea as a preventative, but in places where salt is not used much, adding salt to food can help.

Everyday Health In Western countries with safe water and excellent human waste disposal systems we often take good health for granted. In years gone by, when public health facilities were not as good as they are today, certain rules attached to eating and drinking were observed, eg washing your hands before a meal. It is important for people travelling in areas of poor sanitation to be aware of this and adjust their own personal hygiene habits.

When staying in a village clean your teeth with purified water rather than straight from the tap. Avoid climatic extremes: keep out of the sun when it's hot, dress warmly when it's cold. Avoid potential diseases by dressing sensibly. You can get worm infections through walking barefoot or dangerous coral cuts by walking over coral without shoes. You can avoid insect bites by covering bare skin when insects are around, by screening windows or beds or by using insect repellents. Seek local advice: if you're told the water is unsafe due to jellyfish or sharks, don't go in. In situations where there is no information, discretion is the better part of valour.

Climatic & Geographical Considerations
Sunburn In the tropics you can get sunburnt surprisingly quickly, even through cloud. Use a sunscreen and take extra care to cover areas which don't normally see sun – eg your feet. A hat provides added protection, and you should also use zinc cream or some other barrier cream for your nose and lips. Calamine lotion is good for mild sunburn.

Prickly Heat Prickly heat is an itchy rash caused by excessive perspiration trapped under the skin. It usually strikes people who have just arrived in a hot climate and whose pores have not yet opened sufficiently to cope with greater sweating. Keeping cool but bathing often, using a prickly heat or mild talcum powder, or even resorting to air-con may help until you acclimatise.

Heat Exhaustion Dehydration or salt deficiency can cause heat exhaustion. Take time to acclimatise to high temperatures and make sure you get sufficient liquids. Salt deficiency is characterised by fatigue, lethargy, headaches, giddiness and muscle cramps and in this case salt tablets may help. Vomiting or diarrhoea can deplete your liquid and salt levels. Anhydrotic heat exhaustion, caused by an inability to sweat, is quite rare. Unlike the other forms of heat exhaustion it is likely to strike people who have been in a hot climate for some time, rather than newcomers.

Heat Stroke This serious, sometimes fatal, condition can occur if the body's heat-regulating mechanism breaks down and the body

temperature rises to dangerous levels. Long, continuous periods of exposure to high temperatures can leave you vulnerable to heat stroke. You should avoid excessive alcohol or strenuous activity when you first arrive in a hot climate.

The symptoms are feeling unwell, not sweating very much or at all and a high body temperature (39°C to 41°C). Where sweating has ceased the skin becomes flushed and red. Severe, throbbing headaches and lack of coordination will also occur, and the sufferer may be confused or aggressive. Eventually the victim will become delirious or convulse. Hospitalisation is essential, but meanwhile get victims out of the sun, remove their clothing, cover them with a wet sheet or towel and then fan continually.

Fungal Infections Hot-weather fungal infections are most likely to occur on the scalp, between the toes or fingers (athlete's foot), in the groin (jock itch or crotch rot) and on the body (ringworm). You get ringworm (which is a fungal infection, not a worm) from infected animals or by walking on damp areas, like shower floors.

To prevent fungal infections wear loose, comfortable clothes, avoid artificial fibres, wash frequently and dry carefully. If you do get an infection, wash the infected area daily with a disinfectant or medicated soap and water, and rinse and dry well. Apply an antifungal powder such as Tinaderm. Try to expose the infected area to air or sunlight as much as possible and wash all towels and underwear in hot water as well as changing them often.

Motion Sickness Eating lightly before and during a trip will reduce the chances of motion sickness. If you are prone to motion sickness try to find a place that minimises disturbance – near the wing on aircraft, close to midships on boats, near the centre on buses. Fresh air usually helps, reading or cigarette smoke doesn't. Commercial antimotion-sickness preparations, which can cause drowsiness, have to be taken before the trip commences; when you're feeling sick it's too late. Ginger is a natural preventative and is available in capsule form.

Jet Lag Jet lag is experienced when a person travels by air across several time zones (each time zone usually represents a one-hour time difference). It occurs because many of the functions of the human body (such as temperature, pulse rate and emptying of the bladder and bowels) are regulated by internal 24-hour cycles called circadian rhythms. When we travel long distances rapidly, our bodies take time to adjust to the 'new time' of our destination, and we may experience fatigue, disorientation, insomnia, anxiety, impaired concentration and loss of appetite. These effects will usually be gone within three days of arrival, but there are ways of minimising the impact of jet lag:

1. Rest for a couple of days prior to departure; try to avoid late nights and last-minute dashes for travellers' cheques, passport etc.
2. Try to select flight schedules that minimise sleep deprivation; arriving late in the day means you can go to sleep soon after you arrive. For very long flights, try to organise a stopover.
3. Avoid excessive eating (which bloats the stomach) and alcohol (which causes dehydration) during the flight. Instead, drink plenty of non-carbonated, non-alcoholic drinks such as fruit juice or water.
4. Avoid smoking, as this reduces the amount of oxygen in the aeroplane cabin even further and causes greater fatigue.
5. Make yourself comfortable by wearing loose-fitting clothes and perhaps bringing an eye mask and ear plugs to help you sleep.

Diseases of Poor Sanitation
Diarrhoea A change of water, food or climate can all cause the runs; diarrhoea caused by contaminated food or water is more serious. Despite all your precautions you may still have a bout of mild travellers' diarrhoea but a few rushed toilet trips with no other symptoms is not indicative of a serious problem. Moderate diarrhoea, involving half-a-dozen loose movements in a day, is more of a nuisance. Dehydration is the main danger with any diarrhoea, particularly for children where dehydration can occur quite quickly. Fluid replacement remains the mainstay of management. Weak black tea with a little sugar, soda water, or soft drinks allowed to go flat and diluted 50% with water are all good. With severe diarrhoea a rehydrating solution is necessary to replace minerals and salts. Gastrolyte is a very useful treatment – sachets, with instructions, are available from pharmacies in Vanuatau.

In an emergency you can make up a solution of eight teaspoons of sugar to a litre of boiled water and provide salted cracker biscuits at the same time. You should stick to a bland diet as much as possible as you recover.

Lomotil or Imodium can be used to bring relief from the symptoms, although they do not actually cure the problem. Only use these drugs if absolutely necessary – eg if you *must* travel. For children Imodium is preferable, but under all circumstances fluid replacement is the main message. Do not use these drugs if the person has a high fever or is severely dehydrated.

In certain situations antibiotics may be indicated:

- Watery diarrhoea with blood and mucus. (Gut-paralysing drugs such as Imodium or Lomotil should be avoided in this situation.)
- Watery diarrhoea with fever and lethargy.
- Persistent diarrhoea for more than five days.
- Severe diarrhoea, if it is logistically difficult to stay in one place.

The recommended drugs (adults only) are either norfloxacin 400 mg twice daily for three days or ciprofloxacin 500 mg twice daily for three days.

The drug of choice in children would be co-trimoxazole (Bactrim, Septrin, Resprim) with dosage dependent on weight. A three-day course is also given.

Ampicillin has been recommended in the past and may still be an alternative.

Giardiasis The parasite causing this intestinal disorder is present in contaminated water. The symptoms are stomach cramps, nausea, a bloated stomach, watery, foul-smelling diarrhoea and frequent gas. Giardiasis can appear several weeks after you have been exposed to the parasite. The symptoms may disappear for a few days and then return; this can go on for several weeks. Tinidazole, known as Fasigyn, or metronidazole (Flagyl) are the recommended drugs for treatment. Either can be used in a single treatment dose. Antibiotics are of no use.

Dysentery This serious illness, which is common in Vanuatu, is caused by contaminated food or water and is characterised by severe diarrhoea, often with blood or mucus in the stool. There are two kinds of dysentery. Bacillary dysentery is characterised by a high fever and rapid onset; headache, vomiting and stomach pains are also symptoms. It generally does not last longer than a week, but it is highly contagious.

Amoebic dysentery is often more gradual in the onset of symptoms, with cramping abdominal pain and vomiting less likely; fever may not be present. It is not a self-limiting disease: it will persist until treated and can recur and cause long-term health problems.

A stool test is necessary to diagnose which kind of dysentery you have, so you should seek medical help urgently. For bacillary dysentery, norfloxacin 400 mg twice daily for seven days or ciprofloxacin 500 mg twice daily for seven days are the recommended dosages.

If you're unable to find either of these drugs then a useful alternative is co-trimoxazole 160/800 mg (Bactrim, Septrin, Resprim) twice daily for seven days. This is a sulpha drug and must not be used by people with a known sulpha allergy.

In the case of children, the drug co-trimoxazole is a reasonable first-line treatment. For amoebic dysentery, the recommended adult dosage of metronidazole (Flagyl) is one 750-mg to 800-mg capsule three times daily for five days. Children aged between eight and 12 years should have half the adult dose; the dosage for younger children is one-third the adult dose.

An alternative to Flagyl is Fasigyn, taken as a two gram daily dose for three days.

Alcohol must be avoided during treatment and for 48 hours afterwards.

Viral Gastroenteritis This is caused not by bacteria but, as the name suggests, by a virus. It is characterised by stomach cramps, diarrhoea, and sometimes by vomiting and/or a slight fever. All you can do is rest and drink lots of fluids.

Hepatitis Hepatitis A is common in Vanuatu due mainly to the often poor sanitation of many villages. With good water and adequate sewage disposal in most industrialised countries since the 1940s, very few young travellers from these countries now have any natural immunity. Protection is through the new vaccine Havrix or the antibody gammaglobulin. The antibody is short-lasting.

The disease is spread by contaminated food or water. The symptoms are fever, chills, headache, fatigue, feelings of weakness and aches and pains, followed by loss of appetite, nausea, vomiting, abdominal pain, dark urine, light-coloured faeces, jaundiced skin, and the whites of the eyes may turn yellow. In some cases you may feel unwell, tired, have no appetite, experience aches and pains and be jaundiced. You should seek medical advice, but in general there is not much you can do apart from rest, drink lots of fluids, eat lightly and avoid fatty foods. People who have had hepatitis must forego alcohol for six months after the illness, as hepatitis attacks the liver and it needs that amount of time to recover.

Hepatitis B, which used to be called serum hepatitis, is also common here. It is spread through contact with infected blood, blood products or bodily fluids, for example through sexual contact, unsterilised needles and blood transfusions. Other risk situations include having a shave or tattoo in a local shop, or having your ears pierced. The symptoms of type B are much the same as type A except that they are more severe and may lead to irreparable liver damage or even liver cancer.

Although there is no treatment for hepatitis B, an effective prophylactic vaccine is readily available in most countries. The immunisation schedule requires two injections at least a month apart followed by a third dose five months after the second. People who should receive a hepatitis B vaccination include anyone who anticipates contact with blood or other bodily secretions, either as a health-care worker or through sexual contact with the local population, particularly those who intend to stay in the country for a long period of time.

Hepatitis C is another recently defined virus. It is a concern because it seems to lead to liver disease more rapidly than hepatitis B. The virus is spread by contact with blood – usually via contaminated transfusions or shared needles. Avoiding these is the only means of prevention, as there is no available vaccine.

Often referred to as the 'Delta' virus, hepatitis D infection only occurs in chronic carriers of hepatitis B. It is transmitted by blood and bodily fluids. Again there is no vaccine for this virus, so avoidance is the best prevention. The risk to travellers is certainly limited.

Worms These parasites are common in rural parts of Vanuatu, so a stool test when you return home is not a bad idea. They can be present on unwashed vegetables or in undercooked meat and you can pick them up through your skin by walking in bare feet – hookworm is endemic, so in rural areas keep your shoes on unless you're at the beach. Infestations may not show up for some time, and although they are generally not serious, if left untreated they can cause severe health problems. A stool test is necessary to pinpoint the problem and appropriate medication is often available over the counter.

Diseases Spread by People & Animals

Tetanus This potentially fatal disease is found in undeveloped tropical areas and is present in Vanuatu, although it is not a major health risk. It is difficult to treat but is preventable with immunisation. Tetanus occurs when a wound becomes infected by a germ which lives in the faeces of animals or people, so clean all cuts, punctures or animal bites. Tetanus is also known as lockjaw, and the first symptom may be discomfort in swallowing, or stiffening of the jaw and neck; this is followed by painful convulsions of the jaw and whole body.

Tuberculosis (TB) Although this disease is widespread in Vanuatu, it is not a serious risk to travellers. Young children are more susceptible than adults and vaccination is a sensible precaution for children under 12. TB is commonly spread by coughing or by unpasteurised dairy products from infected cows. Milk that has been boiled is safe to drink; the souring of milk to make yoghurt or cheese also kills the bacilli.

Ciguatera Common in Vanuatu, ciguatera is an often serious illness which occurs when a certain toxic organism in plankton is consumed by reef fish. Although the fish appear to be unharmed, the poison in them can prove fatal to humans.

Ciguatera's symptoms include vomiting, diarrhoea and cramps, alternating fevers and chills, and tingling in the skin and mouth. Outbreaks of the disease seem to coincide with major traumas to reefs such as cyclones and earthquakes, both of which are a regular occurrence here.

The best precaution is not to eat reef fish. In contrast, ocean-dwelling and deep-water species are considered safe.

Parasite Infections Parasitic infections (from parasites such as Angiostrongylus cantonensis) of the spinal cord are endemic in Vanuatu and can be contracted by eating uncooked, green leafy vegetables – particularly watercress and lettuce. The parasite larvae are excreted by the introduced African snail, which eats both of these vegetables, and are thus passed on to human consumers.

The condition is usually benign but can become dangerous – its symptoms are headaches and pains in the limbs. As a precaution, do not eat either watercress or lettuce unless it's been hydroponically grown in a snail-free environment – such produce can be purchased at supermarkets.

Sexually Transmitted Diseases Sexual contact with an infected sexual partner spreads these diseases. While abstinence is the only 100% preventative, using condoms is also effective. Gonorrhoea and syphilis are the most common of these diseases; sores, blisters or rashes around the genitals, discharges or pain when urinating are common symptoms. Symptoms may be less marked or not observed at all in women. Syphilis symptoms eventually disappear completely but the disease continues and can cause severe problems in later years. The treatment of gonorrhoea and syphilis is by antibiotics.

There are numerous other sexually transmitted diseases, for most of which effective treatment is available. However, there is no cure for herpes and there is also currently no cure for AIDS.

HIV/AIDS HIV, the Human Immunodeficiency Virus, may develop into AIDS, Acquired Immune Deficiency Syndrome. HIV is a major problem in many countries. Any exposure to blood, blood products or bodily fluids may put the individual at risk. In many developing countries transmission is predominantly through heterosexual sexual activity. This is quite different from industrialised countries where transmission is mostly through contact between homosexual or bisexual males or contaminated needles in IV drug users. Apart from abstinence, the most effective preventative is always to practise safe sex using condoms. It is impossible to detect the HIV-positive status of an otherwise healthy-looking person without a blood test.

Insect-Borne Diseases

Malaria This serious disease, which is spread by mosquito bites, is Vanuatu's major health risk. Only Port Vila and Futuna Island are considered free of malaria, so it's extremely important to take malarial prophylactics when travelling out of town. Symptoms include headaches, fever, chills and sweating which may subside and recur. Without treatment malaria can develop more serious, potentially fatal effects. A number of ni-Vanuatu die each year from the disease.

Antimalarial drugs do not prevent you from being infected but kill the parasites during a stage in their development.

There are a number of different types of malaria, with falciparum malaria being of most concern. This form is responsible for the very serious cerebral malaria. It is also the predominant form in Vanuatu. Contrary to popular belief cerebral malaria is not a new strain. And because of its serious effects, prevention of falciparum malaria is far better than treatment.

The problem in recent years has been the emergence of increasing resistance to commonly used antimalarials such as chloroquine, maloprim and proguanil. Newer drugs such as mefloquine (Lariam) and doxycycline (Vibramycin, Doryx) are often recommended for chloroquine and multidrug resistant areas.

If taking doxycycline, ensure that you do so only as recommended using plenty of fluids. Do not lie down immediately afterwards. Ulceration of the oesophagus can result by not observing these simple rules.

Expert advice should be sought for malaria treatment, as there are many factors to consider when deciding on the type of antimalarial medication. These include the area to be visited, the risk of exposure to malaria-carrying mosquitoes, your current medical condition, and your age and pregnancy status. Don't forget to discuss the side-effect profile of the medication, so you can work out some level of risk versus benefit ratio.

It is also very important to be sure of the correct dosage of the medication prescribed to you. Some people inadvertently have taken weekly medication (chloroquine) on a daily basis, with disastrous effects. While discussing dosages for prevention of malaria, it is often advisable to include the dosages required for treatment, especially if your trip is through a high-risk area that would isolate you from medical care.

HIV/AIDS can also be spread through infected blood transfusions; most developing countries cannot afford to screen blood for transfusions. It can also be spread by dirty needles – vaccinations, acupuncture, tattooing and ear or nose piercing can potentially be as dangerous as intravenous drug use if the equipment is not clean. If you do need an injection, ask to see the syringe unwrapped in front of you, or better still, carry a needle and syringe pack in your luggage – it is a cheap insurance against infection with HIV.

Fear of HIV infection should never preclude treatment for serious medical conditions. Although there may be a risk of infection, it is very small indeed.

Cuts, Bites & Stings

Cuts & Scratches Skin punctures can easily become infected in hot climates and may heal with difficulty. Treat any cut with an antiseptic such as Betadine. Where possible avoid bandages and Band-aids, which can keep a wound wet, although if there are flies about you'll need to cover it straight away to avoid infection.

Coral cuts are notoriously slow to heal, as the coral injects a weak venom into the wound. Avoid coral cuts by wearing shoes when walking on reefs. Clean any cut thoroughly with hydrogen peroxide if available, then apply Betadine.

Bites & Stings Bee and wasp stings are usually painful rather than dangerous. Calamine lotion will give relief or ice packs will reduce the pain and swelling. There are some spiders with dangerous bites but antivenenes are usually available.

Certain cone shells found in the Pacific can sting dangerously or even fatally. There are various fish and other sea creatures which can sting or bite dangerously or which are dangerous to eat. Again, local advice is the

---

The main messages are:

1. Primary prevention must always be in the form of mosquito avoidance measures. The mosquitoes that transmit malaria bite from dusk to dawn and during this period travellers are advised to:
- wear light-coloured clothing
- wear long pants and long-sleeved shirts
- use mosquito repellents containing the compound DEET on exposed areas
- avoid highly scented perfumes or aftershave
- use a mosquito net – it may be worth taking your own
2. While no antimalarial is 100% effective, taking the most appropriate drug significantly reduces the risk of contracting the disease.
3. No one should ever die from malaria. It can be diagnosed by a simple blood test. Symptoms range from fever, chills and sweating, headache and abdominal pains to a vague feeling of ill-health, so seek examination immediately if there is any suggestion of malaria.

Contrary to popular belief, once a traveller contracts malaria he/she does not have it for life. One of the parasites may lie dormant in the liver but this can also be eradicated using a specific medication. Malaria is curable, as long as the traveller seeks medical help when symptoms occur.

Dengue Fever There is no prophylactic available for this mosquito-spread disease, of which outbreaks occur from time to time in Vanuatu. One epidemic killed seven people and affected 400 others in 1989.

The main preventative measure against dengue fever is to avoid mosquito bites – the mosquitoes that carry the disease bite throughout the day. A sudden onset of fever, headaches and severe joint and muscle pains are the first signs. Then a rash starts on the trunk of the body and spreads to the limbs and face. After a further few days, the fever will subside and recovery will begin. Serious complications are uncommon. ■

best suggestion (also see Fauna in the Facts about the Country chapter).

Bedbugs & Lice Bedbugs live in various places, but particularly in dirty mattresses and bedding. Vanuatu's hotels and tourist guest houses maintain a high standard, but you may find bedbugs and other nasties in the leaf houses of remote villages. Fleas are often a problem in such places.

All lice cause itching and discomfort. They make themselves at home in your hair (head lice), your clothing (body lice) or in your pubic hair (crabs). You catch lice through direct contact with infected people or by sharing combs, clothing and the like. Powder or shampoo treatment will kill the lice and infected clothing should then be washed in very hot water.

Ticks Vaseline, alcohol or oil will persuade a tick to let go. You should always check your body if you have been walking through a tick-infested area.

Women's Health
Gynaecological Problems Poor diet, lowered resistance due to the use of antibiotics for stomach upsets and even contraceptive pills can lead to vaginal infections when travelling in hot climates. Keeping the genital area clean, and wearing skirts or loose-fitting trousers and cotton underwear will help to prevent infections.

Yeast infections, characterised by a rash, itch and discharge, can be treated with a vinegar or even lemon-juice douche or with yoghurt. Nystatin suppositories are the usual medical prescription. Trichomonas is a more serious infection; symptoms are a discharge and a burning sensation when urinating. Male sexual partners must also be treated, and if a vinegar-water douche is not effective, medical attention should be sought. Metronidazole (Flagyl) is the prescribed drug.

Pregnancy Most miscarriages occur during the first three months of pregnancy, so this is the most risky time to travel. Miscarriage is not uncommon, and can occasionally lead to severe bleeding. The last three months should also be spent within reasonable distance of good medical care. A baby born as early as 24 weeks stands a chance of survival, but only in a good modern hospital. Pregnant women should avoid all unnecessary medication, but vaccinations and malarial prophylactics should still be taken where possible. Additional care should be taken to prevent illness and particular attention should be paid to diet and nutrition. Alcohol and nicotine, for example, should be avoided.

Women travellers often find that their periods become irregular or even cease while they're on the road. Remember that a missed period in these circumstances doesn't necessarily indicate pregnancy. You can seek advice and have a urine test to determine whether you are pregnant at any of Vanuatu's hospitals.

WOMEN TRAVELLERS
Although Vanuatu is considered a safe place for women, you'd be well advised to practise a few common-sense precautions, particularly if travelling by yourself. These include taking a taxi or remaining in busy areas at night, and not swimming or sunbathing alone at isolated beaches.

Like it or not, Vanuatu is an impregnable bastion of male chauvinism, and females are often considered second-class citizens – or worse. Some of the restrictions placed on women may seem draconian and silly (see the section on Culture in Facts about the Country), but as they are wont to say: when in Rome...

The office of the Vanuatu National Council of Women, in Vila, can provide you with all the information you'll need in this regard (see the section on Tourist Offices earlier in this chapter).

DANGERS & ANNOYANCES
No one goes into the pot these days, not even on Malakula. In fact, apart from malaria and stomach upsets, there's really nothing for you to worry about in Vanuatu. It's true that

sharks and venomous sea creatures can be a danger, but unless you're either very unlucky or very foolish these are most unlikely to bring you undone.

Your belongings will normally be quite safe in your hotel room. However, petty theft is on the increase and you should never leave any valuables, wallets or handbags lying about unattended.

Politeness and honesty are great virtues of the ni-Vanuatu people, so it's unusual for anyone to give you a hard time. The major exceptions are drunks (fortunately not common) and the more unscrupulous, or desperate, form of taxi driver.

WORK

Visitors are prohibited from taking up employment or any other remunerative activity while in Vanuatu. All nonresidents intending to work locally must obtain official permission to do so. Except for family members of foreigners already working in Vanuatu, all processing of work permits must be completed prior to your arrival in the country. The same applies to business licences for the self-employed.

ACTIVITIES

With only eight or nine days to spend in Vanuatu, the average package-tour visitor is quite content with the attractions in and around Vila and will seldom venture far beyond it. Two weeks are easily filled if you add on a coach tour or rental car ride around Efate, a scuba-diving and sightseeing excursion to Santo and a visit to the Yasur volcano on Tanna.

Vanuatu is a very small country in terms of its land area, but if you really want to see everything of interest – and have sufficient time and vatu to enjoy it – you'll certainly need much more time than is allowed by your basic one-month visa. In fact, enthusiasts for culture, diving, trekking, yachting and nature generally, will have no difficulty spending three months getting to know the country.

Sports

The best place to play or see any sport is in Vila. Teams from throughout Vanuatu and neighbouring countries come to play here. Favourite sports include soccer, cricket, cycling, basketball, volleyball, boxing, netball and athletics. You can also watch a Vanuatu 'special' called handball, which is similar to Gaelic football and is played using hands and feet.

Vanuatu's few golf courses and tennis courts are all in or near Vila and Luganville. The only squash courts are in Vila.

Water Sports

Many of Vanuatu's usually sun-drenched beaches are ideal for swimming, and there are countless coral reefs seemingly created with snorkellers and scuba divers in mind. The country also boasts the world's premier shipwreck dive: the SS *President Coolidge* off Santo.

There's an excellent choice of marine activities around Vila, where you can go on boat cruises, sail, windsurf, waterski, snorkel, scuba dive and parasail, among other things. Most of the capital's boat cruises offer coral viewing, often in a glass-bottom boat. You can take a yacht cruise from either Vila or Luganville from one to five days, or longer if you want. Game and bottom-reef fishing are also on offer.

Things are less organised on the other islands. Still, regardless of where you are you can generally go swimming or snorkelling, and perhaps rent a traditional canoe.

Fishing There's plenty of good fishing around the reefs and in deeper water. However, unless you're a yachtie, the best opportunity for most visitors to go fishing is with one of the specialised tours operating from Vila. As well, you can often hire a canoe on the outer islands, or pay a villager to take you out in a speedboat. Fishing gear is readily available in Vila and Luganville, but the best approach in other areas is to go prepared.

River fishing is also worthwhile, particularly for freshwater crayfish, prawns and eels. Several islands, especially Efate, Aneityum, Santo and Malakula, have either fast-flowing creeks or broad, lazy estuaries where you can land some good-sized catches. Gaua and Ambae boast large crater lakes where prawns and eels are the main attraction. As always in Vanuatu, check whether the water and the fish in it belong to anyone before casting your line.

Swimming Vanuatu has a huge number of sandy, coral and stony beaches ranging from several km to just a few metres in length. The sandy ones are invariably black or grey in volcanic areas, but otherwise either white or golden. Coral beaches are a nightmare to walk on barefooted. The dead coral can make the soles of your feet itch like mad for a few minutes after walking on it.

Scuba Diving

Vanuatu boasts a full range of dive spots, including wrecks, coral gardens, caves, wall and night dives, and marine life. Many islands offer excellent potential, with a number of world-class dives scattered through the archipelago.

The waters around Vila and parts of Santo have been well explored and attract the most attention from tour operators; Vila is considered to have the best range of underwater geography in a relatively small area, while Santo has the best wreck, coral and fish dives. Elsewhere, Vanuatu's underwater world is largely virgin territory.

Remember that it's good manners to ask permission at the nearest village if intending to dive or snorkel near the shore. You may or may not be charged a small fee for the privilege.

Specialist Dive-Tour Operators Operating out of Vila are Hideaway Island Dive and Nautilus; also check whether or not Pro Dive has started up on Iririki Island. In Luganville you'll find Aquamarine, Santo Dive Tours and Exploration Dive, while Bokissa Island Dive is on nearby Bokissa Island. The recognised expert on the SS *President Coolidge* is Allan Power of Santo Dive Tours, with over 25 years experience diving on the wreck. Allan now concentrates solely on shore dives to the Coolidge and nearby Million Dollar Point.

Nautilus is the only company offering extended dive tours. Its dive-boat *Kirio* can carry 10 passengers and does seven-day return trips between Vila and Santo, visiting the Tongoa Wall and other major dive spots en route. The daily all-inclusive cost is A$195.

Water Temperatures Vanuatu's sea temperatures reach their annual maximum of 30˚C between December and February. In June and July it falls to 20˚C.

It's quite warm enough to scuba without a wet suit during the southern summer, though there's always the likelihood of coral grazes – remember that these can quickly become infected. However, it can get unpleasantly cold without a suit during the cooler months, especially if you're night diving. A four-mm thick Lycra suit is usually warm enough and will protect you from the coral.

Visibility Vanuatu's underwater visibility is usually more than 30 metres and sometimes reaches up to 50. However, it can also be considerably less than this depending on such variables as weather and tide.

Equipment Rental A complete range of diving kit can be rented from the tour operators mentioned above. Wherever you are, you'll have to show your certification first.

Learning to Dive As long as you're over 12 and healthy, you can learn to scuba dive. Most local dive-tour operators offer beginner courses. These cost between 25,000 and 30,000VT for a four-to five-day training course, which will bring you up to international open-water certification standard.

Decompression Facilities There is no decompression chamber in Vanuatu, the nearest one available being at Townsville on Australia's north-eastern coast. ■

The majority of beaches offer perfectly safe swimming. However, as sharks and strong currents are a danger in some areas, it's always smart to seek local advice before plunging in. If white sand is considered safer than black sand in terms of shark attack, it's probably because sharks are easier to see against the light background.

Snorkelling Vanuatu has countless good snorkelling spots, many of which can be explored from the shore. These include Hideaway Island, which is considered the best of the easily accessible spots near Vila. Samoa Point in Havana Harbour (check the Vila side of the point) is another great location on Efate Island.

As well, most boat tours around Vila cater for snorkellers. Otherwise, you can usually accompany a scuba group for around 1000VT a time, handfeeding the fish or viewing colourful coral gardens while the rest of your party explores the depths.

Remember that if you're starting from a coral ledge you'll find it comparatively easy

Yellow-red vasiform sponge

to enter the water but often fearfully difficult to get back onto dry land – especially if the sea is anything but calm. For this reason, always plan your exit point before entering the water.

Keen snorkellers should bring their own equipment with them as the cost of either buying or hiring it in Vanuatu can be high.

Bushwalking

There are many fine walks in Vanuatu and the relatively cool winter months are the perfect time in which to do them. Quite apart from the scenery, which is often nothing short of superb, walking gives you an excellent opportunity to meet the people and learn something of Melanesian village life.

It doesn't matter whether your preference is for tough trekking or gentle strolls, there's plenty here to keep you occupied. A number of islands have high, steep-sided, jungle-clad mountains that virtually climb out of the sea. Mt Tabwemasana (1879 metres) in southwest Santo is the country's highest point and there are many more around the 1000-metre mark. Other islands are ideal for easy half, one or two-day coastal walks through coconut plantations, gardens, rainforest and friendly villages.

If billowing smoke, bubbling lava and having the earth move beneath you are your passion, see Volcanoes & Earthquakes in the Facts about the Country chapter.

A small sample of the suggested longer walks on offer are: the four-day trek around south-west Erromango; the two-day walk from north to south visiting the volcanoes on Ambrym; the one and two-day walks in the proposed national park at Big Bay on Santo; the two-day return walk to Lake Letas and Siri Falls on Gaua; and the two-day loop walk around the western half of Aneityum.

There are several options when it comes to planning a walk. You can organise it yourself, join either the Alliance Française or the Vanuatu Natural Science Society (both in Vila) on one of their regular social walks, or take a tour with operators such as Frank King Tours of Vila, Butterfly Tours of Santo and Lolihor Adventure Tours of Ambrym.

Watching Wildlife

For most visitors, Vanuatu's wildlife only becomes a highlight when they put on the goggles and slip beneath the water near a colourful coral reef. Also worth mentioning are the tame dugong at Resolution Bay on Tanna and at Laman Bay on Epi (one apiece). Apart from marine fauna, however, the average person will see little apart from a few birds, some small lizards and maybe a rat scurrying across the road.

Yet for hard-working enthusiasts there's plenty of potential in the country's birds. Among the more notable opportunities: the big lake on Gaua has a large breeding population of ducks; the cloud forests of Santo are home to the endemic mountain starling; Emae has a sizeable population of peregrine falcons; and tiny Laika, off Epi, has a significant colony of shearwaters (also known as mutton birds). Unfortunately, the most common bird in inhabited areas seems to be the introduced Indian mynah. The most obvious of the birds in forested areas are the parrots and pigeons – you may not see them, but you'll certainly hear them.

Visiting Archaeological Sites

Almost all islands contain significant evidence of the much larger populations that existed in the past. Relics include the sites of ancient villages, ceremonial grounds and burial places. Stone foundations and drystone walls are common throughout, while the stone monoliths that mark past dancing grounds are more widespread in northern areas.

Gaua is probably the country's most outstanding island in terms of stone remains. Aneityum is particularly interesting for its ancient irrigation systems and prehistoric petroglyphs, or rock carvings. These typically represent the sun, moon and animals, with other symbols of more obscure meaning. North Pentecost also has numerous petroglyph sites.

As each one of Vanuatu's thousands of archaeological sites has a traditional owner, you will have to ask permission to see it. You may also have to pay a small entry fee.

Collecting Shells

Many visitors like to collect sea shells, although in this age of environmental enlightenment the practice is increasingly frowned upon. In fact, due primarily to the tourist trade, Vanuatu's more attractive varieties of shells are in danger of being overfished – you can appreciate why when you visit the local markets. You should think twice before collecting even dead shells, as these provide a potential home for creatures such as hermit crabs.

If you simply must go shell collecting in rural areas you will need the permission of the village chief, as each reef has a custom owner. Shells are regarded as a source of income, and several chiefs have created small, coastal marine sanctuaries to prevent overexploitation. Apart from angry chiefs, the major risks involved with shell collecting are poisonous cone shells and stonefish.

Cone shell

Traditional Life & Ceremonies

Despite the modern world on their doorsteps, a small and ever-diminishing number of villages in Vanuatu have managed to retain their traditional lifestyles, dress and religions. They are generally in the least accessible parts of the larger islands, particularly Santo, Pentecost and Ambrym. On the other hand, the people of Yakel and Yaohnanen in Tanna live only about seven km from the island's capital. Generally, the people who live traditionally do so because their chiefs have rejected modern ways.

Several such villages, such as Yakel, Matantas on Santo, and Fanla on Ambrym, welcome visitors on guided tours. They provide an ideal opportunity to see how ni-Vanuatu lived before the missionaries arrived. The emphasis is on 'see', because obviously there's no chance to participate in village life on such fleeting visits.

Others allow tourists to witness seasonal dances and other ceremonial activities that have their origins in the mists of time. These include the Toka dancers of Tanna and the land divers of south Pentecost.

For a suitable fee you can often have a dance provided 'out of season' for your benefit, but of course the atmosphere won't be anything like the real thing. At the latter you can watch pigs being killed by being repeatedly bashed over the skull with a heavy club. This is not a sight for animal liberationists, or anyone with a weak stomach or a great love of pigs.

Ceremonial dances are staged throughout the country during the annual Independence Day celebrations, especially in Vila. Fortuitously, this takes place on 30 July, right in the middle of the peak tourist season.

HIGHLIGHTS

It would be fair to say that almost every island in Vanuatu has something to offer the visitor, whether it be coral reefs, idyllic scenery, walking tracks, history, culture, wildlife or friendly people. Of course it depends where your interests lie, but there are a number of highlights that shouldn't be missed.

Efate Island has the capital, Port Vila, which boasts the country's major resorts and most of its tour operators. There is almost no end to the activities on offer in and around the town. For starters, you can wine and dine at some of the Pacific's best restaurants, get in some excellent duty-free shopping, indulge in world-class scuba diving, or take a yacht cruise to the small islands off the coast.

Scuba diving on the SS *President Coolidge* is arguably the main attraction on Santo, the country's largest island. Any diver who's done the wreck will tell you that the experience will blow your mind. There are some magnificent beaches up the north-east coast, and unforgettable hiking in the rugged

south-west. Of interest also is the proposed national park at Big Bay, in the north.

Another destination for walkers is Ambrym Island, where the Mt Benbow and Mt Marum volcanoes breathe smoke and ash over an unbelievably desolate landscape. Other attractions here include the annual Rom festival and the traditional wooden carvings of north Ambrym.

Tanna is best known for the Mt Yasur volcano, which puts on Vanuatu's most spectacular show. A night visit is unforgettable for its sound effects and fireworks displays, so put it on your list. You can also visit custom villages, watch the colourful Toka festival and get an insight into the unusual Jon Frum cult.

Culture is a highlight of Malakula and Pentecost, the latter being the home of the famous land divers. Tall forests and rugged coastal scenery lure the walker to Erromango, while Ambae, Aneityum and Gaua also offer excellent walking. None of these islands is developed for tourism, although there are some basic facilities.

ACCOMMODATION

If you like comfort with an element of luxury, there's an impressive selection of hotels in and around Vila and, to a much lesser extent, Luganville. However, you'll probably get a fright if cutting costs is your aim. Several accommodation houses in the two major towns can claim to be of backpacker standard, but very few charge backpacker prices.

Larger villages and remote missions and schools often have guest houses which, although not intended for tourists, will take you in if there's a vacancy. As well, in recent years, a commercial style of guest house aimed at tourists has sprung up in rural areas around the country. Both types tend to be very basic, and usually have only primitive facilities.

At the rock-bottom end of the accommodation scale are village huts set aside for visitor use. These are generally spartan in the extreme, and as a consequence are very cheap. Almost all rural villages have such a hut; if not, the chief will probably be able to find a vacant house for you to spend the night in. Alternatively, you may be able to stay in the nakamal, as these are also often used for overnight visitor accommodation. Traditional Melanesian hospitality is such that you'll rarely if ever be left to your own devices.

In a village you should never simply appear on the doorstep and ask for a bed. This may cause your intended hosts some embarrassment, quite apart from the fact that their visitor quarters may be full. Courtesy as much as common-sense dictates that they be given advance warning so that they can get ready for you. If you can't contact them by telephone or teleradio, send a service message over Radio Vanuatu. Alternatively, ask the local council office, mission or whatever to pass on a message for you.

Camping
Vanuatu doesn't have official camping grounds, although a handful of accommodation houses will allow it. Camping isn't encouraged in populated areas. In fact, there's no need to camp as most villages have quarters of some description which are available for visitors. If you're really keen to indulge in some out-of-the-way camping on a delightful stretch of coast, for example, the local chief may be prepared to give approval. You can only ask! However, in remote areas there's sure to be disappointment that you don't wish to accept the village's hospitality.

Village Leaf Houses & Nakamals
The majority of rural families live in oblong huts made from sago palm leaves. In Bislama such a hut is called a *lif haos* (leaf house). Together with nakamals, which are of similar construction, these are the country's most basic form of visitor accommodation.

Leaf houses and nakamals usually have a bare earth floor – the occupants invariably sleep on pandanus mats on the dirt, or on rough beds. Anything you don't want chewed by rats should be secured in some way. To avoid being kept awake by fleas, spray the floor with insecticide and yourself with repellent, and sleep in a sleeping bag inner sheet. Hopefully, this will work, or maybe there won't be many fleas!

Leaf-house facilities are invariably rudimentary. Food is cooked outside on a wood-fuelled, open-hearth fire or in a small hut specifically set aside as a kitchen.

Washing takes place either outside in a bowl or bucket behind a screen, or simply by splashing in either a creek or the sea – the latter is usual where there's a chronic shortage of fresh water. Toilets, where they exist, are almost always of the pit variety.

It may cost you up to 250VT to stay overnight in a leaf house, depending on its standard. Alternatively, you can often pay with a small 'thank you' gift, such as a packet of cigarettes or some items from the local trade store. Remember that you will have to share the leaf house with any islanders who also happen to be visiting.

Hostels & Guest/Rest Houses
Places in the 800 to 1500VT per person range include church hostels, private guest houses, and government rest houses. This style of accommodation varies enormously in standard, and rats can be a problem here as well. Although generally very basic, which is why they are cheap by the country's standards, most do provide clean bedding and limited communal cooking facilities.

Where cookers aren't provided in remote areas you should have no difficulty in arranging for meals to be provided by the villagers. However, local foods can be extremely bland to jaded western palates, so pack some sauces, herbs, tinned sardines or whatever to give your meals a lift.

Keep in mind that government guest houses are primarily for the use of government workers. If there's a shortage of beds and a government employee turns up looking for one, you may have to move out. In this case you'll invariably have no difficulty finding somewhere else, although it may not be as flash.

It's also worth mentioning that the toilet and ablution facilities at some guest houses

Top: Beach at the Meridien, Port Vila (AV)
Middle: Boy in canoe, Erakor Lagoon, Efate Island (AV)
Bottom: Beach, Le Lagon Pacific Resort (AV)

A: Stone artefact (AV)
B: Wooden artefacts at handicraft stall, Port Vila (AV)
C: Carved tree-fern figures, Ambrym Island (DO)
D: Tamtams (slit drums) (AV)

are as primitive as those at leaf houses. Take some toilet paper as well, just in case.

Women's Clubs Many villages include a simple building that's used as a women's club, which is invariably linked to the local church. Here the women gather during the day and conduct various activities, while at night the building is unoccupied. They make ideal overnight accommodation for visitors, and in fact some even have beds for this purpose. The women will be pleased to cook for you if there are no facilities available for your use.

One of the best places to learn the location of women's clubs is the Vanuatu National Council of Women office in Vila. If there are any areas they aren't sure of they can put you in touch with someone who will know. Alternatively, you can try the head offices of the various religious denominations in Vila. For more details see the Tourist Information section earlier in this chapter.

Village Resorts In recent years a number of locally owned guest houses aimed specifically at the tourist market have been developed in rural areas. Most are constructed of traditional materials and generally have primitive washing and toilet facilities. Meals – typically island-style – are usually provided, as are bedding and mosquito nets and/or coils. Sometimes the management and staff of such places are inexperienced in dealing with tourists. However, they will always make every effort to ensure your happiness and enjoyment of the visit.

It's rather a pity that these establishments tend to call themselves resorts, as most are far from the accepted meaning of the word. Just looking at the name in the tourist brochure might deter the adventurous sort of visitor who would really appreciate them.

Resorts, Hotels & Motels

Vila dominates Vanuatu's tourist industry and has accommodation to match. Most of it is expensive, although there are a handful of motels both here and in Luganville where you'll pay under 5000VT for a double/twin room. Some have air-con rooms, while others provide ceiling or bedside fans. Most of the places in this category have either communal cooking facilities or an attached dining room and bar. Generally, their standard ranges from spartan to basic.

If you'd prefer something a little more sophisticated, you'll find a number of places charging between 6000 and 10,000VT for a double/twin room.

Above this price are Vanuatu's international-standard hotels and resorts.

On most styles of accommodation, with the notable exception of most of the lower brackets, you can usually get a price reduction by negotiating a weekly or longer-stay rate. You may even be able to get a discount simply by asking for it, especially in their summer low season.

There are often attractive packages on offer from Australia, New Zealand and New Caledonia in particular, so make sure to check all your options before making the big decision.

FOOD

Thanks largely to the French influence, Vila is very well known in the Pacific for its international cuisine and boasts a couple of the region's more famous restaurants. Fortunately, however, you can eat out and not blow your budget as there are a number of cheap eateries which serve substantial meals – but you won't enjoy them if you don't like white rice! If you're wanting to cook your own meals, you'll find that the larger supermarkets carry a good range of local and imported foods.

Luganville offers the best cuisine outside the capital. Elsewhere, restaurants are very scarce and those found in remote villages tend to have very restricted menus. Often you get two choices: chicken and rice, or rice and chicken. Fortunately, local government rest houses have communal kitchens and there are usually well-stocked stores in the larger villages. As a general rule, in remoter areas you should carry a selection of favourite foods as local trade stores – there's at least one in every sizeable village – can have little on the shelves. Often all you'll find is white rice, sugar and tinned meat and fish. If you're eating island-style meals, you may find that something to liven up the taste is beneficial.

You'll find regular markets in all the major population centres as well as most other, smaller central areas. There's no bargaining as all prices are set and very fair. Coconuts, bananas, pawpaw, yams, taro, cucumbers, lemons, limes, oranges, grapefruit, tomatoes and a host of other fruit and vegetable species are usually available. These are all grown in village gardens.

If cooking for yourself, bottled gas is available at most larger stores in Vila and Luganville.

Dining Out

If eating out is your fancy, Vila will be far and away your favourite town in Vanuatu – although the meals at the Bougainville Resort at Luganville also stand out.

Particular local specialities include *roussette* (flying fox or fruit bat), *crevettes* (prawns), coconut crabs, *nautou* (green-winged ground pigeon), *escargots* (snails) and *grenouilles* (frogs' legs). Both roussette and nautou are particularly good when served *au vin* (in red wine), while coconut crab is especially tasty in garlic sauce.

Other delicacies are *poulet* fish (given this name because it tastes like chicken), mangrove oysters, and *nems* (Vietnamese spring rolls). Another favourite is Tahitian raw fish salad. In this dish, seafood is first marinated in lime juice, then sweetened with coconut milk. Finally, there are good-quality beef steaks from Efate's many herds of Charolais and Limousin cattle.

Traditional Dishes

Laplap Vanuatu's national dish is laplap. It's made by grating either manioc, taro roots or yams into a doughy paste. The mixture is then put on to taro or wild spinach leaves,

and soaked with a milky juice made from grated coconut diluted with water. Next, pieces of pork, beef, poultry, fish, prawns or flying fox are added. Taro or banana leaves are then wrapped around the doughy mix and tied up with strands of vine. The packages are then placed in a ground oven, with hot stones above and below, where they cook beautifully.

Other Dishes *Tuluk* is very similar to laplap. It's basically a pork-filled manioc pudding, prepared and cooked the same way.

Nalot is a vegetable dish made from roasted or boiled taro, banana or breadfruit mixed with a cream made from grated coconut and water. The cream is placed in the centre, with a hot stone in it to keep it warm.

Local Foods

Coconuts The primary food of the Pacific, Vanuatu included, is the coconut. In addition to being the staple diet, it has other valuable uses. It provides roofing materials, sennit for weaving and fibres for fire-making.

Each of the nut's five growth stages provides a different form of food or drink. The first stage is ideal for drinking, because as yet there's no flesh inside. The next is when tasty, jellied flesh appears inside.

The best eating stage is the third, when the flesh inside is firm but thin and succulent. After this, the flesh becomes thick, hard, and ideal for drying into copra. At its fifth stage, the nut begins to shoot while the milk inside goes crispy, making what is known throughout the Pacific as 'coconut ice cream'.

Other Local Foods There's a large number of other edible fruits and nuts which you may come across in Vila. These include *nakatambol*, a small, clusterlike fruit. Each one is cherry-sized and turns yellow when it's ripe. Another common one, similar to a mango, is called a *naus*.

You're sure to see the occasional rose apple tree as you travel around the archipelago. Also called 'bush', 'Malay', 'New Guinea' or 'Kanak' apple elsewhere and *nakavika* by ni-Vanuatu, this small pink-and-white fruit has an apple-like flesh beneath its skin. Villagers often flavour their food with its blossom, calling this the *kakae flaoa* (food flower).

Several edible nuts are grown around the country. The most common are 'cut-nuts', also called *narli-nuts*, *narveli* or *namambe* depending where you are. In other parts of the Pacific, these are also known as 'Tahiti' or 'island chestnuts'. The edible part of the cut-nut is the light-brown inner kernel concealed inside a hard, brown, outer shell. This has to be cut with a firm stroke using a bush knife, hence its name.

Equally plentiful is an oval, nut-containing fruit called *nangae* (pronounced 'nanyai'). Its edible part is the crispy white kernel inside the nut's greenish-black outer surface. It tastes rather like an almond.

There are also worms and grubs which islanders have traditionally favoured as food. The best known is the *palolo* worm, collected from certain coral reefs when the creatures swarm in their millions every November throughout the Pacific. When it's served on toast, palolo looks like green caviar. Another delicacy is a tasty mauve grub which is found in decaying logs.

DRINKS
Alcohol
The only one true pub in Vanuatu is the Office Pub, in Vila. However, almost all hotels, restaurants and private clubs are licensed. Most supermarkets in Vila and Luganville carry a good range of French and Australian wines and spirits, and local and Australian beers.

Preparing kava

You can buy takeaway alcohol in urban centres as soon as the shops open each morning at 7.30 am, and until restaurants close around 11.30 pm. There's a weekend rule barring shops from selling alcohol between 11 am on Saturdays and 7.30 am on Monday mornings, but there's no such restriction on hotels, restaurants or private clubs.

Kava

Often called *aelan bia* (island beer) in Bislama, kava is the drink preferred by many ni-Vanuatu men. It is made from the roots of the *Piper methysticum* shrub, or 'intoxicating pepper' as Captain Cook called it. Widespread in the archipelago, this member of the pepper family is related to the betel nut, which itself is common in countries to the north. In Vanuatu, betel nut is found only in the Torres group.

The term kava is similar to the Polynesian word *ava* meaning 'intoxicating drink'. However, it's more likely that kava spread from Vanuatu eastwards into Polynesia rather than the other way round. This is because of the large number of varieties of the plant growing in the archipelago: 40 in all.

Kava drinking is an evening ritual throughout the country. If you're asked to drink some at a village consider yourself honoured, as the invitation amounts to a formal welcome. To decline kava when it is offered is to decline friendship. So even though it may taste worse than anything you can possibly imagine, you've got to gulp it down and appear impressed.

Ceremony Traditionally, there are strict rules for preparing and drinking kava. As well as being used as a form of welcome, it's also used to seal alliances, to start chiefly conferences, and to commemorate births, deaths and marriages.

Preparation procedures vary throughout the archipelago. In some of the more traditional areas, such as on Tanna, kava roots are brought to the nakamal late each afternoon by prepubescent boys. Once the roots have been washed, the boys prepare them by chewing them into a mush and spitting the hard bits onto leaves. The mush is then placed in a container, water is added and the ingredients are stirred and worked around with the hands. Then the mud-coloured liquid is filtered through coconut fibres.

In Ambae, Maewo and northern Pentecost, men prepare kava in wooden bowls, grinding it up with a phallic-shaped piece of coral. In other areas, the roots may simply be pounded in a plastic bucket, or the drink may be prepared from a commercially packaged powder.

Once the liquid mixture is ready for drinking, it's poured into a bowl made from an empty half-coconut shell, which serves as a cup – for this reason a draught of kava is usually known as a 'shell'. First the chief drinks it, followed by any honoured guests. Then the other men drink in order of precedence. In most parts of the country, kava drinkers consume two to three half-coconut cupfuls in a session. Etiquette requires each man to drink his kava in a single gulp, any remaining liquid being poured on the ground.

In some parts, kava is drunk in silence. In others, it's drunk with a great deal of slurping to show appreciation. Sometimes your companions will quietly clap as you drink.

While kava is being drunk, except for the clapping stage, conversation and loud noises are kept to a minimum. Islanders feel it's best drunk when there's an atmosphere of quietness. Frivolous, irrelevant, negative or critical conversation is frowned on, but praise is always welcome.

As you'll quickly discover, kava makes the eyes sensitive to glare, so any strong lights, especially flashbulbs, are considered most intrusive. If you really want to take a photograph, be sure to ask permission and limit yourself to one or two shots. Any more and you'll be in danger of becoming a nuisance.

Effects Kava has a pungent, muddy taste. If the brew is a strong one, your lips will go numb and cold, like after a dental injection.

Then your limbs will feel heavy and your speech will become quiet and slow.

You'll begin to be affected within 10 to 25 minutes. Even if it's only a mild brew, you'll probably want to do nothing more than lie down and think about life, feeling sedated and with a general sense of well-being. You may also experience some minor perceptual changes, both in your emotions and your vision. If the brew is a strong one, you'll probably experience a mild form of double vision, and want to sleep for a few hours.

Some islanders claim to have repeated religious experiences after drinking kava. Most sightings of the Tannese god, Jon Frum, have occurred at such times!

Social Effects Kava has helped Vanuatu to retain its ancient customs longer than many other neighbouring countries. Its rituals have reinforced the traditional authority of chiefs, even when villagers have moved to the capital.

Many people attribute the capital's low crime rate to the calming effects of kava. Unlike alcohol, which often produces aggressive and irresponsible behaviour, kava produces amiability, peacefulness and acceptance of life. Sadly, however, alcohol consumption is on the increase and with it violent crime, particularly domestic violence.

Medicinal Uses Some of the 40 subspecies of kava are too strong to drink freely, and are used instead as bush medicines.

Different kinds of kava plants produce differing effects, which are strengthened or reduced depending on whether the drink is prepared by chewing, straining or pounding. On Pentecost, six subspecies have medicinal use, while eight can be used to make the drink. On Tanna, only five can be used medicinally, but 12 types can be drunk.

In scientific terms, kava is an amalgam of up to 14 analgesics and anaesthetics, and has natural pain and appetite-suppressant features. The root also has antibacterial, relaxant, diuretic and decongestant properties. It's been recommended for cancer and asthma patients, and also for people suffering from stomach upsets. No scientist has yet studied what the effects of a lifetime of kava drinking are. However, there are plenty of elderly ni-Vanuatu men who have drunk copious quantities on a daily basis for years, yet appear to be well and mentally alert. Many long-term expats have taken to kava like ducks to water, and they certainly seem a lot healthier and sharper than the average alcoholic!

In the early 20th century, islanders drank kava to heal themselves of gonorrhoea and blackwater fever (a complication of malaria). It proved extremely beneficial as a remedy for these diseases as it keeps the bladder and kidneys working overtime. Indeed, the people of kava-drinking areas suffered much less severely from venereal diseases than did others.

Female Kava Drinkers In most tradition-conscious parts of Vanuatu, drinking kava is an exclusively male activity – the original kava plant is generally believed to have sprung from the loins of a woman, hence the tabu. However, on some islands, such as the Shepherds, Banks and Torres groups, and also central Pentecost, women are free to drink it along with the men.

In custom-oriented areas of Tanna, it's tabu for women to even see kava being made. Elsewhere on the island, especially in the Jon Frum cult villages around Sulphur Bay, it is quite acceptable for women to partake.

In Vila, where long-held customary rules are usually relaxed, an increasing number of ni-Vanuatu and expatriate women enjoy a regular shell at the various nakamals.

ENTERTAINMENT

Some of the best places to look for information about upcoming events in Vila and Luganville are the notice boards in the various supermarkets and stores. To find out what's on when travelling around the islands, either ask your hosts or enquire at trade stores along the way.

Cinemas

The only regular film shows are in Vila and Luganville, where they are mainly French language or English with French subtitles. Elsewhere there'll be a film shown in a school or public hall whenever a plane or ship brings the reels.

String Bands

This term often includes rock groups, though most of the country's genuine string bands are more like 1950s skiffle groups. Usually these include a number of singers, guitarists and banjo players, backed by a homemade bass or drum made out of a converted tea-chest. However, conventional drum sets are increasingly taking over. Other locally made instruments include xylophones made out of water-filled bottles – they produce a fascinating sound. String bands are extremely popular entertainment throughout Vanuatu.

Discos

For visitors, by far the best disco entertainment is in Vila. A number of villages have discos and you might find it an education to visit one, but don't forget the ear plugs!

THINGS TO BUY
Duty-Free Shopping

Vila is by far the country's most important duty-free port. The consensus among travellers seems to be that local prices are on a par with, if not better than, most other duty-free ports around the world.

When purchasing duty-free alcohol and tobacco you must produce your passport and advise the shopkeeper of your departure details. The shop will then deliver the goods to you at the airport or main wharf. You shouldn't open them until you have passed through customs and immigration.

Mother Hubbard Dresses

Although there are several shops in Vila selling the latest French fashions, ni-Vanuatu women seldom follow the rigorous demands of *haute couture*. Instead, you will see plenty of local women dressed distinctively in what is called a 'Mother Hubbard' dress or 'mission gown'. These are loose-fitting outfits which are usually decorated with ribbons, lace and colourful floral patterns. Most ni-Vanuatu women in Vila seem to wear these dresses, although they are not popular in Luganville.

Mother Hubbard dresses were designed by moralistic missionaries in the late 19th century. The churchmen of the time felt that dresses which revealed the shape of a curvaceous female figure would only excite base male sexual desires, thus distracting their newly converted flock during church services. The result is not an elegant design.

This style of dress is readily available from the Chinese stores in Vila and Luganville. While they don't rate highly as souvenirs, a female tourist who wears one occasionally in rural areas is making a statement that will be well received by the local women.

Handicrafts

Vanuatu's major handicraft outlets are in Vila and Luganville. Elsewhere, purchasing is usually by direct contact with village artisans. Generally, examples of all the nation's various handicrafts are available in Vila.

The country offers a wide range of traditional and contemporary handicrafts, with woven leaf products and carvings in wood and stone being most popular. You can buy woven baskets and mats, pottery, shell necklaces, headdresses, bows and arrows, and ankle rattles. Items carved from wood include masks, miniature canoes, animals, pig-killing clubs, walking sticks and spears. Of the wood carvings, those from northern Ambrym have by far the best reputation for quality and artistry.

Wherever you are, keep in mind that the heavier wooden objects may not have dried out and thus may crack in the future.

You also need to make sure that your souvenir isn't at risk of being confiscated by customs when you get back home. For example, Australia has very strict quarantine and import laws.

Fortunately, the only objects likely to require fumigation are those made from tree ferns and those that have soil or feathers on them. Anything with fresh borer holes will also require treatment. Fumigation takes a minimum of 24 hours (with costs up to 800VT). Most specialty shops will arrange this, otherwise you'll need to organise it yourself at one of the country's two quarantine stations. These are near the airport in Vila (☎ 23130) and behind Customs at Luganville's main wharf (☎ 36223).

You'll also require a CITES (Convention on International Trade in Endangered Species) exemption form for objects made from either tree ferns or parts of animals, including shells and coral. Shops should be able to organise this as well. If not, go to the Department of Environment Unit (☎ 22423) in the Georges Pompidou Building just north of central Vila and make an application.

Restrictions on Exports

Many countries, including the USA, Australia and New Zealand, restrict imports of body parts of sea and land animals as well as objects made from certain plants. Although there are many beautiful shells to be found in Vanuatu's waters, they may be embargoed in your country. As well, the importing of turtle shell is banned by many nations.

Vanuatu is determined to protect its cultural heritage. Although the country's traditional artefacts are avidly sought by museums worldwide, the government has banned the export of all magic stones and antiques – that is, any artefacts more than 50 years old. If one of your purchases could possibly be taken for a restricted item, make sure to obtain a certificate proving that it's been made recently.

Getting There & Away

The basic problems with getting to Vanuatu are first that it's a long way from most places, and secondly that the major airlines don't exactly vie with each other for the honour of flying there.

About 60% of visitors to Vanuatu arrive on cruise ships, while the remainder – except for a very small percentage of yachties – come in by air. Nearly 80% of all visitors originate in Australia (over 50%), New Zealand and New Caledonia.

AIR

The relatively small number of flights in and out of the country are usually heavily booked during the most popular times of the year. Busy periods are Christmas and the start and end of major Australian and New Zealand school holiday periods, particularly the mid-year and September breaks. If you're thinking of going then, make sure to book well in advance.

The following international airlines have either offices or agents in Vila: Air Caledonie International office and Air France agent (☎ 22019); Air Pacific and Air Niugini agents (☎ 22836); Air Vanuatu office (☎ 23838); Qantas and Solomon Airlines agents (☎ 23848); Air New Zealand, Aerolineas Argentinas, British Airways, Scandinavian Airlines and Thai International Airways agents (☎ 22666).

Air Vanuatu, Air Caledonie International, Solomon Airlines and Air Pacific are the only international airlines currently providing direct services to Vanuatu.

Buying a Plane Ticket

The plane ticket will probably be the single most expensive item in your budget, and buying it can be an intimidating business. There is likely to be a multitude of airlines and travel agents hoping to separate you from your money, and it is always worth putting aside a few hours to research the current state of the market.

Make sure to start your research early: some of the cheapest tickets have to be bought months in advance, and some popular flights sell out early. Talk to other recent travellers – they may be able to stop you making some of the same old mistakes. Look at the ads in newspapers and magazines, consult reference books and watch for special offers. Then phone around travel agents for bargains. (Airlines can supply information on routes and timetables; however, except at times of inter-airline war they do not supply the cheapest tickets.) Find out the fare, the route, the duration of the journey and any restrictions on the ticket. Then decide which is best for you.

You may discover that those impossibly cheap flights are 'fully booked, but we have another one that costs a bit more...' Or the flight is on an airline notorious for its poor safety standards and leaves you in the world's least favourite airport in mid-journey for 14 hours. Or they claim only to have the last two seats available for that country for the whole of July, which they will hold for you for a maximum of two hours. Don't panic – keep ringing around.

Use the fares quoted in this book as a guide only. They are approximate and based on the rates advertised by travel agents at the time of research. Quoted air fares do not necessarily constitute a recommendation for the carrier.

If you are travelling from the UK, South-East Asia or the USA, you will probably find that the cheapest flights are being advertised by obscure 'bucket shops' (low-cost, independent air-ticket centres) whose names haven't yet reached the telephone directory. Many such firms are honest and solvent, but there are a few rogues who will take your money and disappear, to reopen elsewhere a month or two later under a new name. If you feel suspicious about a firm, don't give them all the money at once – leave a deposit of 20% or so and pay the balance when you get the ticket. If they insist on cash in advance, go somewhere else. And once you have the ticket, ring the airline to confirm that you are actually booked onto the flight.

You may decide to pay more than the rock-bottom fare by opting for the safety of a better known travel agent. Firms such as STA, who have offices worldwide, Council Travel in the USA or Travel CUTS in Canada are not going to disappear overnight, leaving you clutching a receipt for a nonexistent ticket, but they do offer good prices to most destinations.

Once you have your ticket, write its number down, together with the flight number and other details, and keep the information somewhere separate. If the ticket is lost or stolen, this will help you get a replacement.

It's sensible to buy travel insurance as early as possible. If you buy it the week before you fly, you may find, for example, that you're not covered for delays to your flight caused by industrial action.

Air Travellers with Special Needs

If you have special needs of any sort – you've broken a leg, you're vegetarian, travelling in a wheelchair, taking a baby, terrified of flying – you should let the airline know as soon as possible so that they can make arrangements accordingly. You should remind them when you reconfirm your booking (at least 72 hours before departure) and again when you check in at the airport. It may also be worth ringing around the airlines before you make your booking to find out how they can handle your particular needs.

Airports and airlines can be surprisingly helpful, but they do need advance warning. Most international airports will provide escorts from check-in desk to plane where needed, and there should be ramps, lifts, accessible toilets and phones. Aircraft toilets, on the other hand, will present a problem for some physically disabled people; travellers should discuss this with the airline at an early stage and, if necessary, with their doctor.

Guide dogs for the blind will often have to travel in a specially pressurised baggage compartment with other animals, away from their owner, though smaller guide dogs may be admitted to the cabin. All guide dogs will be subject to the same quarantine laws (six months in isolation etc) as any other animal when entering or returning to countries currently free of rabies such as the UK, Australia and Vanuatu.

Deaf travellers can ask for airport and in-flight announcements to be written down for them.

Children under two travel for 10% of the standard fare (or free, on some airlines), as long as they don't occupy a seat. They don't get a baggage allowance either. 'Skycots' should be provided by the airline if requested in advance; these will take a child weighing up to about 10 kg. Children between two and 12 can usually occupy a seat for half to two-thirds of the full fare, and do get a baggage allowance. Pushchairs (strollers) can often be taken as hand luggage.

Round-the-World Tickets

Round-the-World (RTW) airline tickets have become very popular because you can often pick up some real bargains. Since Vanuatu is on the other side of the world from Europe or the east coast of North America, it may work out cheaper to keep going in the same direction rather than buy a return ticket.

The official airline RTW tickets are generally put together by a combination of two airlines, who will permit you to fly anywhere you want on their routes as long as you don't backtrack. Other restrictions are that you must usually book the first sector in advance with cancellation penalties then applying. There may also be a limit to how many stops you can make. Such tickets are normally valid from 90 days up to a year, with typical prices for South Pacific RTW tickets being in the UK£1900 to UK£2100 (US$2900 to US$3500) range.

An alternative type of RTW ticket is one put together by a travel agent using a combination of discounted tickets. A UK agent such as Trailfinders can put together some interesting London-to-London RTW combinations.

Also worth investigating is the Explorer Fare – a RTW ticket put together by Qantas and British Airways. The number of stops on this ticket is usually limited to six.

Circle Pacific Tickets

Circle Pacific tickets are similar to RTW tickets, and use a combination of airlines to circle the Pacific. As with RTW tickets, there are advance purchase restrictions and limits on how many stopovers you can make. Most fares range between US$2200 and US$2500.

You may be able to design a ticket that takes in Vanuatu, among other Pacific destinations.

Visit South Pacific Pass

The Visit South Pacific Pass is a two-to-eight coupon pass costing between US$150 and $300 depending on the length of the flight. It is offered on flights throughout the southwest Pacific by all regional international airlines but is available only to overseas visitors travelling from North America, Asia, and Europe (VSPP only issued there). It's issued in conjunction with full-fare tickets

---

Air Travel Glossary

Apex Apex, or 'advance purchase excursion' is a discounted ticket which must be paid for in advance. There are penalties if you wish to change it.

Baggage Allowance This will be written on your ticket: usually one 20 kg item to go in the hold, plus one item of hand luggage.

Bucket Shop An unbonded travel agency specialising in discounted airline tickets.

Bumped Just because you have a confirmed seat doesn't mean you're going to get on the plane – see Overbooking.

Cancellation Penalties If you have to cancel or change an Apex ticket there are often heavy penalties involved, insurance can sometimes be taken out against these penalties. Some airlines impose penalties on regular tickets as well, particularly against 'no show' passengers.

Check In Airlines ask you to check in a certain time ahead of the flight departure (usually 1½ hours on international flights). If you fail to check in on time and the flight is overbooked the airline can cancel your booking and give your seat to somebody else.

Confirmation Having a ticket written out with the flight and date you want doesn't mean you have a seat until the agent has checked with the airline that your status is 'OK' or confirmed. Meanwhile you could just be 'on request'.

Discounted Tickets There are two types of discounted fares – officially discounted (see Promotional Fares) and unofficially discounted. The lowest prices often impose drawbacks like flying with unpopular airlines, inconvenient schedules, or unpleasant routes and connections. A discounted ticket can save you other things than money – you may be able to pay Apex prices without the associated Apex advance booking and other requirements. Discounted tickets only exist where there is fierce competition.

Full Fares Airlines traditionally offer first class (coded F), business class (coded J) and economy class (coded Y) tickets. These days there are so many promotional and discounted fares available from the regular economy class that few passengers pay full economy fare.

Lost Tickets If you lose your airline ticket an airline will usually treat it like a travellers' cheque and, after inquiries, issue you with another one. Legally, however, an airline is entitled to treat it like cash and if you lose it then it's gone forever. Take good care of your tickets.

No Shows No shows are passengers who fail to show up for their flight, sometimes due to unexpected delays or disasters, sometimes due to simply forgetting, sometimes because they made more than one booking and didn't bother to cancel the one they didn't want. Full fare passengers who fail to turn up are sometimes entitled to travel on a later flight. The rest of us are penalised (see Cancellation Penalties).

On Request An unconfirmed booking for a flight, see Confirmation.

Open Jaws A return ticket where you fly out to one place but return from another. If available this can save you backtracking to your arrival point.

and must be completed within the validity of the original international ticket.

To/From Australia

In Australia, STA and Flight Centres International are the major dealers in cheap air fares. Check the travel agents' ads in the Yellow Pages and ring around.

Brisbane The cheapest fare between Australia and Vila is an excursion return from Brisbane on either Air Caledonie or Air Vanuatu. This costs A\$675/745 low/high

season, or 68,800/79,500VT if you buy your ticket in Vanuatu.

Air Vanuatu has two outward and inward flights per week along this route, whilst Air Caledonie has one weekly service out of Brisbane via Noumea – it may be possible to include a stopover in Noumea for the same cost. There's a five or 10-day minimum stay rule on these fares, depending on which airline you choose.

Sydney Air Vanuatu and Air Caledonie have direct flights between Sydney and Vila. Both airlines charge A\$803/870 for their low/high

---

Overbooking Airlines hate to fly empty seats and since every flight has some passengers who fail to show up (see No Shows) airlines often book more passengers than they have seats. Usually the excess passengers balance those who fail to show up but occasionally somebody gets bumped. If this happens guess who it is most likely to be? The passengers who check in late.

Promotional Fares Officially discounted fares like Apex fares which are available from travel agents or direct from the airline.

Reconfirmation At least 72 hours prior to departure time of an onward or return flight you must contact the airline and 'reconfirm' that you intend to be on the flight. If you don't do this the airline can delete your name from the passenger list and you could lose your seat. You don't have to reconfirm the first flight on your itinerary or if your stopover is less than 72 hours. It doesn't hurt to reconfirm more than once.

Restrictions Discounted tickets often have various restrictions on them – advance purchase is the most usual one (see Apex). Others are restrictions on the minimum and maximum period you must be away, such as a minimum of 14 days or a maximum of one year. See Cancellation Penalties.

Standby A discounted ticket where you only fly if there is a seat free at the last moment. Standby fares are usually only available on domestic routes.

Tickets Out An entry requirement for many countries is that you have an onward or return ticket, in other words, a ticket out of the country. If you're not sure what you intend to do next, the easiest solution is to buy the cheapest onward ticket to a neighbouring country or a ticket from a reliable airline which can later be refunded if you do not use it.

Transferred Tickets Airline tickets cannot be transferred from one person to another. Travellers sometimes try to sell the return half of their ticket, but officials can ask you to prove that you are the person named on the ticket. This is unlikely to happen on domestic flights, on an international flight tickets may be compared with passports.

Travel Agencies Travel agencies vary widely and you should ensure you use one that suits your needs. Some simply handle tours while full-service agencies handle everything from tours and tickets to car rental and hotel bookings. A good one will do all these things and can save you a lot of money but if all you want is a ticket at the lowest possible price, then you really need an agency specialising in discounted tickets. A discounted ticket agency, however, may not be useful for other things, like hotel bookings.

Travel Periods Some officially discounted fares, Apex fares in particular, vary with the time of year. There is often a low (off-peak) season and a high (peak) season. Sometimes there's an intermediate or shoulder season as well. At peak times, when everyone wants to fly, not only will the officially discounted fares be higher but so will unofficially discounted fares or there may simply be no discounted tickets available. Usually the fare depends on your outward flight – if you depart in the high season and return in the low season, you pay the high-season fare. ∎

season excursion returns, or for 56,400/64,900VT if you purchase the ticket in Vila. Air Vanuatu has three round trips per week while Air Caledonie has only one.

Air Pacific, Qantas and Air Vanuatu have combined to offer routes from Australia that include Vanuatu, a choice of New Zealand or Fiji, and return to Australia. The New Zealand option starts at A$886 while a ticket via Fiji starts at A$1117. These tickets are valid for two months.

Melbourne The only way you can fly from Melbourne to Vila is on the weekly service offered by Air Vanuatu, whose one-way ticket costs A$988/1054 low/high season. There are no excursion fares out of Melbourne.

Anyone entering Vila by yacht and wanting to fly out to Melbourne will find that it's cheaper to buy a low season excursion fare out of Vila rather than a one-way fare.

Australian Visas All visitors to Australia require an entry visa and it's only New Zealanders who can get it on arrival. These are valid for up to six months and can be extended to 12 months. While the Australian High Commission in Vila may supply one if you can show proof of return or onward passage out of Australia, there is no guarantee of this. The best approach is to arrange your visa before leaving home.

To/From the Pacific

Fiji Air Pacific flies twice weekly both ways between Nadi in Fiji and Vila, with tickets starting at F$369 (Fijian dollars) or US$318. There's also an excursion return of F$560 (US$484) between Nadi and Vila, with a six/28-day minimum/maximum stay rule.

In addition there's a triangle fare with either Air Pacific or Air Caledonie that connects Nadi, Vila and Noumea in New Caledonia. This starts at F$785 (US$678) and the only rule is that you have a stopover in each country lasting at least 24 hours.

Note that some citizens, particularly of former communist countries, must apply to a British consulate or a Fijian high commis-

sion for an entry visa to Fiji. Others will be issued a visa at the Nadi airport provided they can produce onward tickets. Don't forget to check with your travel agent or airline in case there's been any recent tightening of the rules.

New Caledonia Tontouta, Noumea's international airport, is Vila's closest overseas destination. You can fly between the two centres with Air Caledonie International for 20,500CFP (the French Pacific Currency), or about US$206. If you buy your ticket in Vila, it'll cost you 18,700VT (US$160) each way.

Air Caledonie also does an excursion fare between Vila and Noumea. This is for six/28 days and costs 30,300 CFP/33,800VT or about US$330/300.

A twice weekly Noumea-Santo return service operated by Vanair opened recently. The excursion fare is 39,300CFP and is for a maximum of 28 days.

New Caledonia issues three-month visas to citizens of the EU, most other European nationals, a number of formerly French African countries, Australia and New Zealand. Most other nationalities, including the USA, Canada, Israel and Pacific island countries, get 30 days. All non-French visitors must show proof of onward passage.

Air Vanuatu is proposing to introduce a direct service between Tanna Island (in Vanuatu) and New Caledonia, so check the latest on this.

New Zealand As in Australia, STA and Flight Centres International are popular travel agents in New Zealand.

Air Vanuatu's service between Vila and Auckland operates twice weekly in both directions. Its six/20-day excursion fare costs NZ$906/62,400VT.

Cook Islanders, Australians and British citizens are free of visa requirements for New Zealand. Others who are similarly favoured are people from the USA, Canada, Japan and most Western European countries, but excluding some Mediterranean ones and Austria.

Papua New Guinea Air Niugini has no direct flights to Vila but Solomon Airlines offers a once-weekly connection to/from Port Moresby via Honiara in the Solomon Islands. One-way/return economy tickets cost K544/1080 (kina, PNG's currency) or about US$345/692. You can also get a 30-day excursion fare for K702, or US$450 for the round trip.

You can get a seven-day visa on arrival at Port Moresby for K10. This is available to most Western European citizens, North Americans, Australians, New Zealanders and Pacific Islanders. All other nationalities must have a visa prior to arrival. There are PNG consulates in Vila (☎ 23930) and at 100 Clarence St, Sydney, Australia (☎ (02) 299 5151).

Solomon Islands Solomon Airlines operates twice-weekly return flights between Honiara and Vila. Its one-way economy ticket costs US$267.

The airline also offers a Discover Pacific Pass costing US$599 for four coupons, which will take you anywhere on their network for up to 30 days. It's available only in Europe, the USA, Canada and Asia. It cannot be purchased in Australia or New Zealand unless you're holding a ticket issued in the above areas.

Officials in the Solomons give you either a two-week or a one-month visitor's permit on arrival at Henderson Field, the airport for Honiara. This applies to most Commonwealth citizens, some Western European nationalities, and US passport holders. Most other nationals, including French, Irish and Germans, may only enter for one week without a visa. These are available from British consulates.

To/From Asia

Hong Kong is the discount plane ticket capital of the region. Its bucket shops are at least as unreliable as those of other cities. Ask the advice of other travellers before buying a ticket.

STA, which is normally reliable, has branches in Hong Kong, Tokyo, Singapore, Bangkok and Kuala Lumpur.

A reasonably cheap way to get to or from Vanuatu via Asia is to go through Australia first. Qantas and Singapore Airlines both have advance purchase fares to Sydney or Brisbane from Singapore for S$1396/2144 (Singapore dollars) one-way/return. These are infinitely better than the one-way economy fare of S$2027.

One-way excursion fares from Singapore have no advance purchase requirements. However, the return excursion fare has a maximum validity period of 60 days. There are daily flights between Sydney and Singapore, and four per week in Brisbane's case.

If you're coming from Vanuatu and aiming for Asia, both South Pacific Travel (☎ 22836) and Surata Tamaso Travel (☎ 22666) in Vila can arrange special one-way fares using various airlines to get you to Bangkok/Singapore/Hong Kong for 93,000/93,000/98,000VT (US$797/797/840) via Sydney.

To/From Europe

London is the best place in Europe to find cheap air fares. If you check the travel agents and bucket shops you may be able to fly to eastern Australia for around £450. These tickets are written on normal IATA airlines such as British Airways, Qantas etc, but are considerably discounted compared to normal air fares. If you use a bucket shop, make sure you are perfectly clear about what sort of ticket you're buying. Don't hand over your money till you've got your ticket!

Trailfinders in west London produces a lavishly illustrated brochure which includes air fare details. STA also has branches in the UK. Look in the listings magazine *Time Out* plus the Sunday papers and *Exchange & Mart* for ads. Also look out for the free magazines widely available in London – start by looking outside the main railway stations.

Most British travel agents are registered with some kind of traveller-protection scheme, such as that offered by the ABTA (Association of British Travel Agents). If you have paid for your flight to an ABTA-registered agent who then goes out of business, ABTA will guarantee a refund or an alternative. Unregistered bucket shops are riskier but also sometimes cheaper.

Depending on the season, most major airlines offer one-way fares to Sydney from £606 to £1002, while return prices are from £960 to £1500. Once in Australia, you can take Air Pacific's excursion from Sydney to Vila via Nadi or Brisbane.

The cheapest fares from Vanuatu to Europe and the UK are obtainable from South Pacific Travel and Surata Tamaso Travel in Vila. They can get you from Vila to London via Sydney from 139,000VT (US$1206).

To/From North America

The *New York Times*, the *LA Times*, the *Chicago Tribune* and the *San Francisco Examiner* all produce weekly travel sections in which you'll find any number of travel agents' ads. Council Travel and STA Travel have offices in major cities nationwide.

The magazine *Travel Unlimited* (PO Box 1058, Allston, MA 02134) publishes details of the cheapest air fares and courier possibilities for destinations all over the world from the USA.

In Canada, Travel CUTS has offices in all major cities. The *Toronto Globe & Mail* and the *Vancouver Sun* carry travel agents' ads, while the magazine *Great Expeditions* (PO Box 8000-411, Abbotsford BC V2S 6H1) also has useful information.

Qantas and Air New Zealand offer a return trip from the western USA and Canada to Vila via Nadi starting at US$1078. They also have a Los Angeles-Sydney fare via Nadi from US$829 one-way and US$1098 return. A maximum stay of three months in Nadi is permitted on both. However, these fares are restrictive and you must understand the rules before buying. For example, there are charges for cancellation and changing dates.

Both airlines have five flights per week between Los Angeles and Nadi, and daily flights from Sydney. Once in Nadi it's only a hop, skip and jump to Vila.

If your destination or departure point is Vancouver, Canadian flies daily to Sydney via Nadi. The three-month excursion costs from C$1189 one-way and C$1488 return, with restrictive rules as above.

If you're looking for the cheapest fare back to North America from Australia, having made your excursion to Vanuatu, contact STA and Flight Centres International for up-to-date information.

If you're flying to North America from Vanuatu, South Pacific Travel in Vila can get you to either San Francisco, Los Angeles or Vancouver via Nadi on a one-way excursion from 121,000VT (US$1037).

Arriving in Vanuatu by Air

Vanuatu has only one international airport, Bauerfield, six km from Port Vila (air code VLI). Luganville's airport is being upgraded and will become the country's second gateway.

There are usually only two immigration officers to meet each flight at Bauerfield, but you shouldn't have to wait long to be processed. The airport boasts a new terminal with a well-stocked café, duty-free shop and a Westpac bank agency – if the bank's closed you can still make purchases with the more common foreign currencies. The staff at the information desk speak English and French.

Getting from the airport into town is easy, as taxis, transfer coaches and minibuses meet each flight (see the Getting Around section in the Efate chapter). If you've already booked into a hotel you'll be assigned to a transfer coach which will take you to the door.

SEA

Vanuatu has international deepwater ports at Vila and Luganville. Both have full customs and immigration facilities, and are authorised ports of entry.

Cruise Ships

Vila hosts a cruise ship on average about once a week for a day or two at a time. Regular visits are also made to tiny Inyeug

Island, off Aneityum, and Champagne Beach in north-eastern Santo.

If you're planning to travel to or from Vanuatu by liner on a one-way ticket, you'll find the fare is rather more than a comparable flight. However, excellent food, cabin accommodation (shared) and a variety of entertainments are all included in the price. This option isn't encouraged by the cruise company, but it's not impossible.

South Pacific Shipping (☎ 22205) in Vila can advise whether or not there's a spare berth on any cruise ship sailing onwards from Vanuatu. You can book through South Pacific Travel, right next door.

Two cruise lines currently visit Vanuatu on a regular basis from Sydney: P&O Lines with the *Fairstar*; and the Pacific Cruise Company using the *Russ* and the *Mikhail Sholokov*. Both companies will allow you to get on or off in Vila. Their Australian addresses are: P&O Lines (☎ (02) 13 2469), 201 Kent St, Sydney 2000; and Pacific Cruise Company (☎ (02) 9235 0444), 10th Floor, 109 Pitt St, Sydney 2000.

Sailing Ship The Danish-built 19th-century brigantine *Søren Larsen* is now operating out of Auckland and offers an annual programme of cruises throughout the South Pacific. This includes 12 nights among the islands of Vanuatu for US$1660, or 10 nights for US$1380. Alternatively, you can spend 39 nights sailing from Fiji to New Caledonia via Vanuatu for US$5140. You're taken on as a crew member, which means you get to participate in the various aspects of shipboard life. You can contact Square Sail Pacific (☎ (09) 445 9044), PO Box 32247, Devonport, Auckland, New Zealand.

Yachts

Entry & Departure Procedures Touring yachts are not permitted to make landfall in Vanuatu until they have cleared customs and immigration at either Vila or Luganville. If you break this rule, the local police will take your passport and order you to proceed direct to Vila to face court. The fine is usually about 100,000VT per yacht.

Yachts clearing customs wait either at the quarantine buoy near the seawall in Vila Bay or in the Segond Channel opposite the immigration office in Luganville. There is a landing fee of 700VT for the first 30 days and 100VT per day thereafter. Once you've paid the money, you are free to sail wherever you wish during the period of your visa.

Every visiting yacht must check in again at Vila or Luganville before leaving Vanuatu. However, permission is normally given if you want to visit some of the archipelago's outer islands as you make your way out of the country. This allows you to visit Tanna's Yasur volcano if you're going south-west to New Caledonia, or the Banks and Torres groups if you're sailing north to the Solomon Islands.

Although New Caledonia's formalities for a one-month visit are minimal, you'll find the Solomons' regulations are as strict as Vanuatu's. Yacht crews arriving in the Solomons have to report to the nearest police station and proceed within two weeks to Honiara. Once you've done this, you will be allowed a two-month visa from the date of your entry.

Information The best source of general information on yachting matters is the Vanuatu Cruising Yacht Club (☎ 24634), PO Box 525, Vila. It produces a free cruising guide to the country.

Prevailing Winds The best season to sail north through Vanuatu is in winter from late April to mid-November when the south-easterly trade winds blow. If your tack is southwards, the optimum time is summer, particularly December and January when the wind changes direction and generally blows from the north-west.

Repairs Yachts needing repairs should make for Vila or Luganville. There's a ship chandlery at Yachting World, near the Iririki Wharf in Vila. The Palikulo Bay fish factory near Luganville is the only place in Vanuatu where you can get a yacht slipped, although its slipway is designed more for trawlers than small yachts.

Hitching a Ride Finding a berth on a yacht is usually much easier than getting aboard a freighter. The best way is to hang around yachting marinas. You'll find plenty of good places on the US west coast and along Australia's north-eastern seaboard. Auckland, Tahiti and Noumea all have sizeable yachting communities, and Honiara has a small one too. In Vila, try the seawall near the market, the Vanuatu Cruising Yacht Club and next door at the Waterfront Bar & Grill.

Yacht skippers will charge up to US$30 per day per berth. They'll also require you to have an onward or return air ticket if you're planning to travel on to another country with them. Otherwise, you'll be dropped off (so to speak) at either Vila or Luganville.

Before going on a long trip, try to get in a few days' sailing to test your sea legs and see how prone you are to seasickness. If you do become seriously ill, every moment will be torture, and your skipper will heartily regret having you on board.

Cargo Boats

The days when tramp steamers took on travellers with little or no fuss are long gone. Even so, it's sometimes possible to find a berth on a freighter through an experienced shipping agent in a major port. In Vila, the people to approach are South Pacific Shipping (☎ 22205, and Vila Agents (☎ 22490, 23804).

Currently, the only freight company offering a passenger service into Vanuatu is Bank Line, which operates from Europe to the Pacific via Singapore. Its ships can each carry eight passengers, so book well in advance. The local agent is South Pacific Shipping.

TOURS

Although unlikely to suit budget travellers with time to spare, package tours are ideal for those who have only one or two weeks to spend in the country.

Surprisingly, a well-selected package holiday can turn out much cheaper than a budget trip, and with high-class facilities thrown in too. This is because package deals take into account so-called reverse discounts. These can include free car-hire, subsidised hotel prices, vouchers to dine out around the capital, and free water sports.

If you prefer the freedom of a holiday alone, you'll find most package tours will allow a single supplement. Sometimes these range from as little as a 20% surcharge on top of the normal price, though other tour companies may add around 40%.

Generally, the best package deals to Vanuatu out of Australia and New Zealand are those offered by Connection Holidays, Swingaway and Pacific Orient – the three major operators. However, there are numerous options available, so keep checking the various agents until you find the one that fits your requirements.

LEAVING VANUATU BY AIR

There's a 2000VT airport tax charged against all international passengers leaving Vanuatu. Exemptions are for people who transit Vila within 24 hours, and children under two years old.

To avoid your airline cancelling your booking, you should confirm your onward flight either on arrival in Vanuatu or at the latest 72 hours before your departure.

WARNING

The information in this chapter may change – prices for international travel are volatile, routes are introduced and cancelled, schedules change, special deals come and go, and rules and visa requirements are amended. Airlines and governments often make price structures and regulations as complicated as possible. You should check with the airline or a travel agent to make sure how a fare (and ticket you may buy) works.

In addition, the travel industry is highly competitive. The upshot of this is that you should get opinions, quotes and advice from as many airlines and travel agents as possible. The details given in this chapter are only pointers.

Getting Around

Although Vanuatu is rapidly opening up to tourism, many villages do not welcome casual visitors unless they're on a guided tour. A good example is Yakel village, on Tanna. Others, such as the Small Nambas of south-central Malakula, may not want tourists at all.

If you're travelling independently it's always wise to check the current situation before venturing off the beaten track. This particularly applies in the more remote areas. A list of useful sources of information is contained in the section on Tourist Information in the Facts for the Visitor chapter.

Some of the outlying islands are very isolated, as are the east coasts of Maewo, Pentecost and Ambrym, and the west coasts of Santo and Malakula. Here the only access may be by walking track or speedboat. For many places, the major contact with the outside world is provided by the small cargo boats that operate mainly out of Vila and Luganville. The national road system is continually growing, but many islands still have no roads at all. All the larger islands and most major centres are serviced at least weekly by air services from Vila or Luganville.

AIR

There is only one domestic air carrier in Vanuatu – Vanair. Its schedules and fares change periodically so check for current details with the head office (☎ 22643) on Kumul Hwy in central Vila. Alternatively, contact its Luganville office on ☎ 36421.

The only alternative means of air transport is provided by Helicopters Vanuatu, which offers a charter service of US$700 per hour for a maximum four passengers. If the pilot isn't flying you can usually find him at Tropical Adventure Tours (☎ 22743), near El Gecko Cafe in the centre of Vila.

Air Club Vila (☎ 22514) has applied for an open charter licence and is confident of getting it, so check the latest on this.

Vanair offers scheduled flights into 30 airfields using its small fleet of 14-seat Twin Otters. Only the airfields at Vila and Luganville have concrete runways. All other strips have natural surfaces – usually grass or coral – and can be subject to temporary closure after heavy rain.

Vanair allows children under two years of age to travel for 10% of the adult fare, and those between two and 12 to fly half-price. Students are granted a 25% discount on presentation of satisfactory proof such as an International Student Identity Card.

There's a 200VT tax on all internal flights, though this is sometimes incorporated into the ticket price. Only children under two years old are exempt.

All stopovers are charged. For example, Vanair's Vila-Luganville nonstop price is 9800VT, but you are charged sector fares if you decide to stop over at Norsup in Malakula; this raises the fare to 11,600VT.

Vanair's baggage allowance is 16 kg, although the limit may be waived for passengers on outer-island routes. This allows you to carry food into isolated destinations.

It always pays to book your seat well in advance, particularly on the more popular routes such as from Vila to Luganville and Tanna. Don't despair if you're told that the plane is booked out. If you turn up at the airfield just prior to departure there's at least a 50% chance of a vacancy.

Finally, it's a wise precaution prior to departure at each bush airfield along the way to check that your baggage hasn't been accidentally unloaded. As well, always make sure that it gets off when you do.

SEA

About 30 small, coastal cargo vessels provide shipping services of varying regularity and reliability from Vila and Luganville to ports throughout the country. Few of these exceed 70 tons, and for passengers it's often a case of standing room only. As well, the government has about a dozen vessels up to

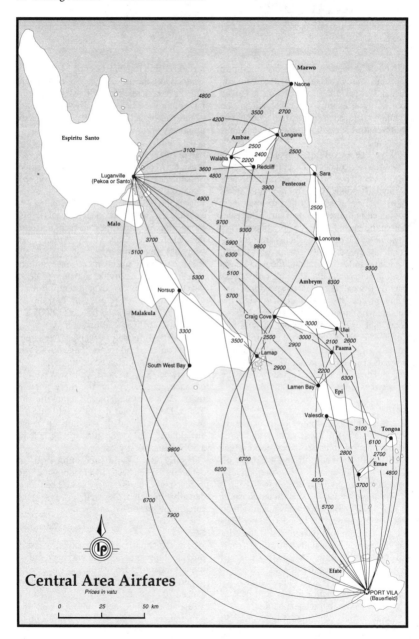

Central Area Airfares

Prices in vatu

0   25   50 km

200 tons, but none of these carry paying passengers.

Inter-Island Shipping Services

The two most reliable operators both have their head offices in central Vila: Ifira Shipping Agencies (☎ 24445) at the BP wharf, and Toara Coastal Shipping (☎ 22370) near the Au Bon Marché Supermarket. If all else fails you can try Dinh Shipping on ☎ 22865. Neither Ifira nor Toara operate to schedules, so there's not much point asking for a timetable. However, they do work to a pattern. In Ifira's case, the 115-ton MV *Saraika* (the country's largest privately owned vessel) does a round trip of a fortnight from Vila, servicing ports on Epi, Paama, Ambrym, Pentecost, Ambae and Santo. Then it does a three-day southern loop to Tanna and Erromango before heading north again.

Toara provides a similar service to various northern ports with its 100-tonnes MV *Aloara* and 15-ton MV *Marata*. The *Aloara* visits Emae, Tongoa, Epi, Paama, Ambrym, Pentecost, Malakula and Santo. The *Marata* services the Shepherds and Epi from Vila.

These three boats are rugged craft with few comforts for passengers. But if you've got the time, they are cheap compared to Vanair and will certainly provide a more colourful and interesting travel experience.

An alternative weekly service from Vila to Santo via Malakula's east coast is provided by the little MV *Saratoka*. You can book at the Ifira office in Vila, or on the wharf at Luganville.

The Malakula Local Council (☎ 48453) in Lakatoro runs the 15-metre launch MV *Mangaru*, which does a weekly service connecting Malakula's east coast with the islands of Pentecost, Ambrym and Paama.

If you're looking for a boat to take you around northern Vanuatu, enquire at Luganville's Chinese stores, as several act as agents for trading boats. The main ones are Dinh Shipping (☎ Luganville 36750, Vila 22865) and the Lo Chan Moon (LCM) Store (☎ Luganville 36530). The boats they will tell you about are small trading vessels which buy copra and other produce from villages en route and sell or exchange stores, tools, clothing etc.

Shipboard Travel Where they exist, the facilities on these vessels are spartan and conditions are often very crowded. For example, the *Saraika* leaves Vila with 100 passengers maximum, but during the voyage it can end up carrying far more than that. The *Aloara* has bunks, although conditions below deck make the open air the best place to be – things in general can become very unpleasant if the sea is at all rough, which it often is. You'll usually be able to find a vacant space somewhere to unroll your sleeping mat, even if it's on top of the cargo.

There's a good chance you'll be the only foreigner aboard. However, you're unlikely to be alone for long as other passengers almost certainly will soon engage you in conversation. They'll be only too pleased to tell you all about their home island, and when the boat arrives may offer to show you around. If nothing else, these boats are a great way to meet people.

Although drinking-water on board will probably be ample, food can be a different story. Basic meals are provided on Ifira's and Toara's three boats (and are included in the fare), but the others usually leave you to fend for yourself. If in doubt, make sure to carry sufficient food for the voyage plus whatever you need to cook and eat it with. In the Melanesian fashion, a bit extra to give away will enhance your reputation.

Don't count on being able to buy fruit and vegetables en route. Crew members will often trail a fishing line from the stern. When a large fish is caught, everyone aboard gets a piece. If you want to do some fishing of your own, colourful squid lures are particularly good for catching kingfish and tuna.

Canoes & Speedboats

When ni-Vanuatu talk of speedboats, they mean motorboats or dinghies powered by an outboard motor. Canoes are simply dugout craft with outriggers, usually powered by paddles and occasionally sails.

Canoes are still widely used as commuter

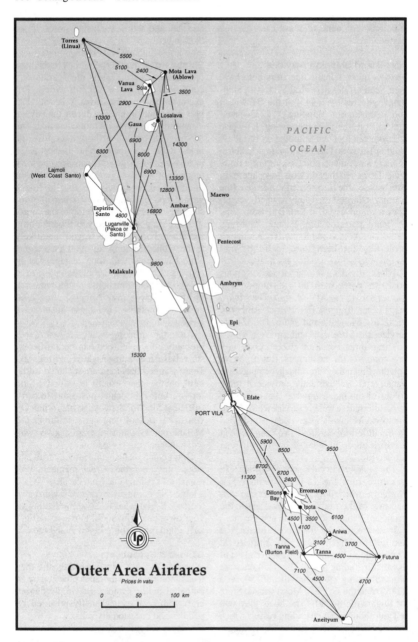

Outer Area Airfares

Prices in vatu

0   50   100 km

craft, particularly where people live on small offshore islands. They are also popular for fishing. Thanks to the outriggers they are remarkably stable craft and can be pushed along at a good rate. In most areas, however, aluminium speedboats seating four to 10 passengers have largely replaced canoes for all but the shorter journeys.

Speedboat prices can be very high and bookings are unreliable; it can really damage the budget if you undertake a longish journey on which you're the only passenger. For example, the 40-km, three-hour trip from Craig Cove to Ranon, on the west coast of Ambrym, costs 8000VT shared among the passengers.

Regular speedboat services connect some areas, such as Luganville with Malo and Aore Islands. The charges are generally much cheaper if you wait for the scheduled departure rather than ask the boatman to make a special trip. Always find out the cost of your ride before you leave, and make sure anything you don't want to get wet is protected.

Generally you won't have any difficulty finding someone with either a canoe or speedboat who's willing to take you where you want to go. But don't count on it – a recent cyclone may have smashed all the boats, as happened at some villages on the south coast of Ambrym in 1994.

Yachts

Vanuatu is a popular destination for yachties, some of whom may be prepared to give you a berth on an island cruise. The best place to find out what's offering is the noticeboard at the Waterfront Bar & Grill in central Vila. In Santo, check at the Natangora Café in the main street. See also the section on Yachts in the Getting There & Away chapter.

LAND

Vanuatu has about 1400 km of government-maintained roads, of which almost half are found on Santo, Malakula and Efate. Santo and Malakula each have in excess of 200 km of roads, Efate has 185 km, and Tanna and Pentecost have between 100 and 150 km each. Of the remainder, only Malo, Ambrym, Epi, Erromango and Ambae have more than 50 km of roads.

Only Vila and Luganville have bitumen roads, and these are mainly confined to the town areas. Major unsealed roads on Efate and Santo are generally of reasonable quality and have had irregular maintenance since most were built by US forces in WW II. The roads on other islands range from good to indifferent, with many being little more than 4WD tracks. Often these routes are seriously damaged by the heavy rain associated with cyclones.

Bus

There are no government bus services, but privately owned 10 to 14-seat minibuses are everywhere in Vila and Luganville. They don't run fixed routes, instead zooming all

Man in outrigger canoe

over the place at the whim of their passengers. As well, a regular but limited minibus service operates on the east coast of Santo between Hog Harbour and Luganville. Tanna and Malakula also have limited minibus services.

These vehicles are like taxis, only much cheaper, as they'll deliver you to where you want to go for a fraction of the cost of a cab fare. You simply flag them down by the roadside – they'll stop if there's a spare seat.

For an additional charge the driver may be prepared to take you to destinations out of town. In these cases you should always find out what the fare will be before getting on the bus. (Ask the driver if they can take you to such-and-such a place, and if they say yes, ask how much.)

Try to tender the correct change, particularly early in the morning. Most drivers prefer you not to smoke.

Taxi

Virtually all islands with roads have taxis of one form or another. In Vila and Luganville they are mostly conventional sedans, while in rural areas the usual taxi is a 4WD truck or utility.

Taxis in Vila and Luganville should have their meters on for trips within the town area. If the meter is off, ask that it be switched on. For longer journeys you can negotiate a price with the driver, and having agreed on the fare make sure you stick to it. Some drivers will try to add extra at the end of the trip.

The minimum charge in urban areas is 100VT, and for a straight point-to-point charter you can expect to pay around 100VT per km. If there are three or four of you, taxis offer a potentially cheaper alternative to organised tours. Ask at your hotel if they can recommend anyone suitable rather than take pot luck down at the taxi rank. Day trips can generally cost between 6000VT and 10,000VT, and sometimes much more, depending on factors such as competition, road conditions and the distance that has to be travelled.

Inevitably, the more tourists there are, the more it costs to hire a taxi (or a speedboat, or

anything else for that matter). Even if the fare asked for is patently absurd, the driver often won't reduce it. Generally, however, the prices tend to come down if you can speak Bislama or have a local intermediary.

Any taxis in the area will always meet the scheduled Vanair flight. However, in some places, such as Dillons Bay, there are only a couple of taxis at the best of times. If you're a little slow getting off the mark, and there's no space left for you in the back, you can usually arrange for the cabbie to come back after the others have been dropped off.

The best immediate source of information at the airfield is the Vanair clerical staff, who usually speak at least some English. If you have a contact name they can easily point you in the right direction.

Car & Moped

Rental You can hire cars and 4WD vehicles in Vila and Luganville, and mopeds in Vila. If you're under 23 years old you can't rent a car, but you can rent a moped. The minimum age for renting a moped is 17, however, you must hold a valid driving licence.

International driving permits are accepted for up to six months after arrival in Vanuatu, as are most current national driving licences. You must have held your licence for at least a year.

Road Rules & Conditions There's a speed limit of 50 km/h in Vila and Luganville. On the roads out of town there is no formal speed limit, however, they are often dictated by road conditions. Vehicles drive on the right-hand side of the road, as in France. You should always give way to traffic coming from the right.

In rural areas be wary of people or animals on the road. Driving fast is not advisable, particularly near villages. In addition, some roads can be very rough, with numerous gutters, potholes, sharp crests and blind corners. Closures due to flooding and fallen trees are common during the cyclone season.

One of the main problems with driving yourself around both Efate and Santo is the almost complete lack of road signs. There's also a shortage of up-to-date road maps.

Bicycle

Although it's rare to see tourists travelling around on bicycles, Efate, Santo, Malakula, Tanna and Pentecost all have sufficient roads and tracks to make mountain-biking a viable option. You can hire bikes in Vila and Luganville, but don't expect them to be either of high quality or in top order. You'd be much better off bringing your own.

There shouldn't be much difficulty bringing a mountain bike with you on your international flight, but of course you should check this when booking your ticket. If you're travelling in a group, you can expect to have trouble fitting more than two bikes into the cargo space of Vanair's Twin Otters.

Bring a good range of spares and tools with you, as professional bike shops are non-existent in Vanuatu. The best place for repairs is Sportzpower, next to the Rossi Restaurant in central Vila. Alternatively, you could try the Chinese stores either in Vila or Luganville.

Hitching

People in Vanuatu don't hitchhike in the sense that Westerners do. If you want to hitch a ride in rural Vanuatu, you should flag down a passing vehicle and ask the driver the cost of a lift to wherever. Many will give you a free trip, but others may charge a modest fee. There are no hard rules on this so you have to play it as it comes. Generally, however, the lack of traffic on most rural roads makes hitching a poor choice if you're on any sort of schedule. Coupled with this is the fact that most vehicles you'll see will already have a full load.

ORGANISED TOURS

There's a wide variety of tours on offer, although the bulk of them are concentrated in and around Vila. Some, such as yacht cruises, game fishing and scuba-diving tours, offer experiences most visitors would never be able to organise by themselves. Sadly, there are no tours designed specific-

ally for the backpacker market, although prices can become competitive if the season is slow. The number of tours is increasing all the time as Vanuatu opens its arms wider to visitors.

The major tour operators in Vila are Aliat Wi Tours (☎ 25225), Frank King Tours (☎ 22808), Pacific Tours (☎ 25200, 25800), Surata Tamaso Tours (☎ 25600), Tour Vanuatu (☎ 22745, 22733) and Tropical Adventure Tours (☎ 22743, 25155). Surata Tamaso mainly looks after the outbound clients of its parent, Surata Tamaso Travel.

On Santo there's Espiritu Santo Travel & Tours (☎ 36391).

Culture Tours

Unless you master Bislama, don't expect too many of these tours to give you a deep and meaningful insight into ni-Vanuatu lifestyles and traditions. That said, cultural spectacles such as the Pentecost land dives and the Toka festival on Tanna have such great atmosphere, colour and drama that you shouldn't miss them.

Frank King Tours, Tour Vanuatu and Tropical Adventure Tours all offer various options for a visit to the Pentecost land diving. Expect to pay through the nose for the experience. For example, a one-day excursion (flying both ways) with Tour Vanuatu costs 40,000VT per person.

Tour Vanuatu can also get you to the Toka festival on Tanna, although the dates for this are usually uncertain until the last minute. The Small Nambas put on some great dancing in north-east Malakula, and you can see this through Pacific Tours.

Most tour operators in Vila offer Melanesian feast nights at outlying villages, such as Mele and Pango, where you can sample traditional cooking, listen to string bands and watch custom dancers. These usually work out at around 2500 to 3500VT per person.

One of the most interesting and relaxing culture tours available is the nature walk at Maga-liliu, near Vila. This 1.5-hour stroll with an expert guide gives you an excellent introduction to the different ways in which ni-Vanuatu use the plants of the forest. After the walk you're served lunch on the beach, following which you can swim, snorkel or go paddling in a dugout canoe. The tour costs 3300VT and can be booked through Tour Vanuatu and Frank King Tours.

Also worth doing are the natural history and garden walks on offer at Ngergarr, near Luganville. Bookings for these can be made through Espiritu Santo Travel & Tours.

Visits to the custom and Jon Frum villages on Tanna are probably best arranged through White Grass Bungalows and the Tanna Beach Resort. At any of these you're much more likely to get the full treatment if you turn up as part of a larger, pre-booked group.

Yacht Cruises

Only a handful of small operators offer

Walking

All the common-sense rules for walking in hot climates apply in Vanuatu. You'll need protection from the sun and mosquitoes – see the relevant sections under Health in the Facts for the Visitor chapter – and you should always carry plenty of drinking water. Warm clothing and rain jackets are appropriate in some areas.

In populated areas you must have the relevant custom owner's permission before walking on their land. You can usually obtain this through either the local council office or, failing that, the curator of the Cultural Centre in Vila (see Tourist Information in the Facts for the Visitor chapter). Either source will be able to advise you on whether or not there are likely to be any problems with your proposed route.

Guides A guide is pretty well essential for walks away from the main roads in rural Vanuatu – in fact, you should never go off by yourself unless you're sure it's OK to do so. There are many advantages in having the assistance of someone with local knowledge and fluency in local languages. Not the least of these is to ensure that you don't unintentionally break any tabus. A guide can also smooth your way by obtaining meals and arranging assistance for the next section of your walk.

One way to hire a guide is to make prior contact with the local council office either by telephone, radio or – as a last resort – by 'special message' broadcast over Radio Vanuatu (see Post & Telecommunications in the Facts for the Visitor chapter). Alternatively, you can contact the curator at the Cultural Centre on Kumul Hwy, Vila. The centre has field officers on most of the inhabited islands, and its curator will contact them on your behalf to arrange for guides. You'll be given a letter of introduction if the officer can't be reached by radio or telephone.

Regardless of how you arrange it, always allow for a delay of a day or so when you arrive at the guide's village. This will enable final preparations to be made before you start the actual walk.

You can expect to pay up to 1000VT per day per carrier and/or guide, while a man who does both jobs will cost up to 1500VT. You may have to provide these people with food, bedding and warm clothing on the trek, so make sure to sort this out before leaving.

Just to confuse the issue, some guides may only require a modest gift in return for their services – a packet of cigarettes will make you a friend for life in the remoter parts of Vanuatu. Either the Cultural Centre or bushwalkers from the Alliance Française and Vanuatu Natural Science Society (see Information below) can advise you on payments.

It often happens that the one guide you requested will grow into a small group. However, if you haven't asked for the services of additional people, you don't have to pay them or provide food. Most times they won't expect you to, but you never know.

Information The Vanuatu Natural Science Society in Vila holds monthly talks on natural history and other topics of interest to bushwalkers. You can contact the society through Frank King of Frank King Tours, diagonally opposite the Vila market. Alternatively, ask at the Alliance Française, behind the French Embassy. As well, these organisations will probably be able to direct you to locals who've done the walks you're interested in.

For information on walking in Santo and Gaua, you can contact Glen Russell of Butterfly Tours in Luganville. Glen can be reached through Espiritu Santo Travel & Tours. Until recently, Fred Kleckham, the manager of Club Hippique in Vila, operated bushwalking tours on Santo. ∎

extended yacht cruises around the archipelago. When they're in port, the captains of the *Response* (a 42-foot sloop) and *Galaxie* (a 72-foot ketch) can usually be contacted through the Waterfront Bar & Grill in Vila. Tour Vanuatu handles advance bookings for both these yachts. The *Response* can take five passengers and is the cheapest option, costing 40,000VT per day for the boat only.

Also in Vila, South Pacific Cruises runs trips of up to three days off Efate with the 72-foot ketch *Coongoola*. Sailaway Cruises mainly stays in sheltered waters with the *Golden Wing*, a 42-foot trimaran.

On Santo the only yacht currently doing overnighters is the 59-foot *Miz Mae*. The captain requires at least 48 hours' notice, and you can leave a message at either the Hotel Santo, the Natangora Café, or Espiritu Santo Travel & Tours. The day rate is 30,000VT without lunch.

Bushwalking Tours

Frank King Tours, Tour Vanuatu, Espiritu Santo Travel & Tours and Lolihor Adventure Tours, of Ambrym, between them offer a good range of day and overnight bushwalking tours. Usually these are by arrangement. A number of the out-of-town accommodation houses, such as Nagar Resort (Efate), Wala Island Resort (off Malakula), the Port Resolution Yacht Club and Tanna Beach Resort (both on Tanna) and Milee Bungalow

(Ambrym), will also arrange a number of bushwalks for you.

Coach Tours

The various operators on Efate, Santo and Tanna offer a variety of day and shorter tours. If you want to do the round trip of Efate, contact Aliat Wi Tours, Frank King Tours, Tour Vanuatu and Tropical Adventure Tours. They all charge around 4000VT per person. Frank King has a half-day 4WD tour up Mt Erskine for 3500VT.

On Santo, bookings for Sandy's Hibiscus Tours and Butterfly Tours are handled by Espiritu Santo Travel & Tours. The Tanna Beach Resort and White Grass Bungalows offer a number of tours in their 4WD minibuses. Most popular is their Mt Yasur excursion, costing 4000VT.

Aerial Tours

The only operators offering aerial tours in Vanuatu are Air Club Vila and Helicopters Vanuatu. Both have some interesting options apart from the usual scenic flights. For example, Helicopters Vanuatu has jungle or island drop-offs including champagne and a picnic for 8000VT per person. Air Club Vila will take you on a low-level tour of the Lopevi and Ambrym volcanoes, including a landing on the Ambrym ash plain. This half-day tour costs 14,000VT per person for a minimum of three passengers.

Efate Island

Since the 1840s Efate, pronounced 'Ef-ART-ay', has attracted more attention from foreigners than any other of Vanuatu's islands. This is because it has two of the country's best deep-water anchorages: Vila Bay and Havannah Harbour. Today, it has the country's principal airport and the national capital, Port Vila.

In 1774 Captain Cook became the first European to visit the island, which he named Sandwich Island after Lord Sandwich, the British patron of his voyage. However, this name was soon replaced by the islanders' own name for it: Efate, or Vaté in French.

For visitors, the island's many attractions include secluded beaches, jewel-like islands, gourmet restaurants, excellent diving and snorkelling, good fishing (including game species), a relaxed tropical lifestyle and, of course, the rich culture of Melanesia. As the

PLACES TO STAY

4 Nagar Beach Resort
6 Takara Resort
15 White Sands Country Club

OTHER

1 Manga'asi
2 Lelepa Landing
3 Valeafu Cave
5 Quoin Hill
7 Forari Wharf
8 Manuro Resort (abandoned)
9 Eton Beach
10 Eton Blue Hole
11 Dry Creek Beach
12 Rentabao Bridge
13 St Francis' Beach
14 White Sands Beach
16 Bauerfield Airport

Efate Island

0   5   10 km

country's most popular tourist destination Efate offers accommodation styles from backpacker standard to luxury resort. There's a large number of different tours and activities on offer, and more are appearing all the time. For these reasons, relatively few overseas visitors venture far beyond the capital.

History

Efate was pushed above the sea by volcanic action during the Pliocene age, between two and five million years ago, and remained free of human occupation until about 500 BC.

Its first settlers were probably one of the peoples of the Lapita culture, who left behind remnants of a distinctive kind of pottery. Later, in the first millennium AD, a new ceramics style evolved. This was named after Manga'asi, an early occupation site on Efate where many ancient deposits have been found.

European settlement began with the arrival of whalers, sandalwooders and missionaries. In September 1842, an American sandalwood expedition under Captain Henry sailed into what is now Havannah Harbour with 60 Tongan sailors aboard. The Tongans quarrelled with the Efatese, shooting 40 of them on the mainland and 20 on neighbouring Moso. Another eight were driven into caves and deliberately suffocated by smoke from fires lit outside.

These battles were not all one-sided, however. Several trading ships were attacked and many crew members killed by vengeful islanders. HMS *Havannah* was dispatched in 1849 to control the situation and several other British warships also did a turn of duty throughout the 1850s.

Meanwhile, Christian missionaries had begun to arrive seeking converts. Though they enjoyed some early successes in south Efate, a number of the missionaries who went to the north coast died of malaria.

By the mid-1860s there were 30 European settlers, mostly British, growing cotton on the flat coastal plains of Havannah Harbour. Cotton prices collapsed at the end of the US Civil War, so they turned first to maize and then to copra. In the late 1870s, French agents began buying up large parcels of land for the establishment of plantations. Britain refused to register or protect its citizens' land claims, placing the British planters at a serious disadvantage. Many sold up and left.

In 1886 French troops landed at Havannah Harbour – then site of the main settlement on Efate – and refused to withdraw. This forced Britain to register land claims and, as a result, British settlers began to return to settle permanently on the island. Most of these new arrivals came from Australia.

With France's defeat by Germany in 1940, the UK took full control of the island's administration. Two years later, in May 1942, a US fleet arrived and bases were constructed at Havannah Harbour and Port Vila. The US forces arrived mistakenly believing that the Japanese had already landed, so it's fortunate they didn't sail in with guns blazing. Over 100,000 service personnel, most of them from the US, passed through the island en route to the North Pacific.

In the 1970s Efate became the centre for Vanuatu's independence movement. Although the period leading up to independence in 1980 was marred by violence on Santo and Tanna, Efate remained calm. Since then the capital has grown enormously as many people from other islands have moved there in search of employment.

Geography

Efate is 46 km long, 33 km across at its widest point, and has an area of 980 sq km. It's the third largest island in Vanuatu.

The island is generally low and undulating, though inland there are several hills over 300 metres in height. Its major peak, at 647 metres, is rugged Mt MacDonald. The highest hills are in the north, with a pronounced rain shadow affecting the vegetation on the western side of the range. Efate's wettest zone is on the exposed eastern coast. Once, large coconut plantations virtually encircled the island on its flat coastal areas. Since the copra price crashed in the early 1990s, these have mostly been either abandoned to the jungle or cleared for cattle grazing.

While the island has many fine beaches, the coastline tends to be ragged and is generally fringed by sharp coral reefs. The volcanoes that created Efate have long been dormant, although there is still minor geothermal activity in the north-east.

Population & People

The 1989 census recorded Efate's population as 30,422, of whom nearly 19,000 lived in Vila. Most of the remainder lived in small villages dotted around the northern and eastern coast. The island's interior was almost totally uninhabited, a big move away from traditional patterns. Several thousand more people were living on the islands off the north coast.

Port Vila

Built around the shores of a horseshoe bay, the national capital rises up steep hillsides that offer stunning views over Iririki and Ifira Islands. Its scenery and tropical vegetation, including coconut palms and huge banyans, combine with its faded French atmosphere to make it one of Oceania's most attractive towns.

History

Early Days Vila was initially overshadowed by the settlement at Havannah Harbour. After a long drought in 1882 and several malarial outbreaks around Havannah, Efate's commercial centre moved to Port Vila on Vila Bay. In the 1890s, the town borders included the short-lived settlement of Franceville. This early centre was established in an attempt to impose French authority over all the island's inhabitants.

In 1906, Vila was declared the seat of the newly proclaimed Condominium government and thus became the national capital. At the time its main street was little more than a bush path connecting the warehouses belonging to Burns Philp (British) and the

SFNH (French). It was a seedy town, much favoured by beachcombers and freed convicts from New Caledonia.

Vila's original hotel, now long gone, was an absolute bloodhouse in the 1920s. Drunken plantation owners used to gamble over the 'years of labour' of their Melanesian workers. Islanders would be lined up along the wall, their employers changing at the throw of a dice several times a night. Long after the USA's Wild West was tamed, Vila was the scene of the occasional gunfight and public guillotining.

By the 1930s, life in Vila had become more sedate for the Europeans, who now numbered 1000. Official functions were the order of the day, with the British Resident Commissioner holding weekly cocktails for the British elite. Meanwhile, the French planters and their wives preferred tennis, social drinking and soirées.

The native islanders were only allowed to live in Vila if they were employed there, otherwise they were given 15 days to leave. They were also subject to a nightly curfew of 9 pm. Ni-Vanuatu had to be off the street by then or face the likelihood of a night in the lock-up.

Hibiscus

Modern Vila The establishment of Vila as a tax shelter and financial centre in 1970 fuelled a construction boom that saw its ramshackle, colonial dwellings replaced by concrete structures. The building of the main wharf in 1972 soon brought up to 40 cruise ship visits each year. This marked the beginning of Vila's role as a tourist destination. By 1980, one sixth of the country's population were living there.

Climate
For most of the year the climate is affected by the south-east trade winds. These keep temperatures and humidity down so that Vila's average maximum is a pleasant 30°C in the warm, wet summer. Winter maximums are down around 25°C, with minimums averaging five degrees less. Monthly rainfall varies from a wet season high of around 300 mm from January to March, down to about 100 mm in the dry season from May to October. The average annual rainfall in the capital itself is 2150 mm.

The best time to visit is during the southern winter from June to August. However, many visitors come in summer during the Christmas school holidays. This is a time when rains deluge the country, and when hot, humid conditions can create discomfort for those used to a more temperate climate. Summer is also the height of the cyclone season.

People
In 1993 Vila's population was estimated at 26,000, which is a huge increase on the 1989 census. It was made up of about 90% ni-Vanuatu, 5% European, 3% Chinese and Vietnamese, and 2% from other Pacific countries. The growth is mainly due to migration from outer islands, as young people in particular come seeking work and a more exciting lifestyle.

Orientation
Vila's banks, most of its commercial buildings and its main shopping precinct are concentrated in an area measuring only about one km by 250 metres, so it's easily explored on foot. The main street is Kumul Hwy, which winds along parallel to the waterfront. Known as Rue Higginson prior to independence, it was renamed in 1980 to honour Papua New Guinea's Kumul Force after its successful mopping up of the Santo Rebellion. Cruising yachts and charter boats usually line the seawall between the Rossi Restaurant and the Waterfront Bar & Grill. Inter-island copra boats moor at the Burn Philps (BP) Wharf.

Coming in from the south, where most of the hotels and resorts are located, the best place to start exploring is the Vila market on Kumul Hwy. Most days this is a hive of activity, with villagers setting up small stalls to sell garden produce, seafood, shells etc. Almost opposite is the former centre of the now defunct Condominium. This ugly, modernistic structure, currently housing various government offices including customs, is now called the Constitution Building.

Continuing north along the highway you pass the GPO on the right, then you're into the main shopping area. From here for the next 500 metres or so the footpaths are lined with duty-free shops, banks, cafés, restaurants and other businesses. The narrow road is chaotic with vehicle traffic, but horns are rarely sounded and motorists are generally very considerate. This is fortunate, as pedestrian crossings are hard to find.

About 300 m from the GPO you come to the Cultural Centre on the left, with the money exchange Goodies opposite. The NTO is upstairs above the Nissan dealership, with its entrance a little way up Rue Pasteur.

Keep going up Rue Pasteur for about 250 metres, crossing over Rue de Paris, and you come to the UK and Australian High Commissions in Melitco House. Rue de Paris runs through the middle of Chinatown. This area with its interesting shops lies on both sides of the intersection.

Back on Kumul Hwy, continue past the Cultural Centre, then turn sharp left before the ANZ Bank to find the Rossi Restaurant down on the waterfront. This is arguably Vila's most famous eating house and is noted for its fish. A lawn with palms and benches

EFATE ISLAND

runs along the waterfront from here back to the market, making a pleasant venue for a picnic lunch.

Just past the ANZ Bank is Fung Kuei, the largest duty-free shop in town. Keep walking around the bend and you come to the Office Pub, which more-or-less marks the northern end of the main business district. It only takes about 15 minutes to walk from the market to this point. The pub is owned by two expat Dutchmen and is a great spot for a cold beer.

Central Vila is hemmed between the harbour on one side and steep hills on the other. To the north are the mainly residential areas of Melcofe, Anabrou and Tebakor. To the east on a chain of hills are Fres Wata (Bislama for fresh water), the French Quarter, Seaside and Tassiriki. In the southern part of town are Nambatu, Nambatri and Elluk, and Wharf Rd (which runs to where the cruise ships berth).

As French people settled mainly around the harbour in the early years, most of the streets in central Vila have French names. The English ones tend to be concentrated to the east of Independence Park where most of Vila's British residents lived prior to independence. All street signs (when you can find them!) are in English and French, eg Rue Bougainville Street.

Information

Tourist Office The NTO (☎ 22685) is your first stop in Vila if you haven't booked accommodation. Its literature and reception staff may be lacking when it comes to providing details on activities and the more basic styles of accommodation in the outer islands, but the staff should at least be able to direct you to alternative sources of information.

The NTO is open from 7.30 am to 4.30 pm on weekdays, except for lunch, and 7.30 to 10.30 am on Saturdays. Alternatively, you can fax them on 23889 or write to PO Box 209, Port Vila.

The Facts for the Visitor chapter has details of a number of other organisations based in Vila that can provide helpful information. The Cultural Centre is particularly worth visiting.

Money Foreign exchange is handled by the ANZ Bank, the Banque d'Hawaii, the National Bank of Vanuatu and the Westpac Bank, all on or near Kumul Highway. There are also two or three privately owned money exchanges. The best exchange rates in Vila are given by Goodies. For bank and exchange opening hours see the Facts for the Visitor chapter.

Post & Telecommunications Also called Hôtel des Postes, Vila's general post office is open Monday to Friday, 7.30 am to 3.30 pm, and 7.30 am to noon on Saturday. Its postage, parcel and poste restante service are all reliable. There's a philatelic counter on the left inside the main entrance.

Public call boxes are outside on the right. The international phone and fax booths, which are inside on the left, are open from 7.30 am to 8 pm during the week and to noon on Saturday.

Useful telephone numbers include: teleradio HF/VHF ☎ 22759/22221, switchboard operator ☎ 90, and directory enquiries ☎ 91.

Travel Agencies South Pacific Travel (☎ 22836) and Surata Tamaso Travel (☎ 22666), both on Kumul Hwy in the south and north of central Vila respectively, can sort out your travel arrangements to and from Vanuatu. Both are agents for various international airlines (see the section on air travel in the Getting There & Away chapter).

Medical Services Vila's Central Hospital (☎ 22100) is in the Seaside district overlooking the beautiful Erakor Lagoon. The hospital is open for outpatients during normal business hours. It also has its own dentist and dispensary.

In addition, the hospital also has a number of qualified private practitioners. There are three well-stocked pharmacies in central

Vila. If you're in urgent need of medication, contact the Drug Store (☎ 22789), Healthwise (☎ 25722) or the Pharmacie de Port Vila (☎ 22446), all of which are on Kumul Highway.

Emergency Numbers For hospital and ambulance service, call (☎ 22100); for police call (☎ 22222); and for the fire brigade, call (☎ 22333).

Foreign Embassies & Consulates See the Facts for the Visitor chapter.

Bookshops Vila's best selection of reference books on the region is provided by Le Kiosque, in Rue Bougainville just up from the Iririki Centre Ville Hotel. Most of its books are written in French; it also sells New Caledonian newspapers.

Snoopys, near the Vila GPO and diagonally opposite the Vila town market, and Stop Press, across from the French Embassy, both sell Australian and British newspapers and magazines. A limited range of Australian publications is kept by the Chew Store, directly opposite Le Kiosque. The store's main advantage is that it's open all weekend.

Vila's only source of French magazines and national (French language) newspapers is the Centre Point Supermarket, opposite the Banque d'Hawaii on Kumul Hwy in central Vila.

Libraries Vanuatu's main public library forms part of the Cultural Centre in Vila. It's the main place to go to read back issues of the international press.

The Alliance Française behind the French Embassy has a small library where you can read the major French newspapers and magazines. Similar facilities are available at the Australian and New Zealand high commissions.

Vanuatu's best source of scientific reference books on the region, including New Caledonia, is the Orstom Library upstairs from the Public Solicitor's Office, behind El Gecko Restaurant in central Vila. The library isn't well known, so to find it you should ask

where the solicitor's office is. Its books are in French and English, and it's open Monday to Friday during normal business hours.

Vila's branch of the University of the South Pacific (☎ 22748) is a little out of the way, but has the best library in Vanuatu. It's open during normal business hours Monday to Friday, and may be used with the librarian's permission.

Things to See
Cultural Centre Vila's Cultural Centre comprises a museum and a library which are open from 9 to 11.30 am and 2 to 5 pm weekdays. Entry is free, although a small donation is requested if you visit the museum.

Outside the centre is a large cast-iron cauldron that was used on Aneityum for melting oil from whale blubber during the 1850s. No, it wasn't used for cooking missionaries.

There's an interesting display of cultural artefacts in the museum section. It includes wooden slit-gongs and tree-fern figures from Ambrym, and teenage male initiation masks, funerary objects and headdresses from south-western Malakula. There are also pig-killing clubs, bows and arrows, spears, pottery, traditional types of currency and many more items representing the rich cultures of the ni-Vanuatu.

Here you'll see a huge anchor from the *Astrolabe*, one of the two French ships, commanded by La Pérouse, that sank in a violent storm in the south-eastern Solomons in 1788.

The museum also houses collections of stuffed birds, shells, reptiles, insects, early photographs and rare postage stamps. In the rear is a lecture room, where regular video sessions about island customs are held. In addition the museum has a large and excellent collection of recordings of island legends and music. Some of these are for sale.

The adjoining library has a good and extensive lending section. The section includes a comprehensive array of books in both English and French. There is also an equally large and interesting research collection of learned articles about Vanuatu and its

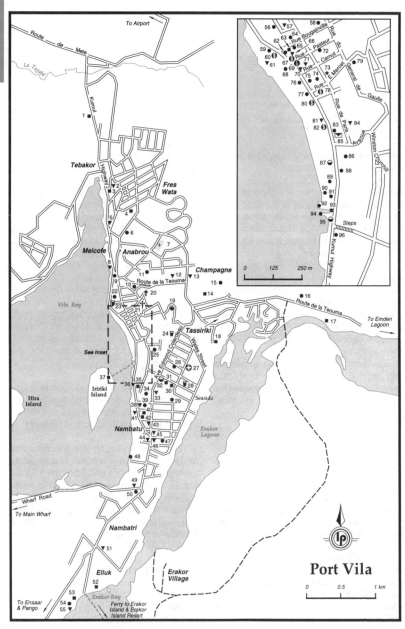

Port Vila

PLACES TO STAY

1 Kalfabun's Guest House
3 Coral Apartments
4 VNWC Guest House
14 USP Guest House
17 Vila Chaumières
18 Le Meridien
30 Talimoru Hotel
31 Ah Tong Motel
35 Marina Motel
37 Iririki Island Resort
40 Windsor Hotel
42 Kaiviti Motel
52 Le Lagon Pacific Resort
53 Pacific Lagoon Apartments
63 Iririki Centre Ville

PLACES TO EAT

2 Crow's Nest Restaurant
5 Harbour View Restaurant
8 Trader Vic's & Pisces Restaurant
12 La Parisiene Bakery
13 Binh Dan Restaurant
23 The Office Pub
33 Bamboo Royal Restaurant
36 Waterfront Bar & Grill
38 Le Bistrot
41 Le Rendez Vous
43 Manwah Restaurant
44 Au Bon Marché
45 Ebisu Restaurant
46 L'Houstalet
49 La Cabane
51 Golden Dragon Restaurant
55 Chez Gilles et Brigitte
57 Food Stalls
61 Rossi Restaurant
66 El Gecko Restaurant & Café

70 Ma Barker's Restaurant
.71 Mondia Restaurant
81 Le Flamingo
84 Club Vanuatu

OTHER

6 Lycée Bougainville
7 Cemetery
9 Surata Tamaso Travel
10 Georges Pompidou Building
11 Stadium
15 University of the South Pacific (USP)
16 Korman Stadium
19 Supreme Court
20 Porte du Ciel Roman Catholic Church
21 Roman Catholic Sacré Cœur Cathedral
22 Swedish Consul
24 PJ's Nakamal
25 Independence Park
26 Sutherland House
27 Central Hospital
28 Red Light Nakamal
29 Chiefs' Nakamal
32 Taxi Centre
34 Parliament House
39 Cine Hickson
47 People's Republic of China Embassy
48 Fisheries Department
50 Island Stream Rentals
54 Michoutouchkine & Pilioko Foundation Art Gallery
56 Radio Vanuatu
58 Vanuatu National Council of Women
59 Fung Kuei
60 ANZ Bank

62 Air Caledonie
64 Aliat Wi Tours
65 Orstom Library (upstairs)
67 Goodies Money Exchange
68 Cultural Centre
69 National Tourism Office (upstairs)
72 UK & Australian High Commissions (Melitco House)
73 Police Station
74 Alliance Française
75 Maison des Combattants & French Embassy
76 New Zealand High Commission (upstairs)
77 Immigration (upstairs)
78 National Bank of Vanuatu
79 Town Hall (Mairie)
80 Banque d'Hawaii
82 Westpac Bank
83 Tour Vanuatu, Air Vanuatu, Vanair
85 General Post Office (Hôtel de Poste)
86 Frank King Tours
87 Taxi rank
88 Constitution Building (includes Customs)
89 Covered market
90 Fish market
91 South Pacific Travel
92 Burn Philps (BP) Wharf
93 Club Marine
94 Iririki Wharf
95 Taxi Stand
96 Pacific Tours

history. These may only be read on the premises. The reading room has a selection of newspapers and magazines, mainly from the UK, France and Australia.

Chinatown Rue Carnot in central Vila is sometimes called 'Hongkong Street' because of its many Chinese shops. There are more round the corner in Rue de Paris. This whole area, containing almost all of Vila's Chinese shops, is often known simply as Chinatown. Most shops are crammed with an amazing array of merchandise, and you'll sometimes find fascinating bric-a-brac that looks as if it's been hiding away there for decades.

Market Vila's market is on the waterfront at the southern end of the central business district. The market is open from 6 am to noon or later on Wednesdays, Fridays and Saturdays. The largest, busiest markets are held on Saturdays, when it pays to get there early if you're serious about buying.

On market days the marketplace under its high roof is normally higgledy-piggledy with tables and mats piled with fresh produce from Efate's numerous villages. The goods include a wide range of fruit and vegetables, seafood, flowers, firewood, shells, bracelets, clothing and artefacts. Usually the stalls are in the care of village women wearing colourful Mother Hubbard dresses.

Fruit and vegetable prices here are rock bottom. For example, coconuts, ripe pawpaws and huge grapefruit normally start at around 30VT each. You could pay as little as 150VT for a small squid cooked in coconut milk and served on a slab of manioc pudding – a meal for one person.

As with all Melanesian commerce, there's no bargaining. Prices are fixed and clearly marked, so if you feel the price is unreasonable, just keep moving to the next stall. No one ever hassles you to buy anything you don't want.

If you don't recognise the tropical fruits or vegetables on sale, ask either the stallholder (who probably won't speak either English or French) or an expat for advice on selection

and preparation. You can usually identify expats from visitors by the fact that they seem to know what they're doing.

Independence Park The large area of lawn and shady trees up the hill from the post office on Ave Winston Churchill is Independence Park. Formerly known as the British Paddock, it's rather like an English village green, surrounded by houses, a church and government buildings. Cricket is played from March to September on Saturday afternoons.

The Condominium was proclaimed here in 1906, with British and French flags ceremoniously raised together. The former British Residency is the large, wooden-shuttered building on the park's upper (eastern) side; the former French Residency is 300 metres to the north. During Condominium rule a daily check was made to ensure that the Union Jack was flying at the same height as the Tricolour at the French Residency – each partner was terrified that they might be upstaged by the other! No wonder their attempts at government were often laughingly referred to as the Pandemonium!

French Quarter Just north of central Vila is the Quartier Français (as it is still called) where many French speakers live. It is bordered to the south by the Georges Pompidou building, a former French hospital that now houses several Government departments.

Close by is the Porte du Ciel Vietnamese Roman Catholic church which is designed like a Quonset hut, with a semi-circular cross-section. Also nearby is the modern Roman Catholic cathedral of Sacré-Coeur, and several colonial-style houses built in typical French fashion with wooden-louvred windows.

From beside the WW I war memorial, at the top of nearby Rue Emile Mercet, you can gain fine and expansive views over Vila Bay. Across the road is the Mairie, or Port Vila Town Hall. This town hall has been designed and built to the same design as many grand and official buildings in mother France.

There's another fine viewpoint 400 metres away to the south, along the Rue du General de Gaulle, and just above a splendidly colourful grove of African tulip trees.

Supreme Court Vanuatu's Supreme Court is the fine old wooden structure on the hillside 500 metres inland from the Mairie (Town Hall). This is the former Joint Court of the Condominium.

The Joint Court was supposed to dispense justice to islanders, and arbitrate in disputes between the British and French. But this seldom happened. Not only did it fail to protect villagers' interests against colonial greed, but it made eccentric judgements concerning Europeans. For example, it permitted a French man who murdered an Australian in front of witnesses to remain at large on his home island. In contrast, a French woman who dared to insult a magistrate was rewarded with one month in the lock-up.

Nambatu & Nambatri One km south of the post office and on a hill overlooking Vila Bay is the Nambatu district, and a km further on is Nambatri.

There is a curious story about the naming of these districts. During WW II, US forces established three large radar stations in Vila. These were known as Number One, Number Two and Number Three. Inevitably a small village of camp followers, caterers and entertainers established themselves around each installation. The names Number Two and Number Three have been preserved in Bislama form. Nambatu and Nambatri are now among Vila's plushest residential areas, with many fine views of the bay. 'Nambawan' was in the south-eastern corner of the British Paddock, now Independence Park.

Cemetery The town cemetery in Anabrou, reflects the varied origins and backgrounds of Vila's population. Of particular interest are its large, exotically decorated Chinese and Vietnamese tombstones.

Iririki Island This small island, only 300 metres from the Port Vila waterfront, is connected to the mainland by a free 24-hour ferry service from Iririki Wharf. The British Resident Commissioner lived on top of the hill in Condominium days but now the only residents are the staff of the luxurious Iririki Island Resort. Visitors are allowed onto the island during daylight hours, or longer if they're eating at the restaurant.

The walk around Iririki Island takes you through lush tropical bushland and is easily accomplished in 30 minutes. En route you pass a popular, shallow snorkelling spot on the west coast. Pedaloes, catamarans, windsurfers etc are for hire at the little beach just south of the resort. You can also enjoy a cool drink up at the restaurant, where the swimming pool boasts a marvellous view of Vila.

Michoutouchkine & Pilioko Foundation Art Gallery This Oceanic art gallery and artists' studio is on the way to Pango about one km from the entrance to the Le Lagon Pacific Resort. You may wander around the gallery's beautiful private garden and admission-free display between 10 am and 5 pm daily. It's also visited by the various town tours.

The art centre is named after its two resident artists, Nicholas Michoutouchkine, a Franco-Russian, and Aloi Pilioko, a Wallis Islander. It houses a fascinating collection of Pacific bric-a-brac and memorabilia, including ornate carvings and masks produced by the master craftspeople of southern Malakula. Interspersed among these are stunning batik cotton prints and embroideries.

University of the South Pacific Based in Suva, Fiji, the University of the South Pacific (USP) has a large annexe in Vila's Champagne district. Students from all over Oceania, including New Zealand and Australia, come here to study Pacific languages and law.

Activities

Scuba Diving & Snorkelling Each of Vila's three established dive companies offers the tuition required to give you internationally recognised scuba certification. These courses last from four to five days and introduce you to many of the area's underwater attractions. The specialist dive-tour operators based in Vila are Hideaway Island (☎ 26660) on the island of the same name, and Nautilus (☎ 22398) on the waterfront just south of central Vila. At the time of this update, a fourth operator, Pro Dive, was in the throes of starting up on Iririki Island. Sailaway Cruises and South Pacific Cruises both offer scuba diving as an extra on their tours.

Prices for single dives start at 3700VT. All dive companies have air compressors and a full range of equipment – you can confidently take nothing but your certification. Some dive sites can be snorkelled, and if you'd rather do this than scuba you can join a tour for around 1000VT, inclusive of kit. All operators charge for pick-ups and returns before and after a tour.

Scuba Sites in Vila You'll find plenty of interesting scuba and snorkelling spots without even leaving Vila Bay. The sites below are close to Vila, but there are many more a little further away (see the Around Vila section later in this chapter).

Star of Russia – About 300 metres west of the main wharf, this iron-hulled, timber-decked, 89-metre schooner lies upright 33 metres down. Her masts and hull are still intact and some rigging survives. She's now the home of thousands of colourful fish and a large, amiable groper.

Tasman – Close inshore, but lying in 38 metres of water, this Sandringham flying boat with its 40-metre wingspan sank after striking a reef in Vila Bay. It sits upright on the bottom, but unfortunately the visibility in the area is not good.

Resolution – Just off Quai Wharf and 40 metres down, this is the wreck of a 19th-century trading boat built of Norfolk pine.

Malapoa Point – Cases and belts of .30 calibre ammunition were discarded here in 10 to 18 metres of water by US forces at the end of WW II. The coral gardens of Malapoa Reef are just beyond.

Sports The old Stadium, north of central Vila in the district known as Stade, is the most popular venue for netball, volleyball, handball, soccer and rugby union football. It's closed from late December to January.

Vanuatu's newest sporting complex, Korman Stadium, was originally built for the South Pacific Mini Games in 1993. It has a number of excellent facilities for sports such as athletics, basketball, boxing, indoor vol-

Star of Russia

leyball and soccer, as well a gymnasium. Updates on programmes for both stadiums can be obtained from the Department of Youth & Sport (☎ 25106).

The Port Vila Tennis Club (☎ 22437), also known as the Cercle Sportif, is just beside the old Stadium. The club has five hard courts, two squash courts, a gymnasium, aerobics classes and a small swimming pool.

An alternative venue for squash is Club Vanuatu (☎ 22615), in Rue de Paris. The White Sands Country Club (☎ 22090), 16.5 km from Vila, has the only lawn tennis courts in Vanuatu.

There are small golf courses at both the Royal Palms and Le Lagon resorts. The Port Vila Golf Club (☎ 22564), four km from Vila on Route de Mele, and the White Sands Country Club both have 18-hole courses.

Horse Riding Trail rides through the tropical bushland and coconut plantations above Emden Lagoon are offered by Club Hippique (☎ 23347). Beach riding is the major attraction at the Ranch de la Colle (☎ 22071) near Mele.

Club Hippique is open to visitors from Tuesday to Saturday, when rides cost 2000VT per hour for a maximum of two hours. You can get there by minibus from Vila's town centre for around 200VT each way.

The Ranch de la Colle opens at 1.30 pm every day except Monday, with rides costing 2400VT per hour for as long as you like. You can catch a minibus from town for 70VT if it's heading that way. Otherwise expect to pay more.

Swimming Not many locals swim in Vila Bay, thanks to pollution and its often busy aquatic traffic. The most popular swimming spots near town are Black Sand Beach, near the golf club, and Mele Beach opposite Mele Island.

Boating You can hire catamarans, windsurfers and pedaloes from Watersports on Iririki Island and from the Le Lagon Resort.

Typical prices are 1000VT an hour for catamarans and 800VT for windsurfers.

With Watersports you can also parafly for 3500VT a flight and waterski for 3500VT per half hour.

Fishing With permission of the appropriate custom owner you can fish anywhere on the reefs, shorelines and rivers of Efate. Unless you have your own gear and transport, the only way to get in a day's fishing is with one of the specialised tours operating out of Vila.

Club Marine have the best range of fishing trips. Their half-day rates per adult (children under 12 half price) are 3500VT for bottom-reef fishing and sports fishing for 6000VT. They also offer big-game fishing for 20,000/50,000VT per half/full day for the boat.

The MV *Calliamanda* (☎ 26557) and Frouin Rémy with *Ymer* (☎ 22649) concentrate on big-game fishing. Both have day and extended excursions.

Organised Tours
A number of pleasure craft based in Port Vila offer a range of tours such as fishing, diving and coral viewing. Tours by helicopter and light-aircraft are also available. Alternatively you can stay on land and either explore Vila or be taken all the way around Efate.

The principal operators offering tours of Efate are Frank King Tours (☎ 22808), opposite and along from the market, Tour Vanuatu (☎ 22745, 22733), near the post office, and Tropical Adventure Tours (☎ 22743, 25155), opposite El Gecko. Aliat Wi Tours (☎ 25225) in Rue Bougainville is also worth trying.

Land Trips Most of the above offer good and interesting two to three-hour tours of Vila, with visits to such points of interest as the Tusker brewery, a silk-screening factory and a coconut mill. Expect to pay around 2000VT for these tours. They also run excellent Melanesian feast nights in nearby villages. The price for these can range to upwards of 2500VT. Frank King has the best and most varied of short (half day only) tours in and around Vila. These include a visit to a kava bar (3000VT) and the local market (1500VT with breakfast).

Frank King also has the widest range of island day tours, with three on offer for 4500VT each. One tour concentrates on the eastern side of the island, another on the west, and the third takes you all the way around. If you want to organise things yourself, he'll hire you a minibus, car or 4WD and guide for around 1700VT per hour. Aliat Wi Tours have the cheapest round-island tour, at 3800VT per person.

Bushwalking Frank King has four tours available ranging from six hours to two days. His two-day walk across the island's rugged, uninhabited centre from Onesua to Vila airport costs 20,000VT and is classed as 'very strenuous'. The walk over Mts Erskine and Bernier takes 10 hours, costs 6000VT and is merely 'strenuous'. Both these walks are by arrangement.

Sea Trips A wide choice of glass-bottomed boat trips as well as day, half-day and sunset cruises is available, with a number of operators vying for your vatu. Frank King Tours and Club Marine (☎ 26660, 24952) have the greatest variety of harbour excursions. Club Marine also offers various tours to the Hideaway Island marine sanctuary, off Mele, and is generally very competitive.

In addition, there are several specialist operators whose cruises can be booked either direct or through Aliat Wi Tours, Tour Vanuatu and Tropical Adventure Tours. If you're interested in a day's yacht cruise beyond the harbour, the ones to contact are *Response* (the Waterfront Bar & Grill can let you know if skipper Jim is in port), Sailaway Cruises (☎ 22743, 23802), South Pacific Cruises (☎ 25020) and Tiva Charters (☎ 25888). These tours include scuba diving and/or snorkelling.

As a guide to costs, expect to pay upwards of 2500VT for a two-hour trip, 3000VT for a half-day, and 5000VT for a full day. Sunset cruises with or without night coral viewing

are around 3000VT including wine and nibbles.

Places to Stay
Vila is well endowed with hotel rooms, for a town of its size. However, other than some hostel-style accommodation, these are mainly in the middle and upper price bracket. Vila's three top resort hotels compare well with the best anywhere, with numerous activities to keep you occupied.

All hotels have to pay a 10% tourist tax, and this is included in the rates given here.

Bottom End The cheapest place to stay in town is *Kalfabuns' Guest House* (☎ 24484) in Tagabe, about halfway between central Vila and the airport. Don Kalfabun and his friendly family have three rooms and three bungalows they rent to guests for 1500VT per person. Use of the kitchen is included in this price.

Located in Anabrou about 10 minutes walk from town, the *VNWC Guest House* (☎ 23108) charges 1500VT per person for a bed and 500VT to camp in the grounds. It's run by the Vanuatu National Women's Council and has a kitchen and laundry as well as a kava bar and small store.

Close to the Central Hospital is the Presbyterian Church-owned *Sutherland House* (☎ 22722) which is mainly used by visiting ni-Vanuatu. This basic hostel has cooking facilities and its three double rooms cost 1750/3500VT for singles/doubles.

As its name suggests, the self-catering *USP Guest House* (☎ 22748) is in the grounds of the University of the South Pacific. Its eight spartan rooms cost from 1500VT per person.

A cut above the guest houses but still quite cheap, the *Talimoru Hotel* (☎ 23740) offers itself as a backpackers lodge. It is conveniently located next door to a seven-day supermarket (which has lots of yummies) and the Taxi Centre. Its 42 spartan but clean rooms cost 2500/3685VT single/double without balcony and 2750/ 3850VT with, including a sizeable continental breakfast. The facilities are shared; sadly, the solar hot-water services often can't keep up with demand. The hotel has a bar and lounge, a reasonably priced restaurant, and a relatively up-market kava bar outside.

Middle Located on Kumul Highway about 1.5 km from central Vila, the *Coral Apartments* (☎ 23569) has 10 self-contained, fan-cooled units costing 4950/5500/6050VT for singles/doubles/triples. Discounts apply for extended stays: eg it costs 83,380VT for a single person for one month.

Close to the centre of town, the *Iririki Centre Ville Hotel* (formerly the Hotel Olympic) (☎ 22464) is equipped for business guests. It has a restaurant, ISD telephone dialling to each room and free use of the catamarans and windsurfers at Iririki Island Resort. Its 20 air-conditioned standard rooms cost 9350/10,450VT for singles/doubles, while the apartments are 13,200VT a night.

Conveniently positioned at the south end of Vila's main shopping area, and with a view of Iririki Island, the *Marina Motel* (☎ 22566) has 10 self-contained, air-conditioned studio units with kitchenettes. The charge per night is 6500/7200VT for singles/doubles and 1800VT for each extra person.

The refurbished *Windsor Hotel* (☎ 22150), which is a few hundred metres further up the hill, is definitely worth a look if you're with a few friends. It has two restaurants, three bars and a swimming pool, as well as 85 air-conditioned or fan-cooled rooms catering for couples, families and groups. Its cheaper rates are 7300VT for studios (four beds),10,500VT for one-bedroom apartments (three beds) and 11,000VT for two-bedroom apartments (five beds). There are two small gaming lounges on the premises.

Right next door, the *Kaiviti Motel* (☎ 24684) is a more down-at-heel but friendlier place with a bar and swimming pool. Its 28 fan-cooled studios cost 7500/8500VT doubles/triples; the nine two-bedroom apartments are 10,000VT for up to four guests, and 1000VT each for two extra persons on rollaway beds. All units have kitchenettes. Manager Joy Wu, from Queensland, has lived in Vanuatu over 20 years and can point you in the right direction for most things.

The *Ah Tong Motel* (☎ 23218), near the Talimoru, supermarket and the Taxi Centre, has 10 airy, twin rooms with kitchenette, TV and air-conditioning or ceiling fans. The price per room is 6800/30,000/80,000VT on a day/week/month basis. From here it's about 10 minutes' walk to town.

Top End Most central of Vila's three principal hotels and across from the old BP Wharf is the *Iririki Island Resort* (☎ 23388). Connected to Vila by a free 24-hour ferry service, the resort has great views, 72 air-conditioned bungalows, a swimming pool, artefacts shop, restaurant, bar and regular floor shows. Its bungalows cost upwards of 13,200VT per night for singles/doubles.

Twenty minutes' walk east of central Vila, the *Le Meridien*, formerly the Royal Palms Resort, (☎ 22040) has 145 rooms in a magnificent setting near the top of Erakor Lagoon. Most of its rooms sleep up to three people and start at 14,000VT per room. There's a swimming pool, two private beaches, a small island with its own golf course, two tennis courts, water sports facilities, a disco, video room and tour desk. Its bars and restaurants are among Vila's best. The hotel used to be called the Radisson, which is how most locals still refer to it.

Le Lagon Pacific Resort (☎ 22313) is set on the shore of Erakor Lagoon about three km south of central Vila. Its 109 air-conditioned rooms and bungalows start at 11,550VT per night for singles and doubles. The resort has a number of facilities. These range from its own islet, a private beach, a golf course, tennis courts, a disco, a video room, restaurants, bars, swimming pools, an outdoor spa, a handicrafts and artefacts shop, any number of water sports and even a tour desk.

Vila's Outskirts A saunter about 500 metres down the road, towards Pango from Le Lagon, is the comfortable *Pacific Lagoon*

Apartments (☎ 23860) which has 12 lovely, fan-cooled, fully self-contained apartments right on the mouth of Erakor Lagoon. Each unit sleeps up to six people and costs from 6000 to 9000VT per night, making it very good value for groups. A minibus to town costs 70VT.

The *Erakor Island Resort* (☎ 22983) boasts a beautiful, tropical island setting across the water from Le Lagon and Pacific Lagoon Apartments. It has a very nice open-air restaurant on the beach, plus 13 fan-cooled bungalows costing 7200/8400/10,800 for singles/doubles/triples, with four of its larger bungalows able to sleep five people for the price of a triple. Access is by a free 24-hour ferry service to and from a small jetty on the mainland near Le Lagon.

About 3.5 km from Vila, in a lush garden setting on the north side of Emden Lagoon, is *Vila Chaumières* (☎ 22866). Its four fan-cooled, self-contained bungalows sleep up to three people each and cost 8000VT for singles and doubles – a third person costs 2000VT extra. Children under 16 years are not accepted. The resort has a romantic restaurant on the waterfront, and you can work up an appetite with free use of a dugout canoe on the lagoon.

Out of Town *Hideaway Island* (☎ 26660), out past the airport 10 km from town, lost its accommodation in the 1993 cyclone. However, check it out as there are plans to construct thatch bungalows and backpacker rooms. The resort offers excellent snorkelling and diving – there's a dive shop on site – as well as a pleasant beach restaurant and bar. A ferry service connects this delightful island to the mainland 200 metres away.

On the south coast 16.5 km from Vila, the *White Sands Country Club* (☎ 22090) has 10 fan-cooled, Melanesian-style bungalows costing 7000VT for singles and doubles. Extra adults cost 3500VT, but children under 16 years are free. The club also has a pool, bar, restaurant, an 18-hole golf course and tennis courts. A courtesy bus provides a daily service to and from Vila on request.

The only other accommodation houses on

Efate outside Vila are the Nagar Resort and Takara Beachcomber, both on the north coast. These are described in the Around Efate section later in this chapter.

Places to Eat

Vila has made quite a name for itself in culinary excellence throughout the South Pacific. Wining and dining are often top class, and there is a wide variety of European, Asian and Pacific cuisines on offer. With around 50 eating establishments to choose from you shouldn't have any difficulty finding something to suit your tastes and budget.

Supermarkets The cheapest option is to buy a stick of French bread at a shop and flavour it with some fruit from the market. There are a number of supermarkets and corner stores in Vila. The large ones, of which there are several scattered about town, carry an excellent range of fresh and processed local and imported foods, beer and wine. Most are open seven days a week from 7.30 am, and several remain open until 9 pm.

Fast Food & Takeaways *La Parisienne Bakery*, near the Stadium (Stade) is open early in the morning. It serves deliciously warm French bread, as well as tasty and wholesome meat pies (known as pâtés), chaussons (apple turnovers), croissants and a variety of soft drinks.

Across from the Iririki Wharf, the *Calvo Store* has a limited but cheap selection of simple takeaways. These include such things as meat pies and spring rolls. Remember that it is closed for the lunchtime siesta.

Chengs, near Frank King Tours opposite the market, sells delicious Chinese snacks and takeaways. It's open seven days a week. A typical rice dish costs 220 to 300VT per serving.

Standard fast-food fare is the order of the day at *Natapoa Take Away*, in Rue de Paris, and *Ma's Take Away,* Rue Carnot next door to *Ma Barkers*. Both are open from breakfast until late evening.

If you're after a pizza for supper, *Trader Vics* on Kumul Hwy at the northern end of central Vila, the *Sunset Bar* in the Windsor Hotel, and *La Pizza* in L'Houstalet Restaurant, at the other end of town, can satisfy your craving. Trader Vics also sells fish and chips; the quality of their takeaways is excellent, but the prices will make your eyes water.

Snack Bars, Cafés & Cheap Eats Vila's cheapest place for lunch is a group of modest food stalls out front of Radio Vanuatu, at the northern end of central Vila. Here you can buy a heaped plate for 200VT, so not surprisingly it's popular with local workers.

The *Club Vanuatu*, in Rue de Paris has good-value lunches and dinners, with its specials (usually a choice of three) costing 400VT. These come with either white rice or chips – unless you're a white-rice addict take the chips, as these give you better value. Nonmembers must sign in and you must wear socks and shoes after 7 pm.

In Nambatu, *Au Bon Marché* supermarket has a cafeteria area selling snacks for 100VT and rice meals from 200 to 450VT. It's open from 6.30 am seven days a week and is best for breakfast and lunch as it tends to run out of food after lunch.

Shells Café in Le Meridien is open 24 hours all week for snack meals. It's the only place in Vila where you can go for coffee and a quiet chat regardless of the hour.

Tucked away off Rue Bougainville between Rue Pierre Lamy and Kumul Hwy, *La Viennoiserie* is a French bakery offering bread, cakes and pastries as well as small-sized meals averaging 300VT. It's open from 6.30 am to 5.30 pm Monday to Friday and mornings on weekends.

The main town area has several cafés, most of which are open seven days. Classiest of these are *El Gecko*, opposite the Cultural Centre, and the *Harborside Café*, in the Ballande Centre opposite Iririki Wharf. Their breakfasts start at around 400VT, and you can pick up large sandwiches for

upwards of 350VT. Full meals are also available.

La Tentation, opposite Tour Vanuatu, is a popular meeting place thanks to its pleasant alfresco setting. Almost next door, *Jill's Café* has delicious American style snack meals – burgers start at 150VT. Further up the street, the sidewalk eating area of *La Terrasse* is fine if you like traffic noise and exhaust fumes.

Worth mentioning is *The Office Pub*, at the northern end of central Vila, where you can enjoy typical pub meals from 600VT. It's a dimly-lit, friendly place that stays open until late every night.

Le Bistrot, near the Windsor Hotel, specialises in French cuisine. It opens at 7 am and serves excellent breakfasts from 550VT. Lunches are equally enjoyable, if somewhat more expensive. Attached is a delicatessen where you can buy a range of French foods and wines.

Middle On the waterfront in the centre of town, the *Rossi Restaurant* (☎ 22528) is one of Vila's dining institutions. It's famous for its seafood, such as the giant platters costing 6600VT which will easily feed three adults. Go there at sunset for a marvellous view of Vila Bay.

Close by are *El Gecko Restaurant* (☎ 25597) and *Ma Barkers* (☎ 22399), both of which offer lunches and dinners starting at around 1000VT. Ma Barkers wins on atmosphere while El Gecko is ahead on food.

Also in central Vila, the very relaxing, open-air *Waterfront Bar & Grill* (☎ 23490) is open every day but Sunday for lunch and dinner. A large, juicy steak or piece of fresh fish plus as much as you could possibly eat from the salad bar costs 1200VT. This is the place to be if you want to learn what's happening in local yachting circles.

A spectacular view is the major attraction at the *Crow's Nest* (☎ 25257), which overlooks the harbour from a spectacular cliff-top perch out at Tebakor. Unfortunately, it's closed on Sundays, but is thankfully open all other days for OK lunches and dinners. It serves international cuisine of which the Thai is recommended.

With one of the most imaginative menus in town, *L'Houstalet* (☎ 22303) offers fare such as frogs' legs, snails, flying fox and green pigeon. Open only for dinner, it's the oldest French restaurant in town and one of the best. As a bonus, if you're into dancing, there's a disco on the premises. L'Houstalet is across the road from Au Bon Marché supermarket in Nambatu.

Almost next door, *Ebisu Restaurant* (☎ 23612), is the only place in Vila currently specialising in Japanese cuisine. Don't be put off by the unpromising exterior as its meals are usually excellent.

La Cabane (☎ 22763), also known as Chez Felix, is on the road to the main wharf. This restaurant has a pleasant, island-style atmosphere, and serves a variety of international cuisine. Main courses for lunch start at 1100VT, while dinner is a little more expensive.

The Vietnamese *Binh Dan Restaurant* (☎ 22287) near USP is reasonably priced for a quality eating house. Another Vietnamese establishment is the *Mondia Restaurant* (☎ 22450), in Chinatown. Both are open for dinner only.

Vila has four Chinese restaurants: the *Manwah Restaurant* (☎ 23091) in Nambatu; the *Golden Dragon* (☎ 3933) in Nambatri; the *Bamboo Royal* (☎ 22806) in Rue d'Artois across from Parliament House; and the *Harbour View* (☎ 23668) in Anabrou. These are all reasonable value, with main courses from around 800VT.

As well as all these, the resorts and major hotels between them have a number of bars and restaurants offering a range of styles to suit most budgets.

Top End *Le Rendez Vous* (☎ 23045), opposite the Windsor Hotel and poised high above Vila Bay, serves delicious French cooking. Open for lunch and dinner, it's famous for its soufflés as well as the views across to Iririki Island.

Specialising in Italian cuisine, the *Pisces*

Restaurant (☎ 24940) is open for dinner only and has a truly superb atmosphere. It's on the waterfront behind Trader Vic's at the northern end of central Vila.

Vila Outskirts Main meals in the *Erakor Island Resort's* island style restaurant cost 1000 to 2500VT, while snack meals average 750VT. Coconut crab and lobster are the house specialities. Their Sunday lunchtime barbecue with salad bar and live music is very popular at 1400VT.

'Laid back' is raised to an art form at the *Hideaway Island Resort*, where you eat beachcomber style at shaded tables on the white sand. The restaurant opens between 8 am and 4 pm daily and has a single menu covering all meals. Costs start at 750VT. Their regular Sunday evening beach barbecue of fish and beef costs 1200VT and starts at 5 pm.

Vila Chaumières is open daily for lunch and dinner. Situated on the edge of palm-fringed Emden Lagoon, it has a wonderful atmosphere, particularly in the evenings.

Out past Le Lagon, in the Michoutouchkine & Pilioko complex, *Chez Gilles & Brigitte* serves superb French dishes in an idyllic setting on the waterfront. It's open for lunch and dinner most days, except Saturday lunch and Sundays.

If you're touring, the restaurant at the *White Sands Country Club* is open from 7 am to late. Breakfast costs 400 to 950VT, the lunchtime snack menu averages 750VT and dinner main courses average 1500VT.

Further afield on Efate, the only other restaurants are found at the *Nagar Resort* and the *Takara Beachcomber*. These are both covered in the section on Around Efate later in this chapter.

Entertainment

Vila doesn't have much in what you could call a vibrant and bustling nightlife. There is, however, a couple of reasonable, though not entirely jumping, discos and casinos, but otherwise don't expect to be raging after midnight.

Casinos The Palms Casino in the Le Meridien is open from midday until early morning daily for blackjack, roulette, baccarat and poker machines.

In the Windsor Hotel, the Club 21 Gaming Lounge's poker machines are open from 10 am to at least midnight daily. The Club Vanuatu also has pokies and keeps the same hours.

Discos & Piano Bars Vila's cheapest and most basic night spots are the ni-Vanuatu discos scattered about town. If you want to visit one, take ear plugs and preferably go with someone who knows the ropes.

L'Houstalet is the best of the ni-Vanuatu discos. It's open from 9 pm to 3 am on Mondays to Thursdays, and to 4.30 am on Saturdays and Sundays.

By far the classiest disco in town is Le Flamingo, in the main street of central Vila. It opens daily at 5 pm (there's a 'happy hour', when the price of drinks drops by about a third, from Monday to Friday from 5 pm until 8 pm) and closes late. According to the blurb, it has the best sound, lighting and video systems in the South Pacific.

Private Clubs In Rue de Paris the double-storey Club Vanuatu (☎ 22615) offers a range of facilities including a bistro, bar, squash courts, snooker, darts, satellite TV and live bands on weekends. It's open from 10 am to midnight daily and overseas visitors are welcome. If you're a short-term visitor you gain entry by signing the visitor book. Otherwise, temporary membership costs 100VT a week up to three months.

The Maison des Combattants (☎ 22947), behind the French Embassy, is a French-language social club open for coffee and light snacks between 10 am and 1 pm, and again from 4 to 10 pm most days.

In the same building, the Alliance Française de Port Vila offers a variety of entertainments and activities. These include bushwalks and plays. It also has a small library where the major French newspapers and magazines may be read.

The Yacht Club of Port Vila (☎ 23030) at Malapoa Point and the Vanuatu Cruising Yacht Club (☎ 24634) in central Vila, next to the Waterfront Bar & Grill, welcome all yachting people and sailors.

Kava Bars There are well over 100 kava bars or nakamals in Vila, with most being little more than iron sheds or open shelters. The sunset kava cup, served in a coconut shell or glass bowl, is a ritual for many of Vila's expat citizens as well as ni-Vanuatu. The most popular kava bars with expats are PJs. This is located up the hill from the Taxi Centre on Avenue Edmond Colardeau, and the Red Light Nakamal past the Talimoru Hotel. The going rate is 50VT for a small shell (about 150 mm) and 100VT for a larger one.

Although kava is generally reserved for men elsewhere in Vanuatu, female expats and tourists are more than welcome at most nakamals in Vila. If you're not sure whether it's appropriate, ask an expat or a taxi driver.

Many of these establishments have rather poor hygiene in that they often don't wash the shells between servings – this is about as good a way as possible of transmitting hepatitis A. If you're concerned about this (and who wouldn't be?) it's advisable to take your own shell or bowl. (See also the Health section in the Facts for the Visitor chapter.) It's hard to imagine anything nasty surviving in the kava itself.

Plays A great splash of posters go up all over town announcing the imminent staging of a play. There are a number of drama groups associated with the Alliance Française and the Club Vanuatu put on several shows a year. As well, the Wan Smolbag Theatre offers regular plays during the dry season. These are usually popular and interesting productions and are almost always well worth attending.

Feasts, String Bands & Custom Dancing The major resorts put on a number of regular string band and custom dance shows. These are usually done to provide entertainment to diners during meals. For example, Le Lagon's Melanesian feast nights include cooking demonstrations, a kava ceremony, black magic demonstrations, a string band and dancers from Futuna Island.

As well, most local tour operators offer village feasts which include traditional foods, string bands and custom dancers. These cost upwards of 2500VT including transport.

Cinemas The Cine Hickson near the Windsor Hotel is Vila's only movie house. It shows French language and subtitled films nightly except Thursday.

Things to Buy

Handicrafts Vanuatu has a wide range of traditional and contemporary handicrafts available, and you'll almost certainly find what you're looking for in Vila.

The largest number of traditional objects is offered by the thatch-roofed Handikraf blong Vanuatu, beside the Cultural Centre on Kumul Hwy. Prices here are among the cheapest in Vila as it's supposedly a non-profit venture acting on behalf of the artisans.

Across the road is Goodies, where you'll find a huge variety of quality artefacts and handicrafts with most islands represented. Ask to see their pig-killing clubs and masks.

The Treasure Chest, whose main shop is at Le Lagon, always has a good range of carvings and artefacts for sale, including examples from the Solomon Islands. Its other branch is at the Iririki Island Resort.

Duty-Free Stores You'll find a number of shops selling duty-free products in the main street between the market and just beyond the ANZ Bank.

Probably the best range in town is offered by Fung Kuei, next door to the ANZ Bank, which carries cameras, electrical goods, watches, Chinese porcelain, gift ware, liquor and perfume, among other things.

If you're particularly interested in jewellery and watches, both Tiffany's, next to the Cultural Centre, and the Sound Centre across from the ANZ are worth trying.

Paris Shopping, across from the GPO, and Proud's, opposite the French Embassy, both specialise in French imports. Their perfume and cosmetics counters are very tantalising. The French Perfumery in the Centre Point building next to the Centre Point Supermarket is another good spot for these items.

La Cave du Gourmet, opposite the Banque d'Hawaii, is probably the best place to go for wines, spirits and French crystal.

Chinese Stores Generally speaking, Vila's Chinese shops (most of which are concentrated in the area known as Chinatown) are chock-a-block with an amazing range of goods. In any given store you may find anything from Japanese stereos and watches to straw hats, Chinese cigarettes and balls of wool. Prices are often a lot cheaper here than on the main street, so have a good look around before you start spending. These are probably the best places to buy minor camping equipment if you haven't brought your own.

Getting There & Away

All international flights, and most cargo boats and yachts, arrive at Vila to clear customs and immigration. See the introductory Getting There & Away chapter for details on international flights and ships to and from Vila.

Within Vanuatu, most of the larger islands have several flights a week to and from Vila, or a connection via Luganville on Santo. Tanna, Luganville and Norsup in Malakula have daily air services to and from Vila. Even the smallest islands are connected at least weekly to the capital, provided, of course, that they have an airfield.

The northern islands (that is, between Vila and Luganville) and the Tafea region to the south are connected to the capital by weekly or fortnightly cargo-boat services. Also see the Getting Around chapter.

Getting Around

To/From the Airport Airport shuttle buses cost 400VT per person to or from Vila. Alternatively, if you don't have much luggage, you can catch a minibus for 70VT or a cab for around 600VT to the town centre.

Minibuses are not allowed to pick you up outside the main terminus doors as this area is reserved for taxis and shuttle buses. Instead, all you have to do is to walk about 100 metres to the start of the exit road towards Vila and wave the first bus down. If there are no buses around, walk 1.6 km to the Tagabe roundabout and catch one there.

Whenever you need to go back to the airport from town, flag a minibus down and ask the driver if you can be taken there. If the driver says yes, ask how much it'll cost before getting in.

Minibus The cheapest way around Vila is to travel by 14-seater minibus. They come in all colours and usually the only way you can tell them from private vehicles is by the red letter 'B' beside their number plates.

The main routes into the town centre are usually thick with minibuses between 6 am and 7.30 pm; all you do is flag them down at a bus stop or anywhere else along the roadside where it isn't dangerous for them to stop. Fares are a uniform 70VT wherever you go within the wider town area, unless you want them to divert far from their usual circuit. Then 30VT extra should be sufficient. It is best if you can offer correct change.

Taxi There are over 200 taxis operating in Vila, and as there's sufficient work for only 70 or so the service tends to be very competitive. At the same time, however, the fact that most drivers are paying their cabs off forces some of the less successful to cheat. Apart from blatantly ripping you off, a common ploy is to pretend to have no change.

There are a couple of things to be aware of when hiring a taxi in Vila. First, for town trips make sure the meter is turned on – beware of cabs with their meters concealed in any way. All taxis should have working meters and the driver's ID card and photo should be clearly displayed.

Second, if you're going on a longer trip you should ask how much the fare will be before committing yourself. If it sounds high ask someone else. Always pay the fare stated, no more and no less.

The Taxi Centre (☎ 25135) in Nambatu offers a 24-hour service, but charges you the fare from the depot to your pick-up point as well as to your destination. Vila's main taxi stands are beside the marketplace and Iririki Wharf. The minimum cab fare is 100VT.

Moped Island Stream Rentals (☎ 22470), at the town end of Wharf Rd, rents out 50 cc mopeds for 500/2200/9200/15,000VT an hour/day/week/month plus 1000VT for insurance. This includes a crash helmet. Rentals are limited to daylight hours and the Vila area.

Club Marine (☎ 24952, 26660), near the Iririki Wharf, has motor scooters for hire at rates ranging from 1000VT for one hour to 3500VT for a full day.

Car Rental There are four car-hire companies in Vila, and all of them offer the luxury of collision damage waivers. Remember to make sure you read and understand the insurance conditions before renting, because an accident without protection will quite likely knock a huge hole in your holiday funds.

Competition can be very fierce and different packages are offered. It would be wise and sit down and really study the figures, but on the face of it, the cheapest rates are offered by Thrifty. The smallest four-seaters offered by Thrifty cost 3800VT per day for one to two days, plus 1100VT per day collision damage waiver. This includes driving for upwards of 160 km per day, after which you pay 25VT per km. The good news is that you're unlikely to do more than 160 km in a day unless you drive around the island and make a few extensive detours en route.

But, on reflection, there's really not a lot in it. Hertz, probably the most expensive car-hire companies, rents its smallest vehicles for 5100VT per day for one to two days, plus 1300VT waiver. With them you get unlimited kms.

As for tempting deals, Budget and Discount Rentals both offer a free night's accommodation at the Takara Beachcomber in north Efate for car rentals of two days or more. Discount Rentals will also give you one free day's rental if you take a vehicle for between three and six days.

Only Hertz has a desk at the airport. In town, Hertz (☎ 25700, 25600) has its main office on the Route de Téouma in Stade, Budget (☎ 23170) is in the Iririki Centre Ville courtyard, as is Discount Rentals (☎ 23242). Thrifty (☎ 23228) has an office in the Handikraf blong Vanuatu at the Cultural Centre.

Bicycle Sportzpower (☎ 26326) near the Rossi Restaurant has bicycles for hire at 1300VT a day or part thereof. There's also a tandem available for 1600VT per day.

Walking Almost all destinations in Vila's central area are only five minutes apart by bus, or 20 minutes on foot. Traffic drives on the right, so beware if you are not used to this. Also the hilly terrain away from the shore can be tough on your leg muscles, but it's worth persisting for the fine views. After a few fattening meals in the cafés and restaurants you'll probably need the exercise!

Vila's streets are mostly poorly lit at night, and some of the potholes seem like tank traps; until you've learned where the main pitfalls are, it's a good idea to carry a torch.

AROUND PORT VILA

Just outside Vila are a number of interesting, easily accessible places, several of which are definitely worth visiting.

For example, if you're looking for peaceful tropical surroundings in which to forget the workaday world, a day on Erakor or Mele (Hideaway) Islands is hard to beat. The snorkelling around Mele Island is excellent, while the Mele-Maat Cascades are one of the prettiest spots in the whole of Efate. If you

want to go swimming, Black Sand and Mele Beaches are popular with local people.

Distances given in the following section are from the post office in central Vila.

Ifira Island

Also known as Fila Island, Ifira is a 10-minute speedboat ride from central Vila. The island is only half a sq km, yet has 600 people living on it.

Ifirans are the traditional owners of Iririki Island and therefore its resort, and also own a sizeable amount of the commercially valuable land in Vila. This right to ownership puts them quite firmly among the country's wealthiest ni-Vanuatu people. The Ifirans are known for their fine handicrafts, which include a variety of model canoes, bows, arrows and an assortment of multipronged fishing spears.

Ifirans have a similar dialect to Rotumans, the people of a small, isolated Polynesian island north-east of, and governed by, Fiji. Some Ifirans are descended from Samoan missionaries and thus claim a relationship with that country. Although most Ifirans are physically similar to Melanesians, they contend that their ancestors reached southern Efate before any Melanesians did, and that intermarriage has produced their dark skin. Against all the odds their original language has somehow remained intact.

As elsewhere in Vanuatu, it is etiquette that visitors should see the chief first to ask permission to swim or perhaps explore. If you're respectful and dressed tidily he will probably say yes.

Things to See There's a secluded and charming beach on the island's southern side and, in front of the village, a sandy strip of beach facing Iririki Island. Beside the church are the forlorn graves of a number of early missionaries. The site also include the buried remains of the first Ifiran chief to be converted to Christianity.

Getting There & Away There are a number of speedboats and cruisers travelling back and forth between Iriki Wharf and Ifira Island throughout the daylight hours. Ask one of the boatmen if he'll take you over. The usual fare is about 100VT each way.

Pango Point Area

This road travels from Vila southwards through Ensaar; Pango is two km beyond. Five hundred metres before Pango the road passes one of the largest banyan trees around Vila – it's a monster with a canopy at least 70 metres across. Once you get to the village be careful of the speed bumps.

Pango (5.5 km) The village gets its name from the Samoan missionaries who arrived here in the 1840s. They came from Pago-Pago (pronounced Pango-Pango) in what is now American Samoa.

Pango people were less prepared than Erakor and Ifiran islanders to accept oncoming Christianity and the resulting new order that was soon to be thrust upon them. They preferred to stick to timeless traditions, which included the slaughtering and eating of a trading party of 21 Moso Islanders in 1852.

The main cottage industry here is the

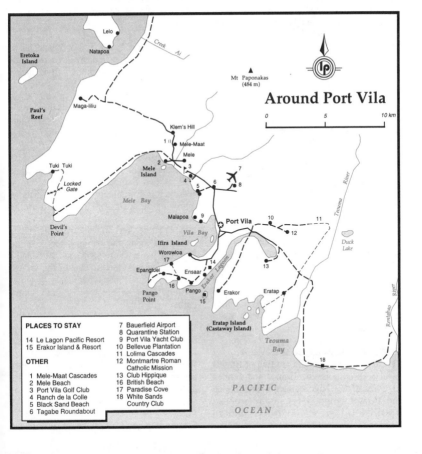

PLACES TO STAY

14 Le Lagon Pacific Resort
15 Erakor Island & Resort

OTHER

1 Mele-Maat Cascades
2 Mele Beach
3 Port Vila Golf Club
4 Ranch de la Colle
5 Black Sand Beach
6 Tagabe Roundabout

7 Bauerfield Airport
8 Quarantine Station
9 Port Vila Yacht Club
10 Bellevue Plantation
11 Lolima Cascades
12 Montmartre Roman
   Catholic Mission
13 Club Hippique
16 British Beach
17 Paradise Cove
18 White Sands
   Country Club

weaving of mats and bags from pandanus leaves. Fishing is another important activity – you'll see a large bamboo fishtrap jutting out from the shore just before you reach Pango. There are several similar traps scattered along the coastline here.

A sign says that outsiders who wish to swim or enjoy the privacy of the beaches in this area must pay 100VT per vehicle. There's often moderate but consistent surf, although the coral reefs can be dangerous. Ask the villagers if you want to ride the waves.

Several tracks cut northwards through the thick bush just beyond Pango. One of these crosses the peninsula to Paradise Cove, a popular sunbathing and snorkelling spot for charter boat groups. The villagers will be happy to give you directions.

For more details on scuba diving and snorkelling sites, see the following Dive Sites In & Around Mele Bay.

You can visit Pango either independently by minibus from Vila or with Aliat Wi Tours on their regular day tours and Melanesian feast nights. The manager of this company is from Pango.

British Beach (6.5 km) This cove was a popular picnic spot for British residents in Condominium days. Villagers use it for fishing and you should ask at Pango for permission to visit.

Epangtuei (9 km) The road is blocked by a gate at Epangtuei, which is the original site of Pango village. Although the gate is often left open, you should ask permission at Pango if you want to go through it to Pango Point. A secluded sandy beach and opportunities for snorkelling and diving are its main attractions.

Erakor & Emden Lagoons
To the south-east of Vila are two of Efate's most scenic spots, the Erakor and Emden lagoons. Erakor Lagoon is sometimes called the First Lagoon. Beyond the wooden Tassiriki Bridge, it's known as Emden Lagoon (or Second Lagoon).

Club Hippique (8 km) Located on the southeastern shore of Emden Lagoon, this popular horse-riding school offers trail rides through the bush above the lagoon. See Port Vila's Activities section for more details.

Erakor Island (4.5 km) At the mouth of Erakor Lagoon lies Erakor Island, one of the jewels of Vila. The island is long, narrow, more-or-less flat and covers about nine hectares.

Polynesian religious teachers arrived here in 1845, and 15 years later Erakor Island was a mission stronghold. Between 1872 and 1893 two Presbyterian missionaries, Reverend and Mrs McKenzie, lived and taught here.

Things to See & Do Erakor Island has a white sandy beach near the resort at its northern end, while the southern half is like a natural botanic garden of infinite variety. If you don't plan to leave Vila, a quiet stroll around this beautiful island will give you a tantalising glimpse of what many other islets in the archipelago are like. The old mission site (the McKenzies' graves are nearby) is a popular place for open-air weddings. Mrs McKenzie and her three infant children, as well as two Samoan teachers, are buried nearby. It is possible to visit their graves by following the main walking track from the hotel.

At low tide you can walk from the end of the island along the fringing reef over to Erakor Village, whose people are the island's custom owners. One km east of the village along a footpath is another sandy beach at Ekapum Inlet, where there's good swimming.

Getting There & Away There is a 24-hour free ferry service that links the Erakor Island Resort to the mainland at a small jetty just south of Le Lagon. To summon the ferry across from the island, the trick is to simply press the buzzer at the landward end of the jetty.

Erakor Village (5.5 km) The Erakor Island

Top: Sunset at Mele Island (AV)
Middle: Canoe park on beach (DO)
Bottom: Mele Island (AV)

A: Sun setting on the Pacific (AV)
B: Coconuts grown to produce copra (DO)
C: Champagne Beach, Espiritu Santo Island (AV)
D: Le Lagon Pacific Resort, Port Vila (AV)

villagers lived there until 1959, where they canoed to the mainland on a daily basis to tend their gardens. A cyclone in that year levelled their huts and, as a result, the people set up present-day Erakor Village on the ridge just across the lagoon. You'll often see the villagers fishing from dugout canoes in the waters around the island.

Other Destinations

Worowloa (5 km) Two km beyond the main wharf is Worowloa's pleasant quiet beach. Although the village faces Vila Bay, the beach is behind it facing the open ocean. Sometimes you can see people spearfishing in the shallows between the beach and nearby Ifira Island.

Lolima Cascades (10 km) Just north of Emden Lagoon are these year-round flowing cascades. To get there, turn northwards onto the unpaved Route de Bouffa about 500 metres beyond the new USP complex. The road passes below the Bellevue Plantation's French-style, white-timbered homestead.

Shortly before the Montmartre Roman Catholic mission, you'll see a track branching northwards which ultimately turns into a footpath leading towards the falls. Seek permission from any villagers you see to visit the cascades, and ask them to point out the route. One of them may be prepared to show you the way – you may need a guide along the footpath for the 2.5 km from the end of the track through the bush to the waterside. The cascades have several large pools and a persistently strong flow of water.

Bauerfield Airport (4 km & 1.6 km side-road) West of Vila, and half a km beyond the quarantine station and agricultural school, is the US-built WW II airfield which now serves as Vila's international airport. There's a plaque inside the terminal commemorating Lt Colonel Bauer, a US fighter ace who was based here in 1942.

Black Sand Beach (4.5 km & 1.5 km side-track) Turning left at the Tagabe roundabout,

the road to Mele passes a plantation containing stud herds of sand-coloured Limousin cattle. Half a km further, on the left, is the dirt road to Kaweriki village and Black Sand Beach.

During WW II, US marines regularly practised beach-landing techniques both here and further east at Mele Beach prior to the real thing in the Solomons and New Guinea.

Ranch de la Colle (6.7 km) The horse riding school is on the south side of the road. See Port Vila's Activities section for more details.

Port Vila Golf Club (8.4 km) The club house for Vanuatu's principal golf course is on the south side of the road. Visitors are welcome, and you can also use nearby Black Sand Beach.

Mele Village (9 km) Turn right at the crossroads to get to Efate's largest village. Mele has grown considerably since its founders evacuated nearby Mele Island after the devastating 1959 cyclone. Although the original inhabitants were descended from Tongans, many others have Samoan ancestry, or have come more recently from French-ruled Wallis Island. Despite intermarriage with Melanesians, many of the people have retained their Polynesian language and their unique customs.

Mele (Hideaway) Island (9.5 km) The short dirt road on the left, almost opposite the turn-off to Mele village, leads down to Mele Beach, which is a continuation of Black Sand Beach. Barely 200 metres across the water is the Hideaway Island Resort. A nice touch is provided by a flagpole on the beach. It carries a sign in Bislama that invites you and your party to raise the flag to summon the ferry. There is an entry fee of 500VT payable at the bar.

Mele Island may only be about two hectares but those hectares are covered with dense tropical growth cut by narrow, and at times, barely passable, pathways. Just offshore is the best potential for snorkelling close to Vila. On the edge of the reef you'll find a bewildering variety of corals in shades of blue, purple, green, yellow, maroon and brown, as well as swarms of colourful, friendly fish. You can hire snorkelling gear at the dive shop for 800VT a day, or take a ride over the reef in a glass-bottom boat for 1000VT.

Mele-Maat (10.5 km) In early 1951, 300 villagers from Maat in south-eastern Ambrym were resettled here after a volcanic eruption engulfed their homes and gardens.

The pretty Mele-Maat Cascades is nearby, immediately before the hairpin bend at the base of Klem's Hill. Entry is subject to a fee of 250/500VT per child/adult, and if you want a guide it'll be 200VT extra.

From the parking area, you follow the path past small cascades and crystal-clear pools to a 20-metre-high waterfall shaded by rainforest. Beside it is a small grotto where villagers catch freshwater crayfish and prawns in season. The large tree in the pool below the waterfall was dumped there by a landslide after a cyclone in 1994.

Devil's Point (22 km) Instead of turning inland to Mele-Maat and following the main road around Efate, continue straight on along the gravel road to Devil's Point. The road ends at the point, which is too rough and rocky for swimming. However, if you turn right just before the ruins near the point you'll come to a coral beach that fronts a sheltered cove. The largish ruin here was once a plantation homestead.

Dive Sites In & Around Mele Bay

There's a host of scuba sites in Mele Bay, at Pango Point and north of Devil's Point, and more are being discovered all the time. These include wrecks, coral gardens, fish colonies and interesting topography, with several being shallow enough for snorkellers.

Paul's Reef Located to the south of Magaliliu, Paul's Reef is about 400 metres offshore and only four metres below the surface. The reef, which has grown around an extinct submarine volcano, features several tunnel swim-throughs, sheer plunging walls, coral gardens and abundant fish life. There is a custom tabu against fishing here because bad spirits make it too dangerous.

Tuki Tuki This is one of Vanuatu's most exciting and spectacular dive spots thanks to its amazing topography of enormous chasms and swim-throughs. The visibility is usually excellent.

Maringa Reef This small shallow reef, six to 12 metres down, has a large, colourful range of soft and hard corals including purples, pinks, reds and greens. Maringa Reef is sometimes called House-maid's Reef because of its rather picturesque 'feather duster' worms that reveal themselves at night.

Gotham City This intriguing and colourful reef was just as intriguingly named for its large population of curious bat fish. There are an amazing array of fish life and some strikingly beautiful corals found here.

Mele Reef Surrounding Mele Island like a horseshoe, this reef is home to a profusion of undersea life: coral growths, small tropical fish and large pelagic creatures from the deep. This very fecund reef also has great masses of black gorgonia fans on the coral rock wall at the reef's southern side. In other places you're just as likely to see black coral whips.

The whole area of reef is a sanctuary, and it has many shallows. It's a rewarding spot for snorkellers, but unfortunately, the most illuminating areas are a little too far to swim out from the island.

Black Sand Reef This reef is also known as Ghost Train. Its large coral outcrops, complete with a number of caves and tunnels, make for an extremely popular dive spot just off Black Sand Beach.

MV *Konanda* Sitting upright on the seabed and only 24 metres down is this former 45-metre island trader. Scuttled in 1987, its upper works are less than five metres down, so they can be explored by snorkellers.

Semle Federesen This 46-metre cargo vessel was sunk as a dive site in 1985 after many years of inter-island service. The stern, cabins and wheel- house all lie in 39 metres of water, with the bow 10 metres deeper down. It's the best wreck dive near Vila and is suitable only for experienced divers.

Big Bommies Near Epangtuei is a group of large, fan-covered coral heads in about 30 metres of water. It's easily the best chance to see this type of coral in Mele Bay. You may find, however, that visiting the coral heads may depend on the weather.

The Cathedral Off the tip of Pango Point is a whole warren of underwater holes, flutes, elevations, stipples and tunnels. The formation looks remarkably like an underwater cathedral, about 20 metres down. This is one of the most interesting dives in Mele Bay.

1 MV *Konanda* Wreck
2 *Star of Russia* Wreck
3 Sunken Drop Front Barge
4 *Resolution* Wreck
5 *Tasman* Wreck
6 Quai Wharf
7 Star Wharf
8 Main Wharf
9 *Semle Federesen* Wreck

Paul's Reef

Maga-liliu

Mele

Mele Island
(Hideaway Island)

Gotham
City

Mele
Reef

Acropora Reef

Kaweriki

Tuki
Tuki

Maringa Reef

Black Sand
Reef

Tebakor

The Caves

Malapoa
Point

Melcofe
Reef

Malapoa Reef

*Vila
Bay*

Port Vila

The Cabbage Patch

Ifira Island

Iririki
Island

Devil's Point

*PACIFIC

OCEAN*

The Pinnacles

1

3

2

4

5

Island Reef

8 7 6

Twin Bommies

Worowioa

Erakor Lagoon

Big Bommies

9

Epangtuei

Pango

Erakor
Island

Pango Point

Erakor

**Dive Sites In &
Around Mele Bay**

The Cathedral

0   3   6 km

AROUND EFATE
Getting There & Away
The central point for arrivals and departures in Efate is Port Vila. See the Port Vila Getting There & Away section for details.

Getting Around
The coastal route around Efate is 138 km and you can do it with one of the regular tours, hire a car, take a taxi or hitchhike. There's plenty to see and do along the way, and you have the option to visit some of the off-shore islands if you're travelling independently.

Tour Groups Aliat Wi Tours, Frank King Tours, Tour Vanuatu and Tropical Adventure Tours all do full-day bus trips around the island. These take place most days, except when a cruise ship is in port, and cost around 4000VT for adults. The tours pass through villages, subsistence gardens and huge, largely abandoned coconut plantations, stopping to allow you to enjoy the coastal views and to swim at some of its secluded beaches.

Hire Cars The best way to get around and at the same time have the day to yourself is to rent a car. You can easily do the circuit in a day, but if you want to stop and see everything – as well as enjoy the occasional swim or walk – you should allow for at least one overnight stop.

Taxi A daytime round trip by taxi costs about 8000VT, which is a relatively cheap way of seeing the island if there's three or more passengers. The best approach is to find a driver who speaks good English or French and who has a reliable-looking vehicle. Ask him for his price, and if this is acceptable arrange for him to pick you up early the next morning. You may find that the people at your hotel can recommend a driver, so ask them first.

There are advantages in taking a cab in preference to either a bus tour or hire car. First, if it breaks down or has an accident it's the driver's worry, not yours. Second, if your driver is a good guide you'll learn quite a bit

about the island as you travel around. Third, you can stop whenever you want to.

Hitching The road is normally quiet but you may be lucky if you want to hitchhike. Generally, however, the private vehicles that use the road are already full of people. Remember that well-stocked stores and supermarkets are scarce outside Vila, as most people live off their own garden produce.

Efate Mainland
It may pay to bear in mind that most facilities in Efate are concentrated in Vila. These facilities include a health clinic at Paunagisu, which is located in the north, and small resorts at Paunagisu, Takara and White Sands Beach. You'll find that most villages along the way have small convenience stores. Here you'll be able to purchase a collection of foodstuffs including cool drinks and canned food. However, vehicle fuel and puncture repair facilities are unfortunately only available in Vila. If you're going by vehicle, it's wise to make sure to fill the tank as well as thoroughly checking the spare tyre and jacking equipment before setting out.

Almost the entire route around Efate is unsealed. It goes without saying then that much of it is poorly maintained. As a result, it's often rough and rugged and occasionally washed out. This applies particularly on the island's western and northern sides. It's fortunate that the traffic is normally light, but as the road tends to be narrow with numerous blind corners, it's unlikely you'll be able to travel at any sort of speed. In fact, the maximum safe speed is usually only 40 km/h and often less.

There is another important point to remember and that is, when wet, the road is impassable to conventional vehicles that are travelling in a clockwise direction around the island. The reason for this is because of the steep, slippery hills your vehicle has to climb.

The following distances given in this section are clockwise from the Port Vila post office. Again, it is wise you remember that the major points of interest closer than 11 km and Devil's Point are described in the Around Vila section.

Klem's Hill (11 km) The road leaves the coastal plains after Mele-Maat and climbs sharply to 200 metres above sea level. Near the top is a parking bay from where you get a superb view over extensive coconut plantations on the coastal plain towards Vila and Mele Island.

Klem's Hill apparently gets its name from the US engineer who supervised the construction of the road during WW II.

Seven km further, by which time the sealed road has given way to gravel, you crest another steep hill to see Eretoka, Lelepa and Moso Islands and Havannah Harbour stretching before you. You may see the charter yacht *Coongoola* tied up at its usual anchorage off the southern end of Lelepa Island.

Maga-liliu (18 km & 2 km sidetrack) The beach at this small village is the spot from where the body of 13th century Chief Roymata was carried by canoe to its final resting place on nearby Eretoka (Hat) Island.

Manga'asi (18.5 km) Hidden in the bush between the road and the sea is the long-abandoned site of the capital of ancient Efate. First occupied around 500 AD, the settlement reached its zenith under Chief Roymata's benevolent rule in the 1250s. It went into decline following his death, but wasn't finally abandoned until about 1700. Ask one of the local villagers if they'll show you the site.

Lelepa Landing (22 km) The small, open landing area is where you can get a speedboat ride across the Hilliard Channel to Lelepa Island. This will cost you around 1000VT return. If no one's there when you arrive, sound your car horn or bash on the gas cylinder that's hung up in a tree for that purpose. The villagers will hear you across the water and come over. For more informa-

tion on Lelepa Island see the section later in this chapter.

There are untended wayside fruit stalls at several places near here and further north. You pay your money into the small honesty boxes placed beside the produce. The number '1' means 10VT, '2' equals 20VT and so on.

Samoa Point (28 km) The north-west tip of Efate has many sandy coves interspersed with rocky headlands. One of these, named after the Polynesian missionaries who taught here in the late 1840s, is Samoa Point. Used in WW II as a US seaplane base, it's now a pleasant swimming spot by a small sandy beach. There's good snorkelling in shallow water on the Vila side of the point.

Ulei (30.5 km) Pronounced 'Oo-lie', this village is on the site of the former Havannah Harbour settlement. This was Efate's main population centre until a combination of drought, collapsing world cotton prices and malaria drove the European settlers to Vila in the early 1880s.

Havannah Harbour earned its name from HMS *Havannah*, the first British warship to regularly patrol the archipelago. Its narrow eastern end is an ideal location for fishing, snorkelling and other water-related activities.

Ulei came back to life in WW II. This was the time when US warships formed up in Havannah Harbour's protected waters prior to the critical Battle of the Coral Sea in mid-1942. Later, the Americans used the area as a naval base.

On the seaward side of the road near central Ulei is the American Pool, which used to serve as a water source for the ships in Havannah Harbour. Just beyond the American Pool is an old wartime jetty from where you can see the shiny wing of a sunken US seaplane only five metres below the surface. The rest of the aircraft is scattered a little further out in 27 metres of water.

One km beyond, on the inland side of the road, is a ruined building that was used as a US navy officers' mess.

The coconut plantations start again 32 km from Vila and keep you company most of the way from here to beyond Eton, on the south-eastern coast.

Siviri (40 km) A road bears northwards off the main road through a coconut grove to Siviri, half a km beyond. Just before the village, and behind a modern pump house, is the Valeafau Cave. This small, moist cavern has many interesting formations as well as a freshwater lake. It is said that an expedition of scuba divers once travelled five km into it before turning back.

Permission to enter may be gained at the pump house. The cave has an interesting custom story and your guide will be happy to tell you about it.

There are magnificent views from Siviri across Undine Bay towards Nguna, Pele, Kakula and Emao Islands. There's also a thick stretch of onshore reef in front of the village. At low tide you can use it to walk across to Moso Island.

Paunagisu (51.5 km) The seaside village of Paunagisu is noted for its carved ceremonial clubs. The Nagar Resort (see below) is the best spot to arrange a speedboat ride across to the islands. For prices see the Getting There & Away section for the Nagar Resort.

The modest but friendly *Nagar Resort* (☎ 23221) on the beachfront at Paunagisu is one of the best places to hang out in the whole of Efate. Two of its four fan-cooled bungalows sleep two people for 2,200VT per bungalow and the others sleep four for 7700VT, both rates including a continental breakfast. For a small fee you can pitch a tent in the attractive grounds.

The resort sells all meals to casual visitors at very sensible prices, with lunch and dinner starting at 550VT. You can eat either in the licensed restaurant, or alfresco on the beach with a view across to nearby Kakula and Pele Islands. The resort also offers a variety of interesting and very inexpensive activities such as bushwalks, picnics, fishing, canoeing and visits to nearby villages. Attractive

two-and three-day packages are available, including transfers from Vila.

Getting There & Away The one-way taxi fare from Vila to Paunagisu is about 4000VT. Alternatively, if there's a spare seat, you may be able to get a ride with one of the tour coaches on their round-Efate trips. Otherwise contact the resort and ask if they know of anyone who can give you a lift.

Return, shared speedboat rides cost 2000VT to Kakula Island, 3000VT to Pele Island and 4000VT to Nguna Island. It's best to ring the resort first and arrange your ride to suit the tides.

Quoin Hill (55 km) The US wartime fighter strip at Quoin Hill is nowadays only used by light aircraft. The most prominent feature at the roadside end of the runway is a concrete sentry box.

Bauvatu (55 km & 0.5 km sidetrack) Two US WW II fighter planes lie in the shallows close to this French-speaking village. Apparently they ran out of fuel coming in to land at Quoin Hill.

Takara (56 km) Takara is a quiet, windswept spot that's popular with Vila residents on weekends. From the beach there's a fine view of nearby Emao Island, an extinct volcano. Looking beyond Emao you can see towering, pinnacle-shaped Mataso Island with smaller Etarik (Monument Rock) on the right. American pilots used the latter as a target to calibrate their machine guns during WW II. In the distance are the beckoning, misty outlines of the rest of the Shepherds Group.

Just south of the Takara Beachcomber bungalows is a swimming pool. It's kept filled with water pumped from a hot spring. You can go scuba diving by arrangement, or fir the adventurous, snorkel on a nearby WW II plane wreck. Bottom-reef fishing can also be arranged at 2500VT per hour for the boat and basic gear.

The *Takara Beachcomber* (☎ 23576) is on the shore and has six fan-cooled, blockwork bungalows, a bar and restaurant. The bungalows, which sleep four and eight, cost from 4250/5600VT for singles/doubles. Breakfast starts at 350VT and lunch and dinner each cost upwards of 800VT.

Getting There & Away Air transfers from Vila to Quoin Hill in a four-seater plane can be arranged for 8000VT return, shared. Otherwise access details are as for Nagar Resort, above.

Speedboat rides to Wiana on Emao cost 5000VT return in a 10-seater boat, but you need to arrange this in advance.

Saraa (59 km) The village has a minimarket selling local fruits and vegetables, processed foods and handicrafts.

Some of Efate's best scenery lies along the road between Saraa and Forari. One minute you're passing close to small beaches with grassy shores that alternate with coral rock fringed by cyclone-tattered she-oaks. The next you're driving through overgrown coconut plantations, thick bush and enormous banyans that overhang the road. It's obvious from the vegetation that the eastern coast is much wetter than the regions you've just come through, particularly the northwest.

Epau (69 km) This is a large village with many dwellings, some of which are made of local materials and others of corrugated iron sheets. As elsewhere in Vanuatu, people with money build with iron and concrete blocks, while those who are less well off make do with thatch.

There's a rest stop here selling refreshments and handicrafts. On the roadside is a sign advertising a visit to Pounarup Cave for 200/500VT per child/adult. It promises 'an adventurous chance that you should never miss'.

Forari (81 km) A manganese mine operated at Forari from 1961 to 1978. For a short time afterwards, pozzolana, a type of volcanic ash used in making hydraulic cements, was also extracted. Since then the town that once

housed 1000 people has been abandoned, and reclaimed by the bush. You can get there by following the old powerline, but thick bush makes it difficult to reach.

On the shore is a huge ship-loading gantry which formerly conveyed manganese ore straight into the holds of waiting ships. This was turned into a heap of twisted scrap by cyclone Prima in 1992. From here, a rusted conveyor system leads inland to the open-cut mine.

Manuro Point (83 km & 4 km sideroad) Two km past the old wharf, a turn-off takes you east, past the village of Poi to Manuro Point, where a track heads south to the abandoned Manuro Paradise Club Resort. The thatch buildings are in a pleasant grassed area beside a small beach.

There are plans to resurrect the resort. In the meantime, check at Poi as to whether or not you can camp there.

La Cressonnière Cascades (87.5 km) The road crosses the Ewor River just beside these small cascades. Inland from here, but shrouded in bush, are a collection of hot springs. You can ask at the farmhouse if you'd like to visit them.

Eton (90.5 km) Shortly before this village is one of Efate's most attractive beaches. It has an abundance of soft white sand and there is plenty of good swimming. The entry fee of 500VT per car can be paid at the house beside the parking area.

Eton Blue Hole (91.5 km) Just south of Eton, and on the eastern side of the road, is a deep blue hole, which is fed by the ocean. However, it is partially concealed by a number of trees and is easy to miss. Scuba divers come here to observe the large fish, including sharks, that collect near its entrance. This area is owned by Eton village, so ask there for permission before taking the plunge.

Past Eton you enter cattle country. From here almost to Vila much of the forest and coconut plantations have been cleared and the region is now under lush pasture.

Dry Creek (96 km) Also known as Banana Beach, this is an ideal spot for a picnic in calm weather – and because it's a public beach you don't have to ask permission or pay a fee.

Rentabao River (111 km) The bridge here has a hazardous approach, so take it slowly. Locals refer to it as 'the river where the Japanese died', alluding to a fatal crash that claimed the lives of several Japanese tourists. Their car failed to take the bend and went over the bridge into the flooded stream.

Three km past the bridge, a resort is being constructed at an area known as the Blue Holes. Whether it will ever open is a topic of much local speculation.

St Francis' Beach (118 km) Also known as Tessa's Beach and Public Beach, this small stretch of sand boasts a quiet lagoon and is another good picnic spot. On the rocks at the eastern end is a large rusted boiler, all that remains of the steamer *Bucéphale*.

White Sands Beach (121.5 km) This rather exposed beach has a tattered fringe of screw-trunked pandanus palms. For details on the nearby White Sands Country Club see the section on Port Vila, earlier in this chapter.

Teouma Bay (125 km) Some people will tell you that this sheltered little cove isn't safe for swimming because of sharks; once there was an abattoir here, and the sharks are said to be still hanging around looking for a feed. Others will laugh at the tale. Who is correct? Dive in and find out.

Teouma River (129 km) This, Efate's largest river, drains from Mt MacDonald in the island's north. Near the bridge, the plantations have been cleared to make way for crops of squash grown for the Japanese market. The deep water at the bridge makes it a popular swimming spot.

Eratap Island (130 km & 4 km on foot) Half a km beyond the bridge over the Teouma River is a track southwards through Eratap to tiny Eratap Island. This is a picnic spot for boat tours, which advertise it as Castaway Island.

From the turn-off, central Vila is about eight km away.

Eretoka, Lelepa & Moso Islands

These small islands sit just off Efate's north-western shore.

Eretoka Island With a multitude of spellings, uninhabited Eretoka is also called Chapeau, or Hat Island, because from a distance that is exactly what the island looks like.

The legendary Chief Roymata conquered coastal Efate and its northern neighbours including the Shepherds group in the 1250s, which helped to bring a long period of peace to the region. Following his death in about 1265, his body was taken to Eretoka where his 18 chiefs, their 21 wives and Roymata's own wife were buried alive beside him. Most went willingly, though a few reluctant ones had to be killed first. It was easier for the men, who were first stupefied with a super-strong brew of kava. Apparently, by all accounts, the women were not given the salve of kava.

Once the funeral was over, Roymata's burial place was declared tabu. In the late 1960s a French archaeologist, José Garanger, decided to test the local legends. He subsequently took it upon himself to excavate the site. Garanger found 41 skeletons, one of which had many rings around its feet. The corpse was also wearing a valuable necklace, which indicated chieftaincy. Obviously, this could only be the legendary Roymata.

For the detailed history of Roymata and his burial, the best place to start is to visit the Cultural Centre in Vila.

The graves are clearly marked by stone walls surrounding the site. However, it is best to first ask the Lelepa chief's permission to visit them.

The island is surrounded by extremely clear water, often with 50-metre visibility. Large ocean fish, coral gardens, underwater caves and deep crevasses make for excellent diving. There are also some shallows at either end suitable for snorkelling.

Eretoka is reached from Lelepa (see Lelepa Landing under in the Efate Mainland section). A speedboat ride from Lelepa to Eretoka is around 4000VT over and above your return charter trip to Lelepa Landing. However, you'll need permission from the chief at Lelepa before you go. If he won't approve your visit, Sailaway Cruises and South Pacific Cruises both include the island on their regular tours from Vila.

Lelepa Island Formerly called Protection Island, Lelepa has about 500 inhabitants who live mainly at Natapao on the south coast.

On the island's eastern side is a long sandy beach with a wrecked US WW II Corsair fighter in the bush beyond. Much of Lelepa's south-eastern coast, and also part of its northern shore, is fringed by beautiful coral gardens.

Of particular significance is Feles Cave, a very large, deep cavern in compressed ash and calcium on the coast west of Natapao. The legendary chief, Roymata, is believed to have died here in about 1265. High up on its rocky walls are black wall-paintings of men, fish and birds which have been dated to approximately 900 AD. You can visit the cave with Sailaway Cruises, of Vila, who give a particularly good commentary.

On the island's northern tip are the remains of a WW II anti-aircraft gun emplacement, with a crashed Corsair a short distance away. There's a classic white beach on the shore facing Mallao Bay in the north-west. The bay offers good snorkelling for novices.

Lelepa people are proposing to build a guest house overlooking the beach on Mallao Bay.

To get to/from Lelepa, catch a speedboat at Lelepa Landing. See the Lelepa Landing section, above, for details.

Moso Island Known formerly as Deception or Verao Island, Moso has only one village, called Sunae, and about 200 people.

Deep caves pit the uplifted coral cliffs on the island's northern side. There's golden sand at the eastern end, and another small sandy beach in the south-west.

The coral reefs around Moso and neighbouring Nguna Island have been devastated by the crown-of-thorns starfish and are unlikely to recover before the turn of the century. Ask at Sunae if you want to dive anywhere around Moso.

To get to Moso Island, walk across from Siviri at low tide (see the Siviri section, above). Alternatively, you could try to charter a speedboat at Ulei, although there aren't many about.

Nguna, Pele, Kakula & Emao Islands

These high, steep-sided volcanic islands lie three to six km off the north coast of Efate. A fourth island – tiny Kakula – is only one km from Paunagisu. The major islands are stunningly beautiful and their inhabitants are invariably friendly and welcoming. Their generally upland terrain, cooling sea breezes and lack of marshland make them a particularly healthy part of Vanuatu.

There's a medical clinic at Silimoli on Nguna.

Nguna Island Although Captain Cook named it Montague Island, Nguna (pronounced 'Noona') is the name its residents have always known it by. Its large population, currently around 1000, has always enabled it to dominate its neighbours in Undine Bay.

Ngunese, a tongue with some Polynesian influences, is also the language of a number of regions of the various islands including Pele, Emao, the western side of Emae in the Shepherds group, and Efate's north-eastern corner.

History Prior to European contact, Nguna's main activity was war. In contrast to generally peaceful Efate, village fought village, particularly archrivals Utanlang and Tikilasoa.

As on so many of Vanuatu's islands in the past, there was great animosity between hill dwellers and coastal peoples. Conflicts frequently broke out over suspicions of fruit and yam stealing, or the causing of illnesses through suspected sorcery.

In the 19th century, fatal epidemics often accompanied the visit of a European ship. However, few of these were as catastrophic as the 1845 dysentery outbreak that followed a cannibal feast at Tikilasoa, Nguna's main village – 30 Utanlang men were the main course at this fateful meal.

Reverend Peter Milne of the New Zealand Presbyterian church arrived on the island in 1870. From this moment on, every established pattern of Nguna's life began to change.

Milne remained on the island for 54 years until his death in 1924. The severity of his regime ensured that Nguna people, as other islanders say, 'lost their custom' by converting to his very strict form of Presbyterianism.

Milne banned any activity on the Sabbath which could be described as play. In addition, he totally prohibited alcohol and tobacco. Even by the yardstick of his own times, Milne and his wife were extremely puritanical.

Things to See & Do There are excellent walking tracks on Nguna, which has a long white sandy beach on its north-western side. Tall cliffs on its northern coast fall sharply into the sea, while all is dominated by the extinct volcanos, Mt Taputaora and Mt Marow.

Nguna's two main overland routes diverge not far out of Tikilasoa. One follows the western shore as a footpath to Utanlang. The other is a vehicle track, branching off before Woralapa, and reaching Utanlang via Malaliu and Farealapa.

Tikilasoa, which has a 1.5-km sandy

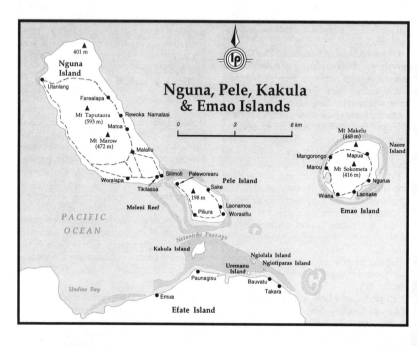

Nguna, Pele, Kakula & Emao Islands

beach, is commonly called 'Tiki' by the Ngunese. Reverend Milne made it his home for most of the time he was on Nguna, and his grave enjoys prominence in the village churchyard.

Set by a sheltered cove, Utanlang is the best place from which to climb 593-metre Mt Taputaora – the name is Polynesian for 'sacred grass', as reeds once grew on its flat summit. The climb is long and arduous, but you'll be rewarded with superb panoramas over the Shepherds and much of Efate.

You can climb 472-metre Mt Marow from Malaliu.

Getting There & Away A shared speedboat ride from Paunagisu to southern Nguna costs 4000VT return.

Pele Island Much of this island is extremely steep, offering little spare room for its 200-or-so inhabitants. And because of its over-population, there has been steady migration from Pele to Nguna's southern end.

As Pele is so close to Nguna, the people of both islands regard each other as coming from the same place. They believe the two will be joined together in due course, either by uplift or through the gradual growth of sandbanks. Already at low tide you can walk between their two closest points, although the practice isn't recommended because of stonefish.

There are some good walks on Pele, but you can't go all the way around, thanks to rocky outcrops and other obstacles. These are mainly on the north-eastern tip.

The island has white sand beaches at Piliura, Laonamoa, and Sake. Fishing isn't permitted.

A shared speedboat ride from Paunagisu to southern Pele costs 3000VT return.

Kakula Island This tiny, uninhabited cay is under lease for yet another resort development. It's connected by an extensive fringing reef to Efate's northern coast.

You can either get a ride in a speedboat for 2000VT return from Paunagisu, or walk across at low tide. If you do the latter, be careful not to step on a stonefish.

Emao Island Called Hinchinbrooke Island by Cook, Emao (pronounced 'Ee-Maow') has suffered drastic depopulation in recent years, with many of its young people moving to the mainland. Now there are only 500 inhabitants, where 10 years ago there were over a thousand.

Paths connect every village, creating a complete circuit of its extinct volcano, Mt Sokometa. To walk this route will take you about three hours. The island is very rocky in the north, but there's a sandy beach at Ngurua. On the western side there's a deep, jungle-fringed lagoon – actually a drowned crater – where you can swim.

Mt Sokometa, which has a central crater some 200 metres deep, rises to 416 metres and makes a tempting target for keen and experienced walkers. There are well-defined paths climbing steeply up the jungle-clad slopes, with magnificent views from the top – arguably the best are from above Mangorongo. Allow at least two hours for the return walk.

A shared speedboat ride from Takara to Wiana costs 5000VT return.

The Shepherd Islands Group

In 1774, James Cook was the first European navigator to see the Shepherd Islands. He named them after Professor Shepherd, an English astronomer friend.

Tongoa and Emae are the largest and most important members of this small archipelago. Tongariki, Buninga, Makura and Mataso are also inhabited, while Ewose, Wot Rock and Falea are not.

All nine islands are volcanic in origin. They rise steeply through dense scrub from mainly black sand shores to inland peaks or high central ridges.

The Shepherd Islands are heavily populated for their small size. Nearly 4000 people live there, with over half on Tongoa.

Overpopulation has caused many families and young, single men to move to Vila looking for work. Shepherd Islanders now comprise by far the largest group working in the capital's building trade, as well as being prominent in the entertainment and sporting worlds. The money they send home is the islands' major source of income.

History
Pre-European The oldest archaeological site in the Shepherds is at Mangarisu in Tongoa. It dates back to around 600 BC, when Lapita people arrived from islands further to the north and decided on settling there.

In the 1250s, the powerful ruler of northern Efate, Roymata, extended his authority over all the Shepherds. He preserved peace by holding a massive feast every five years, during which his leading subjects came to pay him homage.

Island legends claim that Tongoa and its small neighbours, Tongariki, Ewose, Buninga and Falea, were originally all one much larger island. This was known as Kuwae, or Gua as it's sometimes called by Tongariki people.

Islanders believe there was an immense volcanic explosion in about 1475. Not only did this kill many people, but the sea drowned large areas of Kuwae. After the cataclysm only the present-day Shepherds group remained.

A new order was required once the quaking earth had settled down. The hero of the time was a man called Ti Tongoa Liseiriki. His funeral some years later was extremely lavish. When his grave was excavated recently, its contents were just as local myths had described them.

19th & 20th Centuries Other than Cook's passage past the islands in 1774, life in the Shepherds continued along the Melanesian pattern of inter-village and island raiding, followed by much feasting on the flesh of captives.

In the 1860s, a wedding party of Samoan

To Epi Island (7 km)

Tongoa Island

Ewose Island

Falea Island

Emae Island

Buninga Island

Cook Reef

Tongariki Island

Makura Island

PACIFIC OCEAN

To Nguna Island (18 km)

Mataso Island

Wot Rock

The Shepherd Islands

0   10   20 km

church teachers and their guests was blown off-course to Makura and Emae. Because the Samoans had much lighter skin than Emae people, they were mistaken for Europeans, attacked and many killed. The remainder built a stockade on the beach and survived for several months before being overwhelmed. A similar fate befell those who were marooned on Makura.

In 1878, a party of 11 Epi Islanders, returning home from Efate, passed too close to Makura. Eight were killed outright, and three were captured. Parts of the captives were given to the people of neighbouring Emae, Tongariki and Tongoa as gifts!

Like most other parts of the country, the Shepherds suffered considerable depopulation following European contact. In 1860, there were half as many people again in this group as there are now. From 1861 to 1864 there were several measles epidemics with many fatalities and in 1894, about 1000 people died from influenza, whooping cough and pneumonia. By 1908, numbers were down to 2300, about 40% of what they had been 50 years before, with Tongoa experiencing the greatest decline.

Population numbers in the Shepherds began to recover in the 20th century. By the 1930s there were 3000 in the group, and 4000 by the 1960s.

Local Customs

Unlike most parts of Vanuatu, descent in the Shepherds is patrilineal.

Shepherds people have several traditional dances in their repertoire including some light-hearted and comic ones. Islanders living in Port Vila regularly perform at the cultural shows held there for tourists.

As elsewhere, the islanders believed there were a host of sacred places, trees and stones within their island group. These sites were all associated with dead people's spirits. Some were used to guarantee good crops, while others were so tabu anyone visiting them could expect certain death.

Handicrafts

The most common traditional products are hardwood dishes. Rubbed smooth with shells, these resemble birds, fish, turtles or fruit.

Ceremonial clubs of office, made from polished hardwood, mostly come from Tongoa and Tongariki. In addition, mats and bags are woven from dried pandanus leaves.

Medical Services

There are four clinics in the Shepherds group, at Lambukuti on Tongoa, Nofo on Emae, Malakof on Makura, and Lakilia on Tongariki.

Places to Stay

The guest houses on Tongoa were all destroyed in cyclones in 1993 and 1994. To find out about accommodation on the Shepherds generally, it would be wise to call the provincial government office in Nofo (Emae Island) on ☎ 28279, or the provincial government office in Morua (Tongoa Island) on ☎ 28209.

Most visitors to Emae camp by the airfield. See the following information about Emae in the Around the Shepherds section.

Getting There & Away

Air The Shepherds group has two airfields; one on Tongoa (of the same name) and one on Emae, called Emae-Aromai ('Welcome to Emae').

Vanair offers thrice weekly return flights that link Vila with Emae, Tongoa and Valesdir in southern Epi. One-way tickets from Vila cost 3700VT to Emae and 4800VT to Tongoa. From Tongoa it costs 2700VT to get to Emae and 3100VT to Valesdir.

Sea Toara Coastal Shipping's *Marata* services most ports on a weekly round trip from Vila, generally continuing on to Epi. The *Aloara*, run by the same company, calls in to Emae and Tongoa each way on its fortnightly return trips between Vila and Luganville. Fares from Vila cost 1500VT to Mataso and Emau, 2000VT to Emae and Tongariki, and 2500VT to Tongoa.

SHEPHERD ISLANDS GROUP

Getting Around

Inter-Island You can take one of the inter-island cargo boats between Sulua on Emae and south-eastern Tongoa for 600VT. This is a huge saving on the airfare and even more so on a speedboat ride, which will be about 8000VT.

If you're there in April or May, you may be able to hitch a ride in a canoe from Kurumambwe on Tongoa across to Laika Island off eastern Epi to collect young mutton birds. A round trip in a canoe costs about 2000VT.

Tongariki has no airfield, and can only be reached by sea. A chartered speedboat ride to Tongariki from Meriu in Tongoa would be about 4000VT, and about 6000VT from Makatea on Emae. If you're not in a hurry you'd be much better off waiting for the *Marata*.

To/From Tongoa Tongoa's airfield is at Puele. A taxi to Burao costs about 800VT, while the fare to Bongabonga or Meriu is around 1200VT.

Tongoa has the best roads and tracks in the Shepherds. There are some 4WD taxis for hire and these meet each scheduled flight.

To/From Tongariki There are several tracks on Tongariki's western side. You'll have to check with the provincial government office in Nofu, on Emae, as to the availability of transport.

AROUND THE SHEPHERDS
Tongoa Island

Tongoa's people have named their island after the *tongoa* plant, which grows widely in the area. Tongoa has about 2500 inhabitants, making it the most populous member of the Shepherds group.

Tongoa is the group's largest island, measuring eight km long and seven km wide at its broadest point. It's densely forested, with a rugged terrain of 15 extinct volcanic cones and several broad valleys.

The shoreline has many indents and coves. There's black sand along the west

coast, and from Lambukit Point in the south-east as far as Firifini Point to the north.

There are good views northwards of Epi from the island's highest peak, 487-metre Mt Mallamao. Only three metres lower, Mt Tavalapa has similar southward views of the rest of the group, as well as Efate. Mt Akomwa, in the north-east, was used as an American observation post during WW II. The 1½-hour climb to the top provides stunning rewards including a beautiful panorama of the Shepherds group and the island of Efate in the distance.

The northern coast of Tongoa between Nanisukiki and Firifini points is an active thermal area, with a great number of hot springs and fumaroles. In some places, people often cook their food in the naturally heated water. This is a good area to see fauna such as megapode birds. The birds find the warm sand extremely inviting, often laying their eggs there. The best time to see the birds is early in the morning. The northern coast is also very popular with swimmers as they are lured by sea that is warmed by volcanic activity.

Just north of Firifini Point, there's a large seawater blowhole about 13 metres into the scrub. Further west, near Lupalea, a spectacular bluff gives you some fine views across to Pentecost, Epi, Paama and Ambrymislands.

Each village has an average of two to three trade storescand you can also buy supplies at a small general store at Morua.

The following distances are from Kurumambwe at Tongoa's northern tip.

Kurumambwe The villagers are the custom owners of Tefala and Laika islands, off nearby Epi.

Burao (0.7 km) This is Tongoa's main centre for traditional ceremonies. Custom dancers from Burao can be seen wearing wraparound kilts made of tapa cloth, and painting their bodies in black, yellow and white.

Just north of Burao is a *tabu natsaro*, associated with magic, which may not be visited by outsiders. If you do, local tradition says you will get a severe skin infection, with scales, within 24 hours. Another legend claims thunder and rain will follow almost immediately if a certain tree's leaves or branches are broken off.

Puele (2.5 km) There are two nightspots in this village. At weekends, both have either string-band entertainment or operate as discos. On other nights, there are sometimes films.

Lupalea (3.5 km) The cliffs just north of the village offer a spectacular view of islands to

the north. Off the bluff is one of Vanuatu's most outstanding scuba spots: the **Tongoa Wall**. This deep drop-off dive, which features a huge and fascinating concentration of marine life, is visited by tour operators from Vila.

Euta (7 km) Many people in Euta make quality handicrafts. These handicrafts can be bought directly from the skilled carvers themselves.

In the past, during times of war, the villagers would march two km southwards to the sea to consult the oracles at a large rock lying

SHEPHERD ISLANDS GROUP

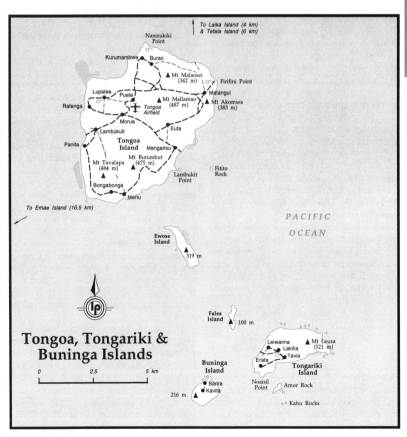

Tongoa, Tongariki & Buninga Islands

close to the shore. If a pigeon flew over they believed they would win the coming battle. If no such bird appeared, they withdrew, fearing they would be beaten.

Ewose Island (9 km & 2.5 km by canoe) Just south of Meriu is Ewose, also called Awoh, which measures 2.5 km long by half a km wide. Its only residents are goats.

Ewose rises to a high central ridge and, from the air, looks rather like an upturned boat. It's extremely rocky, except at the north-western tip where there's a black sand beach.

Tongariki Island

Tongariki has neither beaches nor reefs. There are 500 people here, and the place is noted for its strong kava. Because of population pressures, you'll find plenty of gardens but few coconut trees. The scarcity of land has caused a number of Tongariki people to migrate to Efate.

Although the island's present-day population and also its language are Melanesian, Tongariki's name is Polynesian, as is its social system. A semi-aristocratic society still flourishes, with each adult male resident granted title to specific areas of land. The chief holds court, advised by elders, to decide on the allocation of gardens to the younger men.

The island's main village is **Leiwaima,** but its most attractive one is **Tavia,** deep in the bush. **Lakilia,** in the centre of the island, is also pleasant to visit and has hot springs nearby. **Erata** is high up on a cliff, and has good views of Falea and Buninga islands about three km away.

There are 10 small islets along Tongariki's northern and eastern shores. Five more lie south-east of Noaisil Point, including a 400-metre landmass called Amor Rock.

Falea Island

Falea, also called Valea, is only one km long and in some places only 200 metres wide, and rises to 100 metres. It's populated only by goats.

Buninga Island

Buninga, which lies three km south-west of Tongariki, covers only 1.5 sq km and has many steep hills. It is heavily populated for its small size, with about 200 people living in two villages. Because of this overcrowding, many villagers have emigrated in recent years to Tongoa, Emae and Efate.

The island has an unusual landing beach consisting of millions of large, cannonball-sized rocks.

The best way to get to Buninga is by fishing boat from Tongariki.

Emae Island

This island had four other names or spellings in the past: Mai, Mae, Emai, and Three Hills Island, the last derived from its three peaks, Painga, Talimasa and Lasi.

Emae is 10 km long and three to five km wide. About 750 people, mostly Presbyterian, live on this island which they share with a large number of peregrine falcons.

The interior is mostly highland, except for a central lowland patch between **Sulua,** where the main anchorage is, and **Nofo** on the opposite coast. An onshore reef extends from two km west of Siwa Point to one km north of Mangita.

While most islanders speak Melanesian languages, those living in the north-east speak a similar Polynesian tongue to the people of Rotuma, an island north of Fiji. Physically, however, most resemble their Melanesian neighbours.

Emae is not usually known for shark attacks, though a four-metre shark in 1988 tried to pitch two men out of their canoe. One fell out, but fortunately managed to get back on board before the shark was able to strike again.

The eastern seaboard offers the best vistas in the Shepherds group. Makatea has a very good view of south-eastern Tongoa, Ewose, Falea and Buninga, while the Emae-Aromai airfield is the best place for a glimpse of Makura and Mataso.

Although local villagers are very welcoming, most visitors camp by the airfield in dry weather. However, Emae is plagued with mosquitoes, so bring some repellent. You will need to bring your own food as well.

Cook Reef Five km offshore from Siwa Point is Cook Reef. Also known as Pula Iwa Reef, Cook Reef is a popular scuba site for touring yachts. Although awash at high tide, many parts of the reef are exposed at low water, particularly a chain of sandbars in the southwest. It makes a beautiful sight as you pass over it on Vanair's flight between Vila and Epi.

Makura Island

This island lies about eight km from Emae and is extremely windswept. There are few trees, although its soil is very fertile.

Makura is two km long by one km wide. About 100 people live at **Malakof**, the island's only village. Some of Vanuatu's best string bands come from Malakof, where music is a way of life.

There is a **hot spring** less than one km from Malakof as you walk towards the mountain.

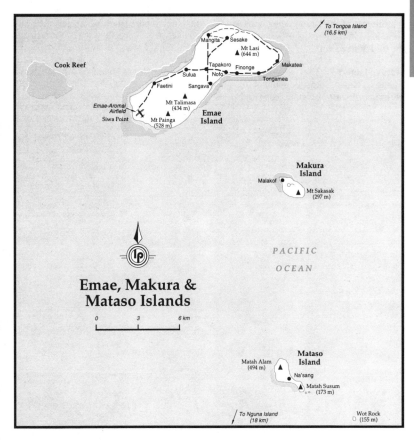

Emae, Makura & Mataso Islands

On the beach is the centre section of the last of Vanuatu's old trading canoes. These were large enough to carry three bullocks each and were used to travel between the further-flung islands. In 1928 the Condominium banned their use for inter-island trading, as a knee-jerk reaction to several islanders being drowned in a canoeing mishap.

Very fine pandanus mats are woven on Makura. As they are of single weave only, they are rather too thin to be used as sleeping mats, but they make fine wall hangings.

Other handicraft products are small model trading canoes. These are assembled complete with outrigger and a crab-claw sail, reminiscent of the large trading craft which were used in many parts of Melanesia until the mid-20th century.

Mataso Island

Mataso is about 11 km due south of Makura, 18 km north-east of Nguna. Also known as Matah, it was aptly named Two Hills Island by 19th-century European seafarers – it consists of two huge, steep-sided rocks rising sheer from the sea and connected by a narrow sandy isthmus.

The only village is **Na'asang**, in the middle of the isthmus. About 100 people live here, and all speak the same language as the people of neighbouring Makura.

Wot Rock Four km south-east of Mataso is Wot Rock. It's also called Wota, Monument, or Wolf Rock, as well as Etarik Island.

Wot rises abruptly from the sea to 155 metres in height. Its isolation makes it an ideal home for seabirds and it has a huge and very noisy population of frigate birds and boobies.

During the war, US-airforce pilots based on Efate used the island as a target for calibrating their guns. Occasionally they used Mataso by mistake, but they fortunately didn't kill anyone.

Epi Island

Known in the past as Api or Tasiko Island, the rather oddly shaped Epi resembles a cockerel with a somewhat protruding backside, wearing a high-heeled boot. It's 46 km from end to end, 19 km at its broadest point, and covers 452 sq km.

Coastal Epi is extremely fertile and largely covered by coconut plantations. However, its rugged, thickly forested interior has discouraged high population growth: only 3600 people live on the island.

Epi has plenty of white sand beaches, as well as some black ones. The west coast is predominantly palm-fringed with whitish shores, interspersed with rocky headlands and onshore reefs. The north-east coast is either rugged or lined with jagged coral rocks, though there are some short stretches of white sand here too.

You'll find several small lakes on Epi. Lake Lapa beside Mt Mariu has clear water for fishing and swimming, and many water birds to watch. Near Mt Beutloa, the rather brackish Imao Lakes attract wild pigs, bullocks and birds. Epi's largest lake, Lake Nalema, is close to Cape Cone. Despite all this water, wet-season flooding is unusual.

Epi has two submarine volcanoes close to its shores. One is just offshore from Mt Nitaia, while the other is close to the tiny islands of Tefala and Tefala Kiki.

Unlike Paama and Malakula, Epi has been spared a history of shark attacks. Villagers swim freely everywhere, with Lamen and Mapuna bays being the most popular places.

History
Epi was one of the first islands to experience

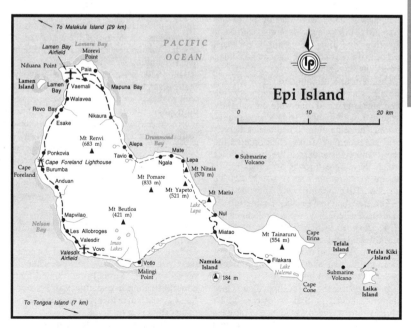

large-scale European settlement and plantations. Before Europeans began arriving in the 1860s it was populated by about 7000 ni-Vanuatu. Seventy years later there were only 1000.

The first of the island's European settlers planned to grow cotton, hoping to capture the world market lost by the USA during its Civil War. However, the recovery of the US economy forced them to grow other crops instead.

The *Carl* Incident One of the worst blackbirding incidents in the Pacific occurred in 1872 aboard the *Carl*. This was a labour ship owned by Dr Murray, a European living on Epi. About 90 villagers from two islands further north were enticed alongside the *Carl* by the offer of trade. Their canoes were sunk, and as the villagers bobbed around in the water, they were seized, hauled aboard and locked below.

On the second night, the captives used their bunks as battering rams to break out of their prison. They were met by pistol fire from Dr Murray and his crew, who kept shooting long after the would-be escapees had been driven back. The slaughter resumed the following night.

On the fourth morning, the crew ordered the survivors to come out. Miraculously, five were unharmed and nine were only slightly wounded, with another 16 in a serious condition. The remaining 60 had been killed.

The murderous Murray then ordered the badly injured islanders to be bound, after which they were thrown over the side to ensure they wouldn't survive to report the incident. Then the ship was whitewashed.

The crew had just finished destroying the evidence when they were challenged by HMS *Rosario*. An officer inspected the blackbirder but didn't do a particularly thorough job. He failed to notice the wounds of the nine injured islanders, or the multitude of bullet holes in their quarters.

In due course the secret slipped out. Once enquiries began in Sydney, Australia, Dr Murray turned Queen's evidence to escape a richly deserved sentence. Also acquitted

were the two chief murderers among the crew. This followed a public outcry over them being charged, let alone convicted!

The Plantation Era Faced with this kind of treatment, many of Epi's islanders gave up hope of ever being treated fairly. In addition to blackbirding, they faced new diseases, alcoholism and despair over loss of land. All of these things combined to take an extremely heavy toll.

In contrast, many of the newly arrived Europeans flourished. Indeed, so many French settlers arrived on Epi in the late 1870s that people in Australia feared France was trying to annex the island, if not the whole archipelago. Their fears were calmed in 1878 by an Anglo-French agreement to prevent this occurring against either nation's wishes.

Prior to WW I, the European settlements were either copra plantations or cattle stations. These were at Mapuna Bay, Votlo, Walavea, Lamen Bay, Valesdir and Rovo Bay. Many had homesteads which were veritable mansions. Some of them survive to this day, though generally in a rather dilapidated condition.

The 1920s were Epi's colonial heyday. Many plantations had their own racecourses with regular race days. Some even printed their own plantation currency. Others recruited large numbers of Vietnamese workers directly from their French-ruled homeland. However, the 1930s' Depression, followed by a succession of powerful cyclones, brought these halcyon days to a sudden close. In contrast to this glamorous past, life on Epi nowadays is extremely quiet.

People

Epi's people live scattered around the coast, mainly in the north-east and west, while the rugged interior is virtually unoccupied. Only about 300 people live south-east of Votlo and Lepa. About half of them are Tongans, whose main centre is at Filakara.

Epi has many dialects. Almost every

village has some slightly different words from those used by its nearest neighbours.

Local Customs

Many Epi people play magical games which include invoking ancestral spirits. However, genuine sorcery, or *shu* as it is called on this island, is now very rare. But in the past many people would use it to kill, or bring sickness to, their rivals. Young male islanders used love magic to win the object of their heart's desire. As on Ambrym and Ambae, local islanders believe that sorcery works strongest close to volcanoes – in Epi's case, submarine ones.

Medical Services

Epi's only hospital is at Vaemali, but there are clinics at Burumba and Ngala.

Places to Stay

There are guest houses in Lamen Bay and Valesdir, and a government rest house in Rovo Bay. See the information on these places in the Around Epi section, below.

Getting There & Away

Air Epi's two airstrips are at Lamen Bay and Valesdir. The Lamen Bay strip, which is right on the shore, gives you a stunning introduction to the island as you come in low over coral reefs and crystal-clear turquoise water. It's only natural to want to get into it as soon as possible.

Vanair has thrice-weekly return flights between Vila and Ambrym (Craig Cove and Ulei) which pass through Lamen Bay. Two of these call in to Paama as well. One-way tickets from Lamen Bay cost 2900VT to Craig Cove, 2600VT to Ulei, 2200VT to Paama and 5700VT to Vila.

Valesdir is visited on a thrice-weekly return service from Vila via Emae and Tongoa, both in the Shepherds group. Fares from Valesdir are 2800VT to Emae, 3100VT to Tongoa and 4800VT to Vila.

Sea Ifira Shipping's *Saraika* visits Lamen Bay, and occasionally Valesdir, on its fortnightly return voyages between Vila and Luganville. Toara Coastal Shipping's *Aloara* provides a similar service but usually visits more ports. They both charge 2800VT from Vila to Lamen Bay, and about 500VT from Lamen Bay to Paama.

Toara's little MV *Marata* mainly services the Shepherds from Vila, with Epi being the turn-around point on its fortnightly round trips.

Speedboat A charter from southern Paama to Lamen Bay would cost in the vicinity of at least 4500VT.

Yacht There are several good anchorages in the north. Probably the pick of the bunch is Lamen Bay. The other worthwhile anchorages are Mapuna Bay, Rovo Bay, Walavea and Cape Foreland. These, however, can often be unsuitable depending on the wind direction.

Getting Around

Air Vanair flights between Lamen Bay and Valesdir are by request only, and cost 2500VT one-way.

Road Epi's roads are not the best, being very basic. Many of the island's villages are connected by road, but there are several sections where a footpath is all the thoroughfare that there is.

A taxi truck from Lamen Bay to Tavio costs about 1000VT. The price would be

2000VT down to Valesdir, and then a further 1000VT to Votlo.

Speedboat Speedboats connect Lamen Island with the mainland. See the information on Lamen Island in the Around Epi section, below.

AROUND EPI
Western & Southern Coasts
The following distances are from Lamen Bay.

Lamen Bay Local people consider Lamen Bay's 1.5-km beach to be Epi's best. There's white sand on the southern side of the bay and beside the airstrip to the north, with plenty of shallow coral for snorkelling. The bay is home to several **dugong**, one of which – a male – is quite tame. The village has three small stores and a fishery base, where you can buy ice and fresh fish.

Between the airstrip and the water's edge is a canoe park used by villagers from nearby Lamen Island.

Places to Stay & Eat The fishery base has a three-bedroom *guest house* where beds cost 1000VT. You can either cook your own meals or buy them at the nearby restaurant, which sells excellent cheap meals. Tasso is the man to see at the fishery. He can advise you on most activities in the area.

Lamen Island (2 km by canoe) This very small but beautiful island is almost surrounded by a white sand beach. About 450 people live here, although it's only 1.25 sq km. From Lamen you can see the volcano on Lopevi Island rising over the top of nearby Epi. There's a **hot spring** near the north-eastern tip.

In the 1890s, the island earned a degree of notoriety when some men who had recently returned from the overseas canefields used it as a base from which to raid other settlements and kidnap females.

Canoes paddle the two km to the mainland all through the day. You'll often see islanders using coconut palm-leaf sails if the wind is

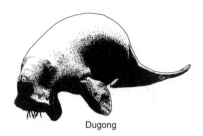
Dugong

favourable. These sails can often prove to be extremely picturesque against the sunset.

Speedboats also go back and forth. If you want to wait for one, it'll only cost you about 300VT. But if you decide to charter, the fare will just as likely quadruple, and be around 1200VT.

Walavea (3.5 km) Several large, abandoned, rather gloomy plantation buildings stand here. Nearby are stretches of black sand beach which are separated by rocky headlands. If you want to get to them, the only access is by canoe.

Rovo Bay (5.5 km) Rovo Bay was formerly called Ringdove Bay, and is now Epi's administrative centre. If you wish to stay here, it has a provincial government council *rest house* (council office ☎ 28258) with two double bedrooms. Each of the rooms costs 1000VT.

Valesdir (27 km) In the 1920s, the Valesdir plantation had the privilege of having its own coinage. On one of the coins was marked 'five centimes' squarely on the front and 'six pence' on the reverse.

Rows of coconut palms invitingly stretch along the road for almost three km in either direction of the plantation's buildings. These buildings are, surprisingly, still operational. There's also a strip of white sand beach nearby.

The *Valesdir Plantation Guest House* (☎ 23916) has five bungalows and one dormitory block with cooking facilities and costs 1500VT per person.

From the guest house you can easily walk the six km or so to the **Imao Lakes,** which are known for their wild ducks. There's also horse riding on the plantation and snorkelling along the beach. Melanesian feasts and custom dancing can be arranged at nearby **Vovo**.

Votlo (41 km) There are five km of coconut trees before you reach this coastal village and the two hot springs close by.

Namuka Island (41 km & 8.5 km by boat) This small, unoccupied islet off Epi's southern shore offers clear water for swimming, coral viewing on its fringing reef, and a white sand beach on its northern side. The island is the top of a mountain poking out of the sea and rises steeply to a height of 184 metres.

Filakara (58 km) There's a hot spring just north of this village.

Eastern Epi
The following distances are from Mapuna Bay.

Mapuna Bay Five km over the hills from Lamen Bay, Mapuna Bay has a white sand beach and some attractive coral gardens.

Alepa (8 km) There's a small hot spring here, and another less than one km further on at **Tavio**.

Ngala (14 km) Most of the people here used to live around the base of Lopevi, the huge volcano off Paama. They were evacuated to Ngala after a series of eruptions in 1958 and 1959.

Mt Nitaia (19 km) Three km offshore is a submarine volcano which periodically steams or bubbles up. Sometimes, when it's being particularly vigorous, rising steam makes the evening sky glow a deep scarlet. Meanwhile, spray and flakes of pumice spurt out of the sea in all directions.

Nul (29 km) Nearby are high white cliffs that remind British expats of Dover. These are quite spectacular and a major landmark for yachties.

Laika & Tefala Islands Another submarine volcano is intermittently active five km offshore from Cape Cone. It's about one km south of Tefala, and the same distance west of Laika's tiny neighbour, Tefala Kiki.

Laika boasts one of the largest colonies of wedge-tailed **shearwaters** (or mutton birds) in the Pacific. The birds lay their eggs from January to February. A couple of months later, the people of Kurumambwe on Tongoa – they are the custom owners of both islands – come across to feast on the young birds and collect others to sell on their home island. If you're hungry, you can buy one for 40VT in the local markets there.

There are no shearwaters on Tefala because it's too rocky, but there are large colonies of **flying fox**. The island is composed of glossy black and brown basalt with obsidian, which indicates the cataclysmic events that created it.

EPI ISLAND

Tafea

The Tafea province gets its name from Vanuatu's five most southerly populated islands: Tanna, Aniwa, Futuna, Erromango and Aneityum. Also within its far-flung boundaries are the tiny volcanic outcrops of Matthew and Hunter islands, both of which are uninhabited. Isangel on Tanna is the administrative centre for the region's 22,000 people.

The three larger members of the Tafea group – Erromango, Aneityum and Tanna – are the least racially mixed of all Vanuatu's Melanesian-populated islands. In contrast, Aniwa and Futuna have a strong Polynesian influence.

Tanna Island

While traditional Vanuatu is easy to find on Tanna, the island's major drawcard is its active volcano, Mt Yasur. This is one of the world's most accessible volcano, and a visit to it offers an unforgettable experience of nature's raw power.

As well, visitors to Tanna can learn about the fascinating Jon Frum cult, meet penis-sheathed and grass-skirted custom villagers, watch age-old festivals, go bushwalking and swim with a tame dugong.

While it's possible to fly in and out of Tanna and see Yasur all in one day, the volcano is most spectacular when seen at night. The island's other features also have much to offer, so you may find yourself tempted to stay on for an extra two or three days.

Before you make any firm arrangements to visit Tanna you need to do your homework in Vila on the available options and costs. Package tours seem expensive, but you could easily find that you won't save very much at all by doing it in other ways.

You also have to consider that independent travel isn't encouraged on Tanna. In fact, you can't visit any of the major attractions without a licensed guide.

History
Early History & Cook's Arrival Tanna emerged from the sea only about one million years ago, which was much later than other islands in the archipelago.

According to archaeologists, people moving southwards through central Vanuatu first occupied Tanna in about 400 BC. Their descendants traded with other islands in the Tafea area, and occasionally as far afield as New Caledonia.

Early in August 1774, the redoubtable Captain James Cook, seeing a great glow (the Yasur volcano) in the sky one night, went to investigate and came to Tanna the following day. Landing in a small bay, he named the area Port Resolution after his vessel, HMS *Resolution*. He wanted to climb the volcano, but because it was tabu the islanders wouldn't allow him to do so.

Cook made friends with an elderly chief

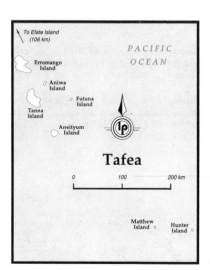

called Paowang. While trying to converse, he pointed to the ground and asked the old man what the place was called. Paowang, probably thinking he wanted to know their name for ground, replied *muk-tana*. Cook only heard the second part, and this is how the island got its name.

Traders In 1825 sailors from Rotuma, a Polynesian island about 400 km north of Fiji, told Peter Dillon, an Irish trader-explorer, that there was abundant sandalwood on Tanna. Most of the trees proved to be on Erromango, but as some were found later at

Port Resolution, a trading station was established there in 1847.

Traditionally the Tannese were enemies of the Erromangans and feuded constantly with them. In an attempt to get the upper hand, the people of Port Resolution offered the European sailors three pigs for every Erromangan captive brought to them. The bride price at the time on Tanna was 10 pigs.

The most popular trade goods after stick tobacco were axes and guns. Axes made gardening and canoe-building much easier, leaving more time for inter-clan fighting and ceremonies. Occasionally the guns were

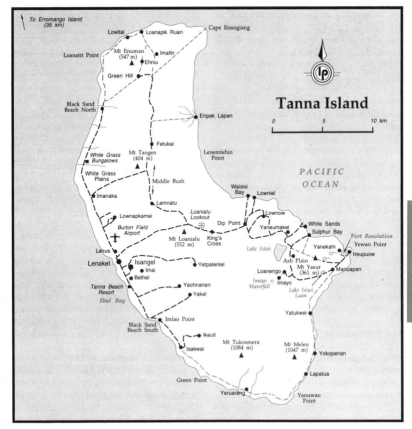

Tanna Island

TAFEA

used against Europeans. In 1874 a Tannese man shot a particularly obnoxious labour recruiter called Lewin, causing several other Europeans to flee.

Three years later a British naval party executed a Tannese islander after another trader had been killed. Too bad the condemned man was innocent. These were the days when punitive raids were official British policy. Deterring islanders from further killings was considered more important than justice.

Missionaries Meanwhile, Tanna's first missionaries landed in mid-1842, but were forced to flee a few months later. The islanders believed a devastating epidemic of dysentery that took place at the time had been caused by sorcery, which was their initial impression of Christianity.

Polynesian religious teachers replaced them three years later, but another epidemic occurred and they were blamed. A fresh group arrived in 1846, only to have smallpox bring their work to a premature end six years later.

John Paton arrived at Port Resolution in 1858. He was a fundamentalist missionary of the fire-and-brimstone type, and condemned all those customs which the Tannese delighted in. He forced his male converts to work for the mission, to have only one wife, to stop fighting, to take over garden work from the women, and to wear European clothes rather than nambas.

The Tannese revolted against Paton's blind bigotry in 1862, and he fled. Returning on HMS *Curacao* in 1866, he persuaded the crew to bombard several villages, killing a number of people. His credibility destroyed on Tanna, he moved on to 'civilise' Aniwa.

The 20th Century By the 1900s, Presbyterian missionaries dominated Tanna's religious and political life. The church people had their own courts, and sentenced Christian offenders to perform menial tasks for the missionaries as punishment.

There were official moves against Tanna's Presbyterian theocracy in 1912, with many attempts by Condominium staff to restrict its excesses. But after WW I, Presbyterianism again flourished, leaving custom worshippers to number only 25% of the island's population.

Eventually, a home-grown religion called the Jon Frum movement emerged as a form of resistance to missionisation (see The Jon Frum Movement in this section). It blossomed to such an extent that by the end of WW II it was one of Tanna's three main religious groups, the others being Presbyterians and custom people. Although widely regarded as simply a cargo cult, it is in fact a hybrid of Christianity and traditional beliefs in which cargo (or wealth) is secondary. However, it's this aspect of the cult that has most appeal to tourists.

In the early 1970s, as the call for national independence grew louder, Tanna became highly politicised. Jon Frum cultists and a Tannese custom group called Kapiel allied themselves in 1979 with the secessionist Nagriamel group in Santo and the Modérés in the rest of Vanuatu.

The Modérés were especially active after the 1979 election. They alleged electoral fraud when their party narrowly missed winning a majority in Tanna (by 2% of the vote).

Galvanised into action by the Santo rebellion of May 1980, Tannese Modérés struck. They seized two British government staff, who were freed by police action two days later. Although many Modérés were arrested, Protestant islanders, fearing a civil war, fled into the bush.

On 10 June 1980, 300 Modérés attacked Isangel, where their friends were being held prisoner. In the ensuing shoot-out a Modéré leader was killed. Arrests were made and the Tannese insurrection fizzled out soon afterwards.

The Jon Frum Movement During the 1930s considerable resentment had built up among Tannese people over the arrogance of European planters and the rigid rules of the local Presbyterian church. In 1936, people in western Tanna began talking about a mys-

TAFEA

terious person called Jon Frum (or Frumm). He was claimed to be the brother of the god of Mt Tukosmera.

The story said Jon Frum had come from the sea at Green Point and had announced himself to some kava drinkers there. He told them there would be an abundance of wealth and no more of the epidemics that had killed so many people. However, all Europeans had to leave the island before this could happen.

The Pacific War Soon after, US troops, including Blacks, landed in Efate and Santo and many Tannese went to work for them, including a number of Jon Frum worshippers. They saw that the troops had huge quantities of steel ships, jeeps, aircraft, refrigerators and radios as well as endless supplies of Coca-Cola and cigarettes. But most of all, the Tannese saw how generous the US servicemen were, especially Blacks, who were surely Tannese in disguise. Jon Frum must certainly be from the USA.

Shortly after WW II, dozens of small red crosses were erected all over Tanna. To the islanders, the red-cross sign in WW II meant expert medical treatment, free of charge. So villagers began putting up red crosses, hoping this would bring free medical attention to their island too. Nowadays red crosses remain a feature in Jon Frum villages.

Europeans and Americans explained there was no Jon Frum. This was interpreted on the island to mean that foreigners were still trying to deprive the Tannese of their rightful wealth.

For a long time after the Pacific war, cultists would examine any plane they saw, in case Jon Frum was inside. Any Americans they met were asked if they had any messages from him.

Jon Frum Prophets Several people have claimed to be Jon Frum's prophet or even Jon Frum himself. To justify their claim, they've recited details of dreams they've had about their god, their revelations often leading to a fresh revival of the faith. At times these testimonies have produced an alternative interpretation of the religion's basic princi-

ples, yet this has been no obstacle for its many believers.

The movement has at times been vigorously opposed by missionaries and officials. Even now, cultists won't pay any taxes or use government schools.

Waiting for Jon Frum Over the years, some Jon Frum supporters, keen to hear his latest message, have made imitation radio aerials out of tin cans and wire. Others have built an airfield in the bush and constructed wooden replica aircraft to entice his planes full of cargo to land on Tanna. A third group has erected wharves where his ships can berth.

Some cultists recommend a return to a totally traditional lifestyle, including wearing nambas. Others continue to wear European clothes, feeling this will be more to their messiah's liking and therefore hasten his arrival.

When will he come? His followers have waited since the early 1940s and nothing has happened yet. 'How long have Christians waited?' they ask. 'Nearly 2000 years, yet we've waited only 50!'

Jon Frum's Name Who was Jon Frum, anyway? No-one knows for sure, but there are at least six possible explanations.

The first says the name stands for 'John from America'. The second claims that a US medical corps member called John, with a red cross on his sleeve, landed on Tanna during WW II and handed out large amounts of free medicine.

A third tells how Nampus, an early Jon Frum leader, returned from prison in 1951 wearing a US medical aide's discarded jacket with red crosses on its sleeves. He apparently told villagers that Jon Frum had told him this was to be the cult's insignia.

Some cultists say Jon Frum is a mispronunciation of Jon Broom. He is the broom that will sweep Tanna clean of Europeans and their influences.

A fifth story claims that either wartime Black US troops or pre war abolitionists told the Tannese about John Brown's fight against slavery in the USA in the 19th

TAFEA

century. Some cult members claim John Brown visited Tanna prior to the US Civil War in the early 1860s.

Lastly, it's said that Jon Frum stands for John the Baptist, the baptiser of Jesus Christ. Jon Frum people respect Jesus, but John the Baptist was clearly senior to him, so that's why they worship Jon Frum, or John the Baptist, instead.

Geography

Tanna's 565 sq km is a compact mix of savannah, thick forest, plains and rugged mountains. The north-west, being in the rain shadow of the central ranges, is covered with grassland and scrub.

In the centre is a fertile area of denser bush, aptly called Middle Bush by the islanders. This is the garden area of Tanna and one of the most productive in Vanuatu. As well as the ubiquitous coconut, coffee and a host of vegetables and fruits are grown here for export to other islands in the archipelago. Kava is a major cash crop – or at least it was until a severe drought in the early 1990s. The kava crop was devastated by drought but will become a major crop again when it is ready for harvesting in three or four years.

Much of Tanna's south-western interior is mountainous. Two peaks – Mt Tukosmera and Mt Melen – rise to over 1000 metres. Mt Yasur, a mere 361 metres high, dominates the island's south-eastern corner.

Climate

Tanna's weather is usually drier and milder than most other islands in the archipelago. Isangel's average summer maximum is 30°C. Winter nights can be quite cool, making a light pullover necessary. In fact, something heavier is often required for night visits to the exposed rim of Mt Yasur.

People

The 1989 census recorded Tanna's population as 19,825, but it's certainly much larger now. Numerous villages and family stations are concentrated in a central belt from Imanaka in the west across to Port Resolution on the east coast.

Most Tannese are accustomed to European visitors. However, children from the island's most remote villages often never see a European face until they reach school age.

Local Customs

In the handful of Tannese villages where custom reigns supreme, females dress in grass skirts while men wear nambas.

The Role of Chiefs A Tannese chief is called a *yeremanu*. With the title comes the authority to cast spells and to regulate the behaviour of his villagers.

Tanna has about 1000 chiefs. There's one per village and another, more senior chief for each grouping of four villages.

According to Tannese custom, there are up to 15 other positions in each village to which men can aspire. However, authority has its price: the more senior a man is, the less land he can have.

In the island's interior, minor offences are dealt with under custom law. A council, whose members are all chiefs, has the power to penalise such law breakers. They usually order the guilty party to compensate the plaintiff with pigs or kava.

Custom Medicine Although the island has two modern hospitals, many villagers still have more confidence in traditional medicine. The standard treatment is to have the skin of your back cut. Herbs are then placed over the incisions. This is also done after a woman has had her first menstruation, and at each new child's birth. Teenage boys are cut in this way at their circumcision. Mothers with large families, or people who've been chronically sick, have many scars on their back.

Sorcery Witch doctors (*klebers*) cast spells both to heal and to harm people. If a sorcerer wants to kill someone, he collects items of this victim's clothing and weaves a curse over them. Then he warns the victim how long he or she has to live.

Some sorcerers claim power over the seasons and climate. Rainmakers can call up wet weather, and others will try to stop cyclones.

The Tannese (along with most other ni-Vanuatu) believe in ghosts, and many believe that the spirits of the dead reside in Yasur.

The Niel Always a rare event, the Niel ceremony was originally a special feast where male islanders rejuvenated themselves by eating their dead enemies. It has now evolved into a surplus-sharing ceremony.

In the late 1880s the adventurous British artist Charles Gordon Frazer chanced upon a Niel ceremony at Yanekahi, near Port Resolution. His famous painting of it, called *A Cannibal Feast on the Island of Tanna*, shows three men, bound and waiting to be eaten. They are surrounded by villagers who are either preparing the fire, collecting yams, or just waiting for the meal. There's a copy of the painting in the Cultural Centre in Vila.

Kava Ceremony Tannese kava is renowned throughout Vanuatu for its strength, so there's a good market for it in Vila. Women in Jon Frum-influenced parts of Tanna, but not elsewhere, are allowed into the village nakamal to prepare and drink it.

The kava ceremony on Tanna is a very special occasion, and any male visitors invited to one should treat it as a real privilege. By contrast, female tourists visiting custom-oriented areas are forbidden to watch kava being drunk, let alone consume it themselves.

Male Initiation Rites Young boys are initiated by circumcision when they are eight to 12 years old. Usually they are kept in seclusion for three months between June and November. During this period, their male elders teach them the custom traditions and how to behave like grown men.

While in seclusion the boys may not see any women, even young girls. If they move from their camp, they must advise everyone by blowing a warning note on a conch shell.

Boys are circumcised with a knife made from sharpened bamboo. Once they've healed, they come out from the bush to be ceremoniously received by their families. Huge amounts of food are served, followed by a night of dancing.

Finally mats are presented to the boys, and up to 100 pigs are clubbed to death. Afterwards, the boys leave to reside in a young man's house for a time before returning home. Numerous circumcision rituals occur on Tanna every year, involving 10 to 20 young boys each time.

Traditional Dances There are dozens of custom dances held throughout the year on Tanna, and each one recounts a different story or legend. Participants usually perform in traditional nambas or grass skirts.

As elsewhere in Vanuatu, dancing plays a unifying role in village life. The ceremonies are intricate, so dancers need to practise together over a long period. Whole villages will rehearse together when there's a major event coming up, such as the Nekowiar festival. People use these occasions to restore old friendships and make new ones. Disputes can be laid aside in the face of the common task of perfecting the performance.

The Nekowiar & Toka Ceremony Everyone describes the Toka as Tanna's most awe-inspiring dance, but in fact it is only one section of a huge, three-day ceremony called the Nekowiar. This functions as an alliance-making process between several neighbouring villages.

Though a Nekowiar may not be needed by every village every year, there's usually at least one held on the island sometime between August and November. The timing usually depends on how wet the winter has been.

If you get a chance to go to a Nekowiar, do so. Rumours that it's about to start will be rife several weeks beforehand, but the actual date is often only announced a few days in advance. You may need to camp out, like the villagers, and will have to pay up to 5000VT to watch.

The Tannese Nekowiar has some similarities to Papua New Guinean sing-sings.

TAFEA

Villages hosting the ceremony try to outdo their neighbours in the number and quality of gifts presented to their guests. The guest villages will give a return feast two to three weeks later, the aim being to put on an even more lavish show than that give by their previous hosts.

The ceremony also brings clan leaders together to organise marriages between youngsters from different clans. For several months after the dance, there are continuous marital negotiations.

Rehearsals The preparations for the Nekowiar are exhaustive. Three dances are practised at the rehearsal site or *yimwayin*. No photography is allowed at this stage.

Beauty Magic Just a few days before the Nekowiar begins, 'beauty magic' takes over. Males and females of all ages, using powder paints mixed with coconut oil, colour their faces a deep red from their noses across to their ear lobes. The lower face is decorated with thin stripes of black and yellow paint. Every dance group tries to outdo the others in stylishness.

The Napen-Napen Finally the Nekowiar is ready. Up to 2000 people of all ages assemble for it. As the guests arrive, the hosts display between 60 and 100 pigs, all tied by the feet and suspended on poles.

The first night begins with the host village's young men dancing. Their aim is to invite the women to dance. When they respond, the Napen-Napen begins. This is a dance by the women that represents their toil in the fields, and continues throughout the first night. It's a spectacular display, with women of all ages arrayed in red, yellow, blue, green and mauve grass skirts.

The Toka This begins the next morning, sometimes before dawn, and reaches its climax that night. All the male guests take part. During the night the women huddle protectively in small groups. If the Toka dancers make a circle and capture a woman, she's tossed up and down between them.

There's plenty of touching of her normally private parts throughout this time.

Tourist women may watch, but they would be wise to remain well protected, too. If you don't want to be carried shoulder high by excited men, keep back. Otherwise your body will be very sore from being pinched. Male tourists can move more freely, although they still need to keep an eye out. The dance on the second day may go on all night. Any man may have as his night's companion any woman he catches – including a female tourist.

The Nao On the third day the Kweriya is produced. This is a three-metre bamboo pole with white and black feathers wound around it and hawk's feathers on top. Carried by the chief of the host village, its appearance announces that the Nao – the host village's dance – is about to begin. The Nao continues throughout the morning. The men dance in lines facing each other and enact routine events from everyday life, such as hunting and wrestling.

The Climax Finally, in the afternoon, the pigs are brought out. With them comes a huge pile of kava roots, woven mats, grass skirts and massive quantities of laplap. The pigs are ceremonially clubbed to death, with the host villages presenting everything to their guests. This is the climax of the Nekowiar. Everyone then inspects the display to assess their hosts' generosity. The pigs are then cooked and a huge feast begins.

Medical Services
There are hospitals at Lenakel and White Sands, plus clinics at Green Hill, Isakwai, Ikeuti, Loanengo and Yokopenan.

Places to Stay
If you've got the vatu, the most comfortable places to stay are *Tanna Beach Resort* just south of Lenakel and *White Grass Bungalows* to the north. Cheaper, more basic options are provided by the guest houses at Isangel, Lenakel, Port Resolution and Dip

Point. For more details see the following Around Tanna section.

Places to Eat

The only restaurants are at the *Tanna Beach Resort* and *White Grass Bungalows*. (The restaurant in Lenakel was blown away by a cyclone early in 1994, but there are plans to replace it.) These places are covered under the Ebul Bay and White Grass Plains sections, below.

If you're on a strict budget you won't like the restaurant prices at the two resorts – but then, if you were on a budget you wouldn't be staying there. You can purchase usually limited processed food lines in the stores in Lenakel and elsewhere, and this can be supplemented with fresh produce from local markets. The Lenakel market takes place on Monday, Wednesday and Friday from dawn until 4 pm.

Getting There & Away

Air The only commercial airfield on Tanna is Burton Field, near Isangel. Vanair provides return services between Vila and Burton Field at least once every day. It also has twice-weekly return services between Tanna and Aniwa, Aneityum, Futuna and the airfields at Dillons Bay and Ipota on Erromango.

The one-way flight from Vila to Tanna costs 8700VT. From Tanna it's 3100VT to Aniwa, 4100VT to Ipota and 4500VT to Dillons Bay, Futuna and Aneityum.

A direct service between Tanna and New Caledonia is due to start in 1995.

Sea Toara Coastal Shipping sails from Vila to Tanna every two weeks or so, visiting Lenakel and Port Resolution en route to other islands in the Tafea group. Tickets cost 4000VT one way.

Ifira Shipping's MV *Saraika* does one return trip on average every two or three weeks from Vila to Tanna via Erromango for the same price.

Both companies charge 2000VT one way between ports on Tanna and Erromango.

Yachties take note: in 1994 there was a push for Port Resolution to be made an official entry and exit point to the country, so check the current situation on this.

Anchorages are rather scarce around Tanna's coast. The best ones are at Lenakel, Port Resolution, Sulphur Bay and Waisisi Bay.

Getting Around

There's a road along the west coast, and another from the island's northern end to its south-eastern tip. Two other roads cross the centre. A 4WD track runs around the southern coast, while footpaths provide access to villages in the far north.

There's a fair amount of rivalry between different villages as to who gets the tourist dollar and, if the truth be known, the people aren't interested in visitors turning up as it pleases them. Accordingly, 'unescorted' tours by any foreign visitors are strictly prohibited by the Tafea Council. Probably the only acceptable options are to hire a taxi or take a tour.

To/From the Airport Transfer costs vary depending on where you're staying. One-way transfers cost 900VT to Tanna Beach and 2500VT to the Nikity Guest House at Yaneumakel. To get to Resolution Bay you can either transfer to Tanna Beach and arrange a ride from there – it'll cost you 2000VT – or find a taxi in Lenakel. For this reason, it's best to take the morning flight from Vila if you're intending to stay at Port Resolution.

Bus There are no regular bus services. However, some freelance minibuses and taxis operate on the cross-island route from Lenakel.

Walking If you have nothing better to do you can walk across the island from Lenakel to Port Resolution by following the main road. This 41-km route is dusty and climbs some steep hills, particularly in the central range. You'll find a leaf house at most villages along the way, and there's the Nikity Guest House at Yaneumakel.

TAFEA

The Tanna Beach Resort offers a range of half-day and day walking tours to various points of interest in their area. These include the custom villages of Yakel and Yaohanen, and the beautiful Yapilmai Cascades. The day walk covers all three for 9000VT, including lunch.

If you're staying at the Napikinamu Yacht Club at Port Resolution you can do any amount of walks with a guide provided at no charge. You will, however, be up for entry fees. One of the nicest walks from here is the six-hour excursion on forest paths over the central range to Yakel. Your hosts will arrange pick-ups where required.

Tours Although it can be costly, the easiest way to get around Tanna for most visitors is on a tour bus. Tanna Beach Tours offers by far the widest range of activities, with its 4WD minibuses visiting all major attractions on a daily basis. White Grass Tours also offers a good range for much the same price. You can make arrangements in Vila for White Grass through Frank King Tours (☎ 22808) and also Surata Tamaso Tours (☎ 25600), and for Tanna Beach through Pacific Tours (☎ 25200).

The cheapest overnight package is offered by Pacific Tours. For 23,900VT you get air fares to and from Vila, one night's accommodation in the Tanna Beach Resort's Guest House, and a night visit to Mt Yasur. Allow an extra 3500VT per day for meals if eating in the restaurant.

From Tanna Beach, a visit to the Yakel custom village, which is arguably Tanna's second major attraction, is an extra 4000VT. Other tour options from here include night and day visits to the volcano (5600VT), a Jon Frum village (4000VT), the Tanna coffee factory (1800VT) and the tame dugong at Port Resolution (4800VT). Several places (eg Port Resolution and the Jon Frum village) can be visited as extensions to the main tours for a much better rate.

Visitors staying at the Paradise Bay Guest House at Lenakel can organise their own tour of the island by hiring a car and driver from the nearby Tafea Cooperative Store. The daily rate is 6000VT, including fuel. But don't forget you'll have to add custom entry fees. These can range from 200VT to 1600VT per person, depending on where you get your entry fee.

The cheapest of all operators is the Napikinamu Yacht Club, which offers its guests an all-day island tour by taxi for 4000VT plus entry fees. It provides a number of shorter tours, also in conjunction with the local taxi service, and these are all attractively priced.

A guided tour of Mt Yasur from the Nikity Guest House costs 3600VT per person. Its other tours include a visit to a Jon Frum village (2200VT) and Port Resolution (4000VT).

AROUND TANNA
South-Western Tanna

The following distances are from Lenakel.

Lenakel Around 1000 people live in Lenakel, Tanna's tiny commercial centre. It has a handful of shops, including the Tafea Cooperative Store, which sells everything from bananas to barbed wire. Next door is Westpac, where you can change most major foreign currencies, and the main market is across the road.

Places to Stay & Eat Behind the Tafea Cooperative Store is the *Paradise Bay Guest House*, which has modest kitchen facilities including six fan-cooled rooms costing 2200VT for singles or doubles. The guest house was the historic home of Bob Paul, who was once the proud owner of the largest coconut plantations on Tanna. If you wish to stay there, you can make a booking through the store on ☎ 68685.

Nearby is *Stephen's Place* (☎ 68606), where two rooms are available for 1500VT each.

The nearest restaurant to Lenakel is at the *Tanna Beach Resort*. You can get a taxi from town for 500VT, but you'll have to make an arrangement to be collected afterwards if you don't want to walk home.

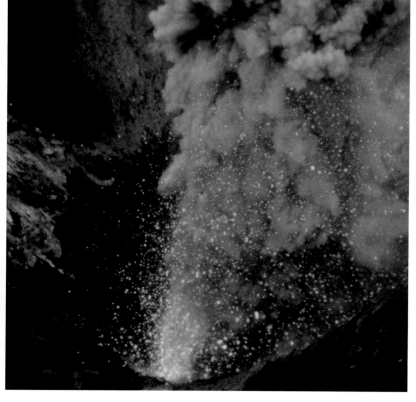

Top: Local villagers on the slopes of Mt Yasur, Tanna Island (AV)
Bottom: Mt Yasur, Tanna Island (AV)

A: Eton Beach, Efate Island (AV)
B: Coconuts - one of Vanuatu's major crops (DO)
C: Sand drawing, Malakula Island (DO)
D: The Blue Hole, Espiritu Santo Island (AV)

Isangel (2 km) The administrative centre for both Tanna and Tafea has about 1200 residents. It's very tidily laid out in an attractive colonial style, with many colourful shrubs and trees, mainly poincianas, pines, banyans and red coral trees.

The government *rest house* (provincial office ☎ 68638) has five rooms sleeping from three to five persons for 2000VT per head. It also has cooking facilities and cold-water showers.

Bethel (2.5 km) Seventh-Day Adventist villagers hold Saturday baptisms on the small black sand beach just before Bethel. Visitors are welcome to watch.

Less than one km behind Bethel is a small Jon Frum settlement called **Imai**.

Ebul Bay (3 km) The *Tanna Beach Resort* (☎ 68626) has a guest house as well as 14 bungalows with private facilities and room for up to five people in each. Accommodation per person costs from 5000VT to 11,000VT depending on the style. The resort, which is among tall coconut palms on the rugged shoreline, also has a swimming pool, restaurant and bar. When the swim-

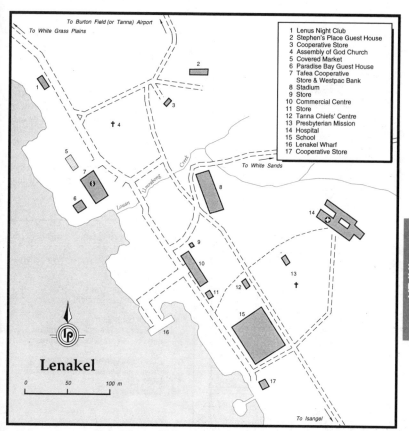

1 Lenus Night Club
2 Stephen's Place Guest House
3 Cooperative Store
4 Assembly of God Church
5 Covered Market
6 Paradise Bay Guest House
7 Tafea Cooperative
   Store & Westpac Bank
8 Stadium
9 Store
10 Commercial Centre
11 Store
12 Tanna Chiefs' Centre
13 Presbyterian Mission
14 Hospital
15 School
16 Lenakel Wharf
17 Cooperative Store

To Burton Field (or Tanna) Airport
To White Grass Plains
To White Sands
To Isangel

Imrabong Creek
Louan

Lenakel

0   50   100 m

TAFEA

ming pool was dug, eight skeletons were found buried in traditional Tannese style with the wives laid across their husbands' bodies.

Yakel (4 km & 4.5 km side-track) Known as 'Custom Village' by ni-Vanuatu tour guides, Yakel is one of the few Tannese villages left where custom reigns supreme. Villagers here wear only nambas and grass skirts, although they do change into Western clothing when visiting other areas. The chief refuses to allow any children to attend school, hoping this will ensure that they'll keep to the old

ways. He seems to be succeeding, as you see little sign of the modern age anywhere here. The major exception is the village truck.

Yakel has a population of about 80 people. It's central to six other villages, so as many as 600 people share the nakamal on the rise above the dwellings. It's used for kava drinking on most evenings, while dancing nights occur on a regular basis.

All the buildings at Yakel are made in the traditional fashion. Most have roofs of coconut thatch and walls of woven pandanus, and about half are on stilts. Each household has two dwellings: a day-to-day house on stilts and a cyclone shelter built into the ground nearby.

If you go on an organised trip to Yakel, after a short tour of the village you can walk up to the edge of the nakamal where artefacts are on sale. These are mainly functional items such as walking sticks, various weapons, woven products and stone axes. When a male tourist wants to buy himself a namba, the seller usually asks his wife what size he needs. It's reckoned she will be less likely to exaggerate!

By now the men will have gathered beside the big banyan that overhangs the nakamal area. High up in its ancient branches is a tree house, where the boys are kept in seclusion after circumcision.

Isangel

0   100   200 m

To Lenakel   To Yetpaleniel

1   Jail
2   Copra Shed
3   Public Works Department Workshop
4   Police Station
5   Radio Mast
6   Huge Banyan Trees
7   Provincial Government Secretary's Office
8   Line of coconut trees marking boundary between former British and French administrative areas
9   Post Office
10   Provincill Government Offices
11   Provincial Government Rest House
12   DOM Church
13   Court House

The dancing begins. Soon the ground shakes as 20 or 30 male dancers form a tight circle and rhythmically stamp their feet. Off to one side are the women, who skip and whirl around while singing in harmony. Deep chanting fills the air. The dust hangs in a white mist at waist level. If it weren't for the cameras clicking on either side you could easily imagine that you'd stepped back into a distant past.

After three or four dances, the performers line up and file past so that each can shake hands with their visitors. They're feeling quite happy because, apart from having earned some cash, they like to show off their skills. As well, your visit gives them an ideal excuse to practise for the next night of dancing in the nakamal.

Imlao Point (5 km) From Imlao Point the road continues south to Isakwai. Here it becomes a 4WD track that continues around the south coast to meet up with the Port Resolution road at Manuapen.

The Tanna Beach Resort maintains a small *bungalow* on the foreshore at Black Sands Beach South, just beyond Imlao Point. It's a good spot for anyone wanting to get right away by themselves.

The walk from Tanna Beach to Black Sands is easy along the little-used road, and there's some nice coastal scenery en route. For something more demanding, you can hike up into the steep, densely-forested country below Mt Tukosmera. Ask at the resort about this.

North-Western Tanna
The following distances are from Lenakel.

Burton Field (2 km) Going north from Lenakel, there's a turn-off to the island's airport just outside the village. The airfield's name comes from an aviator who pioneered air transport in the archipelago.

Imanaka (9 km) There are Jon Frum dances here on Friday night. Visitors are welcome but must accompany a tour from one of the resorts. The entry fee is 3000VT.

White Grass Plains (10 km) The main road turns inland at Imanaka, leaving the coastal route to continue straight on to Black Sand Beach North. The country here is quite different to Tanna's southern end, being flat and covered with hardy grasses. Once the summer rains are over, the grass turns yellow, then white, hence the name.

Unfortunately, you can't expect to see any of the wild horses that tourist brochures tell you live in this area. They may once have numbered in the hundreds, but the vast majority have since been either eaten, captured or killed by drought. If you do see any free-ranging horses you can be sure they belong to someone, which rather takes the fun out of it.

About 10 minutes walk from the White Grass Bungalows (see following) is a large blue hole in the coral reef that makes a good swimming spot at low tide. There are some excellent reef-walking spots right along the coast here.

Places to Stay & Eat Continuing along the coastal track from Imanaka, you'll reach the *White Grass Bungalows* (☎ 68660) after about three km. There are 11 fan-cooled rooms costing 6000/6900/7200VT for singles/doubles/triples as well as a restaurant and bar facilities. The resort is sited on a low cliff with the sea in front and White Grass Plains behind. It's a lonely setting but a very peaceful one, with a beautiful view over the sea.

Black Sand Beach North (17 km) This small, aptly named beach is in a quiet, secluded cove and offers good swimming.

Eastern Tanna & Yasur Volcano
A footpath continues around the north of the island, connecting up with the south-eastwards road near Green Hill and Ehniu.

The following distances are from Green Hill.

TAFEA

Fetukai (7 km) This is the northern end of the Middle Bush area. Vanuatu's main coffee-growing area is found here, with the Tanna Coffee Development Co (☎ 68617) being the major producer. Visitors are welcome to inspect the plantation and factory, but should make enquiries first. Coffee growers are experiencing serious problems with the huge quantities of dust being pumped out by Mt Yasur.

Lamnatu (12.5 km) Some of the people in this area are Jon Frum supporters. At Christmas and New Year, Jon Frummers and Seventh-Day Adventists walk around the district in large groups, singing. You'll recognise the former by the white chalk marks on their faces.

Loanialu Lookout (22 km) Located on top of the main range on the old road from Lenakel to Port Resolution, this lookout point offers a magnificent view of the Yasur volcano. Aniwa Island can be seen in the north-east and Futuna to the east.

The relatively new section of steep, narrow winding road was constructed by British Army engineers in 1990. Travelling along here in the back of a 4WD minibus is quite an experience, and not one for the faint-hearted.

Near the bottom of the main range you pass the *Nikity Guest House* (☎ 68616), which has four rooms costing 2800/9000 per person/family. It's about 30 minutes by car to the volcano – not five as the brochure claims – and is nowhere near the sea. Thanks to the constant rain of fine ash it doesn't enjoy a great reputation for cleanliness. There's a market here on Friday where you can buy local foods, and a small store nearby that sells limited tinned goods.

Waisisi Bay (28 km) At Dip (Deep) Point there's a turn-off to Waisisi Bay, three km to the north-east. This is one of Tanna's few good anchorages. There's also an attractive black sand beach stretching eight km northwards to just beyond Lenemtehin Point.

Yaneumakel (30.5 km) This village boasts a red-painted Jon Frum church. Inside, a large colour poster beside an illustration of Jesus Christ depicts American astronauts who've been to the moon. In the villagers' view the astronauts are Christ's equal because of their lunar visit.

There's also a large red cross and a healing stone inside the church. Villagers say Jon Frum came to their priest in a dream and gave him the right to heal people. To be cured, the sick have to rest their heads on the stone while the priest pours water over their hair. The names of the people who claim to have been healed in this way are on a board on the church's western wall.

As it's tabu for females to see the healing stone, the priest will only allow men to enter the church. He believes he will not be able to converse with Jon Frum if he breaks this rule.

White Sands (30.5 km & 1.5 km side-road) There's a hospital, store, more Jon Frum people and a village council office in this village. True to its name, there's also a white sand beach.

Sulphur Bay (30.5 km & 3 km side-track) This village, also called Ipeukel, is the centre of the Jon Frum cult. Like other villages belonging to the cult, it's built around a square ceremonial ground. The church to one side houses the movement's most sacred red cross, which you may photograph but not touch. Beside it is an unpainted post dedicated to Christ, and used to heal backaches. If you ask, you'll be shown the grave of Nampus, a Jon Frum prophet of the 1950s.

Every Friday evening, cultists come from nearby villages to dance at Sulphur Bay. Unless you have a deep and abiding interest in cults and want to spend more time studying this one in detail, this is probably the time to visit.

Jon Frum's day is celebrated on 15 February. This is the day when Sulphur Bay people believe their messiah will return, bringing all the cargo he has ever promised them. Prayers and flowers are offered at the red cross in the church, followed by a flag-raising ceremony

TAFEA

and military parade. Men carry rifles made from bamboo, painted to look as if they have red bayonets fitted to their ends.

About 100 men, bare to the waist, march under the command of two village elders dressed like US army sergeants. On their bare backs, the soldiers proudly display the red-painted letters 'USA'. Each one considers himself to be a member of the Tannese Army, a special unit – so they say – of the American armed forces.

In essence, Jon Frummers believe that by acting as they think White people do they'll be able to intercept the magic that gives Whites their wealth. They try different things (eg holding military parades and building bamboo aircraft) in the hope that one will do the trick.

Sulphur Bay people consider themselves the traditional owners of the Yasur volcano, although others in the area make the same claim. If you want to walk up the mountain you should check first whether guides are available here. The return walk will take you about six hours depending on how active the volcano is.

Places to Stay As in most rural villages in Vanuatu, there's a small, leaf-style *rest house* in Sulphur Bay where you may or may not have to pay to spend the night. Drifting ash is a problem here, and Yasur's loud explosions may keep you awake all night. Unless it's quietened down you will almost certainly be better off staying at Port Resolution.

Ash Plain (31 km) Towering above you as you pass the lifeless waters of Lake Isiwi, Mt Yasur darkens the sky with great clouds of ash-laden smoke. Over centuries this gritty material has smothered the vegetation, reducing the landscape to a grey moonscape. You can shoot some of the most dramatic scenery in Vanuatu here, with the gaunt shapes of surviving pandanus palms adding a surrealistic quality to the view. In the background, Yasur's stark eroded flanks resemble a huge, smoking coal dump.

Visiting Mt Yasur

Walking up the steep 150-metre path from the carpark to the crater rim, your introduction to the turmoil within Mt Yasur consists of whiffs of sulphur accompanied by whooshing and roaring noises. Then you're on the bare ash rim looking down into a dark central crater about 300 metres across and 100 metres deep.

At the bottom, three vents seem to be taking it in turns to spit showers of molten rock and smoke, like monstrous roman candles. When the biggest one blows there's an ear-splitting explosion that causes heads to disappear into collars. The earth trembles and a fountain of fiery magma soars skywards above the rim. After this come progressively smaller roars until eventually all is quiet, except for the sound of rocks thudding back into the crater. At night you can see glowing boulders as big as trucks somersaulting back down into what looks like the embers of a vast campfire.

Then, just when you're getting used to it, you hear a great 'whoosh' as of indrawn breath, followed by an almighty bang as if a blockbuster bomb has gone off at your feet. The ground underfoot shakes like a jelly as great lumps of red-hot magma shoot high overhead. Black smoke boils upwards in a dense, writhing column, and you may see brief flashes of lightning within. Down below, magma can be seen splashing in the central vent before subsiding again.

After these cataclysmic events you may hear rocks landing behind you, which is a reminder of the ones you passed on the way up. There are no hard hats, of course – there isn't even a guard rail. Mind you, a hard hat wouldn't be much good if a decent-sized rock landed on your head. Neither would a guard rail if the lookout point decided to shake loose and fall into the crater.

Some visitors find Yasur a terrifying experience; it's definitely unforgettable and shouldn't be missed. Common sense dictates that you go at night. Not only are the fireworks more spectacular then, but you can see the rocks coming and thus have a chance of avoiding them. Take a good torch and a warm pullover, and do have your personal affairs sorted out before you go. In early 1995 a guide, a local villager and a Japanese tourist were killed when, while standing on the crater's rim, they were struck by flying rocks. ∎

TAFEA

Imayo Waterfall (36 km) This spectacular waterfall, which is deep in the rainforest behind Imayo, is for serious trekkers only. A local legend says that any White person who swims here will drown. If you still want to go, enquire about guides at the place you're staying before setting off.

Continuing on past the turn-off to Imayo, the track enters a gully on the volcano's southern slopes. Lush tree ferns crowd in on either side, making an almost unbelievable contrast to the desolation that lies just back around the corner.

Yasur Volcano (41 km) Also called Yahuwei, Yasur is one of the world's most accessible active volcanoes. In fact, 4WD vehicles can get to within 150 metres of the crater rim.

There's also a walking route up the mountain's north-eastern slopes from the Ash Plain. The hike takes about 45 minutes and is reasonably easy going. Don't try it at night, though, or you may end up falling into a ravine.

Legends about Yasur In the local language Yasur means 'old man', and people living in the vicinity consider the volcano to be the originator of the universe. In the traditions of south-east Tanna the volcano is another version of heaven, or hell, as this is where a person's spirit is believed to go after death.

Sulphur Bay people believe that Jon Frum lives in the volcano along with a huge army of anywhere between 5000 to 20,000 men, or spirits.

Port Resolution (43 km) Captain Cook landed here in 1774 when he visited Tanna. Nearby is a flat-topped rock called **Cook's Pyramid,** where the explorer took some sightings. Although an earth movement in 1878 raised both the bay and the pyramid about 20 metres, the harbour is still Tanna's best anchorage for yachts.

Port Resolution is the home of a male **dugong** which you can summon by slapping the water with your hands. You can swim with the dugong, but you need to be careful.

It can be aggressive towards males and may try to shepherd females away from shore.

Places to Stay & Eat The *Nipikinamu Yacht Club Guest House* is set on a clifftop with a marvellous view of Port Resolution. It has six traditional bungalows, each sleeping four persons, for 2200VT per person including breakfast and dinner. The food is traditional village fare, so take along some flavourings and tinned food, just in case. Bookings can be made through the Tafea Cooperative Store in Lenakel, or through the NTO, Pacific Tours, Surata Tamaso or Tour Vanuatu in Vila.

Manuapen (42 km) From the 30-metre cliff you can clearly see a large number of sharks in the clear water below. To go to this lookout costs 300VT for casual visitors. The village has basic facilities for camping.

Yanekahi (43.5 km) The black volcanic-sand beach here has two **hot springs** at its north-western end where, in the days before butane cookers, villagers cooked their meals. Thermal steam rises from the rocks near one spring.

Ireupuow (44 km) There's an attractive white sand beach on the southern side of this village, and another beach at nearby Yewao Point.

Erromango Island

A mountainous, forested island, Erromango covers about 900 sq km and is one of the largest members of the Vanuatu group. Yet it has only 1400 inhabitants, all of whom live in the few villages that are scattered around its generally rugged coast.

As with Tanna, Erromango's name is a result of a communication breakdown between Captain Cook and the island people. He asked what they called their island and, confused by his gestures, they replied 'erromango', meaning 'this is a man'. Later, the missionaries named it Martyrs' Island because so many of them met violent deaths there. Traders called it Sandalwood Island because of the abundant supplies of this valuable species of timber.

The heyday of Erromango's sandalwood trade was between the 1840s and 1870s; there were also extensive logging operations in the Ipota area in the 1970s. Since then, logging has been limited to the export of *tamanu*, a local mahogany-like tree, and a small amount of kauri.

There is currently a push by Asian logging companies for large-scale logging of all timber species on the island for export to mills in Asia. This is being resisted by local landowners, who fear massive damage to the environment that supports their lifestyle.

History

Cook's Arrival In August 1774 James Cook landed briefly in Cook Bay, where he offered the people his usual green branch of friendship. But the waiting islanders – fierce cannibals who were accustomed to war – were hostile. When the local chief suggested Cook should bring his longboat ashore, the explorer suspected treachery and retreated

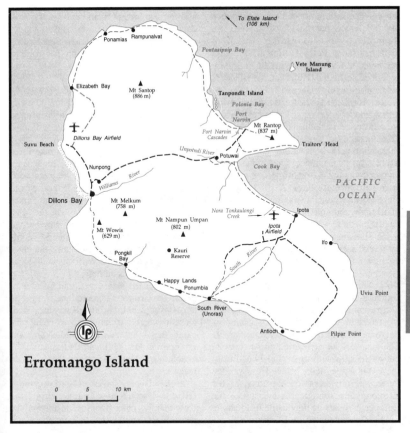

Erromango Island

0   5   10 km

with a burst of gunfire. Following this incident he named the nearby headland Traitors' Head.

Erromangan legends for a long time afterwards described Cook's visit as being made by a *nobu* or god. Islanders told how a huge canoe (Cook's longboat) came with a white god and other ghosts aboard. When the islanders resisted, the mysterious canoe withdrew to a floating village (Cook's ship), which then vanished back into the spirit world (by sailing away beyond the horizon).

Sandalwood Erromangans had no further contact with Europeans until the 1820s, when the crew of an American whaler came ashore. The sailors noticed large quantities of sandalwood but failed to capitalise on their discovery. Soon after, the Irish explorer-trader Peter Dillon arrived and attempted to fill his boat with the delicately perfumed softwood. However, the islanders were indifferent to trade and proved to be too violent for Dillon's taste. He sailed away unrewarded. Others persisted and eventually an industry was established.

In those days sandalwood was in great demand in China, where it was burnt in temples for its fragrance. The Chinese were prepared to pay £30 to £50 sterling a ton – a huge sum in those days. A 10-cm hooped piece of iron would buy a ship's longboat full of sandalwood logs in the south-western Pacific, so there were enormous profits to be made. Humans were also used as trade goods by some unscrupulous skippers. It wasn't unknown for Tannese to be captured and swapped to the Erromangans for sandalwood, after which they became the main course at cannibal feasts.

Erromango was a sandalwood vessel's most dangerous destination and it was essential to be constantly on guard against attack. The islanders were required either to swim out to the ship with their sandalwood or to leave it in a pile on the beach. However, the latter was no guarantee of safety, as the Erromangans soon learned to upset the Europeans' boats as they came in to shore. Ships often retaliated by firing on villages

that had earned their displeasure, and so the cycle of violence continued.

Although many of the missionaries blamed Erromangan ambushes on European crimes, it seems more likely that the islanders thought these trading ships carried unbelievable wealth. They considered that to capture one would reveal huge supplies of cargo, a good return for any casualties sustained in the assault. The most prized item was the longboat, which was a much more versatile craft than any dugout canoe.

The majority of attacks on trading ships in the Vanuatu archipelago occurred in Erromango's waters. In the late 1840s at least nine ships were either attacked or lost sailors ashore there (one of them three times). Sandalwood on the island was almost totally depleted by the 1860s, when blackbirding became the major attraction for foreign vessels.

Missionaries While traders were preaching a message of European avarice and worship of wealth, a few brave missionaries tried to spread other ideals. In 1839 John Williams, who had converted so many people in Samoa and the Cook Islands, decided to take Presbyterianism to Erromango. He first visited Futuna and Tanna, where he was well received. Hoping for a similar response from the Erromangans, he and his colleague James Harris landed at Dillons Bay on the west coast. Unfortunately for them, however, a trading vessel's crew had murdered five villagers and kidnapped a chieftain's daughter a few days previously. Williams and Harris had no idea of this outrage.

Kowiowi, the local chief, told his men to permit the two foreigners to land as long as they stayed near their boat. But if they went close to where a tribal feast was being prepared, they must die. Harris did so and was promptly killed. Williams fled towards the boat, but was clubbed down before he could reach it.

In 1857 George and Ellen Gordon came to Dillons Bay from Canada. This time Kowiowi was more friendly and allowed the newcomers to build a house. Four years later they were still there, despite the fever-bearing mosquitoes that swarmed around Dillons Bay.

In 1861 the island was swept by successive epidemics of whooping cough, dysentery, VD and finally measles, all of which proved disastrous to the locals. The latter resulted when a trading ship deliberately left some infected Tannese on the island as a reprisal for a dispute it had with the Erromangans. Then a tropical cyclone struck and devastated the village gardens.

The Gordons unwisely claimed that all these misfortunes were God's judgement. However, the islanders believed only witchcraft could have caused such a spate of tragedies. The Gordons were held responsible and killed, but their teachings must have had some effect as neither body was cannibalised.

In 1864 James Gordon, George's brother, came to Dillons Bay. He was joined by James McNair in 1867, who died there three years later. Meanwhile, custom-worshipping islanders believed the day of reckoning was coming. If they didn't strike quickly, the new doctrine of Christianity would prevail. Every night Gordon would climb up a ladder into his attic, pull it up after him and seal the trap door. He paid the ultimate price when, early in 1872, he became the last missionary to be killed on Erromango. Another evangelist was quickly sent to replace him.

Depopulation Erromango's population was perhaps as high as 10,000 in Cook's time, but by 1861 a succession of epidemics had reduced it to 4000. Seventy years later, thanks to more epidemics as well as the blackbirding 'industry', it was only about 400. The slide continued until the 1940s, but since then the population has crept up to nearly 1500. Erromangans will tell you that the massive depopulation of their island was God's punishment for their killing the missionaries.

Medical Services
There are dispensaries at Dillons Bay, Ipota and Port Narvin.

Places to Stay & Eat
The custom at all Erromangan villages is that simple beds are always available in the nakamals for the use of visitors. Usually, the only payment required is that you sit and talk with the people until it's time for bed. You should take your own bedding and food, or be prepared to buy food cooked by your hosts. Otherwise, if you go walking, take a tent and ask the local chief for permission to camp.

Contact either the NTO in Vila or the Tafea provincial government office (☎ 68638) in Isangel for details on what commercial accommodation is available.

Alternatively, if you want to check accommodation possibilities before going to Port Narvin, Ipota or South River (Unoras) you can ring the teleradio in Vila and ask to be patched through to these places – they all have two-way HF radios. If possible ask a Bislama speaker to do your talking for you as the person on the other end is unlikely to speak English.

Currently the island's only guest house is at Dillons Bay. (See the following Dillons Bay section for more details.)

Winter nights can often be very cool in Erromango's uplands, while malaria can be a problem at lower levels, especially near the coast.

Ipota, Port Narvin and Dillons Bay have small stores selling a limited range of goods.

Getting There & Away
Air The island's commercial airfields are at Dillons Bay in the north-west and Ipota in the south-east.

Vanair has two weekly return flights between Vila and Ipota and three between Vila and Dillons Bay. Most of these are via Tanna. One-way tickets to Dillons Bay cost 5900VT from Vila and 4100VT from Tanna, and to Ipota cost 6700VT from Vila and 4500VT from Tanna. A ticket from Dillons Bay to Ipota costs 2400VT.

There is also a weekly return service between Ipota and Aniwa – you fly in on one day and out on another – with a one-way ticket costing 3500VT.

TAFEA

Once you're on Erromango you may find that information on air transport out of the island is very limited and can be confusing. For this reason, it's best to arrange everything in Vila prior to departure.

Sea Toara Coastal Shipping and Ifira Shipping both operate a more-or-less fortnightly service from Vila to Dillons Bay, Elizabeth Bay and Cooks Bay. Fares to these ports start at 3000VT, while coming the other way from Tanna will cost 2000VT.

With Toara you can get from Erromango to Aniwa for 2000VT, to Futuna for 2500VT and to Aneityum for 2600VT.

Getting Around

To/From the Airport The truck service between Dillons Bay and the airfield costs 600VT.

Roads There are few well-maintained roads on Erromango. One is the nine-km road between Dillons Bay and the airfield. The others are the logging routes from Dillons Bay to Port Narvin and from Ipota into the southern forests.

Expect to pay upwards of 3000VT for a taxi from Dillons Bay to Port Narvin. You can hire one for the day, but this will cost as much as 15,000VT.

Walking Walking is the main reason most tourists visit Erromango. You can walk across the island along the road from Dillons Bay to Port Narvin then on down the coastal path to Ipota. Alternatively, there's the much more demanding but more interesting walk from Dillons Bay south to South River, then across to Ipota. You must take a guide for the latter.

You'll also find plenty of potential for enjoyable shorter walks in forest and coastal environments, provided you can avoid the logged areas.

Speedboat You can hire speedboats at Dillons Bay, Port Narvin and Ipota.

AROUND ERROMANGO
North-Western Erromango

The following distances are from Dillons Bay.

Dillons Bay Also called Unpongkor, this village of 450 people is Erromango's largest settlement. Now a peaceful spot, its bloody past is recalled by a memorial to the murdered missionaries in the Presbyterian church. This large, sombre building is called the **Martyr's Church** and was built in 1879. Several missionaries – including McNair, the only one to die of natural causes – are buried in a small cemetery on the Williams River's southern bank.

The path on the river's south bank takes you through an area of rainforest where you'll see examples of the sandalwood trees that were once so plentiful on Erromango. In the vicinity is a **rock** that shows the outline of Williams, who was the first missionary to be killed here. His murderers laid the body, which was short and stout, on the rock and and then began chipping around it prior to cooking and eating it. You can ask the villagers and they may show you where the rock is.

There is usually drinking water supplied in tanks at Meteson's Guest House. Otherwise, you'll see the women obtaining supplies from tiny springs at the side of the river. This water is brackish so you should remember to thoroughly boil it before you can even consider drinking it.

Places to Stay & Eat *Meteson's Guest House* (☎ 68692) provides beds and three meals for 4000VT per person per day. The owner, William Mete, is an obliging chap who'll make sure you enjoy your visit. His wife has a reputation as being a fantastic cook.

Nunpong (4 km) Just to the north of Dillons Bay, in a rain-shadow area of white grass, are the ruins of Nunpong, or 'Station' as locals call it. First established as a sheep station by an Australian in the 1930s, it switched to cattle 20 years later and ceased operations in 1980.

Close by is the well-preserved, lichen-covered wreck of a US WW II light bomber. In the bush nearby, along an old track beside the current road, are the remains of two other US WW II planes.

Suvu Beach (6 km) The main attractions at this white-sand beach, which is just below

---

Exploring South-Western Erromango

You can do the walk from Dillons Bay to Ipota via South River (Unoras) in three to four days allowing for some interesting side trips along the way. The route to South River mainly takes you through forest, gardens and cattle-grazing areas along the top of high coastal cliffs, which offer magnificent views. This section is generally easy apart from several steep drops and gruelling ascents in and out of deep, fiord-like valleys.

You can hire a guide in Dillons Bay for the entire route, or you may have to engage one for each section. Expect to pay 500 to 1000VT per day, plus the guide's food.

The following distances are from Dillons Bay.

Dillons Bay to Happy Lands (16 km)

Walking southwards along the track you soon reach a broad ridge halfway up Mt Wowis. As the path climbs upwards, you'll first see yam and taro gardens, then tropical rainforests and open grasslands. Continuing on from Mt Wowis you pass through Demsal, then scramble down the 300-metre-high escarpment to scenic Pongkil Bay. This family station has a nakamal where you can spend the night, and there's good swimming in a freshwater hole behind the beach – this is the last chance for a wash in fresh water before South River. You then have to climb up the scarp to get back onto the path for the remaining four km to Happy Lands.

If you want to shorten your walk you can take a speedboat from Dillons Bay to Pongkil Bay for 3500VT, weather permitting.

Happy Lands

Also known as Umponyelongi, this small village of 100 people has an aid post, an English-language school and a nakamal where you can spend the night for 500VT. It has no store.

If you have the time, spend a day at Happy Lands on a side trip to the nearby kauri reserve. Here you'll find large kauris as high as 40 metres growing on the steep slopes below Mt Nampun Umpan. Enthusiasts will appreciate the diversity of plant life in the area. It's a moderately difficult two-hour walk from the village and you can usually camp there.

Happy Lands to South River (Unoras) (13 km)

The three-hour walk to South River features several high points that offer extensive views along the cliff-girt coast and across to Tanna. There's a final steep descent to South River, which lies beside a picturesque estuary.

South River

The village of South River (Unoras) has a nakamal, where you can sleep, a small general store and a HF radio. If you want to be met by a taxi from Ipota, this is the obvious spot to arrange it.

South River to Ipota (25 km)

You have a choice of two routes, both of which eventually meet up with the logging road network outside Ipota. One path follows the South River, with much boulder-hopping required and shallow fords to be crossed – this track meets the road soonest, so it's the one to take if you're meeting a taxi. The other, which climbs the scarp and crosses higher country, comes out near Ipota airfield. Approaching Ipota you pass through some forestry plantations of a South American hardwood.

Another worthwhile alternative from South River is to do the three-hour walk to Antioch village, then take the path inland to meet the logging road about one hour from Antioch. ■

TAFEA

the Dillons Bay airfield, are two **caves** full of bleached skulls. The larger cave features hand stencils on its walls and ancient skulls encrusted with mineral crystals. The second cave contains much more recent remains. You'll need a guide to explore this area, which is accessible only by canoe or speedboat from Dillons Bay.

Across Erromango & Down the Coast
The 25-km logging road between Dillons Bay and Port Narvin crosses monotonous, undulating forested country for the most part and will take a full day's walking.

If you decide to bypass Port Narvin and go straight on to Ipota, cross the Unpotndi River first at the small settlement of Potuwai. Check here if there are any guides available. Past the village you carry on to the beach at Cook Bay, where you cross the river again.

Port Narvin (25 km) This pleasant settlement of 250 people has a long black sand beach and a nakamal. There are some **cascades** one km inland that are worth seeing.

Towering over the village, and four km to the east, is 837-metre **Mt Rantop**. From the top – it's a stiff climb – is a fine view of Erromango's east coast.

Below Mt Rantop, on its southern side, is a long white sand beach with coral shallows. Six km north of Port Narvin is **Tanpondit Island**, another good spot for coral.

Port Narvin to Ipota (18 km) The path south from Port Narvin heads up a short, steep gradient just beyond the village. Soon afterwards the terrain flattens out and then it's mostly level going as far as Cook Bay.

After you've crossed the Unpotndi River at the shallows in Cook Bay, follow the shore for another 12 km on to Ipota. It's an interesting walk with some nice coastal scenery, but the rugged going makes for slow progress in places.

Ipota The village and its airstrip were built by a French logging company in 1969. Today, 150 people live here and it is once

again the major centre for logging on Erromango. You'll probably have no difficulty finding a place to sleep either in the nakamal or one of the old logging quarters.

Aniwa Island

Covering a mere eight sq km, Aniwa is a low-lying island 24 km north-east of Tanna. Basically a raised coral atoll, its highest point is only 42 metres above sea level. Much of the island's northern half is taken up by a large lagoon, while the south is mainly under subsistence agriculture. Aniwa is an exporter of oranges and is the best place in Vanuatu to see sandalwood. (The trees are found in the gardens and in the secondary growth between them.) Sandalwood is still being exported, mainly to Taiwan.

Aniwa's population of about 400 is basically Melanesian. However, their language has strong Polynesian features, with similarities to Tongan.

History
In 1839 Aniwa became the archipelago's first island to have resident missionaries. They were soon withdrawn, to be replaced in 1866 by John Paton, who had earlier operated on Tanna. He believed the conversion of Aniwa's people to Christianity justified teaching them certain carefully selected falsehoods. For example, he claimed his god was making water surge out of the ground when in fact the missionary had dug a well.

Meanwhile, a trading station had been established on the island in 1860. Paton, jealous of his worldly competitors, roundly condemned the traders for bringing sickness to the area. But when a fatal measles epidemic swept through Aniwa after a visit by a mission vessel, Paton could only describe it as unfortunate.

Medical Services
There's a clinic at Vangaway.

Places to Stay

Make enquiries at the Tafea provincial government secretary's office (☎ 68638) at Isangel, on Tanna.

Getting There & Away

Air Vanair operates two return trips a week connecting Aniwa with Vila, Tanna and Ipota on Erromango. One-way tickets cost 8500VT from Vila, and 3100VT from Tanna and 3500VT from Ipota.

Sea Toara Coastal Shipping visits Aniwa en route to/from Futuna and Aneityum on a needs basis only. To get there it will cost 4000VT from the capital Vila, 2000VT from Erromango, 1000VT from Tanna and 1200VT from Futuna.

AROUND ANIWA

Most of Aniwa's residents live in the southern half of the island, which is crisscrossed by footpaths. A four-km road connects the airport to Ikaokao.

Itcharo Lagoon

This is a classic South Pacific lagoon, with calm blue water surrounded by white beaches and tall coconuts. There is good snorkelling on coral gardens along the reef, but you have to be careful of currents at the entrance. The lagoon is so beautiful that cruise ship companies have asked to visit it. However, landowner disputes have so far prevented this from happening.

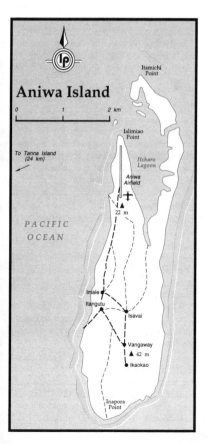

Futuna Island

Covering 11 sq km, and located 73 km east of Tanna, this ancient coral reef rises abruptly to 666 metres above sea level. Futuna is very different to other Vanuatun islands, and its people have a fascinating way of life which has developed largely because of its unusual topography. Basically, the island consists of a great column of limestone surrounded by a narrow coastal belt of lowland. When seen from a distance it resembles a steep-sided volcano rising out of the ocean.

Futuna's seven villages cling to the cliffs of the central plateau, the top of which is used exclusively for taro cultivation. It's too cold for bananas and other tropical crops up high, so these are grown on the lower slopes.

To get from village to village and up to the gardens you walk along narrow paths and scramble up and down ladders. These are made of bamboo poles lashed together with creepers.

In times of plenty the islanders make a mash of either bananas or breadfruit, wrap it

TAFEA

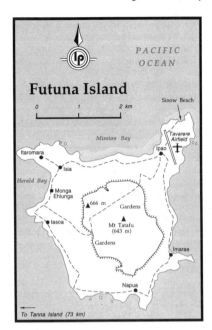

Futuna Island

0   1   2 km

PACIFIC
OCEAN

Sinow Beach

Mission Bay

Tavarere
Airfield

Itaromara

Isia

Herald Bay

Monga
Ehlunga

▲666 m

Gardens

▲
Mt Tatafu
(643 m)

Iasoa

Gardens

Imarae

Napua

To Tanna Island (73 km)

several sources including Tonga and Samoa, is very close to that of the Maoris of New Zealand.

Intermarriage with other ni-Vanuatu has produced physical characteristics in some Futunans suggesting a Melanesian descent. Yet others appear to be pure Polynesians except for their unusually light brown hair.

Local Customs

Futunans share the distinctly Polynesian custom of wearing 'mat', a cloth woven from pandanus leaves. As happens commonly in eastern Oceania, the men wear the mat like a kilt around the waist, although ·it is now used only during traditional ceremonies. At such times the women wear grass skirts.

In typical Polynesian fashion, Futunan chiefs gain their titles through inheritance. Traditional tattooing techniques are preserved.

Handicrafts

Futunans make attractively finished pandanus baskets and elegant mats. As the latter are made from a single weave and are therefore rather thin, they are more decorative than useful. Other local specialties include model canoes and war clubs.

Medical Services

Futuna's sole medical clinic is at Ipao.

Places to Stay

Contact the Tafea provincial secretary (☎ 68638) in Tanna for advice, or you can try to contact the local council office by teleradio.

A house can usually be made available on request, and while meals can be arranged it's best to take your own food. Warm clothing is a must during winter.

Getting There & Away

Air Vanair operates two return trips a week connecting Futuna with Vila, Tanna and Aneityum. One-way tickets cost 9500VT from Vila, 4500VT from Tanna and 4700VT from Aneityum.

in banana leaves and bury it in dry ground. This keeps indefinitely provided the leaves are changed regularly, so it makes an excellent food reserve in the event of disasters such as cyclones or drought.

The islanders' only source of protein is the sea, and they have an ingenious method of catching flying fish. This involves night fishing using a torch made of coconut fronds. The fish are attracted by the light, fly over the canoe and are scooped out of the air with nets. The canoes are similar to those used elsewhere in the country, but have raised freeboards to keep their crews dry in choppy or rough seas.

Futuna is the only island in Vanuatu that's free of malaria.

People

The 1000 present-day Futunans, about half of whom live on the island, say their ancestors originally came from an island in eastern Polynesia. Their language, which indicates

Sea Toara Coastal Shipping visits Futuna every three weeks or so, with deck space costing 5000VT from Vila, 2500VT from Erromango, 1800VT from Tanna and Aneityum and 1200VT from Aniwa.

AROUND FUTUNA

The following distances are from Ipao.

Ipao

Futuna's main village is next to the sandy shore of Mission Bay. From here a footpath connects Ipao with Imarae, 2.5 km away. There's a ladder about one km along this route.

Climbing Mt Tatafu from Ipao requires manoeuvring up a tree past a difficult ledge, but fortunately there are two ropes to hold onto.

Herald Bay (3 km)

It's a particularly difficult walk from Ipao to Herald Bay. Ladders lead up the hillside to Isia, and there's another between there and Itaromara.

Iasoa (4.5 km)

You'll need to use more ladders to get down to sea level at Iasoa. About half a km before you reach this village, you'll see another footpath which climbs by ladder to the top of Mt Tatafu.

Napua (8 km)

There are more obstacles to negotiate in the long, arduous stretch between Iasoa and Napua, and further on to Imarae.

Napua was the island's first true Polynesian settlement. According to the villagers, the first settlers were from East Futuna in the Wallis group. They reputedly found people already living here, but eventually won power through warfare and intermarriage.

Aneityum Island

This island, which until recently was officially called Anatom, covers 162 sq km and rises to 852 metres at Mt Inrerow Atahein. Much of the interior is mountainous and thickly wooded. It was a major centre for sandalwood logging in the 1840s, but only kauri has been exported in this century. Large specimens of this species have virtually disappeared as a result of unrestrained logging.

The land is fertile and there is abundant evidence of old irrigation channels, which points to it having a much higher population in the past. There may have been 12,000 or more people living here before the arrival of Europeans. Now, due mainly to a succession of devastating epidemics in the 19th century, there are only about 550 people living in a few isolated coastal villages.

Aneityum has several attractive beaches as well as a reef that surrounds three-quarters of the island, making it an ideal spot for snorkellers and scuba divers. In addition, the island has 84 species of orchid, more than anywhere else in Vanuatu.

The island is on the itinerary of cruise ships, which call in at tiny Inyeug Island (Mystery Island) every three weeks or so. There are no problems visiting Inyeug, but otherwise tourists are not generally encouraged; check this situation at the Cultural Centre in Vila prior to making any bookings.

The temperate climate has enabled the Australian goshawk to become established, making Aneityum the only place in Vanuatu where you'll find this attractive bird of prey.

Aneityum's flora is different to the rest of Vanuatu, being more akin to that of Australia and New Caledonia.

History

Scattered around the island are rocks decorated with a number of petroglyphs, including representations of the sun, stars, people, birds and fish as well as spirals and other geometrical designs. Islanders claim these are the work of an earlier people.

In the past the Aneityumese traded occasionally with their counterparts in New Caledonia, over 300 km away. When they saw their first sailing ship on 16 April 1793, they thought it was a sea spirit. It was in fact the French navigator D'Entrecasteaux, who was searching for his lost compatriot La Pérouse. After a cursory examination he sailed on. According to island legends, a large offering of coconut and yams displayed on the beach persuaded the mysterious apparition (ie the French ship) to depart.

Traders The first permanent European presence in Aneityum – as well as Vanuatu – was established by James Paddon in 1844. He built his trading station on Inyeug Island and operated it until 1852.

Paddon's main interest was sandalwood, but he also replenished passing whaling ships and satisfied a huge demand for jew's-harps among local villagers. Unlike many traders of his time, Paddon treated the islanders with respect.

Business boomed as up to 40 ships a year called in, mainly for sandalwood. However, by 1852 most of the timber was logged out. Though other traders remained, Paddon moved to Tanna to be closer to Erromango, then the Pacific's richest source of sandalwood. Whalers continued to come ashore, using huge pots to melt their whale blubber into oil, until the industry ceased in the early 1870s.

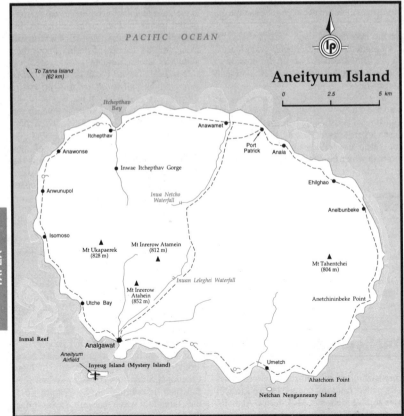

A: Soft coral with extended polyps (MC)
B: Clown fish with anemone (MC)
C: Diver with tomato clown fish and yellow tangs (MC)
D: Soft coral (MC)

A: Port Vila market (DO)
B: Chief Stephan of Amelboas natsaro, Malakula Island (DO)
C: Rom dancers, Ambrym Island (DO)
D: Small Nambas drum orchestra, Malakula Island (DO)

Missionaries John Geddie, a Presbyterian minister of Scottish descent from eastern Canada, arrived in May 1848. This dour, unimaginative man made Aneityum the initial headquarters of the Presbyterian mission in Vanuatu.

In 13 years, Geddie converted 3000 people to his particular brand of puritanical Christianity. This was more than three-quarters of Aneityum's population at the time.

How did Geddie succeed? He learnt Aneityum's main language, translated the Bible into it, and had it printed. As well, he set up schools where islanders were taught to read it.

Geddie banned his flock from dancing, smoking, drinking kava and taking part in traditional ceremonies. But on the positive side he did bring peace to Aneityum, and tried hard to stop the traditional strangling of wives on their husbands' death. To his dismay, however, the women tended to insist on their right to die with their spouses.

All the traders detested Geddie, as he was openly resentful of the way their influence on the islanders rivalled his. Aware of his obsession with Sunday worship, traders would deliberately arrive on the Sabbath in the summer wet season. Gleefully they would leave highly perishable goods and exposed mail on the shore. Then they would have their own brief, solemn service aboard ship, devoutly praying for rain.

And rain it often did! All the letters would be sodden by the time Geddie's services were over, much to the sailors' amusement.

In 1853 France annexed New Caledonia, and Geddie and his Presbyterian friends were afraid Vanuatu would be next. They petitioned Britain, with the backing of all the Christian chiefs, to make Aneityum a British protectorate. However, Britain was reluctant to assume further imperial responsibilities and declined. These petitions were repeated in 1859 but again without success.

Depopulation By 1860, Aneityum's original population of 12,000 people or more had been reduced to about 3500 by catastrophic epidemics of influenza, diphtheria and whooping cough. Early the following year measles, followed by dysentery, swept through the island and killed almost half the remaining population. There were so many dead that the only way to dispose of the bodies was to cast them into the sea.

Although it can hardly be proved, some say it was the mission-donated clothes that killed so many people. These often carried a range of European diseases, including tuberculosis and skin infections, to which the Aneityumese had no immunity.

The deaths of huge numbers of women of child-bearing age was the most serious feature of Aneityum's recurrent epidemics. By 1885 the population was down to around 850. Forty years later it had fallen to 250, and it was not to pass 500 again until the early 1980s.

Climate
Aneityum's climate is Vanuatu's most pleasant. Rainfall averages 300 mm per month in the first quarter and about 150 mm per month for the remainder of the year. Temperatures are at their highest in the wet season from January to March, when they range from 23°C to 30°C. In July and August the average is 16°C to 23°C.

Medical Services
The island's only clinic is at Analgawat.

Places to Stay & Eat
The council office in Analgawat (☎ 68672) can advise you about the guest house on Inyeug Island, plus any other accommodation that may be available. The village has a small shop where you can buy limited food lines. See the Analgawat section, below, for details.

Getting There & Away
Air Aneityum's only airfield is on Inyeug Island. Vanair operates two round trips per week connecting Vila, Tanna, Futuna and Aneityum. One-way tickets cost 11,300VT from Vila, 4500VT from Tanna and 4700VT from Futuna.

TAFEA

Sea Toara Coastal Shipping visits Aneityum every three weeks or so. Its fares are 6000VT from Vila, 2600VT from Erromango, 2000VT from Tanna and 1800VT from Futuna.

Getting Around
To/From the Airport A speedboat connects Inyeug Island with the mainland at Analgawat for about 200VT.

Walking The lovely 51-km footpath around Aneityum is mainly easy going except for the south-eastern section, which is much steeper and rougher. Here it repeatedly detours into the bush away from high cliffs.

The best option is to walk around the west coast from Analgawat to Port Patrick, then return through the middle. This will take two to three days depending on what sort of hurry you're in.

All around the western coastal section you'll find lots of beautiful picture-postcard scenery of white beaches, waving palms and turquoise water. The walking is quite easy, being mainly on the beach, and there is good drinking water to be had from the streams you cross en route.

Along the way you can explore old irrigation channels and village sites in the fringing grassy hills. Some of the channels are still used for the cultivation of water taro, a staple food of the islands.

The 14-km cross-island footpath from Port Patrick to Analgawat crosses the rugged central range, so you may find this section difficult in places. As compensation, the scenery is often magnificent, with large kauris and high waterfalls along the way. The orchids in the forest bloom all year but are said to be at their best in October and November.

Ask at Analgawat about guides for walking on the island.

Speedboat An around-the-island speedboat ride will cost at least 8000VT unless you share. So also will the return trip between Analgawat and Port Patrick.

AROUND ANEITYUM
The following distances are clockwise from Analgawat.

Analgawat
This is a popular anchorage for cruising yachts as it offers a secure shelter from all but the west wind. Consequently, Analgawat was the island's natural centre for whaling and sandalwood activity in the 1840s to 1870s.

John Geddie built a stone church here that was large enough to seat several hundred people, but the epidemic of 1861 ensured it would never be filled. A tidal wave in 1875 left it a ruin, but it is still quite substantial and makes an impressive sight.

Analgawat has a village council office, a large cooperative store (usually well-stocked), a medical clinic and a white sand beach. In thick bush about 4.5 km inland is the impressive **Inwan Leleghei waterfall**, which you can see from the shore.

Inyeug Island (1.5 km by boat)
This beautiful sandy islet now serves as Aneityum's airfield. It's surrounded by a broad sandbank and dazzling coral, while to the south-west is a surf-washed reef.

Inyeug was the site of Paddon's first trading post. The Aneityumese believed it to be the home of ghosts and would not live there, so were happy to sell it to him for some trinkets, a rug and a hatchet.

The self-catering *guest house* on Inyueg has three bedrooms where you can sleep for 1000VT per person per night. You can also hire kayaks. Ask at the Analgawat council office for details. Except on cruise ship days, you'll usually have the island to yourself except for the daily work gangs that come over from the mainland.

Utche Bay (3.5 km)
This pretty bay is fringed by a black sand beach.

Inmal Reef (6 km)
The reef, which is about one km offshore, is visible only at low tide. You can often see

turtles swimming in the channel between the reef and the mainland.

Anwunupol (10 km)
There's a hot-spring site near here.

Anawonse (12 km)
This area was the centre of the archipelago's 19th-century whaling industry. Some huge, rusting cooking pots, once used for melting whale blubber, still lie hidden in the thick bush.

Itchepthav Bay (15 km)
The deep-water anchorage here is considered especially safe for yachts. There are more hot spring sites about 500 metres to the west, while to the south along the creek is the steep, narrow **Inwae Itchepthav gorge**. The wild goats living here are a good source of protein for local villagers.

Anawamet (20.5 km)
From here you can see **Inwa Netcho waterfall**, three km inland. The local people have created a marine sanctuary off Anawanet to protect the numerous turtles that gather to feed along the reef. Elsewhere around the island the turtles are still hunted for food.

Port Patrick (23 km)
This is Aneityum's only village of any size once you've left the south-western coast. There are several long stretches of colourful reef as well as a 2.5-km length of sandy shore. Behind the village is a large plantation of pines.

Anaia (24.5 km)
The village has a long swamp used for taro cultivation. Local tradition has it that freshwater prawns showed farmers where to build the taro bed's water courses.

Ahatchom Point (39.5 km)
Fresh water bubbles up here at the water's edge. It's refreshing and pure enough to be drunk just as it is.

Umetch (42 km)
Looking south-east from here on a clear day you can sometimes see the black volcanic smoke that issues from distant Hunter Island.

You'll find some more **hot springs** about three km along the track towards Analgawat, with another site two km further on. Analgawat is four km beyond this.

Central Mountains
Aneityum's centre is dominated by several mountains, including two extinct volcanoes: **Mt Inrerow Atahein** (852 metres) and **Mt Tahentchei** (804 metres). In island tradition the former and its near neighbour, Mt Inrerow Atamein (812 metres), are married – Inrerow Atamein being the wife. Climb Inrerow Atahein and you'll get an excellent view into the crater on top. From here you can see over most of Aneityum as well as the islands of southern Tafea.

Matthew & Hunter Islands

Far to the south of Aneityum are the two tiny, active volcanic islands of Matthew and Hunter. Matthew was first sighted in 1788 by Captain Gilbert in the *Charlotte*, who named it Matthew's Rock. Its neighbour was discovered 10 years later by Captain Fearn in the *Hunter*.

Matthew Island lies 274 km south of Aneityum and over 320 km from New Caledonia. Hunter lies 77 km east of Matthew.

Both islands are minute: Hunter covers barely half a sq km while Matthew is about a fifth of that. Triangular-shaped Matthew Island has a central cone 142 metres high. Hunter has four small volcanic vents, the highest reaching up to 296 metres. There's always a strong smell of sulphur around both.

Not surprisingly, they're both uninhabited except for gulls.

Disputed Ownership
The people of Aneityum consider both

TAFEA

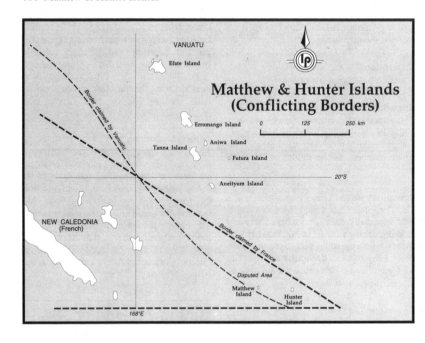

islands to be part of their customary ownership. They tell several ancient stories about them, calling Matthew and Hunter Umai Nyang and Umai Nupne respectively.

The islands were always considered to fall under the Anglo-French Condominium. However, in 1965 the French residency in Vila published a newssheet claiming that the UK had agreed to these two islands being incorporated into New Caledonia. Ten years later, the French navy erected a plaque on Hunter, officially claiming them for France. Soon after Vanuatu achieved its independence, the government removed the plaque and raised its new flag. Shortly afterwards a French patrol boat arrived. Its crew tore down the flag and unfurled the French tricolour. A small party of soldiers stayed behind to enforce France's claim.

Hunter proved to be a very unpopular assignment. Even so, the tiny force remained there until 1985 until the party was finally withdrawn.

Conflicting Borders
French mapmakers draw a triangle around New Caledonia which just includes Matthew and Hunter within its eastern tip. Vanuatu's map has a flowing line roughly bisecting the seas between the two countries. The midpoint on Vanuatu's charts coincides with the spot where the 20th parallel crosses the line of 168° longitude. This firmly places the two islands within Vila's rule.

The fuss is because Hunter's 321-km distance from Aneityum extends Vanuatu's exclusive economic zone by 35% or 230,000 sq km, while France stands to gain about 30,000 extra sq km of sea and two very remote outcrops of volcanic rock.

Getting There & Away
Matthew and Hunter islands' only non-naval visitor is the occasional yacht, making them its last stop in Vanuatu before heading on to New Caledonia or Fiji.

Malakula Island

The most apt and colourful explanation for Malakula's name – which is also spelt Malekula – comes from a tale about some 19th-century French sailors who landed there. The local islanders secretly wanted them to leave. In one version of the story, they sat the Frenchmen down on some furry local plants while everyone drank copious amounts of kava. Unfortunately for the sailors the leaves of these plants contained a strong skin irritant. Once the Frenchmen had sobered up, they all ran around clutching their rear ends, shouting *Mal à cul!* or 'Pain in the arse!' Another version has the Malakulans offering the sailors the same leaf to use as toilet paper – with similar dire effect!

Malakula is Vanuatu's second-largest island. It measures 2069 sq km, and is 94 km long and 44 km at its widest point. It is

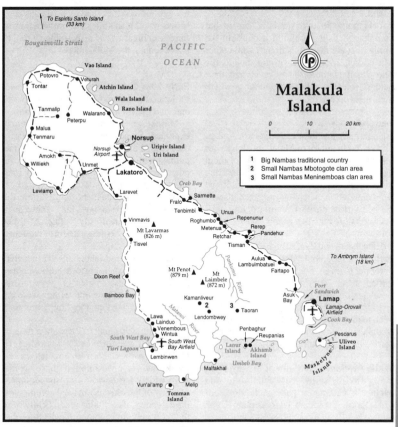

shaped like a sitting hound, having two high-land areas connected by a narrow section often called 'the dog's neck'.

Like many other such islands in the archipelago, Malakula is growing all the time. In 1965 a powerful earthquake raised parts of the northern half by up to 40 cm. The uplands, intersected by narrow valleys, rise to over 800 metres in parts of the island's southern centre. Much of this area and the south-western coast is extremely rugged and inhospitable.

More than 30 different languages are spoken on Malakula, which is Vanuatu's most linguistically and culturally diverse island.

It is home to two similarly named but completely distinct cultural groups. In the north-west are the Big Nambas, while other Malakulans are generally grouped under the title Small Nambas. They've earned their names from the size of the nambas which their menfolk wear.

History

Islanders say that their cultural hero, Ambat, once lived in southern Malakula along with his two children, and that the three of them had white skin and long, straight hair. They introduced the practice of male childhood head elongation, a custom restricted historically to this part of Vanuatu and still occasionally found in the area. (See Customs following.)

Like Adam and Eve, Ambat's two children each ate a rose apple despite their father's order not to do so. For their crime, they were turned black. They were also required to wear nambas and to remain isolated in the island's south. Right up to the 1930s, a European male would often be known to southern Malakulans as Ambat, or by the name of some other local cultural hero.

White Arrivals & Settlement In May 1768, Bougainville sailed between Santo and Malakula, naming the passage the Bougainville Strait. Six years later Captain Cook landed briefly in the south-west.

Although there was no sandalwood on Malakula, it was one of the earliest islands to be settled by Europeans. Much of the eastern coastal plain was cleared to make way for several huge coconut plantations. Although copra returns were initially encouraging, malaria, the humidity, cyclones and the islanders' zest for cannibalism drove many of the early settlers away.

By the 1880s, the French land-development company CCNH had bought up large tracts of the eastern coast. Because of constant friction between English and French planters over land ownership, French troops landed in Port Sandwich in 1886. When they left two years later, the trouble between the two groups of settlers had by no means been sorted out. Meanwhile, the introduction of European firearms and diseases had wrought havoc among the Malakulans.

Early 20th Century By the 1900s, French settlers outnumbered British almost two to one, and owned three times as much land.

Malakulan labourers were frequently exploited. Sometimes they were arbitrarily condemned by planters to work for them as punishment for nonexistent offences. At other times they were required to work long after their original contracts had expired.

Although the islanders didn't know the details of European law, they knew such treatment was manifestly unfair. At times they retaliated by killing settlers or crewmen from recruiting ships.

Some northern Malakulans were determined to retain their customs, refusing any contact with missionaries or government. The least affected by white settlers were the Big Nambas, who at the time numbered about 1000.

The late 1920s and 1930s were a time of catastrophic death rates in southern Malakula, particularly from gonorrhoea and blackwater fever. Although these deaths were widely attributed to the abandonment of many of the old customs and ceremonies, the defenders of tradition paradoxically were the most numerous among the dead, probably because they had much less contact with

Europeans and thus their immunity to disease wasn't well developed.

From 1939 until the early 1950s, an indigenous organisation called the Malakula Native Co-operative Movement, or the 'Malnatco', operated on the island. Initially it traded in copra, spending its profits on village improvement programmes. In WW II it gained a cargoistic element, with members eagerly anticipating the arrival of huge quantities of free gifts from the USA. When the bounty failed to materialise, the movement returned to its prewar commercial origins.

Anthropologists Malakula has long been a favoured stamping ground for anthropologists, thanks largely to its diverse languages, cultures and customs.

Bernard Deacon, a remarkable and tireless 24-year-old Cambridge University graduate, recorded much of the culture of the Small Nambas and the people of the South West Bay area before he died of blackwater fever in 1927. His book *Malakula: A Vanishing People in the New Hebrides* is still the most informative study on the area. Thomas Harrisson, a British Condominium official of the early 1930s, did the same for the Big Nambas and other northern Malakulans in his book, *Savage Civilisation*.

In the 1970s Charlene Gourguechon and two companions visited the Big and the Small Nambas. She recorded many fascinating details of their lives, noting several hitherto unknown features of the two unrelated cultures in her fascinating work, *Charlene Gourguechon's Journey to the End of the World*.

Recent Events Vanuatu's last *kakae man*, or victim of cannibalism, went into a Big Nambas pot in 1969. Only in the anarchic conditions of the Condominium could human flesh have been eaten so recently, and so close to police stations at Norsup and Lakatoro.

At independence in June 1980, the Modérés Party in Malakula announced its secession from Vanuatu and formed a provisional government. Then it joined forces with secessionist groups elsewhere to set up the Provisional Government of the Northern Islands. But by late September the rebellion was over. Papua New Guinean troops nipped it in the bud by arresting 700 Malakulans, mainly in Lakatoro, Lamap and the South West Bay.

Flora & Fauna

Much of Malakula's coastline is lined with mangrove, though there are plenty of sandy stretches. Inland are 20 orchid species, mainly in the upland areas.

Malakula's waters teem with sharks, especially along the east coast. There have been several fatalities over the last few years from Atchin south to the Maskelyn Islands.

The bush is plagued by rats and ferocious wild dogs. If you camp out or sleep overnight in a villager's hut, keep your shoes on: rats like to chew at the calluses on your feet.

Malakula is one of the few islands with a large population of Pacific boas. It is also the principal habitat of the endemic Vanuatu (or chestnut-bellied) kingfisher.

Population

Malakula's 20,000 inhabitants are mainly coastal dwellers, with less than 1000 living inland. Several thousand people inhabit the small offshore islands along the northeastern and southern coasts, with Vao, Atchin and Uliveo being the most populous.

Most of those living in the island's rugged interior reside in tiny, isolated mountain villages. These people are generally smaller and darker than other Malakulans. In the 1930s, they were mistakenly described as pigmies. The highlanders are one of the groups that have, to a large degree, managed to retain their cultural purity.

Malakula's inland population was once much larger, but over the years there was a drift of people down to the missions on the coast. Today, a resurgence of self-identity and a reduction in the stigma attached to living in the bush are promoting a move back to the interior.

MALAKULA ISLAND

Customs

Generally speaking, Malakulans have preserved their traditions more successfully than other ni-Vanuatu. For example, in the southern highlands, villagers still make fire by rubbing sticks together. Paddle dances are still common among the small island communities along the east coast from Vao down to Uliveo. People on Tomman Island have a ceremony commemorating the wife of a long-dead cultural hero: their headdresses represent the woman, while the small figure carried on their hips is her baby.

As elsewhere in Vanuatu, most people, despite Christianity and apparent sophistication, still strongly believe in devils. They also believe that some places are tabu to certain families, and that if their members go there, they will get sick and possibly die. People say medicine, or going to a hospital, seldom helps.

Until recently, sorcerers used to speak into bamboo instruments concealed in the ground. If villagers came for advice or a prophecy, the sorcerer would chant into the

Malakulan man

ground. The resulting, eerily resonating sound was attributed to ancestors. This, of course, left the clients suitably impressed!

A few older men from southern Malakula have elongated heads because their skulls were lengthened in childhood by means of a binding process. The practice was once considered to improve a persons' looks, but it rarely if ever occurs nowadays.

Nimangki grades are zealously followed in south-western Malakula and among the Big Nambas of the north. The most dedicated participants are from South West Bay, where aspiring males have as many as 35 grades to pass in the process of becoming a bigman or chief.

As elsewhere, boars with curved tusks are slaughtered during grade-taking ceremonies and other occasions including circumcisions, funerals, the sale of land, and the paying of a fine for breaking tabu. In the interior, the tusks are used in masks and puppets.

Although nakamals are the traditional meeting place for most ni-Vanuatu men, adult males from Malakula's north-eastern offshore islands often prefer to use a *natsaro*. Many of these clearings have large standing stones and low stone platforms lining one side. The platforms are used either as seats or as 'altars' where pigs are killed during nimangki ceremonies.

These small islands are among the world's last megalithic cultures. This culture has declined dramatically in practice, but the memories are still strong and there is a move towards restoring some of the old sites and customs.

The Big Nambas The Big Nambas were given their name because of the large mass of purple-coloured pandanus fibres the men wind around their penises. The loose ends are curled into a large bunch and secured by several thick bark belts worn around the waist, leaving the testicles exposed.

Although the Big Nambas' traditional territory extends from Nuas and Tenmaru to Unmet, nowadays almost all of them live at coastal missions. Only a few families remain in the northern interior.

History The Big Nambas were extremely well organised in war. Rifles were a powerful status symbol, and in the blackbirding days a man would volunteer to work as an indentured labourer in an overseas canefield just to obtain one.

By the early 1900s the Big Nambas had earned an awesome reputation. No foreigner, whatever his rank, dared venture into their territory without permission. Even police expeditions, which came to punish them for various crimes such as killing traders, were ambushed and dispersed. As a result, the Condominium police could only restrict their practices to the interior, not eradicate them completely.

The Big Nambas kept a stone fireplace where unwelcome outsiders, including Europeans, were ritually cooked and eaten. When a man of another tribe offended them, they would send a messenger to warn him of his likely fate. If he persisted – and few did – his eventual fate was met at the ceremonial fireplace.

Among other islanders their reputation was made worse by their treatment of dead enemies, whose bodies were often denied the usual death and burial rites. Instead of being eaten, the corpses were hung upside down until they rotted.

Until 1932, the lack of European contact helped the Big Nambas to survive the many epidemics of the time. But that year up to 600 of their number died of whooping cough, and a further 100 perished three years later from influenza.

These deaths, allied with the spread of Christianity, the banning of firearms after WW II, and the rising standard of living of their coastal counterparts, ultimately brought the Big Nambas down to the sea.

Daily Life The peaceful side of Big Nambas life has remained essentially the same. Working in the gardens is a women's work, while hypnotising pigs, a Big Nambas speciality which only takes a few minutes, is a male preserve. It's a great honour to be allowed to watch this take place.

The Meleun The last custom-oriented chief of chiefs, or *meleun*, died in the late 1980s. Since then his family has moved down to the coast and Christianity.

The Big Nambas are the only tribe in northern Vanuatu with hereditary chiefs. Traditionally, power is transferred to the eldest son once he reaches full maturity at about the age of 20. This prevents situations arising where authority might lapse because of his father's senility. The father, meanwhile, acts as adviser.

The Erpnavet Big Nambas men call their nimangki grade system the *erpnavet*. The ceremonies are often preceded by lengthy rehearsals, which are tabu for any women to see. If one does, she'll have to pay a fine of one tusked pig.

In the old days, up to 100 pigs would be slaughtered at an erpnavet. Nowadays about 20 suffice. To dress for the occasion the men cover themselves in a mixture of charcoal and coconut oil, tie nut rattles around their ankles and wear feathers in their hair.

Each erpnavet grade requires lengthy preparation and much paying of pigs. When a Big Nambas man has reached the highest grades, he is considered to have symbolically reached the sky. Metaphorically, he is like a bird of prey hovering above his fellow villagers, staring down at all beneath him. Having attained this level, he is given a hawk's name.

The hawk dance is the Big Nambas' ultimate erpnavet ceremony, where a man covered in white paint acts the part of a hawk's spirit. He is called a 'spirit man' while he assumes the actions of a hawk, soaring around the other dancers who are all painted jet black, then suddenly zooming in amongst them.

Women's Traditions Although Big Nambas women do not cover their breasts, it's tabu for a man to see them without their headdresses or grass skirts on.

Women squat when among men. When passing a male, they crouch low to ensure their head and shoulders are never above his. If a female meets a man in the bush who is not a blood relative, she has to conceal her face behind her headdress.

If a Big Nambas woman has truly pleased her husband, he may permit her to take part in the tooth ceremony. In this ritual, which results in much greater status, she has her two front teeth slowly loosened and then knocked out by a stone. The privilege costs her a large number of pigs, which are paid to the meleun, her husband's relatives and the teeth extractors.

Some Big Nambas women still wear traditional headdresses of purple pandanus fibres. These hang down from their brows to below the hips, modestly covering their genitals. This headgear is never removed in public as it's believed that to do so would put the whole tribe at risk. The women also wear a purple pandanus skirt, beneath which is a small mat covering the lower hips.

Small Nambas woman in traditional dress

Kava As elsewhere in Vanuatu, drinking kava in the nakamal is an important pastime for Big Nambas males. It's their traditional method of communicating with the ancestral spirits.

Such ceremonies are frequent and require lengthy preparation. For several hours all the participants, except the meleun, chew kava roots to release the juice which is then drunk from a communal bowl. If you're honoured with an invitation to a Big Nambas kava session, expect it to begin soon after sundown and end close to midnight.

The Small Nambas These days only the isolated Mbotogote and Meninemboas tribes of south-central Malakula are generally referred to as Small Nambas. This is because almost all their fellows elsewhere on the island now wear clothes and have abandoned many old customs. The two tribes have retained their customs longer than any others on the island. However, they stopped eating human flesh in the mid-1950s, which was earlier than the Big Nambas. The following information generally refers to these two groups.

The Small Nambas earned their name because of the small size of their penis sheaths compared to those of the Big Nambas. Tribesmen only wear one leaf around their penises, securing it by tucking it into their bark-type belt, while the women wear a short raffia grass skirt. During ceremonies, most adult men and women wear a bone through their noses.

The few remaining communities are built around a central dance area with up to five permanently standing tamtams. A funeral platform, where dead bodies lie, usually stands nearby, with large tree fern statues erected in front of it. The nakamal is nearby. It's forbidden for women to go anywhere in the dance area, but they may view it from a distance.

There are neither mosquitoes nor malaria in Malakula's mountainous south-central region, whereas the coast, particularly South West Bay, is infested with the disease. Many traditional Small Nambas people refuse to look at the ocean for fear of becoming ill, as they always associate coastal areas with malaria.

The Small Nambas receive little medical attention yet are among the healthiest people in Vanuatu.

Small Nambas men and women live totally separately. While the men have club-houses, ceremonial dancing areas and even some tracks reserved solely for their use, the women's lives revolve around housework and their communal hut.

Sleeping Arrangements The Small Nambas are monogamous. While the husbands will live alone, the wives sleep communally along with all the young children and some of the dogs. Romance is difficult because of the lack of privacy in the women's quarters. It's further complicated by the beds, which are no more than a few banana leaves on the hard floor. This also means sleepers are frequently woken by earth tremors.

Boys' Initiations Boys are circumcised when they are five to eight years old. Circumcision is the final event of a one-year training period.

Art objects made for boys' initiations either identify the actual boys who are about to be circumcised, or are decoys intended to lure malevolent ancestral spirits away. Boardlike figures with elongated eyes on stylised faces, called *namaragi*, represent the boys. Another oblong object, usually with two faces, one above the other and about 1.5 metres high, is called a *nekembao*. One is made for each male who is to be circumcised.

The Male Nimangki The Small Nambas have 19 nimangki grades. However, in contrast to the Big Nambas, they only kill a few boars at a time.

The Female Namanggitenge Unlike most other ni-Vanuatu females, Small Nambas women have their own nimangki system. While they are considered to be inferior to

men in this life, as long as they take their grades their spirits are as powerful as any man's after death. They call their nimangki process the *namanggitenge*.

The first stage requires a female grade-taker to present a pig to the chief. Then she dances with the other women outside the village, beside the women's funeral platform. This continues for six days, though there's an interruption on the fourth when the female grade-taker is taken to a nearby creek. There she's ceremonially but lightly beaten and briefly submerged.

The sixth day begins with a pig-killing. Even if the participants are pre-teenage girls, they must kill their pig, then hand out parts of it to the chief and the other dancers.

The ceremony climaxes when one of the female grade-taker's front teeth is removed by repeatedly striking it with a stone. This can be a lengthy process, but the end result is that she rises to a higher grade.

Death & Sorcery The Small Nambas believe that people only die due to old age or sorcery. When a young person dies, the spirits are consulted because they are believed to be all-seeing. They are asked whether sorcery was involved in the death, which is always suspected when children die. The fine for causing the death of a child is two curve-tusked pigs.

They also believe that an elderly chief who has gone far in his nimangki grades becomes a powerful spirit when he dies. For him, it's the beginning of a new astral life, in which the dead man may haunt his village and family if his spirit is not adequately appeased. His principal male relative has to ensure a complex sequence of funeral ceremonies or suffer the consequences – usually being haunted!

The Rambaramp About eight months to a year after a chief's death, the Small Nambas give him a new body, or *rambaramp*. This is built by covering a tree fern or bamboo frame with vegetable fibre and clay.

To ensure the rambaramp's face really looks like the dead man, the skull is removed from his decomposing body and overlaid with smearings of clay. (Over-modelling is a sculpting procedure whereby the object is constructed from layers of clay and coconut fibres built up over a bamboo frame, a coconut shell or a dead man's skull.) If the skin has not yet completely decayed, it is then smoked off.

The rambaramp, which is the same size as the deceased person, is then painted all over in red, white and black, and fitted with armbands, feathers, armlets, a namba and a bark belt.

The dead chief's effigy remains hidden in the nakamal until it's displayed for one day only. Puppetlike objects are positioned beside it, representing any of his children who have died before him.

Small Nambas men dance before the rambaramp dressed as spirits, completely covered with strands of smoked ferns, their heads shrouded in a mass of spider webs or thick green moss. Then the rambaramp is returned, where it remains until it falls apart.

Few tribesmen reach a high enough nimangki grade for a rambaramp to be made after their death. Consequently, such ceremonies have always been very rare, sometimes occurring only two or three times in a generation.

You won't see a rambaramp unless you're very fortunate, as they're usually concealed in the nakamal. However, there is a good example on display in Vila's Cultural Centre.

Clay Artefacts Prior to each ceremony, the Small Nambas make anew all the over-modelled clay objects they require. These include

Malakulan ceremonial headdresses

large round images of the sun and moon (named *metamieles* by anthropologists), ritual clubs and spears used for the pig kills during nimangkis, masks and headdresses.

Some of the most distinctive over-modelled clay artefacts are *temes nevimbur*, puppetlike objects used in ritual plays where legendary people fight over good and evil. They are slightly less than one metre tall.

A temes nevimbur's head is modelled over a human skull or half a coconut. When the show is over, the ones representing evil are ritually killed, releasing 'blood' – actually red juice from a plant.

The *nambugi* are smaller, puppetlike objects only about 50 cm high. They are simply an over-modelled face on a stick, and are used at funerals of tribesmen who have reached very high grades.

Visitors Although the Small Nambas may be prepared to accept you on a short day-trip basis, they usually aren't interested in receiving visitors. In the past they have been infuriated by the casual breaking of tabus by outsiders who – probably in ignorance – seem to consider such matters of little consequence. Visiting the Small Nambas, in the South West Bay Area section, has more details on this subject.

Handicrafts
Vanuatu's most colourful and dynamic art forms come from Malakula, especially the south-west. Particularly outstanding are masks and headdresses, some of which are on permanent display in Vila's Cultural Centre.

Tree Fern Figures Tree ferns in Malakula are carved to resemble a person or spirit, with their hands held by the side or held across the waist. They are usually life-size and coloured in green and red.

Masks In south Malakula's tribal interior, only men of high rank are permitted to wear dancing masks and ceremonial headdresses. Some of these are carved from tree ferns, while others are over-modelled.

Headdresses A high proportion of south Malakulan ceremonial headdresses are made of clay mixed with vegetable matter, and are surmounted by tall feathers. A variant of these has a small model of a man on top. A third type is designed with two or four faces, one on each side. Lastly, spider webs are sometimes used at the back of a single-faced mask to give the appearance of hair or a wig. Masks such as these are specially made for each occasion. This may be a funeral, a nimangki ceremony or a boy's initiation (ie circumcision).

Medical Services
In addition to the two government hospitals at Norsup and Lamap, there are clinics and dispensaries at Vao, Atchin, Walarano, Tontar, Tenmaru, Leviamp, Unmet, Lakatoro, Vinmavis, Pandehur, Fartapo, Wintua, Melip, Akhamb and Uliveo.

Places to Stay
There are a number of government rest houses in Lakatoro, Norsup, Lamap and Wintua (South West Bay), and village resorts on Wala and Rano Islands. For details see the information about these places in the Around Malakula section.

Places to Eat
There are small, limited restaurants in Lakatoro and Norsup, and at the Wala Island Resort. For information, see the Around Malakula section.

Getting There & Away
Malakula is reasonably well-off for air and sea services, with connections to Vila and Luganville.

Air Vanair flies via Norsup at least once a day on the Vila/Luganville route. Three times a week there's a flight into Lamap from both Vila and Luganville, and there's a similar twice-weekly service to South West Bay. A weekly loop flight from Vila links Lamap with Craig Cove and Ulei, both on Ambrym, and Lamen Bay on Epi.

The one-way fare from Vila is 6200VT to

MALAKULA ISLAND

Lamap, 6700VT to South West Bay and 7900VT to Norsup. From Luganville, it costs 5300VT to get to Lamap, 5100VT to South West Bay and 3700VT to Norsup. To get from Lamap to Craig Cove costs 2500VT, and to Lamen Bay 2900VT.

Sea Toara Coastal Shipping's *Aloara* offers a fortnightly service each way connecting both Vila and Luganville via ports along Malakula's southern and north-eastern coasts. On these trips it also visits other islands, such as Epi, Ambrym and Pentecost. Its major stops on Malakula are at South West Bay, Lamap and Litslits, near Lakatoro.

Fares from Lamap are 800VT to South West Bay, 600VT to Craig Cove (on Ambrym), 2800VT to Luganville, and 2800VT to Vila.

The little MV *Saratoka*, which can carry 20 self-catering passengers, also provides a fortnightly service each way from Vila to Luganville via Malakula. However, its fares are almost twice as much as those on the *Aloara*. You can book a ticket at Ifira Shipping's office in Vila, or down at the wharf in Luganville.

The Malakula Local Council (☎ 48453) in Lakatoro runs the equally modest launch MV *Mangaru*, which offers a weekly service connecting Malakula's east coast with Pentecost, Ambrym and Paama.

Speedboat A chartered speedboat ride for the 24 km from Lamap to Craig Cove is only safe in the calmest weather. It will cost you at least 8000VT each way.

Getting Around
To/From the Airport The Norsup airport is three km from Norsup and four km from Lakatoro. It's 300VT by taxi and 100VT by bus into either town.

Air Vanair offers Norsup/Lamap flights three days a week and Norsup/South West Bay twice a week, with one-way tickets costing 3500VT and 3300VT respectively. There are no regular flights between Lamap and South West Bay.

Motor Vehicle & Walking Northern and eastern coastal Malakula are reasonably well served with roads. There's an all-weather route from near Tenmaru around to Asuk Bay, near Lamap, and another heading straight across to the west coast from Norsup. Other than that, the usual way of getting around is to walk.

Hitching Hitching is possible along the main routes, but you wouldn't want to be in a hurry. A lift from Norsup to Veturah, opposite Vao Island, will probably cost in the order of 500VT. The fare from Norsup to Asuk Bay would be about the same.

Minibus There are a few minibuses operating mainly in and around Norsup and Lakatoro. To get from Norsup to Veturah costs 200VT per person unless you charter.

Taxi A taxi from Norsup costs 2800VT to Veturah and 5000VT to Asuk Bay. Generally, taxis in Malakula are a little cheaper than most other areas, costing about 70VT a km. The best places to find one are Norsup and Lakatoro.

Speedboat Southern Malakula lacks population, roads and footpaths. Consequently speedboats are the most convenient form of long-distance transport south of Tisvel and Lamap. All islands are linked to the mainland with either speedboats or canoes.

AROUND MALAKULA
North Coast
The northern Malakulan coast is one of Vanuatu's most densely populated areas. The heaviest concentrations of people live on seven small islands along the north-eastern seaboard between Vao and Lakatoro. The inhabitants of most islands speak French in addition to Bislama; Atchin and Uripiv islanders mainly use English.

The following distances are from Norsup.

Norsup With over 1000 people living in or around it, Norsup (pronounced 'norrhsoup') is Malakula's largest town. During the Condominium it was the centre for French administration in northern Malakula, and is still mainly French-speaking. It's a strung-out sort of place, with red coral trees, locally called *naradas*, and yellow hibiscus or *burao* trees doing their best to make it attractive.

About 800 metres offshore is small, French-speaking Norsup Island.

Information Norsup's facilities include two well-stocked stores, a bakery, a restaurant, a post office and a market on Wednesdays and Saturdays. Electricity is only guaranteed between 6 am and 9 pm, though lights stay on for an extra hour or so at the weekend.

Things to See Only 300 metres beyond the airport terminal is sandy **Aop Beach**, whose palms and turquoise water make it the prettiest spot around Norsup. It makes an infinitely more appealing place to wait for your plane than the grotty terminal. A long stretch of beautiful coral reef stretches southwards from Aop Beach to Litslits, the main port for this area.

Norsup's commercial activities revolve around the PRV company (Plantations

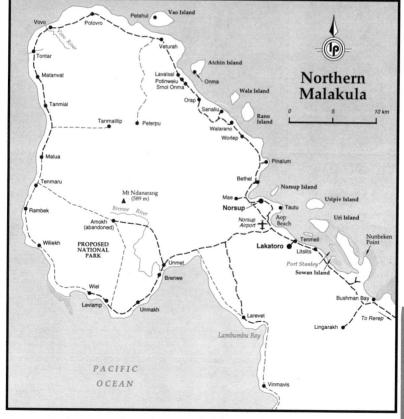

Northern Malakula

Réunies de Vanuatu), whose **coconut plantations** border the town on three sides. This is Vanuatu's largest copra producer as well as being its major agricultural operation.

PRV's block is at the north-western end of Norsup, and you get a clear view of it as you come in to land at the airstrip. Staff huts are lined up along the inland side of the road, with copra dryers opposite them backing onto the sea. At the far end is a Quonset storage hut complex and a small wharf from where PRV's own coastal barges operate. Beyond this are PRV's plantations, which cover 30 sq km.

Places to Stay & Eat The government *rest house* has eight beds in three rooms, and washing and cooking facilities. A night there costs 1000VT. As the caretaker lives on nearby Uripiv Island, you'll need to contact Norsup post office (☎ 48452) first to get her to leave a key. If you arrive on the weekend, you'll have to visit the provincial secretary (☎ 48453 weekdays) at Lakatoro to ask permission to use the house. Alternatively, try ringing Sael Sikoma on ☎ 48491.

Raemon's Restaurant offers a limited menu of rice dishes for very reasonable prices, although the servings aren't overly

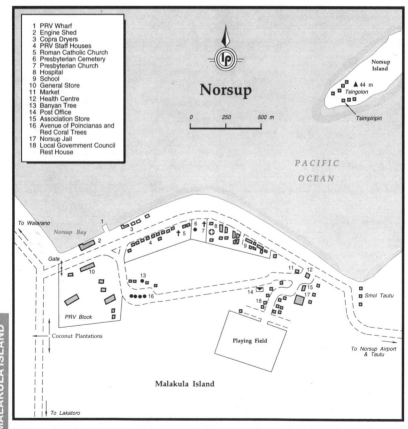

1 PRV Wharf
2 Engine Shed
3 Copra Dryers
4 PRV Staff Houses
5 Roman Catholic Church
6 Presbyterian Cemetery
7 Presbyterian Church
8 Hospital
9 School
10 General Store
11 Market
12 Health Centre
13 Banyan Tree
14 Post Office
15 Association Store
16 Avenue of Poincianas and Red Coral Trees
17 Norsup Jail
18 Local Government Council Rest House

Norsup

Norsup Island

▲ 44 m
Tsingolon

Tsimpiripiri

PACIFIC OCEAN

0   250   500 m

To Walarano

Norsup Bay

Gate

PRV Block

Coconut Plantations

Playing Field

Smol Tautu

To Norsup Airport & Tautu

Malakula Island

To Lakatoro

MALAKULA ISLAND

large. It's open seven days for lunch and dinner.

Getting There & Away See the relevant Getting There & Away information in the Malakula section.

Getting Around The seven-km journey between Norsup and Lakatoro costs 400VT by taxi and 100VT by bus. If you want to go over to Norsup Island the return fare is about 800VT.

Walarano (13 km) The people in this village originally came from the nearby islands of Wala and Rano, hence its name. From here you can hire a canoe or speedboat to take you across to **Rano Island**, where there is a village resort.

Sanaliu, about 1.5 km further north, has onshore coral gardens worth snorkelling over. This village is generally known as Wala mainland, and it's where you get a ride to **Wala Island**. There's a village resort on this island as well.

Wala Islanders are currently restoring their old natsaros, including carving new slit-drums, or tamtams. This is the only place where you can easily see the traditions of the Small Nambas people.

Things to See & Do Peter Fidelio, owner-manager of the Wala Island Resort (see following section) can arrange activities such as kava sessions with local villagers,

---

Amelboas Natsaro

The deep, primeval throbbing of a tamtam shattered the quiet as I walked along the jungle path to Amelboas natsaro. I was with Peter Fidelio, manager of the Wala Island Resort, and we were on our way to see something of the ancient traditions of the Small Nambas people. The drumming had a menacing quality, perhaps because of the gloomy conditions. I knew it was for my benefit, but that didn't stop the hair from rising on the back of my neck.

Suddenly we broke out of the trees at the edge of a large, fenced clearing lined with thatched shelters and carved nimangki figures. Chief Stephan Lelektei, 'bigman' of this particular natsaro, stepped forward with a smile of welcome. He was a young man resplendent in blue and yellow body paint, and wearing only a penis sheath, a headdress and a pig's tusk. The latter hung around his neck as a symbol of his chiefly status.

Once the greetings had been made we settled down to watch the show. A small group of older men started up the drum orchestra opposite. On a signal, about 20 painted male dancers wearing nambas, ankle rattles and tall feather headdresses came into the natsaro to begin the canoe dance. More modestly dressed in pandanus skirts, the same number of women and girls made an appreciative audience on the side.

Forming a canoe shape, the men cleaved the air with brightly coloured paddles as they stamped and chanted in perfect rhythm up and down the clearing. Peter said they were telling the story of travels to Ambae, Ambrym and other islands to buy pigs for grade-taking ceremonies.

The drummers were producing a complex mixture of high and low notes using tall tamtams and small logs, which were beaten with sticks. Chief Stephan's father – the master of ceremonies – sat with a coconut in each hand facing the two largest tamtams. His left hand held a green coconut with which he beat the time on one tamtam. In his right, he held a dry coconut which, when pounded on the second drum, produced a deeper booming note that indicated changes in pattern. His skill was the secret of the dancers' excellent timing and choreography.

I spent three fascinating hours at the natsaro watching several dances, including one by the women, and learning about grade-taking and the different ranks of chiefs. There were also demonstrations of cooking and fire lighting. Towards the end the women offered chicken laplap and delicious fruit, and I was prevailed upon to say grace.

At the close, all the dancers lined up and I was asked to give a small 'tankyu' speech. I'd been learning Bislama as I travelled around, but now – just when I really needed it – my mind was a blank. Still, they were obviously pleased with my poor effort and applauded on its conclusion. Remember: you may well be asked to perform the same services, so don't say you haven't been warned. ■

mainland trekking and fishing. There's also good swimming and snorkelling in the area. Cultural activities include visits to island natsaros (there are five) and Small Nambas custom dancing on the mainland at nearby Amelboas natsaro. This opportunity is currently only available to visitors staying at the Wala Island Resort.

Places to Stay & Eat The modest, traditional-style *Dorano Rapolesi Resort* on Rano Island is an excellent spot to escape the workaday world, but it certainly won't appeal to those who crave their creature comforts. There are three rooms with a total of six beds costing 1000VT per person, plus meals, and you must supply your own bedding. Chief Aleck can arrange various activities such as walks, fishing and custom dancing. Sharks make swimming hazardous near the resort. For bookings, contact Espiritu Santo Travel & Tours (☎ 36391) in Luganville.

Set right on the beach, the neighbouring *Wala Island Resort* is also very welcoming and has English and French-speaking staff. Its facilities are primitive, but Peter Fidelio has had many years' experience in the hospitality industry in Vila and knows how to look after people. As a result, his operation is definitely among the top five of Vanuatu's village resorts and guest houses.

The resort has one family and five twin thatched bungalows costing 2200VT for singles or doubles, including breakfast. These are small but comfortable. Simple, good-quality traditional and European meals are served, with lunch costing 600VT and dinner 800VT.

Bookings can be made through the Norsup post office (☎ 48452), Pacific Tours in Vila (☎ 25200) and Espiritu Santo Travel & Tours.

Getting There & Away The taxi fares from Norsup to Walarano and Wala mainland are 1400VT and 1500VT respectively, while the bus to either costs 200VT. A boat across to either Wala or Rano will cost around 1000VT return.

Atchin Island (31 km) Tiny Atchin covers only 0.8 sq km yet has a population of over 1000 people, making it Vanuatu's most densely populated island. Atchin Islanders are considered to be the wealthiest people in Malakula, owning two shipping companies amongst other things.

Many Atchin people own gardens on the mainland, so every day they must paddle the 300 metres across to **Potinweiu** (pronounced 'fot'n-way') to tend them. They talk of 'Big Atchin' and 'Smol Atchin', meaning Atchin itself and the mainland opposite, between Lavalsal and Smol Onma, where some have moved.

Onma is the largest village on the island. Its sister settlement on the mainland is populated by members of the same clan and is called **Smol Onma**.

Sharks have taken several people near Atchin in recent times. A particularly bad year was 1984, when four people were killed. Islanders have decided not to have any tourist facilities on Atchin for fear of further attacks.

If you want to visit Atchin for a few hours, contact the island's council office (☎ 48402) first. They will arrange a guide to show you around. A canoe ride across the narrows between Onma and Potinweiu will cost 1000VT.

Things to See Atchin has two natsaros. To win membership of either one, an aspirant has to kill a pig there and put his mark on the coconut tree growing nearby. The notches near the treetops have been made by bullets – each bullet hole represents a dead pig.

Handicrafts The island specialty is carved model canoes complete with stylised frigate bird figureheads and sails.

Vao Island (36.5 km) Traditional customs have survived on Vao better than elsewhere along Malakula's north-eastern coastal strip. Nimangki grade-taking still occurs in the natsaros, though nowadays this tends to take place only once every few years.

Until recently, initiation was an important

rite for young boys. Once they had been circumcised, they lived in a special initiates' hut where they were taunted and teased for a month. They had to grin and bear it, because if they didn't they were forbidden to marry.

With a dense population of 1350 in an area of only 1.3 sq km, spare land on Vao has become extremely scarce. For this reason, as at Atchin, many islanders have gardens on the mainland opposite.

Things to See & Do There's a very interesting walk around the island, during which you pass through thick vegetation into small clearings lined with stone monoliths and ancient tamtams up to three metres high. These are the old natsaros, and if you ask your guide (see Getting Around) he'll tell you all about them. You could also ask him to give you a demonstration of drumming.

Petehul, the largest village, has a sandy beach. There's another on the island's north-eastern tip.

Handicrafts Vao Islanders make fascinating wooden masks in addition to wooden clubs, ceremonial bowls and other objects. Your guide will take you to the various carvers, but look around first before buying. You can purchase some excellent work here at much lower prices than in Vila.

Getting Around Some footpaths on Vao are for males only. Others are for females, who aren't allowed to walk through the natsaros. The chief, or one of the elders, will appoint someone to act as an escort to ensure you don't breach any tabus.

Tontar (54 km) There's a very large coconut plantation at Tontar, complete with copra dryers. A small pool of cool, clear fresh water, locally called 'Spring', is ideal for swimming.

Tanmial (59.5 km) Near Tanmial there's a very large and spectacular **cavern** with a hole in its roof. The Small Nambas used to bury their dead chiefs here, believing the

spirits would rise up to the sky through this very same vent.

There are several handprints so high up on the ceiling it seems impossible that humans put them there. The local explanation is that the spirits of the dead chiefs made these marks as they passed out of the cavern.

The entry fee is 300VT fee per person, paid to the cave's guardian at Tanmial – check first with the provincial government office in Lakatoro on the current situation with guardians. It's necessary to enter the cave in pairs for protection against the spirits. Before you go in, your guide will call into a small hole in the cliff at the cave entrance. The eerie trumpeting noise warns the spirits that you're coming.

Malua (68 km) This Small Nambas village is built around a Seventh-Day Adventist Mission. Being in a rain shadow, the surrounding area often experiences prolonged drought. However, numerous streams flow down from the wet interior, and these have been tapped to irrigate the village's market gardens. They make an unexpected sight in this stark volcanic country, which is otherwise covered by dry, scrubby vegetation.

Tenmaru (73 km) This Big Nambas village once warred constantly with neighbouring Malua, but now they're the best of friends. Unlike Malua, the old traditions are still fairly strong here, and custom dancing is popular entertainment. Footpaths lead from Tenmaru up to the Amokh plateau, while a 4WD track continues down the coast another nine km to the beach at Wiliekh.

The Amokh Rd
You may be able to hire a 4WD truck in Unmet or Brenwe to take you up to Amokh, but otherwise it's usually a long wait between rides. Alternatively, the return taxi fare from Norsup is about 4000VT.

Distances are from Norsup.

Unmet (19 km) The last residents of Amokh have all moved to Unmet and neighbouring Brenwe, where missions are busily converting them to Christianity – the church at Unmet is Roman Catholic, and that at Brenwe is SDA. Ask at either of these two villages, or Unmakh further along the coast, if you need a guide for the interior.

Hoping to raise a few vatu, the Big Nambas intend building a custom nakamal at Unmet for tourists to visit.

There's a long stretch of beach from Unmakh all the way round to Larevet. However, local villagers prefer to swim in the Brenwe River rather than risk the sharks in the sea.

Amokh (42 km) Only collapsed houses remain of the last major traditional village of the Big Nambas tribe. It was abandoned in the late 1980s following the chief's death. The old ceremonial dancing circle, now overgrown, is on the edge of the village. Still standing sentinel are tall **tamtams** decorated with two large holes representing eyes and a long slit for the mouth.

To avoid tabus, ask at Unmet or Brenwe before you visit Amokh.

There's been a recent proposal to establish a national park to protect the primeval forest in the general area between Amokh and Wiel, to the south. Ask at the provincial government office in Lakatoro for an update on this.

To Larevet & Further South A road turns south off the Norsup-Unmet route towards **Larevet** and **Lambumbu Bay** where there's a small beach, a sawmill and a large cocoa plantation. A rough track goes on for another six km to Vinmavis, from where a footpath continues to Tisvel.

The very few settlements further south can only be reached by boat or on foot. Most of the coast is coral-lined except for the anchorages at both Dixon Reef and Bamboo Bay. There's particularly good coral growth around **Dixon Reef**, a very small and poor village boasting a new Roman Catholic church which was severely damaged in an earthquake in 1994.

East Coast

The fertile coastal plain of eastern Malakula

was one of Vanuatu's first areas to be settled by Europeans. Coconut plantations now reach from the shore right up to the foothills of the densely forested interior.

Distances are from Lakatoro.

Lakatoro Malakula's administrative capital is attractively laid out on a hillside, with many shady trees. It was once the British government centre in Malakula during Condominium days, and so is mainly English-speaking.

Lakatoro's compact tidiness contrasts markedly with nearby Norsup. Although growing in size, the town still has only about 500 residents.

Orientation Lakatoro is built on two levels. The top half, on the hillside, houses most of the government buildings. Down below is a sizeable playing field, with the town's commercial centre nearby. Across the road is a cocoa research farm.

Information As elsewhere, the first place to ask for any information is the provincial government office.

You'll also find Mr Alpet, at the Department of Agriculture's local office, to be a very useful source for finding guides and for general information on northern Malakula.

Places to Stay & Eat Lakatoro has a government *rest house* with three bedrooms of up to eight beds per room for 1000VT per person. It has basic cooking facilities, sheets, mattresses, flush toilets and cold showers – the water goes off at 9 pm in the dry season. For information contact either the provincial government office on ☎ 48453 or Sael Sikoma on ☎ 48491.

There's another *rest house* in the public works complex with three beds, a gas cooker and cold showers for 1000VT. For those with sleeping mats and bedding there's plenty of space on the floor.

The *Kalpen Restaurant* in the commercial centre is open seven days for lunch and dinner. Its menu is limited (to say the least) and servings cost 300 to 400VT.

The best kava in town is found at the policemen's nakamal, but watch out – it's strong! Beer is sold at the police bar next to the nakamal.

Uripiv Island (1 km & 4 km by boat) The main attraction is a **marine sanctuary** (proclaimed by the chief) that completely encircles the island. This has everything for the snorkeller – beautiful coral, small colourful fish, turtles and many other varieties of marine life.

A *guest house* is proposed here, so check with the provincial government office in Lakatoro for details.

Getting Around To get to Uripiv, arrange for a canoe or speedboat at the Lakatoro jetty. Expect to pay at least 1500VT for the return fare.

Uri Island (1.5 km & 3 km by boat) The **marine sanctuary** at the southern end of this island is designed to protect the mangroves and reef. There is good snorkelling, and a rare chance to see colourful giant clams.

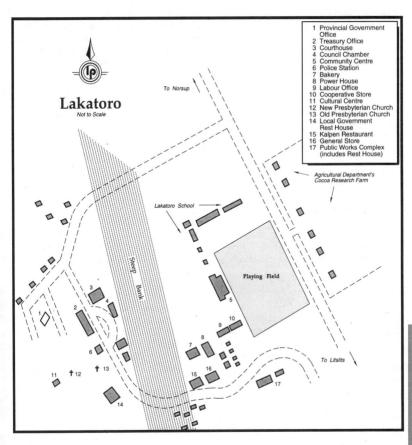

Lakatoro
Not to Scale

To Norsup

1 Provincial Government Office
2 Treasury Office
3 Courthouse
4 Council Chamber
5 Community Centre
6 Police Station
7 Bakery
8 Power House
9 Labour Office
10 Cooperative Store
11 Cultural Centre
12 New Presbyterian Church
13 Old Presbyterian Church
14 Local Government Rest House
15 Kalpen Restaurant
16 General Store
17 Public Works Complex (includes Rest House)

Agricultural Department's Cocoa Research Farm

Lakatoro School

Steep Bank

Playing Field

To Litslits

MALAKULA ISLAND

Access details are as for Uripiv Island, above. You'll probably find the chief in Lakatoro, whose permission you'll need to visit the island.

Litslits (2 km) Lakatoro's port is situated at the entrance to Port Stanley, a wide, seven-km-long inlet that offers the best anchorage on this section of coast.

Sowan Island (4.5 km) This island is basically a very long sandbar plus a few bushes and coral rocks. It's a favourite haunt of wild ducks.

Bushman Bay (12 km) Copra sheds line the shore in front of a large plantation. The bay, which is mainly fringed by mangroves, is another good yacht anchorage.

The remains of an inter-island copra boat lie shattered on the reef at the north-eastern end of the bay at Nunbeken (or Wreck) Point.

Crab Bay (16 km) Ships anchor at a small sandy beach to supply the local coconut plantation. There is plenty of coral growth at the entrance to this inlet.

Unua (26.5 km) Unua has a narrow, white sand beach fringed by coral growth. At one time, men from this village used to land dive from tall banyan trees, just like Pentecost Islanders did before they began building towers. In Unua's case, however, the practice wasn't related to the yam harvest. Instead it was part of the village's grade-taking process.

Pankumu River (31.5 km) The swampy estuary of the Pankumu River, which you cross on a concrete causeway, is an introduction to Vanuatu's longest watercourse outside Santo. Over the centuries, this river has repeatedly changed course between Metenua and Retchar, leaving a large wetland area of isolated oxbows and bayous. It's an excellent spot for birdwatchers.

Further inland, the Pankumu narrows into winding channels, isolated pools and a series of minor cascades.

Tisman (40 km) Up to the 1960s a group known as the Middle Nambas lived in the central interior about 13 km south-west of Tisman. These people were often in disgrace with Condominium authorities because of their liking for human flesh, including women! Their numbers began to decline after WW II as people moved to the coast.

Tisman was the home of the legendary Australian expat planter, Oscar Newman, who became the uncrowned 'king' of Malakula. Newman had six wives, each of whom was housed separately, and numerous children. He died just after independence.

Asuk Bay (61 km) The road from Lakatoro ends at Asuk Bay, or Black Sands, but there are plans to continue it around to Lamap. Again, villagers bathe in the river rather than in the sea for fear of sharks.

This is the best place to find a speedboat to Lamap. The cost, if you share it, is about 500VT per person.

South-East Coast
The following distances are from Lamap's light tower.

Lamap The principal French government centre in Malakula in Condominium days, Lamap was once Vanuatu's third-largest town.

Although there are about 950 people living in the immediate area, the town is a derelict shadow of its former self. You couldn't describe it as attractive and pleasant, which it undoubtedly once was, but it's certainly interesting to explore.

Things to See The mission (see below), the hospital and the small trellis light tower are the only three places in Lamap with electric lighting after sunset. Lamap's other facilities include two small stores, a post office and a branch of the National Bank of Vanuatu.

The town's busiest operation is the **Roman Catholic mission**. There's a large, modern church in its grounds, with several interesting wall paintings modelled on traditional sand-drawing designs.

Lamap's water is not always safe to drink, so it's wise to boil or otherwise treat it first.

The only road in the area connects Port Sandwich (also called Ballande) Wharf with the Lamap-Orovail airfield.

On a clear day there's a good view of Ambrym's two volcanoes, Mt Marum and Mt Benbow, from beside the light tower. You can also see Paama and Epi in the distance.

Places to Stay The government *rest house* (Lamap post office ☎ 48444) in the old French colonial-style government block has six beds in three rooms costing 1000VT

each. As there are so few visitors, there's seldom any need to book in advance. A paraffin lamp is provided, but you'll need to buy fuel for it at the local store. You'll also require mosquito coils as there's no flywire.

The government block has a charmingly rustic setting, with chickens and cows wandering freely outside the official buildings.

Getting Around Taxis and speedboats are available for hire in Lamap.

Port Sandwich (3 km) The first notable visitor to Malakula's safest anchorage was

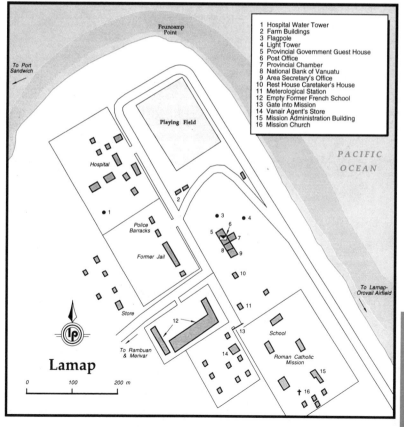

1 Hospital Water Tower
2 Farm Buildings
3 Flagpole
4 Light Tower
5 Provincial Government Guest House
6 Post Office
7 Provincial Chamber
8 National Bank of Vanuatu
9 Area Secretary's Office
10 Rest House Caretaker's House
11 Meterological Station
12 Empty Former French School
13 Gate into Mission
14 Vanair Agent's Store
15 Mission Administration Building
16 Mission Church

Peunoamp Point

To Port Sandwich

Playing Field

Hospital

PACIFIC OCEAN

Police Barracks

Former Jail

To Lamap-Orovail Airfield

Store

To Rambuan & Merivar

School

Lamap

Roman Catholic Mission

0   100   200 m

MALAKULA ISLAND

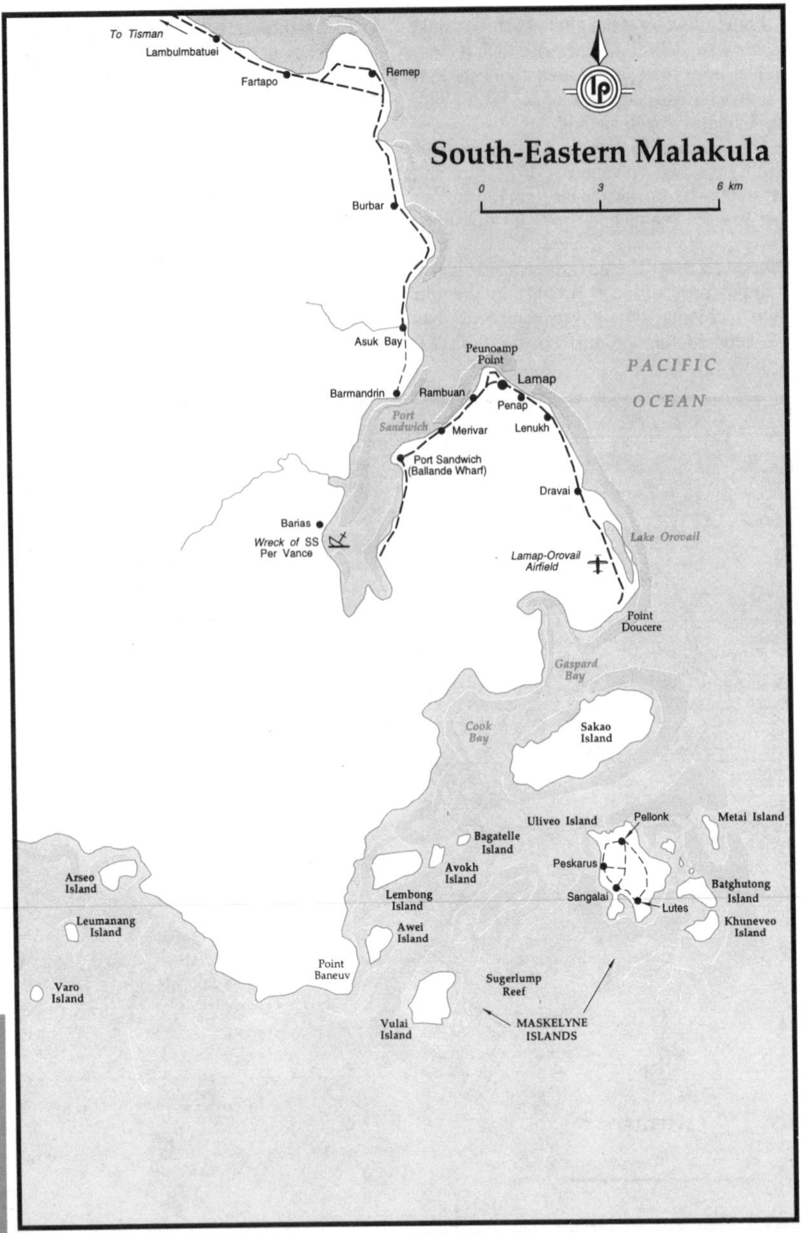

South-Eastern Malakula

To Tisman
Lambulmbatuei
Fartapo
Remep

Burbar

Asuk Bay

Peunoamp
Point
Barmandrin   Rambuan   Lamap
Penap
Merivar   Lenukh
Port Sandwich
(Ballande Wharf)
Dravai

Barias
Wreck of SS
Per Vance

PACIFIC

OCEAN

Port
Sandwich

Lamap-Orovail
Airfield

Lake Orovail

Point
Doucere

Gaspard
Bay

Cook
Bay
Sakao
Island

Uliveo Island   Pellonk
Bagatelle   Metai Island
Island
Avokh   Peskarus
Arseo   Island   Batghutong
Island   Lembong   Sangalai   Island
Island   Lutes
Leumanang   Awei   Khunevo
Island   Island   Island

Point
Varo   Baneuv
Island
Sugerlump
Reef
Vulai   MASKELYNE
Island   ISLANDS

0   3   6 km

MALAKULA ISLAND

Captain Cook. He named the inlet after his patron, the Earl of Sandwich, a former British prime minister. Port Sandwich is favoured by touring yachts.

Things to See & Do It's a pleasant, 45-minute walk from Lamap to the wharf, past a number of several friendly villages including **Rambuan** and **Merivar** (where the store sells cold beer). En route you'll pass many coconut trees, each with a broad aluminium strip around its trunk two to three metres up. This is to prevent rats climbing up to chew holes in the nuts.

At the wharf a small golden beach fringing deep water may tempt you in for a swim. However, it's best to restrain yourself unless you're convinced it's fun being eaten – this is one of the worst places in Vanuatu for shark attacks.

From the wharf you can get a speedboat across to the **wreck** of the SS *Per Vance*, a copra boat which was grounded during a cyclone in the 1950s. The hulk is sitting upright in the shallows and has mangroves growing on top. You can climb aboard and see its old steam engine.

The estuary is one of the best places in the country to find oysters and mud crabs.

Dravai (3.5 km) Several corroded aeroplane engines lie along the beach between Port Sandwich and Dravai, including one on the reef just below the mission at Lamap. During WW II, several US aircraft flying between Efate and Santo ran out of fuel and were forced to land along the coast. After the war, villagers salvaged everything that could be carried away, but the engines proved too heavy to move.

Point Doucere (7 km) The road from Lamap ends at a sandy beach, which is a major landing for canoes and speedboats travelling to and from Sakao and other islands in the Maskelyne group. If you're patient this is a good place to find transport across to the islands. Alternatively, you can hire a speedboat in Lamap (see Getting Around).

The Maskelyne Islands

James Cook named the small islands at Malakula's south-eastern tip the Maskelynes. The group has several fine stretches of coral – particularly around Uliveo, at Sakao's north-eastern edge, around Awei, Lembong, Avokh and Bagatelle islands, and also on the Sugarlump Reef between Vulai and Uliveo.

Some of the islands in the Maskelyne group are very rugged. Others have patches of mangrove-lined coast, or sandy beaches. They are very beautiful, and everyone who visits tends to speak of them in superlatives.

There are many excellent diving and snorkelling spots around the group, but you have to be very careful of strong currents between the islands.

Getting There & Away It's only a 90-minute journey by speedboat from Lamap to Uliveo or Avokh. However, if you're prone to seasickness be warned that it's often very rough until you reach the shelter of Sakao Island. A chartered, half-day return ride costs about 6000VT.

Uliveo Island Called 'Maskelyne' locally, Uliveo is by far the most densely populated member of the group, with 950 of the area's 1150 people.

Uliveo's major village is **Peskarus**. People from the island's other three villages come here to eat, making up a daily roster of staff and cooks at the communal dining hall.

Beyond the villages of Sangalai and Lutes are several small mangrove islets as well as **Khuneveo**, an island surrounded by golden sand. You'll often see villagers hunting for edible sea creatures when the tide is out. There is first-class snorkelling on the coral gardens around the island's south-west tip.

Uliveo's oldest settlement is **Pellonk**. As well as a natsaro, there's a cemetery with several very unusual inscriptions on the graves, including one recounting the exploits of a long-dead drunkard!

Several large sailing canoes operate regularly from Pellonk. All are sturdy enough to

MALAKULA ISLAND

reach destinations as far away as Port Sandwich in all but the foulest weather.

Uliveo's villages are very tidy, party because small fines are imposed by the council on any residents who don't keep their houses and gardens up to scratch.

Places to Stay Peskarus has plans to develop three small *bungalows* for visitor accommodation, so ask about this at the NTO in Vila or the Lamap post office (☎ 48444). Otherwise check with the Cultural Centre in Vila, or the Lakatoro provincial government office, on accommodation facilities and the procedure for hiring them.

Getting Around You can see everything on Uliveo, and meet all sorts of friendly people, in a leisurely three-hour stroll around the island. On arrival, your boatman will introduce you to a member of the Uliveo council who will detail one or two young islanders to show you around. On your departure, even if a fee is charged, show your gratitude by buying your guides some refreshments at the Peskarus store.

Avokh Island Apart from Uliveo and Sakao, this small but attractive island is the only other inhabited member of the Maskelyne group. The return speedboat ride from Peskarus costs about 1500VT.

Vulai Island Also called Harper Island, Vulai is a steep, rocky outcrop with several sharp, upward-jutting rocks around it. A long, narrow stretch of coral, called **Sugarlump Reef**, extends from Vulai almost all the way to Uliveo.

Arseo Island There are some beautiful coral formations over seven km west of the Maskelynes around Arseo Island and its two neighbouring islets of **Leumanang** and **Varo**.

Akhamb Island Akhamb is a small coral outcrop with a sandy shore. It's the prettiest island in Umbeb Bay, and has extensive coral gardens at its south-eastern end. The island's main village is **Penbaghur**.

Getting There & Away The easiest access to Akhamb is from Uliveo. A return speedboat ride from Lamap or Port Sandwich takes about three hours each way and costs at least 12000VT. The return trip from Uliveo is around 6000VT.

South West Bay Area
Ancient traditions are preserved in the south-

Church at Pellonk

western part of Malakula. Several stone circles are still used by custom-oriented villagers, who perform their traditional ceremonies wearing double or four-sided masks. Indeed, a cultural revival is taking place here, with nakamals and dancing grounds being reopened.

Despite their long-held fear of malaria, most highland people have abandoned the interior and now live around South West Bay. There are six language groups in the immediate area, making it the most interesting culturally in Malakula.

The following distances are from Wintua.

Visiting the Small Nambas Most visitors to the South West Bay area come hoping to meet traditional Small Nambas. However, this could be difficult owing to their reticence in receiving foreigners.

If you're interested, call in at the Cultural Centre in Vila and ask the staff about the latest situation. If their advice is against such a trip, accept it. If, however, they have heard that the Small Nambas are being more receptive, they may suggest you contact the South West Bay area secretary, who will then ask the Small Nambas chief if you will be welcome. If the reply is favourable, hire a guide in Wintua for a four-day hike (two days in each direction).

The route to the Small Nambas is long and hard at the best of times. It crosses seemingly endless sequences of steep ridges and narrow valleys, with masses of claggy soil adding weight to your boots. (In the wet season the track is cut by floods for weeks at a time.) When you've finally reached your destination, you'll find the Small Nambas will only permit you to stay a very short while. It may only be long enough to buy a few handicrafts and take some photographs, which of course you'll have to pay for.

Guide fees are normally around 1000 to 1500VT per day. For this price, your guide will carry your baggage, an essential requirement unless you are genuinely fit because of the difficult terrain. However, after taking into account his three or more nights out, plus food, you may find his services costing

in the vicinity of 8000 to 10,000VT for the whole trip.

Getting Around Except for the flight into the local airfield, journeys are either on foot or by speedboat. Ask about guides wherever you go, even around South West Bay, as there are many tabus. Expect any trip into the interior to be strenuous.

Wintua Wintua (pronounced 'win-tor') is the local administrative centre. Behind it is Tsiri Lagoon, which locals say was emptied by an earthquake in 1994 and has subsequently refilled.

There's a beautiful **beach** in front of the abandoned plantation, with good snorkelling on offer.

About 10 minutes' walk from the village is a traditional **nakamal** with a dancing ground used by several different language groups. Custom dances will be performed here on request, with the payment of a suitable fee.

Places to Stay & Eat Bong's Guest House, also known as George's, is near the northern end of the airstrip. It has three bedrooms costing 1000VT per person, and facilities are very basic; you can get delicious seafood meals prepared by the ladies of the local Presbyterian women's group. Direct enquiries can be made to George Thompson, the Vanair agent – George can be contacted through Vanair, or you can try calling him on the community telephone (☎ 48466).

Venembous (3 km) The walk from Wintua to Venembous takes about 45 minutes. This is the best spot to buy artefacts in the area.

The village has a large **nakamal** which doubles as a museum of traditional artefacts. It houses a great array of items including two-sided masks and metamieles. However, tabus restrict entry to adult males. This applies to foreigners also, who may only enter if invited.

Lainduo (5 km) Here there's a dramatically shaped headland with a high cliff that has a deep cleft in its centre. The attractive village is on a steep hillside with a marvellous view across the bay.

Lawa (6 km) A narrow sandy beach extends northwards from Lawa all the way to Dixon Reef. This village is the gateway to the interior, with several walking tracks starting there. It's best reached by speedboat from Wintua, the trip costing about 300VT.

North of Lawa are numerous deserted villages and dancing grounds, with skulls, slit-drums and other interesting things to find. Vila's Cultural Centre has a field officer in the village and he is the best person to see about arranging a tour – you may be able to do this through the curator in Vila.

Tomman Island

Also called Urur, Tomman is yet another extremely attractive island with coral gardens and golden sand. The local people still retain many of their ancient customs, including grade-taking and male circumcision. However, the practice of binding small boys' heads to give them an elongated cranium is all but finished.

In the past, Tomman people made effigies of their dead. They were similar to Small Nambas ones, and called *narambarambs*.

Melip, on the mainland three km east of Tomman, has one of the best beaches in Vanuatu. It's about 1.5 km long and very sheltered, and you'll find it in the bay to the east of the village.

Getting There & Away The 17-km speedboat trip from South West Bay to Tomman is around 6000VT for a half-day return.

Ambrym Island

The few tourists who visit Ambrym mainly come to see the twin volcanoes of Mt Marum and Mt Benbow. Secondary attractions include Vanuatu's best fern carvings and tamtams, and its most skilful sand drawers. There are also traditional magic and conjuring tricks, both of which still feature in village life.

Measuring 43 km from west to east and 30 km from north to south, the 682 sq km island is roughly triangular in shape. It gets its name from another of Captain Cook's misunderstandings. The islanders he met gave him a yam to eat, saying *am rem*, meaning 'your yam'. While they consumed theirs, they said *ama rem*, ie 'our yam'.

Ambrym has also been called the Black Island because of its dark volcanic soils. It's certainly an appropriate name at least for the

area within the enormous central caldera, where the ash surface is largely devoid of vegetation. Elsewhere the island is so lush you'll wonder if the Garden of Eden was ever like this. Paradise does have its down side, however. The island is often devastated by cyclones, and its volcanoes have erupted seven times this century. Whole villages were lost in 1913, 1929 and 1950, while lesser events occurred in 1937, 1946, 1979 and 1993. Drifting ash often creates serious problems by disrupting the fruiting of food plants.

Most of the island's 7000 people live in coastal villages in the north, south-west and south-east. No one lives in the centre of the island, because of its exposure to ash. Generally, the relatively few inland villages are built on hills or ridges because, in the event

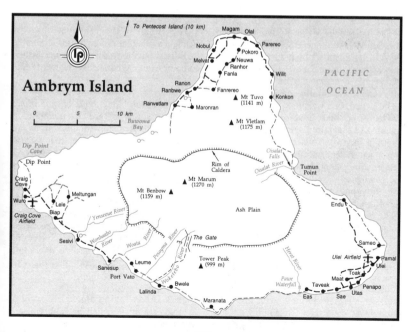

of an eruption, only the higher ground is safe from molten lava.

Few islanders swim in the sea for fear of sharks.

History

Captain Cook landed briefly in western Ambrym in 1774, but there was little foreign contact after this for nearly a century. While 1840 to 1870 was a busy period elsewhere in the archipelago, this was not so in Ambrym as the island had no sandalwood. However, by the 1880s European contact was well established.

A major part of the late 19th-century trade with Ambrym was in alcohol. Many islanders, usually men, took to it rather too enthusiastically.

The 20th Century The stability following the proclamation of the Condominium in 1906 produced a steady influx of new settlers onto the island. Compared to elsewhere in Vanuatu, the local villagers were slow to object.

The indigenous Malnatco trading association of Malakula reached Ambrym during WW II. Its members built several roads in vain anticipation of the arrival of US cargo. Malnatco's successor, the Ambrym Freedom Movement, was briefly active in 1950, but its influence soon waned.

The Nagriamel movement from Santo established several villages on the island in 1970. In June 1980, when much of Vanuatu was in a turbulent state just prior to independence, some Modérés on Ambrym formed their own provisional government, announcing they had seceded. Once the Santo rebellion was mopped up in September 1980, over 500 rebel supporters were subsequently arrested.

Volcanic Eruptions Of much greater impact than political strife has been the frequency and severity of Ambrym's volcanic eruptions. In December 1913, the central part of the island was in turmoil, with six vents erupting at once. Huge quantities of lava flowed like water. On the third day the lava

reached the sea, having demolished a hospital at Dip Point in the south-west. Boats from nearby Paama and Malakula rescued most people, but some lives were lost.

The 1929 eruption was almost as severe. People from one village were trapped between lava pouring from the centre of the island, and three underwater eruptions in the sea surrounding them. A Frenchman braved the boiling water in his launch to rescue the villagers, towing them in their canoes away from danger.

The last major eruption, taking place in 1950, destroyed the village of Maat, forcing most of its 300 residents to emigrate to Efate. They built a new village near Vila called Mele-Maat, where they still live today.

Local Customs

In Vanuatu, the islands with active volcanoes are the ones where magical powers are said to be strongest. Not surprisingly, Ambrym, with its two volcanoes, professes to be the country's sorcery centre, though this is challenged by Ambae people.

The island is the principal base for Vanuatu's sand drawers. Its most notable traditional ceremony is the *rom* dance, which combines both grade-taking elements and magic.

Sorcerers *Man blong majik* or *man blong posen*, as sorcerers are often called in Bislama, are treated with respect by all islanders. Many have seen too many unexplained happenings to regard a good sorcerer with anything but awe. Others, particularly Christians, regard them with wary suspicion.

Sand Drawings Ambrym's sand art is made up of circular loops and lines which join up to create a stylised picture whose message is easily understood by local people. Every one of the island's 180 sand designs refers to a specific object, story, legend, song, dance or creature.

Pigs & Grade-Taking *Maghe* ceremonies, as grade-taking is called in Ambrym, are major customary events, especially in the north. More than 120 pigs may be slaughtered if several men are taking grades together. Although some ceremonies are for one person only, up to six men at a time are permitted to take part in most lower-grade events.

No major transaction occurs without the exchange of pigs. They can also be paid as fines if a customary rule is breached, or as licence fees to the generally accepted owner of a traditional copyright, such as a tamtam design.

The Rom Dance Arguably, the island's most striking ceremony is the rom dance, or *olé rom* as it is called locally. It takes place every August in the north as part of a maghe ceremony, and is followed by a pig kill. In the south-west it's being revived as an annual event for tourists.

The dancers perform first in their home village. Then, for several weeks afterwards, they visit other parts of the island putting on shows.

Rom dress consists of a tall, conical, brightly painted, banana-fibre mask, with a face resembling a baboon's, and a thick costume of banana leaves which conceals the wearer's body.

As the rom dancer represents a spirit, each costume is burned after the dance in case any of the spirit's power remains. If it isn't destroyed, a spirit will take it over and haunt or impersonate the dancer. Consequently, very few rom outfits exist for posterity – one

of these is on display in Vila's Cultural Centre.

The rom dance originally came from the Olal area. As legend has it, a local girl made the first rom costume to gain the love of a young man from her village. She enticed him into the bush, where she revealed who she was. To please him she explained how she had made the uniform. Once he knew the secret he killed her, so keeping the secret to himself. Then he sold the rights to make copies of the rom to his fellow tribesmen, charging a stiff franchise each time in pigs.

It's tabu to see a rom costume made. If you do, you must pay a fine (a pig or its value in cash) to the chief. Villagers will also whip your back with the leaves of a stinging nettle, called the *nangalat*, whose poison will burn your skin like fire for several days. This punishment is extended to ni-Vanuatu and foreigners alike.

Handicrafts

Tamtams Also called *ating ating* in northern Ambrym, the island's tamtams or slit-gongs vary from only 60 cm to six metres high. Those made in northern Ambrym are usually shorter, between two and three metres high, and have an elongated face with huge disc-like eyes, pronounced nose and protruding chin. Often they represent an ancestor.

Tamtams from the southern and western parts of the island are usually very tall and have two, sometimes more, elongated faces, again with exaggerated, rounded eyes.

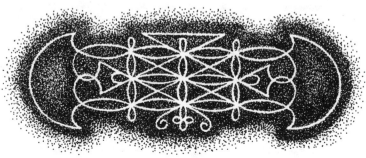

Sand drawing

You'll see plenty of examples of these in Vila, with the largest situated in front of the Royal Palms Resort. The Cultural Centre also has some on display.

Tree Fern Figures Male and female tree fern figures are usually depicted with their hands either clasped across their waists, or hanging down by their sides. Like tamtams they have elongated faces with pronounced chins and noses, and disc-like eyes.

Though often made nowadays as decorations – you see them everywhere in Vila – tree fern figures were originally only made prior to maghe ceremonies. Although some are left at the natsaro after a maghe festival, others are placed in pairs in the grade-taker's gardens to guarantee a good crop.

Different sculptural designs are used depending on which grade an aspirant has reached. While a tamtam has to be made each time grade-taking occurs, a tree fern carving indicates the aspirant has already climbed halfway up the ladder, with only stone statues to follow.

As the grade-taker moves further up the maghe scale, each subsequent stage he takes requires a tree fern to be carved especially for the event. Each one must be more highly decorated than that made for the previous ceremony. They are painted black, red, white and/or green, depending on what rank the aspirant aims to reach.

Each tree fern carver strives to achieve a perfect sculpture. If they succeed, they believe their work will be rewarded by the spirit of an ancestor making its home in the carving.

Stone Carvings One-metre-high volcanic-rock sculptures of very stylised men are occasionally made for the very highest maghe levels. They are similar in design to tree ferns, except they are usually modelled out of a block of pumice.

Much more common are magic stones. Usually half the size of a human hand, these are mainly made to guarantee prosperity or success in love. They are also occasionally used to inflict sickness or accidents on rivals.

Dancing Masks Tree ferns are also used to make ceremonial masks or *tamakes*. All are brightly painted, and decorated with hair made from dried banana palm. These masks are always destroyed after a ceremony because of the danger of the dancer's spirit remaining within them.

Pig-Killing Clubs A large hoe-shaped iron-wood club, called an *atata*, is used at maghe ceremonies to kill the pigs. Many are carved with stylised human features on them. Clubs with two faces carved back to back indicate the owner is a person of considerable rank.

Musical Instruments Some islanders play a single-string bow. Used like a jew's-harp, the musician places it on his lower lip and plays by plucking it with a coconut leaf.

More common is an unusually shaped bamboo flute. Slightly less than a metre in length, this instrument is decorated with geometric designs and has a long, multispiked end piece.

Medical Services

There are five health centres in Ambrym, at Olal, Endu, Biap, Sesivi and Utas.

Places to Stay

There are guest houses at Craig Cove, Ranon and Sanesup. See the information about those places in the Around Ambrym section, below.

Places to Eat

There are no markets on Ambrym and the co-op stores sell only dry goods, so to get fresh fruit and vegetables you must trade with the villagers. The guest houses at Sanesup and Ranon both sell meals. As elsewhere, you'll have no difficulty arranging for the locals to cook meals for you.

Getting There & Away

Ambrym's airfields are at Craig Cove in the south-west and Ulei in the south-east. An airstrip is currently proposed for Nobul, in the north, but at present this area is only accessible by sea.

Sunset, Tanna Beach Resort, Tanna Island (MC)

A	B
C	D
E	F

A: Parliament House, Port Vila (DO)
B: (AV)
C: Jungle gully near Lalinda,
   Ambrym Island (DO)
D: Iririki Island Resort, off Port Vila (AV)
E: Wreck of US warplane,
   Espiritu Santo Island (DO)
F: (MC)

Air Vanair has three return flights each week from Vila to Craig Cove and Ulei, and one per week from Luganville to each of these airfields. Each of the Vila flights includes Epi (Lamen Bay), while Paama is visited on two of the flights and Malakula (Lamap) once. The Luganville flight goes via Paama and Lamen Bay.

A one-way ticket from Craig Cove costs 3000VT to Ulei, 2500VT to Lamap, 2900VT to Lamen Bay, 5100VT to Luganville and 6700VT to Vila. From Ulei it's 2600VT to Lamen Bay, 5900VT to Luganville and 6300VT to Vila.

Sea Each week or so, Ifira Shipping's MV *Saraika* visits ports around Ambrym on its runs between Vila and Luganville. It also calls in to Epi, Paama, Pentecost and Ambae en route. Aloara Coastal Shipping's MV *Aloara* has a similar service, but includes Tongoa, Maewo and Malakula as well as those visited by the *Saraika*.

Ifira charges 3400VT for a ticket between Vila and Craig Cove, while Toara's fare is 3600VT. Both charge 500 to 1000VT if you're just travelling between Ambrym and its immediate neighbours, or between major ports on Ambrym.

The 15-metre launch MV *Mangaru* does a round trip between Lakatoro in north-eastern Malakula, Paama, Ambrym and Pentecost almost always on a weekly basis.

Yacht Good anchorages are few and far between, with the best one being Craig Cove. Sanesup is the only good one on the south coast, while the east has none at all. In the north, the recommended anchorages are Ranon, Buwoma Bay and just north of Ranvetlam.

Yachts visiting north Ambrym must call in to Ranon and pay a fee of 2500VT per week to the Lolihor Development Council. This entitles you to stop at any of the north's three anchorages.

Speedboat A chartered speedboat ride for the 24 km from Craig Cove to Lamap, on Malakula, is only safe in calm weather and will cost you at least 8000VT each way. You can travel from north Ambrym to south-west Pentecost for upwards of 4000VT one way.

Getting Around
In the south, a 4WD road connects Craig Cove with Maranata, and a coastal path continues on to Eas in the south-east. From here a road goes as far as Endu on the east coast, with a path linking up with Wilit in the north. A road connects the coastal villages from Wilit around to Ranvetlam.

The terrain along the uninhabited north-west coast is very rough, with no established path. Consequently most people travel between Craig Cove and Ranvetlam by speedboat. This can be expensive if there's only one or two of you, as the boat costs 8000VT. Arrangements should be made ahead of time either through a service message or by telephone.

AROUND AMBRYM
Southern Ambrym
The road from Craig Cove to Maranata is basically a narrow track that winds along the coast through small villages, coconut plantations and patches of jungle. Numerous paths lead down to the shore, and there are some excellent views from the higher points.

The following distances are from Craig Cove.

Craig Cove The commercial centre at Craig Cove is opposite the wharf and a short walk from the airport. It has a government guest house, wholesale store and a National Bank of Vanuatu agency. You can buy fresh bread at Sulo, which is just above the commercial centre. A hot spring close to the wharf is used by villagers for ablutions and washing clothes.

Places to Stay The basic *Craig Cove Guest House* is a basic iron structure with four bedrooms sleeping 14 people. It's got a gas cooker, bathroom and pit toilet and costs 800VT a night. For bookings you can try ringing the provincial government office on ☎ 48499, but as their phone is often out of order you'd be better off sending a service message. When you get there, ask the store manager for a key.

In the unlikely event that the guest house is full, you may be able to a bed up at the Roman Catholic mission. However, their guest quarters are even more spartan.

Biap (6 km) The village has a health centre with a trained nurse in charge.

Inland from this point, the villages of Meltungan and Lele are reviving the rom festival as an annual event for tourists. Meltungan is the only place in Ambrym where the dance is performed on request. This will cost you 5000VT, with a surcharge for cameras. You can purchase good-quality wood and stone carvings very cheaply at both villages.

Sesivi (9.5 km) A hot spring on the rocky shore below the Roman Catholic mission is a favourite bathing spot for villagers. You'll be quite welcome at the mission's kava bar, which sells some of the best kava in Ambrym.

Sanesup (13.5 km) A beautiful black sand beach begins just beyond Sanesup and extends all the way to Maranata. The taxi fare from Craig Cove to Sanesup costs 2000VT.

Things to See & Do Provided he has notice, Enos Falau at the Milee Guest House can arrange various **tours** by taxi to places such as Meltungan, Sesivi and Long Beach at Maranata. For information on tours to Mt Marum and Mt Benbow see the Volcanoes section later in this chapter.

While you're recovering from (or practising for) a trek to a volcano you can do some pleasant **walks** from Sanesup along the coast and along vehicle tracks in the area. Villagers use the beach as their bathroom, so you've got to be careful early and late in the day that you don't intrude. Enos can provide more information on this.

There's a small copra drier down on the beach a short walk from the guest house. This is usually in operation and will give you

an idea of what is involved in producing copra. The produce is picked up from the beach each week by the *Saraika*.

Places to Stay The *Milee Guest House* in Sanesup has six small rooms sleeping 12 people for 3500VT including three meals. This is a little expensive considering the standard. You'll need your own sheet and sleeping bag. Make bookings through the NTO in Vila, or leave a service message.

However, the English-speaking owner, Enos Falau, is a great character and will go out of his way to make sure you enjoy yourself. He's over 70, but you'd never know it, and is a good source of information on the whole island. He was the president of the former local government council (now provincial government) for Ambrym from 1983 to 1990.

Lalinda (19.5 km) Between Sanesup and Lalinda you cross some dry ash rivers which make a stark contrast to their lush, forested banks. They give you an introduction to what the ash plain is like, although nothing can really prepare you for that awesome moonscape.

The chief at Lalinda is the custom owner of the southern access to the volcanoes and charges you a small fee to visit them. This is where you collect your guide for the walk, which normally starts at a vehicle drop-off point about five km away in the bed of the Woketebo River.

The taxi fare to Lalinda is 2500VT from Craig Cove and 500VT from Sanesup.

You may be allowed to sleep on the floor at either the school or the Presbyterian women's club.

Maranata (27.5 km) Tower Peak rises high above the village, effectively barring access to the volcanoes beyond. This high, steep-sided peak has many narrow, rugged ridges descending abruptly from its summit.

There's an excellent swimming beach at the village with a fine view of Paama and cone-shaped Lopevi to the south-east. The body surfing is said to be quite good, but the villagers are too afraid of sharks to take advantage of it.

Continuing on from Maranata, the path to Eas varies from easy walking along the beach to hard slogging over steep hills.

From Sanesup, the return taxi fare to Maranata is 2000VT.

Eas (38 km) There's a waterfall one km inland on the Herat River, and black sand beaches from here to Endu.

Toak (47 km) This is a large village with a vocational training college. The Presbyterian women's group may let you sleep in their club house. Taxis can be hired in the village.

Endu (57 km) From here it is mostly footpath to Wilit. The path follows the coast most of the way and is often difficult, with numerous steep slopes and rough ground. The only reliable source of drinking water is at Tumun Point.

Tumun Point (65 km) The Oisalat River (pronounced 'Wisalat') flows straight over the cliff into the ocean. Sailing ships used to pull up here to refill their water tanks.

Northern Ambrym

Most of Ambrym's northern coast is extremely rocky. In some places, particularly west of Ranvetlam, high volcanic cliffs rise straight out of the sea. Only Wilit, Parereo, Ranon and Ranvetlam have beaches, of which the latter two are the best for swimming.

Northern Ambrym is where the island's customs and traditions have been least affected by the modern world, especially at Fanla. It's also the area where Ambrym's best carvings come from. Dance clearings in the more traditional villages usually have several tall tamtams standing around them as permanent sentinels.

It's easy in this part of Ambrym to work out whether you're approaching a Christian or a traditional village. The former are built along either side of the road, whilst custom-oriented villages are usually semicircular and constructed beside a clearing used as the natsaro.

Sand drawing is a common practice in northern Ambrym. The local word for it is *tutu*. You'll find sand artists in most villages along the coast from Ranvetlam to Konkon.

Kava is very popular in northern Ambrym, which has many nakamals. Women may enter the nakamals in coastal areas.

The following distances are anticlockwise from Craig Cove.

Olal (81 km) With a population of about 650, Olal is Ambrym's largest village. The Roman Catholic mission has no accommodation, but is proposing to build a guest house. Taxis and speedboats can be hired in the village.

Pokoro (82.5 km) This village is a traditional centre for sorcerers.

Neuwa (84 km) Rom dances are annual events in this semi-custom village, and at nearby Ranhor, where most men are active grade-takers. A major feature is the unusual rooster-head tamtams you'll see in the gardens.

Fanla (86.5 km) The most authentic rom dances are performed in Fanla, the island's principal custom centre. In addition, magic is taught here to youngsters from other northern villages. It has recently accepted Christianity, although many of the older people prefer to worship their traditional god, Barkulkul.

Men and women mix much more freely in Fanla than they do in traditional bush villages elsewhere in Vanuatu. However, there are definite distinctions between individual males, based on their rankings. Local men of very high status still live in tabu, or exclusive, huts where they cook and eat alone – in the past to avoid being poisoned. No female may enter any of these places.

All people believe the surrounding bush is inhabited by spirits, especially at night. If a man goes out into the scrub after dark, he will try to keep any malevolent spirits away by singing lustily. It's believed phantoms don't like loud noises!

Things to See Fanla's maghe clearing boasts several large **tamtams**. During the periodic grade-taking ceremonies, a four-metre-high platform is erected for grade-takers to dance on. This symbolises their newly acquired status. Meanwhile, other dancers gather below, throwing stones at the grade-takers to remind them that they are still mortals.

During the maghe, 30 or more pigs may be killed by each grade-taker. Cash can also be paid to the chief, especially if some of the pigs are considered inferior. It'll cost 1000VT to visit the maghe ground.

Places to Stay The villagers are accustomed to tourists, but will expect you to stay overnight at Ranon, where there's a guest house. And for a minimum of 20,000VT they'll put on a custom dance for you.

Fanrereo (87.5 km) This semi-custom Francophone village is a good starting point for climbing nearby Mt Tuvo and its neighbour, Mt Vletlam. Both offer fine views of Malakula, while Pentecost can be seen from Mt Tuvo. On clear days you can see as far as Santo. It's a one-day round trip to visit either summit.

Local people believe that if you talk to another person while on Mt Tuvo, 'snow' will fall shortly afterwards – snow being their word for heavy fog.

The village's tamtams and nakamal are worth seeing, but you may be asked to pay an exorbitant fee to take photos.

Ranon (88.5 km) Here you'll find the best swimming beach in northern Ambrym, as well as some of its best carvers. Speedboats and 4WD taxis can be hired in the village.

Things to See & Do Douglas, the owner of the Solomon Douglas Guest House (see below), can arrange excursions to Fanla and various natural attractions such as the **lava tube** at Melvat, the Buwoma Bay **hot springs** and the **volcanoes**. You could easily spend several days here doing tours or easy **walks** along the coast and in the nearby hills.

If you're by yourself, the two-day **walk** from Ranvetlam to Meltungan will cost you 5000VT including food, pack, guide and entry fee.

You can either walk to Melvat or take a speedboat from Ranon for 1000VT return – entry to the lava tube costs 500VT. This village is also very good one for **carvings.**

Places to Stay & Eat The *Solomon Douglas Guest House* in Ranon charges 2500VT per person for accommodation and meals, with sheets and mosquito nets provided. Its traditional-style bungalows are right on the beach. To make a booking, call either the NTO in Vila or the Tousi co-op office (☎ 48405). The latter is also the number to call if you want to arrange a speedboat ride to Craig Cove.

Ranbwe (90 km) There are several hot springs between Ranbwe and Ranvetlam, two km to the south-west. This is another place where villagers cook and wash in the thermally heated sea water.

Maronran (91 km) You'll find sites of several abandoned leaf-house villages near here, though the bush has obscured most of their remains. All except Maronran were evacuated during the eruption of 1950.

Buwoma Bay (97.5 km) The bay has two large hot springs, one issuing from a cave while the other is on the shore. It's another good spot for a warm bath, and as a bonus you may see some megapode birds. The return speedboat fare from Ranon is 2000VT (for half a day) and the entry fee is 500VT per person.

The Volcanoes

Columns of white smoke pour constantly from several vents in Mt Benbow's central crater. Although Mt Marum itself is dormant, three vents around its base periodically spew out dense clouds of dark smoke and molten rock. One of them erupted in 1993, sending a river of lava curling away across the ash plain. The dark, brooding outlines of Mt Benbow and Mt Marum are a km or so apart, with Mt Marum, the highest by a hundred metres, rising to 1270 metres. Usually shrouded in smoke and cloud, they dominate the vast area of barren ash that lies within the old caldera. At night, the sky above them glows red from the infernos below.

A Land that Time Forgot

We were about five km from Lalinda when our 4WD truck came to a black, glassy wall of lava that reared out of the sandy riverbed in front. This was the end of the 'road'. Grabbing water bottles and my light pack, my two ni-Vanuatu guides and I climbed out and commenced our walk to the volcanoes.

For the next 30 minutes we followed the old lava flow as it wound between high ridges covered in thick jungle. Although it was early and reasonably cool, I was already sweating buckets. However, my guides, Peter and Jerry, looked cool and comfortable even when we entered a wet, steamy gorge further on towards the caldera. As we walked the trees became progressively smaller due to damage by the constant rain of ash. By the time we reached the caldera the vegetation was mainly slender palms and ferns.

An hour after leaving the vehicle we scrambled up a steep mossy creek, then passed through a thicket of wild cane before bursting out onto the barren emptiness of the ash plain. It was an unbelievable sight. Behind me was tropical lushness, while in front stretched a vast, utterly lifeless wasteland of grey ash. As I stared in amazement, the clouds parted to show dark smoke billowing up from the base of distant Mt Marum. The whole godforsaken landscape looked like a suitable habitat for goblins and other evil creatures from one of Tolkien's books.

For another hour we crunched northwards across the ash plain, crossing dead rivers and climbing up and over low ridges and hummocks. At one point we crossed a 100-metre-wide river of clinker-like lava from the 1993 eruption. Finally we stood before the closest of the three new vents below Mt Marum, whose stark eroded flanks towered overhead. The sound of the vent sucking in oxygen was surprisingly loud. Grasping Peter's outstretched hand, I was able to lean out and feel its fiery breath. Unfortunately, loose edges made it impossible to look down its smoky gullet to where the magma boiled and heaved 100 metres below.

Leaving the vent we walked west towards the forbidding face of Mt Benbow, passing close to several small fumaroles that quietly steamed among great mounds of ash. There were no plants of any kind and no animals – not even an insect. I wondered if this is what the whole of planet Earth will be like when the human race has finished with it.

Progress was slow as we crossed the two km or so of deeply incised ash to the base of Benbow. Here Peter led us into a narrow gully, then up onto an exposed razor-backed ridge that snaked upwards with steep slopes plunging away on either side. It was like being on top of the world, and about as close to walking on a tightrope as I ever want to get.

Twenty minutes later, having survived the most unusual walking experience of my life so far, we arrived at the summit. This proved to be the narrow rim of a huge central crater where, far below on its floor, great columns of white smoke poured from a number of circular vents. Again it brought to mind Tolkien: this is where you'd expect to find a dragon. It was like a glimpse of another world, and not a very friendly one at that.

We decided to eat our picnic lunch on the crater rim, which was only about three metres wide at that point. The food was ordinary, but the view over our naked, water-sculpted surroundings was exhilarating. We'd just finished eating, and I was making noises about walking around the rim, when fog closed in around us. A cold breeze cut through our thin clothes as light rain began to fall. It was time to head back to our pick-up point.

It really is difficult to imagine anything as silent, desolate and lifeless as the landscape of central Ambrym. Its sheer starkness combined with the dramatic results of water erosion and volcanic activity produces something that must be truly unique, and is certainly awe-inspiring. The next time I visit Vanuatu I'll definitely be going back for another dose. ■

Access & Tours The best starting points for walks to the volcanoes are Lalinda and Ranvetlam, with the latter offering the easiest route up Marum. Whichever way you go, you'll need to allow two days if you want to climb both volcanoes. To climb one requires a reasonably long day from either starting point.

Walking Conditions The first requirements are to be fit, reasonably acclimatised and used to walking, as conditions can be difficult whichever way you go.

Starting from either of the vehicle drop-off points near Ranvetlam and Lalinda, the path takes you up dry, soft riverbeds and steep slopes, with thick jungle that can tear at sensitive skin. There's no shade on the barren ash surfaces in the caldera, and the heat there can be terrific. This makes skin protection (including a broad-brimmed hat) and plenty of water essential. Loose-fitting cotton clothing is the most comfortable.

The slopes around the volcanoes are covered with a thin, dry slippery crust. Jogging shoes are not at all suitable for this type of surface because – apart from grit filling them – you might end up using your backside to toboggan down a very high, steep ridge when your feet slip from under you. You'll feel much safer with strong walking boots capable of kicking toe and heel holes in the crust. Good ankle support

is also necessary as you may have some boulder hopping to do, particularly if you're walking from Lalinda.

Tours John Salong of the Lolihor Adventure Tours in Ranon (☎ 48405) operates a walking tour from Ranvetlam to Meltungan, climbing Mt Marum and spending a night nearby on the ash plain. This is one of the best walks in the South Pacific, with plenty of variety and some unforgettable experiences. John provides rucksacks, but not bedding.

If you like, you can take John's walk as part of an interesting five-day package which is offered by the Lolihor Development Council. The deal includes all transport to and from Vila, accommodation and meals at the Solomon Douglas Guest House, various tours and activities in the Ranon area, and the volcano walk. The cost is 46,000VT per person for a minimum group of three.

Alternatively, you can do a day walk from Lalinda. Enos Falau at the Milee Guest House can arrange guides and transport for walks up to the central ash plain and on to the volcanoes. If you're fit, you can easily do the return walk to one of the new vents under Mt Marum and climb to the summit of Mt Benbow in a day. This tour is highly recommended and costs 2500VT all inclusive for a lone traveller.

Paama Island

Formerly called Paum, which means 'to act', Paama was until recently a separate administrative district. Its main centre is at Liro in the north-west.

Measuring nine km long by four km, the island covers 32 sq km and is a uniform oblong. The terrain is mostly rugged and steep, with high forested hills falling sheer to the sea around much of the coast. Cultivatable land is so scarce that the fallow period between crops is only one to two years instead of the usual 15. Fortunately, the soil is extremely fertile – the island is noted for its abundant, high-quality fruit.

Paama has no permanently flowing streams. Freshwater supplies come either from rainwater catchment tanks or from coastal springs at low tide, where water is collected in buckets, basins and cans. Bores have been sunk, but reliable groundwater supplies have only been found at Liro, Tahi and Hingal. Knowing its likely origin, it's common sense to boil all water before you drink it.

The island's population numbers about 1700. Many islanders now live on Efate, Santo, Malakula and Epi because of lack of employment, drinking water and suitable land for gardening on Paama. If you notice that there aren't as many men as women around, it's because they're away working on other islands.

History

There were very few foreign settlers on Paama prior to the arrival of British traders and planters from 1900. They described the villagers as strong and self-reliant.

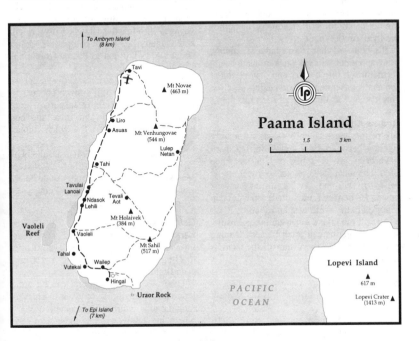

The Ambrym Freedom Movement of the early 1950s spread to Liro, but emigration soon sapped its energy. The Santo-based Nagriamel movement likewise enjoyed only a brief influence on Paama.

Local Customs

Fishing Rights There's good fishing off the south-eastern coast. However, as the best reefs are regarded as valuable items of property, fishing on someone else's 'patch' can lead to serious disputes. These can only be settled by the trespasser making gifts of pigs, mats or money.

Bear this in mind if you plan to go reef fishing here. As long as you have permission to use a particular area of reef, all will be well. But make sure you have asked the right person, not the first person you meet.

Nakaimos Every village claims to have at least one man who can change himself into a shark; such a person is called a *nakaimo*. Only sorcerers may do this, and as women are not meant to perform sorcery, nakaimos are by definition male.

It's believed that if you have an enemy, your opponent will get a nakaimos to transform himself into a shark and devour you at sea. As a consequence, the islanders describe shark attacks as the work of sorcerers.

Sharks & Dolphins

Six people were taken by sharks – mainly tigers – between 1982 and 1986, but there have been only a couple of fatalities since then. The most dangerous places seem to be off Liro, Tahi and Tavulai, all on the west coast. In contrast, no attacks have been reported in the north-east and south.

Not all the island's marine life is hostile. Indeed, dolphins can often be seen leaping playfully through the water off the island's north-eastern corner.

Medical Services

There are clinics in Liro, Lehili and Vaoleli.

Places to Stay & Eat

The only commercial accommodation is a guest house in Liro (see the following Around Paama section). However, most villages have Presbyterian women's clubs where you can sleep for up to 500VT per person.

Getting There & Away

Air Paama's single, short airfield is jammed up against a steep hill right on the north-west coast. Landing here is a real experience in turbulent conditions.

Vanair has three flights each week to the island, two from Vila and the other from Luganville. All three also call in to Craig Cove and Ulei on Ambrym, and Lamen Bay on Epi. One-way fares from Paama are 2100VT to Ulei, 3000VT to Craig Cove, 2200VT to Lamen Bay, 6100VT to Vila and 6300VT to Luganville.

Sea Ifira Shipping's *Saraika* and Toara Coastal Shipping's *Aloara* visit all ports on Paama during their fortnightly return voyages through the islands between Vila and Luganville. Both companies charge about 3000VT to get to Paama from either Vila or Luganville.

Although it's much faster between Epi and Paama by speedboat, it's much cheaper by ship. These vessels only take two hours between Lamen Bay and Liro, and cost between 500 and 1000VT – which is much less than a speedboat.

The launch, the MV *Mangaru*, sails regularly from Lakatoro in north-eastern Malakula. Its return trip starts with Paama and continues via Ambrym and Pentecost.

Getting Around

Land A road runs down the west coast, linking the airfield at Tavi in the north-west to Hingal, on the south coast. Taxis meet each flight.

Otherwise, getting around can be rather arduous, especially if you want to cross the mountainous interior. Footpaths are everywhere, but the steep slopes and lack of water make for trying conditions.

Sea Speedboats provide a quick way around the coast. You can hire them at Liro, Tahi, Lehili, Lulep Netan and Vaoleli.

AROUND PAAMA
The following distances are from Liro.

Liro
This is the island's largest village, having over 500 residents. It's pleasantly laid out around a playing field, which is fronted by a short black sand beach.

Liro has a fruit-and-vegetable market every Friday. There's also a fishery base where you can buy ice and cheap fresh fish.

There's a private *guest house* in Liro belonging to the local mission. It has cooking facilities and two double rooms cost 1000VT per person. They're in regular use, so check the vacancies with Liro's provincial government office (☎ 48411) before heading over. The following distances are from Liro.

Lanoai (3.5 km)
A colourful **reef** stretches the 300 metres between Lanoai and Ndasok and offers good snorkelling. The water teems with sharks, but they're mainly of the harmless reef variety.

Tevali Aot (4 km)
This is the most traditional of Paama's villages, and it's not tourist-oriented.

Vaoleli (4.5 km)
Less than 500 metres from the shore is Vaoleli Reef. The locals say this was once an island, but it was washed away by the sea in a violent storm. Now only the reef remains.

Vaoleli has a black sand beach. There's another one two km further south at **Vutekai**.

Lulep Netan (5 km)
It's a slow, laborious hike across the mountainous interior to the east coast. Once at Lulep Netan, you can get a speedboat over to Lopevi.

LOPEVI ISLAND
Also called Ulveah and Volcano Island, Lopevi is Vanuatu's most dangerous active volcano. Despite considerable activity in 1883, and again between 1958 and 1959, there was a DOM mission on the island until a particularly powerful eruption in 1970. Everyone was hurriedly evacuated and resettled on Epi, and the island is now deserted.

Lopevi has an elliptical base 5.5 to 7.5 km across and rises to a classic cone over 1400 metres high. Officially it's 1413 metres high, but it has almost certainly grown since it was last surveyed in 1979.

The volcano's mood is often calm, but when it's really fired up it hurls out masses of molten rock and spews rivers of flaming lava. Thick grey smoke regularly billows from its towering summit.

Dense vegetation blankets Lopevi's lower slopes, while its upper portion is dark volcanic ash. A subpeak 166 metres high in the south-eastern corner is the remains of an earlier, now dormant, crater.

Getting There & Away
A chartered return trip in a speedboat from Lulep Netan on Paama straight across to Lopevi will cost you at least 3000VT. It'll be more like 4500VT if you want the boat to go all the way around.

PAAMA ISLAND

Espiritu Santo Island

Although officially named Espiritu Santo – Spanish for the 'Holy Spirit' – this island is called Santo by almost everyone. To add a little confusion, Luganville, the island's principal settlement, is also generally referred to as Santo. Just when you feel you've worked out whether people mean the island or the town, someone will start talking about a place called Canal. And where's that? Why, Luganville of course! ('Canal' refers to the Segond Channel off Luganville.)

Espiritu Santo, 4010 sq km in size, is Vanuatu's largest island. For administrative purposes it's grouped with Malo, Aore, Tutuba and Bokissa islands to form Sanma Province.

Tourism is growing in importance, as evidenced by the upgrading of Luganville's airport to Boeing 767 capability – this is due for completion in 1995.

You'll find several hotels, motels and restaurants in Luganville, as well as two resorts reasonably close to town. The island has a fairly good network of unsealed roads that offer access to sandy beaches and friendly villages. Scuba divers come for the world-class underwater attractions close to Luganville, particularly the wreck of the SS *President Coolidge* and nearby Million Dollar Point.

History

Spanish Arrival On 1 May 1606, shortly after he had passed through the Banks group, the Spanish explorer Quiros saw Santo on the horizon. Two days later he sailed into Big Bay with his three galleons. He called it St Phillip & St James Bay, as the day he arrived was the feast day of these two apostles. However, its prosaic name of Big Bay is much more appropriate.

Quiros' first task was to colonise this 'new' land, then spread Christianity and search for gold. Filled with religious fervour, Quiros named the spot where he landed Nueva Jerusalema (New Jerusalem) and the adjacent waters the Jordan River.

Relations with local villagers were the key to the venture's success, but these got off to a bad start. Realising that the land was fertile, with abundant root crops, the Spanish stocked up with food without paying for it.

The villagers of Big Bay couldn't work out whether the Spanish were gods or devils. But when some of them were shot, pigs and other food stolen, and a chief killed, they began to resist. Soon there were constant skirmishes.

Malaria, fish poisoning and general disillusionment brought the new colony to a sudden end. On 21 June 1606, shortly after midnight and while Quiros was asleep on board ship, his crew silently cast off. They had had enough. Unable to make them change their minds, Quiros let them sail straight back to Peru.

Later Explorers There was no further European contact until May 1768, when the French navigator Bougainville with his ships *La Boudeuse* and *L'Etoile* sailed along Santo's southern coast and up to Big Bay. Six years later, in August 1774, Captain Cook also found Big Bay. Clearly, Spanish savagery had been forgotten by then: two members of Cook's expedition walked across eastern Santo without incident.

The French explorer La Pérouse may have landed on Santo in 1788. But we shall never know as his two ships were lost with all hands later that year in the south-eastern Solomons. Some of the debris salvaged from La Pérouse's sunken vessels includes pottery made in the Santo style.

From Traders to Settlers Santo missed the first rush for trading stations in the 1840s as its sandalwood resources were not discovered until 1853. Alluvial gold was found two years later and outside interest mushroomed. By 1856, 16 traders were resident on the

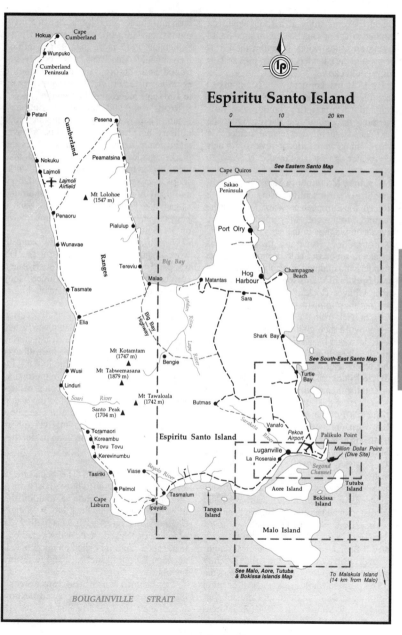

island. Several ships at a time would be moored at various anchorages around Santo taking on sandalwood. In return the Europeans sold the islanders as many pigs as their ships could carry.

By 1871 blackbirders were beginning to cast their greedy eyes on Santo, as the demand for plantation labour was now booming throughout the Pacific. Over the next decade, there were several incidents in which sailors were killed in revenge for acts of violence against islanders.

Resistance Movements Many Santo traditionalists were resentful of the destructive effect of the European presence. Forming the Tamata movement, they made sporadic attacks on planters in the early 1900s.

In 1923 the Ronovuru movement was formed in southern Santo. Ronovuru was an islander who claimed to be able to bring the dead back to life. This soon had people from other villages flocking to his bush home, hoping that long-lost relatives could be brought back from the dead.

Ronovuru then claimed that his wife had been poisoned by an Englishman, and said that only by killing this settler could his wife and other dead people be brought back to life. So Ronovuru and two friends murdered the Englishman, giving away various edible morsels from the body to supporters.

Santo's Europeans were quite outraged. Ronovuru, unrepentant, went to the gallows, promising a return to life for all his followers' ancestors. Despite his death, the cult persisted for a while in Santo's isolated bush villages.

In 1937, Avuavu, a man from the mountains of south-west Santo, called for the expulsion of all Europeans. He was promptly put in prison, where he later died.

WW II Because of Japan's relentless southward drive in early 1942, the Allies urgently needed a secure forward base to buttress the USA's desperate holding action in the central Solomons. Santo's Segond Channel was ideal. From May to July 1942, US forces turned the island's supposedly impenetrable bush into a huge camp city capable of accommodating 100,000 servicemen. Up to September 1945 more than half a million men, mainly Americans, were briefly stationed here before sailing off to battle elsewhere in the Pacific. There were often up to 100 ships moored off Luganville.

Roads were laid throughout south-east Santo. There were over 40 cinemas, four military hospitals, five airfields, a naval repair centre, a torpedo boat base, jetties and market gardens. Numerous Quonset huts were erected for use as offices, stores, workshops and servicemen's accommodation, and many of these can still be seen around Luganville. Despite the area being such a juicy target, only one Japanese bomb landed on Santo. It hit a cow!

Over 10,000 islanders came to Santo to work as labourers or servants for the US troops. To the bushmen, the servicemen seemed fabulously wealthy and indeed, they were also generous, paying much higher wages than the planters.

The most remarkable part of it all occurred once the fighting was over. Santo was turned into a huge junkyard of surplus war material. Local planters as well as people from all over the south-western Pacific came looking for bargains. But there was much more than people would buy. Endless supplies of new equipment were daily trucked to the waterside and dumped in the sea at a place now known as Million Dollar Point. Every night, islanders scavenged for anything useful they could find.

The Postwar Reaction The departure of 100,000 Americans left a huge ghost town at Luganville. As a reaction, a traditionalist movement sprang up in 1946 in Santo's mountainous interior. It was called the Mamara, or 'Naked Cult', and was led by a man called Tsek. He called on his people to abandon European lifestyles and to resume the old ways.

Tsek claimed that all disagreements could be solved by everyone going naked, destroying all their goods and having free sex. He promised 'Amerika' would return, making all Santo people wealthy and immortal. The movement died with Tsek in 1952.

Under the leadership of Atori, another Santo cultist of the same period, a road was built through the bush from Viase to the sea at Tasmalum. This was to facilitate the arrival of American bounty. Atori was jailed for his beliefs but later released.

Finally, in the early 1950s a man called Moli Valiu reaffirmed the need to abandon European religion and principles and to stay loyal to bush traditions. By the mid-1950s these movements, essentially reactions to seeing such unbelievable wartime extravagance and waste, were in decline.

In the 1960s a major cause of dispute was created when settlers began clearing hitherto unused land. Some planters even tried to evict local people from their villages.

European agents had acquired large tracts of land by the early 1900s, but had not put them to use. In custom terms, if you acquire land but then fail to use it, ownership returns to the seller. Between 1962 and 1964, Chief Buluk campaigned against planters extending their plantations; he regularly uprooted fences, earning himself six months in jail on one occasion.

Jimmy Stevens & Nagriamel Moli Jimmy Tupou Putuntun Moses Stevens, one-time bulldozer driver, was of mixed Scottish and Tongan descent. Though skilled in European ways, he also assumed the role of a ni-Vanuatu chief, holding yearly grade-taking ceremonies. The charismatic Stevens was equally at home talking in Bislama to bush people or using commercial language with European and US business interests.

In 1963 Chief Buluk and Jimmy Stevens formed the Nagriamel movement. Its aims were to restore the primacy of custom and to recover from Europeans all undeveloped land. The term Nagriamel was a union of the names of two sacred bush leaves, the *nagria* and the *namele*.

In 1965 Buluk and Stevens made their base at Vanafo. Two years later, they occupied some nearby European-owned land, earning themselves a jail sentence. But in the

eyes of Santo's bush people, they had all become heroes. Word spread to other islands. Soon Nagriamel had a following throughout northern Vanuatu.

Although the majority of Nagriamel's membership were Santo tribespeople, by 1968 the organisation had found some unexpected allies. French planters in Santo were worried that Britain might wish to grant independence to the archipelago; and the US Phoenix Foundation, based in Boulder, Colorado, saw Stevens as an ally who could help create a model free-enterprise tax haven and a retirement paradise for rich US customers. Phoenix began buying land that would be subdivided into plots and sold in the USA.

Although the Condominium passed legislation in 1971 to prevent overseas interests from acquiring land without government approval, the relationship prevailed, providing Stevens with the cash to petition the UN for the country's independence within 12 months. At the same time he announced that Nagriamel had 20,000 supporters.

Pre-Independence Manoeuvring Not everyone supported Nagriamel. English-speaking Protestant islanders were disturbed by Stevens' polygamy: reports said he had over 20 wives. They also opposed his relationship with French and other foreign interests.

The French authorities, on the other hand, encouraged Nagriamel to become anti-British and pro-French by financing various facilities at Vanafo. As the 1970s progressed, Nagriamel united for electoral purposes with other anti-British and anti-independence movements.

Secessionist Talk When Nagriamel and its allies unexpectedly lost the 1975 election, people on Santo began talking of secession. Nagriamel then set the date for secession at 1 April 1976, but deferred it to 10 August the same year. Yet when the day came and secession was proclaimed, no one took any notice.

Throughout the late 1970s, Santo parties grew more hardened in their secessionist ideas. In response to the English-speaking

Vanua'aku Party's increasing dominance of national political life, they allied themselves ever more closely with French settlers and the Phoenix Foundation.

Although barred from entering the country, the Phoenix Foundation continued to finance Nagriamel. It also provided 25,000 passports in the movement's name. At the same time French settlers, fearful of independence, gave constant encouragement. Convinced of France's cultural superiority, they had no desire to accept the authority of the mainly Melanesian, Protestant and English-speaking national administration that was elected in late 1979.

The Coconut Rebellion On 27 May 1980, eight weeks before national independence, Jimmy Stevens and his supporters staged their coup. Armed mainly with bows and arrows, they occupied Luganville and proclaimed Santo's independence, calling their new country Vemarana.

British and French troops were sent to Luganville six days prior to independence, but their orders were to do nothing to cause displeasure to either party. When looting occurred, all they did was to stand by. Because of their failure to control the rebels, they were replaced by Papua New Guinea's Kumul force. The new arrivals arrested the Whites who had supported secession, immediately breaking the rebellion's back.

Vemarana collapsed with Stevens' arrest on 1 September, though mopping up in the bush continued till the end of the month. Stevens' reward for his rebellion was 14½ years imprisonment. He was released from Port Vila prison as part of a general amnesty in 1991, and died three years later.

Geography
Santo is 116 km long, 59 km wide and has Vanuatu's four highest peaks: Mt Tabwemasana, Mt Kotamtam, Mt Tawaloala and Santo Peak, all of which are over 1700 metres. They rise out of the densely wooded mountainous spine which runs almost the full length of the island's western side.

In contrast, the southern and eastern coastal strips are reasonably flat and have been largely developed for cattle grazing and plantations. This is where most of the population lives.

The island is frequently shaken by minor earthquakes. A powerful quake in 1965 raised parts of the island's coastline by up to 40 cm.

Climate
Over the past 20 years Luganville's annual rainfall has ranged from 1165 to 3360 mm, giving an average of 2328 mm. February is the wettest month with 334 mm, while the driest, August, receives 85 mm on average. Maximum temperatures range from 30°C in the summer months to 27°C during winter, while average minimums are about 8°C lower.

Flora & Fauna
The fast-growing American vine covers large areas of forest and secondary growth in south-eastern Santo. Introduced during WW II as a natural camouflage for US bases, it's now a serious pest.

Far preferable are the island's 49 species of orchid. Although some are restricted to densely forested mountainous areas, there are plenty of the more common varieties in the more accessible coastal areas. Also of interest are the huge kauris said to exist in the south-west mountains.

Santo is Vanuatu's richest island in terms of bird fauna, with 55 species including all seven of the country's endemics. Rarest and least known of all is the Santo mountain starling. This rufous bird, about 20 cm in length, inhabits the undergrowth of Santo's cloud forests. It's only found above 1300 metres, so don't count on seeing one without a lot of hard work.

Another highland rarity is the endemic Vanuatu mountain pigeon, which occurs only in primeval forest above 600 metres. A slate-grey bird with bright-red legs, it grows to about 40 cm long. It's usually seen either singly or in pairs, although you may see small groups feeding in the canopy.

Economy

Copra, cattle and fish are the island's principal sources of income. Most of the copra production is exported to France to be processed into soap. Santo carries the bulk of Vanuatu's beef-cattle herd.

Gold deposits have been found in the south-west and, along with copper and silver, in the Sakao Peninsula and Big Bay areas. However, these areas all await systematic exploration.

People

In 1989, Santo's population numbered 22,664, of which 6965 lived in Luganville – the town was estimated to have grown by 2000 four years later. A further 3000 lived on the neighbouring islands of Malo, Aore, Tutuba and Bokissa, of which Malo was by far the most populous.

You'll sometimes see blonde, curly haired children with light-brown skin, a genetic peculiarity that's also fairly common in the Solomon Islands. However, their hair has usually turned brown by the time they reach adulthood.

Local Customs

Santo, like the other large northern islands, is still an important centre for nimangki ceremonies. The strongholds of this custom are Vanafo, the Sakao Peninsula, the west coast and the mountainous centre.

Everyone living along the south-eastern seaboard has adopted European dress. In other parts of the country, such as Butmas and the Big Bay area, many people still wear T-piece genital covers called *mal mal* (these are usually a strip of cloth or a tapa apron) and grass skirts as their everyday dress.

Handicrafts

The only places in Vanuatu where pottery is still made in the traditional way are the villages of Wusi and Linduri on Santo's west coast. Yet pottery-making was once widespread on the island, and when the rainforest is cut back ancient ceramics are often found. Why the practice died out isn't known.

Tourist Information

The best source of tourist information on Santo is Espiritu Santo Travel & Tours (☎ 36391), in Luganville's main street (called Blvd Higginson although the locals refer to it as Main St), next door to the Asia Motel. The NTO doesn't have an office here yet, although this may change with the opening of the new airport.

Medical Services

In addition to Luganville's hospital there are a number of health clinics, dispensaries and aid posts scattered about the island.

Medical facilities and supplies are very limited in western and inland Santo. Most west-coast health needs are met by a monthly tour of a government ship with a doctor and nurses aboard.

Activities

Scuba Diving & Snorkelling There are at least 20 worthwhile dive sites in the channels within 15 km south and south-west of Luganville. Santo's wreck and coral diving are generally superior to Efate's. Most reefs are suitable for snorkelling, as is Million Dollar Point, but the wrecks are out of reach for free divers. The following sites will give you an idea of what's on offer.

SS *President Coolidge* – The world's largest easily accessible wreck lies in 21 to 67 metres of water just off the shore east of Luganville. With virtually no current and visibility up to 40 metres, conditions are normally excellent for diving.

ESPIRITU SANTO ISLAND

SS *President Coolidge*

Swimming along and through the wreck you can view the trappings of a 1930s luxury liner as well as the hardware of a WW II troopship – the holds still contain artillery, trucks, jeeps, personal equipment and much more. At 202 metres long it's far too big to be explored on a single dive. In fact, the experts recommend at least four. (For more details see the section on Around Espiritu Santo, later in this chapter.)

USS *Tucker* – Like the *President Coolidge*, the destroyer *Tucker* was sunk by a 'friendly' mine during WW II. Numerous salvage operations and wartime demolition practice have largely destroyed the wreck's appearance as a warship. It lies broken into two pieces in about 20 metres of water, with visibility averaging 30 metres.

MV *Henry Bonneaud* – This former coastal trading vessel was scuttled in 1989 to make a wreck dive. Now it's the home of many fish and some beautiful soft corals. Sitting upright in 30 to 40 metres of water, it makes an excellent introduction to both wreck and deep diving.

Million Dollar Point – Awesome quantities of equipment and supplies – literally ranging from bulldozers to bottles of coke – were pushed into the sea here at the end of WW II. Even when you see it you won't believe it. The depth ranges from zero to 40 metres, generally with no current and good visibility.

Bokissa Bommie – The main attraction here is fish, including pelagic varieties. A dozen or so whaler sharks live in the area and are the focus of shark-feeding. If you're into thrills this shouldn't be missed.

Tutuba – Off the northern tip of Tutuba Island, this is one of the best coral dives near Luganville. There are also deep crevices, swim-throughs and caves. The depth ranges from five to 30 metres and visibility is excellent.

Tubana – This drop-off dive near Urelapa Island off Tangoa Landing, about 15 km south-west of Luganville, has depths ranging from five to 70 metres. Here you can see huge gorgonia sea fans, black coral trees and swarms of fish life.

Chails Reef – Also known as 'Fantastic', this protected dive site features gorgonia sea fans and the usual array of marine life. The depth ranges from 26 to 42 metres and visibility is usually excellent.

Organised Tours

Several tour operators have main-street premises in Luganville.

Land Trips The principal operators are Butterfly Tours and Sandy's Hibiscus Tours, both of which can be contacted through Espiritu Travel & Tours. They offer a range of standard half-day and day tours in their minibuses, or they'll tailor-make one to suit your requirements. They'll also organise walking tours for you.

One of their day trips is the Santo full circle, visiting Vanafo, Matantas, Champagne Beach and the Matevulu Blue Hole for 4000VT per person (the minimum charge for

Whaler shark

the bus is 20,000VT). Alternatively, you can explore the north-east coast for 3000VT (minimum charge 15,000VT).

You can also hire a taxi and arrange your own tour. A day trip to the Matevulu Blue Hole and Champagne Beach will cost around 7000VT shared. If you just want to go for a swim in the former you'll pay around 3000VT shared.

Sea Cruises The 59-foot *Miz May* offers day cruises for 30,000VT, with lunch not included, and will also do overnight charters. The operators require 48 hours' notice, which makes it a little difficult as they don't have a phone. However, you can leave a message at either the Natangora Café, the Hotel Santo or Espiritu Santo Travel & Tours.

Scuba Diving Santo Dive Tours (☎ 36822) and Exploration Diving (☎ 36638) both have offices in the main street, while Bokissa Island Dive (☎ 36855) is on nearby Bokissa Island. They all offer a full range of rental equipment.

If you just want to dive the *President Coolidge*, then you'll find that Allan Power of Santo Dive Tours is the recognised expert. He should be, he's been diving on the wreck for over 25 years. Allan charges a group rate of 2500VT per dive (a 'group' comprises 10 divers) with transport, guide, air tanks, weight belts and weights provided. He does shore dives only and concentrates on the *President Coolidge* and Million Dollar Point.

For a broader range of dives you'll need to contact Exploration Diving or Bokissa Island Dive. Their rates depend on whether or not you're prebooked – it's much cheaper if you are – and on how many dives you want to book for.

Getting There & Away
Air Santo had five operational airfields during WW II, but now only Pekoa, six km from Luganville, is still active. Wartime pilots knew it as Bomber Two. The island's

only other commercial strip is at Lajmoli, on the north-west coast.

Pekoa is the main feeder airfield for the northern islands. From here you can fly by Vanair to Ambae, Ambrym, Epi, Maewo, Malakula, Paama, Pentecost and the Banks and Torres islands, as well as Vila.

There are at least two, and usually three, return flights daily between Santo and Vila, with tickets costing 9800VT one way. For details of flights and fares to other destinations see the Getting There & Away sections in relevant chapters.

Vanair also operates a twice-weekly return service to New Caledonia. See the section on air travel in the Getting There & Away chapter.

Sea Each fortnight Ifira Shipping's *Saraika* and Toara Coastal Shipping's *Aloara* provide a return service between Vila and Santo, taking a week each way via the larger islands in between. *Aloara* calls in at ports on Tongoa (in the Shepherds), Epi, Paama, Malakula, Ambrym, Pentecost and Ambae; *Saraika* doesn't visit Tongoa and Malakula. A one-way fare including meals costs 5000VT on *Saraika* and 6000VT on *Aloara*.

Several small trading boats ply the northern routes from Luganville and their skippers may be prepared to take you on as passenger. You can check the current situation by asking around at the Chinese stores – the best one to start with is the LCM Store (☎ 36530) on Blvd Higginson (Main St).

Launches & Speedboat Small 'water taxis' link Luganville and its offshore neighbours, departing from the mouth of the Sarakata River beside Unity Park. If you wait for the 'regular' service the fare is about 400VT per person one-way to Aore Island. Charters cost a lot more.

Yacht Luganville has full customs and immigration facilities at the main wharf. The Fisheries Department in western Luganville has a marine repair workshop and professional sail-repair sewing machines. There's a slipway at Palikulo Point.

Segond Channel is the town's main anchorage, but it's somewhat exposed and has poor holding. Most yachts prefer to anchor off Club Nautique at Palikulo Bay, about 12 km from town, where there's a sandy bottom and better wind protection. However, the bay has a tricky entrance due to coral bommies and shallows.

A good anchorage closer to Luganville is at La Roseraie, three km from the town centre, where a number of moorings are available.

Getting Around

Santo has a relatively good network of unsealed roads connecting Luganville with the south-west coast, north and east. However, the mountainous central and western areas have only walking tracks.

To/From the Airport The minibus fare between Pekoa airport and Luganville is 200VT, while taxis charge 400VT shared.

Air Vanair has one flight each week from Luganville to Lajmoli airfield in the north-west. You can fly directly between the two from Luganville, but to return you have to go via Gaua, Vanua Lava and Mota Lava in the Banks group. It's an interesting flight provided you can get a window seat.

Bus Regular minibus services connect Luganville and Port Olry. As their main function is to run workers to and from town, the best way to catch a ride is to stand by the roadside before 7 am if you're heading in and after 5 pm on the outward run. The fare is 200VT each way.

Another east-coast service is operated by the Lonnoc Beach Resort, which charges 500VT each way.

Car The only place you can hire a car in Luganville is the Hotel Santo (36250), on Main St. However, the quality of their few small passenger cars and 4WD vehicles can be a little rugged, so check before you hire. Their minimum rate for a day rental is 3600VT including insurance, plus 25VT per

km. Two to six-day rentals cost from 6100 to 8600VT per day including insurance and unlimited km.

Truck Luganville's market is a good place to make enquiries if you're looking for a ride to outlying areas. You can check the availability of accommodation while you're at it.

Mountain Bike Exploration Diving in the main street just up from Hotel Santo hires mountain bikes for 750/1000/5600VT per half-day/day/week.

Walking There are many excellent walks on Santo, although, as elsewhere, relatively few visitors indulge. If nothing else you should at least do a couple in the proposed national park at Big Bay. Those interested in some serious trekking should contact either Glen Russell of Butterfly Tours or Sandy of Sandy's Hibiscus Tours. Both can arrange anything from coastal walks to climbing the highest mountains, and will tailor walks to suit your requirements.

The record for walking around western and central Santo is held by a government malaria-eradication team. This group did it in the early 1980s in 28 days flat, and somehow avoided catching malaria or being washed away by raging torrents. They set out knowing that if they were injured, there would be little chance of early treatment or rescue. The situation is also the same for bushwalkers today.

Luganville

The country's largest town after Vila is Luganville, Vanuatu's northern capital. Although it's less than 1750 km from the equator, the weather is usually quite pleasant thanks to the breezes coming off Segond Channel.

Before WW II, Luganville was a scattered collection of modest buildings separated by coconut plantations. Then the Americans came and changed its face forever. Today, the main town area sprawls along several km of waterfront. It's a lazy, down-at-heel sort of place, with numerous ageing Quonset huts, rusting steel sea walls and empty concrete slabs remaining as evidence of busier times.

Orientation

Coming from the airport, the first place you reach in Luganville is Simonsen's Wharf, the base for the inter-island trading boats that service northern Vanuatu. Just beyond is Main Wharf, where larger vessels tie up.

It's best to walk once you reach Main St, as it's called by locals but is more correctly known as Blvd Higginson. You'll easily be able to explore the area between the immigration office (at the turn-off to Main Wharf) and Sarakata Bridge on a three-hour stroll.

Information

Post & Telecommunications The post office has two public telephones and is open during normal business hours. Telecom Vanuatu's office in Rue La Pérouse, one block back from Main St, offers national and international telephone, telegram, fax and telex services. It's open from 7 am to 7 pm Monday to Friday and from 7.30 to 11.30 am on Saturday.

Some useful telephone numbers are immigration ☎ 36724, customs ☎ 36225, Vanair's town office ☎ 36421 and their airport office ☎ 36511.

Money Luganville is the only town other than Vila with a good range of commercial banking facilities. These are provided by the ANZ and Westpac banks, Trading Bank of Vanuatu and Banque d'Hawaii on Main St.

Medical Services The hospital (☎ 36213) is perched above the town in Le Plateau, with a commanding view of the Segond Channel. There are two chemists on Main Street.

ESPIRITU SANTO ISLAND

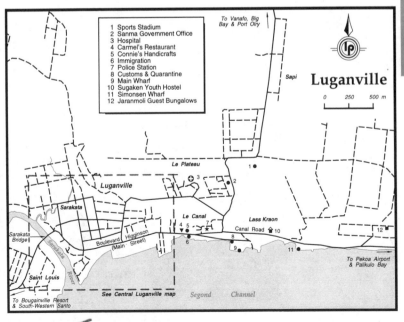

1 Sports Stadium
2 Sanma Government Office
3 Hospital
4 Carmel's Restaurant
5 Connie's Handicrafts
6 Immigration
7 Police Station
8 Customs & Quarantine
9 Main Wharf
10 Sugaken Youth Hostel
11 Simonsen Wharf
12 Jaranmoli Guest Bungalows

To Vanafo, Big Bay & Port Olry

Sapi

Luganville

0   250   500 m

Le Plateau

Luganville

Sarakata

Le Canal   Lass Kraon

Canal Road

Sarakata Bridge

Boulevard Higginson (Main Street)

Saint Louis

Sarakata River

See Central Luganville map

Segond   Channel

To Bougainville Resort & South-Western Santo

To Pekoa Airport & Palikulo Bay

Emergency Relevant phone numbers are police ☎ 36222, ambulance ☎ 36345 and fire ☎ 36333.

Library The library is open on Wednesday and Saturday between 9 and 10 am, although there are plans to extend opening hours.

Things to See & Do

Quonset Huts You'll find a number of these rounded, corrugated-iron huts scattered around town. Some have been refurbished, while others are rusted, tumbledown ruins close to their final demise.

Good places to see them are Main Wharf

PLACES TO STAY

1   Church of Christ
    Transit Hostel
3   Natapoa Motel
8   Unity Park Motel
14 Hotel Santo
22 Asia Motel
24 New Look Motel

PLACES TO EAT

16 Madeline's Bar &
    Restaurant
17 Formosa Restaurant

18 Sports Club
20 Natangora Café
28 Santo Chinese
    Restaurant

OTHER

2   Cine Hickson
4   Library
5   Telecom Vanuatu
6   Fish Market
7   Covered Market
9   Women's Handicraft
    Centre
10 Chiefs' Nakamal

11 Water Taxis &
    Bokissa Mooring
12 Unity Park
13 Santo Dive Tours
15 Westpac Bank
19 Exploration Diving
21 Espiritu Santo Tours
    & Travel
23 Trading Bank of
    Vanuatu
25 Post Office
26 Banque d' Hawaii
27 ANZ Bank

ESPIRITU SANTO ISLAND

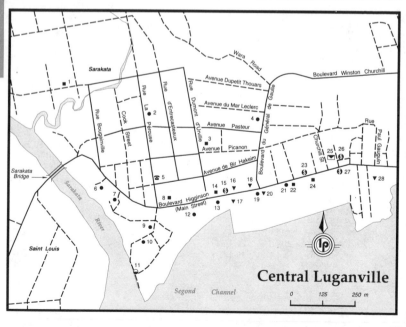

Central Luganville

0   125   250 m

and near Unity Park at the lower ends of Rue La Pérouse and Rue Dumont d'Urville.

Town Market Villagers come from all over southern and eastern Santo to sell garden produce and handicrafts at the Luganville market, on Main St near the Sarakata Bridge. It's open Tuesday, Thursday and Saturday from dawn until late; although they often open the evenings before the market days as well (Monday, Wednesday and Friday evenings).

Handicrafts At Connie's Art Blong Yumi, across from the immigration office, you can watch local craftspersons manufacturing a wide range of traditional and modern handicrafts. Arguably the best-value handicrafts in town are available from the Women's Handicraft Centre, at the western end of Unity Park.

Activities

Sport Soccer, volleyball and basketball are the main activities at the town stadium. Cricket has also started up recently – if you're in the mood for a game, go up on Saturday morning and you'll probably find a place in one of the teams.

There's also a golf course out at Palikulo Bay.

Swimming There are no worthwhile beaches in Luganville. Most are unsuitable because of submerged debris or sharp coral rocks in the shallows.

The best place to swim is at the Club Nautique near Palikulo Point, 12 km from town. A taxi ride there will cost you around 1000VT; fix a time with the driver to come back to collect you, but be prepared for the fact that he may not return unless you offer some strong incentive. There are very few vehicles on the road for hitching.

Places to Stay

Hostels & Guest Houses The *Church of Christ Transit Hostel* (☎ 36633) in Sarakata suburb has five beds per room costing 800VT each. You can call the same number to ask about the *Sugaken Youth Hostel*, near Simonsen's Wharf.

The self-catering *Jaranmoli Guest Bungalows* (☎ 36857) is about a km east of Simonsen's Wharf on the road to Pekoa. (No, it's not the ugly concrete block of flats beside the main road. You turn off here and walk up the hill to the edge of the plantation, then turn right.) Although out of the way, the hostel is very quiet and has a pleasant, rural hilltop setting. Its nine garden-style bungalows cost 1260/2625VT per single/double.

Hotels & Motels The best reasonably priced accommodation in Luganville is the 13-room *Unity Park Motel* (☎ 36052). It has share kitchen and ablution facilities, with most rooms having four beds costing 1320/1980/2310/3080VT per single/double/triple/quad. The larger rooms upstairs sleep three and cost 2750VT per room.

The *Asia Motel* (☎ 36323) has some self-contained double rooms costing 1650/2200VT for singles/doubles. Its single rooms have share facilities and cost 1300VT.

Just up the street above the New Look Store, the *New Look Motel* (☎ 36440) has four double and five single rooms (some of them air-conditioned), with private facilities and shared kitchens. These cost 2750/3850/4950VT for singles/doubles/triples. The motel is popular with long-stay guests, so book well in advance.

Also in demand with long stayers is the *Natapoa Motel* (☎ 36643) off Ave Picanon. Its rooms have cookers, fans and private facilities.

By far the smartest lodgings within the main town area are provided by the *Hotel Santo* (☎ 36250). It has 22 rooms with air-con for 8250/9350/10,450VT per single/double/triple, and another eight with fans for 4290/5390VT per single/double. The hotel has a swimming pool, bar and restaurant. Its buttressed exterior is designed to make it earthquakeproof!

ESPIRITU SANTO ISLAND

Luganville's Outskirts

About five km from the centre of town, the *Bougainville Resort* (☎ 36257) boasts a very pleasant garden setting with views over Segond Channel to Aore Island. Its 18 fan-cooled bungalows cost 8200/9200VT for singles/doubles. This very friendly establishment has a bar, swimming pool and the most sophisticated restaurant on Santo.

If you're going to the Bougainville Resort for an evening meal make sure to prearrange your transport back to town. Otherwise you may be able to get a lift in the minibus that takes the staff home at around 10 pm.

On Bokissa Island, which is about 10 km from Luganville across Segond Channel, there's the *Bokissa Island Resort* (☎ 36855). Boasting an idyllic setting among shady trees on the beach front, its 12 fan-cooled bungalows, each of which sleeps four, cost 9600VT for singles/doubles and 2000VT for each extra person. The resort has a bar, restaurant and swimming pool, and offers scuba diving, fishing, bushwalks and visits to neighbouring islands. Transfers take about half an hour from town and can be arranged through the resort – the launch leaves from the mouth of the Sarakata River.

Places to Eat

Budget Eats The cheapest places to eat in Luganville are the food stalls beside the market and at the western end of Unity Park. These sell simple but decent rice meals starting at 200VT a serve.

Takeaways at the *Formosa Restaurant* on Main St start at 300VT, as do sit-down meals – these are great value – at the nearby *Sports Club*. Both are open seven days.

Cafés & Restaurants There's little to choose between the Asian-style fare of the *Formosa Restaurant* and the *Santo Chinese Restaurant*, which is also known as the Santo Chinese Association. Lunches and dinners at both start at around 700VT for good-sized servings.

The *Natangora Café* specialises in breakfasts, hamburgers and home-made pastries and cakes. Its pleasant alfresco setting, good food and reasonable prices make it popular with local expats as well as ni-Vanuatu. *Madeline's Bar & Restaurant* is another good breakfast spot.

The café-style *Carmel's Restaurant* is the place to go for Sunday breakfast and lunch. It serves hearty Italian and English-style dinners starting at 800VT and is open daily except Monday.

You can eat either on the verandah with the sea breeze or in the pleasant restaurant at the *Bougainville Resort*. It's open daily for lunch and dinner, with the à la carte dinner menu starting at 1250VT for a main course. The resort specialises in French cuisine and seafood, and offers one of Santo's few opportunities for a gourmet experience.

Entertainment

The only nightlife other than that offered by the handful of bars and restaurants is *Cine Hickson*, which has evening film shows starting at 7.30 pm. It's open nightly except Monday and shows French-language or subtitled films.

Kava Bars Luganville has over 30 licensed kava bars, of which the most popular with expats is Kalo's in Sarakata. Most, if not all, will welcome your custom.

Getting Around

Minibus You'll have no difficulty finding a minibus between 7 am and 6 pm, but it's a different story after that. The standard rate anywhere around town is 50VT.

Taxi The minimum cab fare is 100VT. Taxis can be found waiting near Carmel's Restaurant or cruising slowly up and down Main St.

AROUND ESPIRITU SANTO

All distances in this following section are from the Luganville post office.

South-East Santo

The first things you'll notice outside Luganville are the many huge coconut plantations. These are spread in a concentrated belt right along the south-eastern coast, continuing north past Turtle Bay.

WW II Concrete Pay Hut (3.5 km) This small structure in the coconut plantation on the left about 300 metres before the airport turn-off was a wartime strongroom.

SS *President Coolidge* (6 km) Continuing on towards Palikulo Point, you pass a sawmill on the left and then a series of tracks heading down to the coast on the right. Take the third track about 400 metres past the sawmill and you arrive at a small parking area on the shore. Look straight out to sea from here and you'll see a couple of orange floats close to the reef. These mark the wreck of the 22,000-tonne SS *President Coolidge*.

On the morning of 26 October 1942, the *President Coolidge* sank here in 85 minutes after hitting two American mines in Segond Channel. Previously a luxury liner, she had been refitted as a troopship and was carrying over 5000 men. The captain tried to run the stricken ship onto the nearby reef, but it slid backwards into deep water and sank. Two lives were lost.

On the main road about 50 metres past the turn-off to the wreck is a small monument to Captain Elwood Euart, one of the casualties.

Carving from *SS President Coolidge*

Euart was a young artillery officer who was trapped and drowned after assisting some men to escape from the galley.

Million Dollar Point (8.5 km) Just where the main road turns to the north, a well-defined track runs southwards to the nearby beach. In front of the automatic lighthouse was a jetty where thousands of tonnes of US military equipment were dumped at the end of WW II. Everything from bulldozers, aero engines, trucks and jeeps to crates of Coca-Cola, clothing and canned food went into the water.

The US had offered local planters, who were mainly French, and the Condominium government all its Santo war surplus. But the French stalled, even when the price fell to eight cents in the dollar, hoping to get it all. They miscalculated, because finally the Americans decided to dump the lot.

At low tide you'll find coral-encrusted axles and other metal objects littering the beach for a km in either direction. On calm days it's a great snorkelling spot owing to the generally shallow depth, excellent visibility and lack of current.

Club Nautique (13.5 km) Turn right to Palikulo Point at the road junction about four km beyond Million Dollar Point. The Club Nautique is a shed-like structure on a quiet beach beside sheltered Palikulo Bay, just north of the intersection. This is a popular swimming and picnic place, and also an anchorage for yachts. Being a private club it charges nonmembers a small fee to use its premises. Half a km to the north-west is a tug that was beached by a cyclone during the early 1980s.

If you prefer not to pay, there are many other access points to the bay between Club Nautique and the old Palikulo Point fish factory, about 1.5 km to the north.

Palikulo Point (15 km) Previously operated by Taiwanese interests, the old fish factory is now used mainly to produce ice for the Luganville fish market. This makes it probably among the world's most expensive ice in terms of production costs.

Santo Golf Club (15.5 km) Back at the junction before the Club Nautique, the road heads north-west to Surunda. Passing the overgrown remains of the wartime Bomber One airstrip, you come to the Santo Golf Club by Palikulo Bay.

The golf club is mainly active on weekends and visitors are welcome to use the nine-hole course. As an added attraction, it offers a good view of Aese Island and Palikulo Point.

Roman Catholic Cemetery (4.9 km) The inland road from Luganville to Surunda travels through coconut plantations, which continue for most of the way to Turtle Bay. Golden-brown Limousin cattle graze beneath coconut palms in this rustic paradise. The interesting graveyard has several Vietnamese tombs. About 400 metres further is the turn-off for the Vanafo road.

Radio Station (7.6 km) The ruin under the low, shady tree on the right was a WW II US radio station. Between here and Suranda you see quite a few signs of wartime activity.

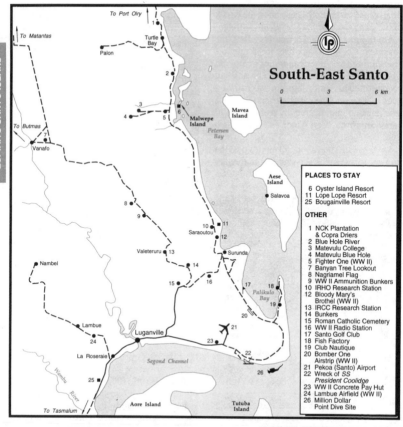

ESPIRITU SANTO ISLAND

South-East Santo

0   3   6 km

To Port Olry
To Matantas
Turtle Bay
Palon
Malwepe Island
Mavea Island
Petersen Bay
To Butmas
Vanafo
Aese Island
Salavoa
Saraoutou
Valeteruru
Nambel
Surunda
Palikulo Bay
Lambue
Luganville
La Roseraie
Segond Channel
Wombu River
Aore Island
Tutuba Island
To Tasmalum

PLACES TO STAY

6 Oyster Island Resort
11 Lope Lope Resort
25 Bougainville Resort

OTHER

1 NCK Plantation & Copra Driers
2 Blue Hole River
3 Matevulu College
4 Matevulu Blue Hole
5 Fighter One (WW II)
7 Banyan Tree Lookout
8 Nagriamel Flag
9 WW II Ammunition Bunkers
10 IRHO Research Station
12 Bloody Mary's Brothel (WW II)
13 IRCC Research Station
14 Bunkers
15 Roman Catholic Cemetery
16 WW II Radio Station
17 Santo Golf Club
18 Fish Factory
19 Club Nautique
20 Bomber One Airstrip (WW II)
21 Pekoa (Santo) Airport
22 Wreck of SS *President Coolidge*
23 WW II Concrete Pay Hut
24 Lambue Airfield (WW II)
26 Million Dollar Point Dive Site

Most obvious of these are the old ammunition roads that cut through the coconut plantation.

Surunda (10 km) The road via Palikulo Point joins up with the main inland northern route at Surunda, the site of a wartime camp for US and New Zealand forces.

There's a fine, half-moon-shaped, golden beach beside the village. About 400 metres beyond it, on the eastern side of the road, is a spring-fed 'blue hole' filled with clear, fresh water.

Just past the village, and on your left, an old bitumen road climbs the hill to the site of a wartime hospital. Down below at the plantation headquarters, on the right, an iron cottage shelters under a huge tree on the beach front. This was Bloody Mary's brothel, of *Tales of the South Pacific* fame. Local legend has it that convalescing soldiers would walk down from the hospital to the brothel, where they'd test their fitness before returning to work. The site is on private property and can only be visited on a guided tour.

Aese Island (10 km & 4 km by boat) Salavoa, the island's only settlement, is built on the site of another US wartime camp. There's a nice sandy beach by the old wharf, and the wreck of a Japanese trawler at the island's southern point.

Saraoutou (11.7 km) You pass the IRHO coconut research station, run by the Department of Agriculture. If you want to look around, come early and ask at the 'bureau' (ie office). To its right is another spring-fed blue hole.

Directly opposite the research station buildings, a track turns off the main road and heads down to the *Lope Lope Resort* on the coast. The small, isolated group of traditional-style buildings is attractively situated by a quiet, shaded beach. The shallow, crystal-clear, freshwater creek fed by the IRHO spring runs into the sea on one side.

This exceptionally basic resort is not well patronised, mainly due to lack of publicity,

so Chief Timothy will be delighted to see you. His two bungalows cost 2000VT each, with meals extra. Washing facilities are the creek or the sea, whichever you fancy. To make a booking, contact Espiritu Santo Travel & Tours in Luganville.

Matevulu Blue Hole (20.5 km) The track on the left takes you up the former US wartime airstrip, Fighter One. About a quarter of the way along it, and on the left, you pass the wreckage of a crashed Grumman Avenger torpedo bomber.

The main track turns left towards the Matevulu Agricultural College about halfway along the strip, but you continue up the strip to the end. Here you swing left and follow the track around to the Matevulu Blue Hole. This is the largest such feature on Santo, being about 50 metres across and 18 metres deep. The fact that it's in the middle of a cow paddock means it isn't as clear as it once was, but it's still a good spot for scuba diving.

Oyster Island Resort (20.9 km) The track through the gate on your right heads down to the landing area for the *Oyster Island Resort* (☎ 36390). This beautiful spot is just 300 metres out on tiny Malwepe (or La Pérouse) Island, one of several in Petersen Bay that shelter behind the raised coral structure of Mavea Island.

The resort's two thatched bungalows are among tall coconut palms on the beach front and cost 2500VT for singles/doubles. Camping is permitted at no charge. Its French restaurant, which serves magnificent seafood, is a popular Sunday lunch spot with Santo's expats. Be prepared to order your meal a day in advance so they can get the food in.

To summon the boat across, either sound your car horn or sing out from the beach. Don't try to swim across as there's a strong current in the channel.

Yachts can get into Petersen Bay, but the numerous coral reefs and shallows make it a risky undertaking.

ESPIRITU SANTO ISLAND

Blue Hole River (23.1 km) The road crosses another pellucid, spring-fed stream. Its solid-looking bridge was built by the US army in WW II.

Copra Driers (26 km) Here you can drive through the headquarters of the huge NCK Plantation by Turtle Bay. On the left is a bank of copra driers, where coconut flesh is dried by the hot-air method. The ramshackle structures on the right are the workers' quarters.

During WW II, Turtle Bay was a US patrol boat and seaplane base. A few concrete structures still remain along the shore, but if you want to explore them you'll have to ask permission at the plantation homestead.

North-East Santo
Shark Bay Blue Hole (29.6 km) This spectacular, crystal-clear spring, which like the others you've just visited creates a creek to the sea, measures about 30 metres across and 15 metres deep. It's an excellent spot for snorkelling. When you dive in you get the impression that you're exploring an underwater moonscape; the water is so clear that, when you look up from a reasonable depth, the fish appear to be swimming in the sky.

An entry fee of 500VT applies and you pay this into the honesty box at the front gate. A change room and toilet are provided.

North-East Santo Viewpoint (51 km) There's a magnificent view of north-east Santo as the road crests a hill two km before Hog Harbour. In the distance you can see forested Elephant (or Lathu), Dolphin (or Thion) and Sakao (or Lathi) islands.

Lonnoc Beach (52 km & 1.5-km side-track) In the days of the Santo Rebellion, this beautiful area was ear-marked as the site of a retirement centre for elderly Americans. However, the proposal foundered along with the rebellion in 1980. You pass the remains of the Lokalee Hotel, which was abandoned at that time, about 700 metres in from the main road.

At Lonnoc Beach are the *Lonnoc Bungalows* (☎ 36850), an excellent budget resort with nine traditional-style bungalows lined up along the beach front. These cost 1000/2500VT for singles/doubles, with 1300VT for each additional person in a room. Allow 3000VT per person per day for meals and drinks.

The resort has a bar and restaurant, with a magnificent white sand beach, good swimming and a stunning view right out the front. It runs a daily return bus service to Luganville for 500VT each way.

Elephant Island This rocky, hat-shaped island, which rises abruptly out of the sea about four km off Lonnoc Beach, is said to be one of the South Pacific's great drop-off dive sites. In places the shore drops off almost sheer to scarifying depths well over 100 metres.

You can arrange for diving equipment to be delivered to Lonnoc Bungalows by Exploration Diving of Luganville. To get out to the island, you can either hire a boat at Lonnoc or get Exploration Diving to meet you on the beach. The reefs are extre,ely close to the island so it's a good snorkelling spot as well.

Champagne Beach (52 km & 2.5-km side-track) From Lonnoc Bungalows you continue along the same track to famous Champagne Beach. There are various explanations for the name. One is that it comes from the swirling that occurs in the water along the beach as fresh water, which runs down in abundance from the nearby scarp, mixes with sea water.

Every four weeks or so between May and October, a cruise ship drops anchor off Champagne Beach. For a day the beach is like Queensland's Gold Coast as up to 1200 passengers come ashore to enjoy themselves. Apart from cruise-ship days and weekends, however, you're almost assured of having it all to yourself. It's certainly a beautiful spot on a fine day, although the tatty shelters along the beach front don't do much for the view.

To use the beach you must place a custom fee of 200VT per car in each of two honesty boxes on the way in. The reason for this is that two local men claim to be the rightful custom landholder of the beach and each wants payment for the right to use it. Usually the claimants, who live nearby, go straight to their box to collect your money. If you haven't paid they'll come over to challenge you.

You can camp at Champagne Beach as long as you get the custom owners' okay.

Hog Harbour (53.4 km) Back on the main road you'll come to this English-speaking village, which was named for the numerous wild pigs of the area. Prior to WW II it was the British government centre on Santo.

The village has a trade store where you can buy beer, fresh bread, ice cream and general items. Unfortunately, fresh fruit and vegetables are not so readily available.

Blue Lagoon (58 km) A ticket-collection point on the right at the start of a steep descent marks the short walking track to yet another spring-fed blue hole. The ticket-collection point is for cruise-ship days. Casual visitors are not usually charged. As you descend through the rainforest you might notice pieces of coconut fixed to the ground. These have been placed as bait to catch coconut crabs.

Between here and Port Olry you pass Golden Beach and Longar Beach, both of which are to be opened up to visitors. Golden Beach is the most attractive of the two and is said to look like Champagne Beach before its overhanging trees were cut down. There are plans to build a guest house at Longar Beach.

Port Olry (68 km) This drab, French-speaking village is built around a Roman Catholic mission that dates from 1887. About 800 metres before entering the town you pass a shrine of the Virgin Mary at a huge banyan beside the road. The villagers believe that its presence will keep evil spirits from making their homes in the tree.

Port Olry's beach is just as beautiful as Champagne Beach, although the water isn't so clear owing to its exposed position. A highlight is the huge *Calophyllum* trees – some reaching 2.5 metres in diameter and 30 metres in height – that grow along the beach front. These towering native hardwoods are adorned with orchids, mosses and other epiphytes; a single tree can have as many as eight species of orchid growing on it.

Permission to camp along the beach can be obtained from either the chief or the mission.

About two km offshore is Dolphin Island, where two small freshwater lakes make excellent swimming holes.

The road continues on past Port Olry to Lotoror, where it ends.

Luganville to Vanafo
The road initially follows the inland route to Surunda, until just after the Roman Catholic Cemetery. You leave Luganville by turning north at the police station and continuing past the stadium out of town.

Bunkers (7.5 km) The rusting bunkers in the cow paddock on the right were used by the Americans to store vegetables, which were grown in large gardens to feed the troops based nearby.

Valeteruru (11.1 km) Tours can be arranged at the Department of Agriculture's IRCC coffee and cocoa research station (☎ 36748) on the left, but they require advance notice.

Banyans (13.1 km) Look in the grove of tall trees on the right and you'll see how some young banyans have become established on the trunks. These have sent down roots to reach the ground; it's a slow process, but eventually they'll strangle their hosts to death. The larger banyan nearby is about 60 years old.

WW II Ammunition Bunkers (16 km) On either side of the road are abandoned US WW II ammunition bunkers, and if you keep an eye out you'll see the old wartime roads cutting across the paddocks. This was part of a huge complex, but you can't see much from the road.

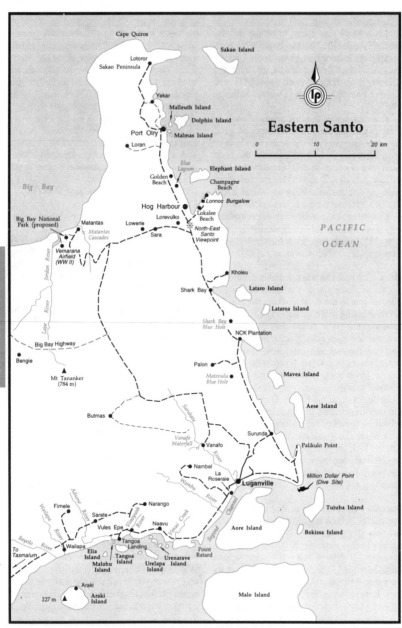

Eastern Santo

Cape Quiros
Lotoror
Sakao Peninsula
Yekar
Malleuth Island
Dolphin Island
Port Olry
Malmas Island
Loran
Sakao Island

0   10   20 km

Blue Lagoon
Golden Beach
Elephant Island
Champagne Beach
Hog Harbour
Lonnoc Bungalow
Lorevulko
Lokalee Beach
Lowerie
North-East Santo Viewpoint

Big Bay
Big Bay National Park (proposed)
Matantas
Matantas Cascades
Sara
Vemarana Airfield (WW II)

PACIFIC
OCEAN

Kholeu
Lataro Island
Shark Bay
Lataroa Island
Shark Bay Blue Hole
NCK Plantation

Jordan River
Lope River
Big Bay Highway
Bengie
Palon
Matevulu Blue Hole
Mavea Island

Mt Tananker (784 m)
Aese Island

Butmas
Sanduata
Vanafo Waterfall
Surunda
Vanafo
Palikulo Point
Nambel
La Roseraie
Million Dollar Point (Dive Site)
Luganville
Tutuba Island

Adsone River
Fimele
Narango
Sarete
Vinyagh River
Neavu
Vules
Epe
Tangoa Landing
Venui Creek
Point Ratard
Bokissa Island
Wailapa River
Wailapa
Elia Island
Tangoa Island
Urelapa Island
Urenarave Island
Bayolo River
Wambu River
Segond Channel
Aore Island
To Tasmalum
Malohu Island

Araki
227 m
Araki Island

Malo Island

Nagriamel Flag (16.7 km) The flag of the Nagriamel movement on the left marks the spot where Eddie Stevens, son of Jimmy Stevens, was shot dead while trying to run a Kumul Force roadblock.

Turn right at the Y-junction at 21.4 km. The road on the left leads to a new hydro-electric power scheme at Vanafo Waterfall. To go to Vanafo turn left at the T-junction at 22.4 km. Go right if you want to by-pass Vanafo and continue on to Matantas.

Banyan Tree Lookout (23.6 km) The huge banyan on the right was a lookout point for Nagriamel sentries, who had their sentry hut built high in its branches. Behind it are the remains of the nakamal where the movement began.

Vanafo (23.8 km) If you'd like to have a look around this historic village call in to the office and talk to Frank Stephens, who'll arrange a guide for you. You'll recognise the office by the flags placed in a circle beside it. Nearby is Jimmy Stevens' grave.

Vanafo's Christians wear ordinary clothes, while custom-oriented males of all ages are naked except for their mal mal. You may also see small girls wearing leaves, and older females in grass skirts.

Your guide will no doubt show you some nagriamel leaves. These are the yellow namele or 'mother plant' and the mauve leaf, which comes from a short, oil-palmlike bush, or 'father plant'. These two leaves were always present during Santo's traditional ceremonies, so Nagriamel people chose them to demonstrate their belief in the primacy of custom.

Ask Frank if his proposed guest house is up and running yet. If it is, it'll make a good base for a day-return walk to Butmas, a custom village up in the hills. Many traditional supporters of Jimmy Stevens left Vanafo after his death in early 1994 and went to live in Butmas.

Vanafo to Big Bay & Matantas

There are two ways to get from Luganville to Matantas, on Big Bay in the island's north.

From the east-coast route, turn off 4.6 km south of Hog Harbour. This road passes mainly through coconut plantations to the intersection with the Vanafo road 11.3 km further on. From here the road narrows as you drive through primeval forest almost all the way to Matantas, which is another 12 km on.

The second route, which is described below, goes from Luganville via Vanafo. (The side-road to Vanafo describes a loop from the Luganville to Matantas road.) This is the more adventurous option due to its narrowness and the lack of traffic and human habitation once you leave Vanafo. There are some straight stretches at first, but the road winds about with many tight turns and a number of roller-coaster sections once it reaches the uplands.

The following distances given are from Vanafo.

Butmas (13.9 km & 6 km side-road) The rough, coral road into this custom village is normally only suitable for 4WD vehicles. On the first km or so you get some fantastic views over jungle-covered hills as the road cuts around the mountainside. Check at Vanafo as to whether or not independent visitors are welcome here.

Big Bay Hwy (26 km) Opened in late 1994, this road is about 28 km long and takes you to Malao village on Big Bay. One of its major features is a truly magnificent panorama of the rugged Cumberland Range as you wind steeply down to the fast-flowing Lape River. A concrete causeway takes you across the river 13 km from the intersection – the water is generally ankle-deep over it during the dry season. There are a few large-sized holes to cool off in near the causeway, and you'll also find a very nice picnic spot on the western bank.

Matantas Turn-off (41 km) From the Big Bay Hwy turn-off, the road travels over flatter, heavily logged country to the inter-

Where the Wild Things Are

Walking down the empty black sand beach from Matantas was easy going. In front, and misty in the haze, the rugged Cumberlands beckoned us to attempt something more vigorous than the hour's stroll we'd planned. On one side, gentle waves lapped the sand. On the other, large spreading trees offered tempting pools of shade on the edge of the forest.

After 20 minutes we decided it was time to cut through the forest and meet up with the 4WD track from Matantas to the Jordan River. Among the trees it was cool, green and quiet, with an atmosphere of cathedral calm thanks to the big trees that closed in overhead to block out the sun. Walking through the forest proved surprisingly easy, as the floor was open except for clumps of bushes and palms. Sandy, our guide, soon indicated the main nasty to watch out for – the aptly named wait-awhile vine. This species has close-spaced, hook-like thorns that you only have to brush against to be held fast. Fortunately we didn't encounter many.

On all sides the trees supported thick vines that wound skywards around the trunks. Sandy stopped to give a lecture on their various uses: this one is used for rope or string; and that one is for the land dives on Pentecost. A particularly thick, gnarled vine is a good source of drinking water. I forgot to ask what uses the wait-awhile might have, other than to remind tourists to keep their eyes open.

At one point we sat on a log to take in the sounds of this primeval place. Thirty metres above our heads the uppermost branches tossed in the wind, forming a background to the main symphony of insects, pigeons and parrots. A large dark pigeon with white on its tail flapped onto a nearby branch and fixed us with its beady eyes. Sandy said that it was called *narwinba*, and was excellent cooked with coconut cream.

To typical ni-Vanuatu the forests are a treasure trove of resources for food, building materials, canoes, artefacts and many other uses. Their lives will be much poorer without them. Local people wanted to preserve the Big Bay forest, but there was pressure from logging companies who were already working in the area. Hopefully, the creation of the park will provide sufficient income from tourism to guarantee its survival. ■

section with the Matantas to Hog Harbour road, where you turn left to get to Matantas.

National Park Boundary (48.8 km) You arrive at the edge of a high scarp and enter the proposed national park on Big Bay. From here the road drops down to the forested coastal plain.

Matantas (53 km) This village is split into two parts, with one being custom-oriented and the other Seventh-Day Adventist. The former is the first part you come to. Here the people dress traditionally, while their neighbours on the other side of the creek wear European clothes. The village headman, Chief Moses, follows custom. He welcomes visitors and will be happy to arrange for a guide to show you around.

In the centre of the village is a low, square-shaped, mortared stone wall. There's a theory that it was used as a fortified camp by Quiros in 1606, but it's more likely to have been built by a French missionary or store-keeper in the 1860s. There are two cotton trees in the village, one very close to the wall. These are both about 130 years old and are relics of the days when European settlers tried growing cotton in Vanuatu.

You may also be shown a tall tree close to the shore which has been damaged by 40 mm shell fire. This occurred in September 1980 at the end of the Santo rebellion when the Papua New Guinea gunboat *Madang* shelled Matantas, forcing the rebel villagers to accept Vanuatu's authority.

A freshwater stream enters the sea just east of the village. With the chief's permission you can swim here and enjoy a picnic on the sandy beach. You can also visit some pretty cascades a short distance upstream.

Just before Matantas, a 4WD track leads through the forest to the mouth of the Jordan River and the disused WW II Vemarana airfield close by. This whole area, being low-lying and swampy, is an ideal place for birdwatching. It's included in the proposed Big Bay National Park.

Big Bay National Park The proposed Big Bay National Park promises to be one of Santo's highlights for anyone who likes trees, birds and bushwalks. Covering about 45 sq km, it stretches along the coast from north of Matantas to the Jordan River, and inland to the top of a 400-metre-high limestone scarp. Half of its area is covered by Vanuatu's largest, reasonably intact, alluvial lowland forest. This is the main reason for its protection.

Forest walks are the park's major attraction, with birdwatching second; you can see 82% of Vanuatu's native land and freshwater bird species here. A range of walking tracks is being developed, so you can do anything from a quiet two-hour stroll to a two-day effort that includes the highest point on the scarp – 449-metre Mt Wimbo. You get superb views of the Cumberland Peninsula right along the scarp. Alternatively, an easy day walk takes you along the beach from Matantas to the Jordan River (there's plenty of shade en route) and you can return along the 4WD track. Guides are available in the village for 1000VT per day.

Also in the development phase are camping and accommodation facilities. As an interim measure, you can stay in a private house in Matantas for about 1500VT, but you'll need to provide your own bedding and food. Ask Chief Moses about this on arrival.

You can get an update on what's happening with the park from the Environment Unit in the Georges Pompidou Building in Vila. If you're in Luganville, Espiritu Santo Travel & Tours should be able to help.

South Coast

The southern coastal road passes many cool, clear freshwater swimming spots. Some are said to have leeches in their shallows, so keep an eye out.

Lambue Airfield (6 km) The turn-off to Nambel is about 4.5 km from the Luganville

post office. On the way in you cross the disused wartime airfield Lambue, formerly called Bomber Three.

There's a small coconut-oil factory at the back of the house on the left about one km past the old strip. This operates most days except weekends and Mondays, and expat Aussie manager Ron Hawkins will be happy to show you around. If you buy some samples of his fragrant skin-care products he'll probably let you in for free. It's an interesting enterprise and well worth the detour.

Wambu River (8.5 km) A crashed but still well-preserved US navy transport plane lies on the coast on the western side of the river not far from the main road. You should get permission from the plantation owner before visiting it.

Point Ratard (13.5 km) This is a very scenic spot with a large, inviting sandbar about 150 metres off shore.

Venui Creek (20.5 km) A freshwater swimming hole lies about 50 metres upstream from the bridge. Just past the creek, an Italian planter has established a vanilla and pepper farm. Ask here if you want to go for a swim.

Neavu (22.5 km) The ford crossing is close to the shore where there is a small beach, which makes an ideal picnic spot. Opposite are four attractive islets covered with coconut palms.

Hooker Plantation (23 km) This coconut plantation dates from 1891, when trader Peter Sawyer and his Malakula servant were murdered here by Santo bushmen. A memorial at the gravesite also commemorates planter Peter Craig and his family, who were killed on the same spot in 1908.

The graves are hard to find, but you may be able to get directions from the owner of the Natangora Café in Luganville.

Vules Epe (26.5 km) Half a km beyond this

ESPIRITU SANTO ISLAND

village, the main road leads northwards to Narango. Another route continues westwards across a ford towards Tangoa Landing.

Tangoa Landing (28.5 km) You'll usually find outrigger canoes and speedboats parked here, so if you're prepared to wait you should be able to get a ride over to Tangoa Island.

The landing has a one-km black sand beach as far as tiny Malohu Island, and there's another sandy stretch beyond with surf. Although it looks like a nice place for a swim, several people and many dogs have been taken by tiger sharks in recent years. It's still a good spot for a picnic, though.

You'll often find a local market operating under the big trees on the beach front.

Tangoa Island (28.5 km & 0.3 km by boat) Traditionally, this island was the first stage in an ancient trade route between southern Santo, Malo and north-western Malakula. The usual product was pandanus leaves for clothing and mat-making. These were in great demand by coastal villagers in north-western Malakula.

Tangoa now houses a Presbyterian Bible college – the island was settled by missionaries in 1887, making it probably the first European foothold on Santo. Most students commute back and forth to the mainland, which explains why there are so many canoes parked at the landing.

Sarete (30 km) The residents of this large village sometimes perform traditional fire dances, which are well worth seeing. For information, contact Espiritu Santo Travel & Tours in Luganville.

Adsone River (31 km) This is the second of the five main streams to be crossed on the road to Tasiriki. It has a concrete underwater causeway which is usually open to conventional vehicles in the dry season. Do not attempt to cross when the river is in flood.

Bayolo River (46.5 km) The road crosses several small fords (ideal for a cooling swim)

The Potters of South-West Santo

The small villages of Wusi and Linduri huddle against the mountains beside a long, black sand beach in south-western Santo. They are the last places in Vanuatu where traditional pottery, known as lapita, is still produced in any quantity. The craft is restricted to women here, although at Butmas, where it has recently become extinct, men were the potters.

At Wusi, the *groanpots*, as they are termed in Bislama, are moulded flat without using a potter's wheel. At Linduri, the layers of clay are built up on a bamboo framework. After being shaped the pots are dried for several days before firing takes place. This procedure is the same at both villages.

In the firing process, the pots are first placed on a platform of volcanic rocks which have been heated in a hardwood fire. Then the women quickly build a teepee-like kiln of dry bamboo over the top and light it. The resulting inferno creates temperatures of 700° C. Bamboo is used both for the heat produced and because the fine ash doesn't harm the pots when it falls on them.

When the fire has died down, and before the pots have a chance to cool, the potter lightly whips them with leafy twigs which have been dipped in salt water. This treatment gives the pots a matte glaze that strengthens them.

The tabus in pot making are complex. For example, the potters must spend lengthy periods confined indoors and only eat special foods before beginning the process. They believe that if a tabu is broken, the pots will break as well!

Both Wusi and Linduri have HF teleradios. They can be contacted through the Sanma provincial government office (☎ 36712) in Luganville at 8 am Monday, Wednesday and Friday. The office will also be able to advise you on any proposed visit.

The one-way taxi fare from Luganville to Tasiriki is 7000VT. It costs 9000VT to hire a speedboat to take you from Tasiriki to Wusi and back. ■

A: Woman at Port Vila market (AV)
B: Adam & Eve Beach, near Forari, Efate Island (AV)
C: Coral reef, Bokissa Island (MS)
D: Mele-Maat Cascades, Efate Island (AV)

A: Land diving, Pentecost Island (MC)
B: Boar with curved tusk (DO)
C: Champagne Beach, Espiritu Santo Island (AV)
D: Safe landing! Pentecost Island (MC)

before reaching the Bayolo R
Like the Adsone, the causew
open but should not be attemp

Beyond Tasmalum (48.5 k
French-speaking village of
road continues to Tasiriki via
final section is restricted to 4
and is open throughout th
during floods.

Beyond Tasiriki there are (
These mainly follow the coa
maori village, on the Kere
five-hour walk from Tasiriki.

The coast north of Tasiriki
the most scenically rugg
Vanuatu. Here, towering cl
jungle-clad mountains plung
to black sand beaches. T
together with the deeply in
usually remind New Zealanders of their
spectacular Fiordland.

West Coast

About 5000 people live on the island's
western littoral and adjacent inland bush
area. Only occasionally do tiny villages and
beaches interrupt the many thickly wooded
mountains that fall abruptly into the sea. As
the population is so dispersed, there are no
telephones and only a few teleradios.

People in western Santo still follow a very
traditional lifestyle. In fact, custom generally
reigns supreme from the south-western foothills all the way to Cape Cumberland in the
north.

Santo Peak South-west Santo has Vanuatu's
highest mountains: Mt Tabwemasana (1879
metres), Mt Kotamtam (1747 metres), Mt
Tawaloala (1742 metres) and Santo Peak
(1704 metres). These are the haunt of the
Santo mountain starling, found nowhere else
in the world.

You'll need to organise an expedition to
climb Mt Tabwemasana, but Santo Peak is
reasonably straightforward. From Tasiriki
the going is very steep and slippery when
wet, which is most of the time, and there is
no well-defined path. For most of the way

Other Destinations With many peaks
higher than 1000 metres, the Cumberland
Ranges are a formidable barrier to people
travelling on foot. However, hard-core
walkers may enjoy the challenge of the two
cross-peninsula routes: from **Pesena** to
Penaoru and from **Malao** to **Elia**. If you're
fit and determined, it's possible to do each of
these in a day if you start early. Actually you
won't have much choice as there are no
camping spots along the way.

Alternatively, you can fly to **Lajmoli** and
walk down the coast to **Wusi**. This will take
about two days, and is often a hard slog over
stones and soft beaches. You can stop overnight at Tasmate's simple *rest house* for
1000VT including meals.

The people of this region are extremely
isolated from outside events. In 1979 a small
launch drifted helplessly off the coast, out of
fuel. Seeing a village, the crew fired flares.
Instead of helping, the villagers fled into the
bush. They later admitted that they thought
the Japanese had invaded at last!

The locals rarely see tourists, so you'll be
assured of an extremely warm welcome at
the various villages you will pass through
along the coast. But because they have so

few visitors, you'll avoid embarrassment by
giving advance warning of your intentions
via a service message through Teleco
Vanuatu in Luganville. This will allo
villagers time to get ready for you.

As always, you must ask the ch
village if you can walk throug
will almost certainly help y
food and accommodatio
should offer a gift of
tobacco, canned foo

...m
...the

...ef at each
...his area. He
...ou with guides,
...n. In return, you
items such as stick
...or rice.

Neighbouring
...ds

MALO ISLAND
Malo's eastern half is highly fertile and given over to coconut plantations – the island has been ranked third or fourth in copra production for Vanuatu. Not all are still active, however. Asavakasa and Malo Prospect were once major centres but are now deserted except for caretakers. Malo Pass has resumed operations under Japanese ownership.

Most of the population of about 2600 live on the southern and western coast, of the island, which is 17 km long and 13 km wide.

History
Archaeology suggests that Malo was Vanuatu's first island to be settled permanently. This took place in about 1400 BC when Lapita people were moving southwards towards New Caledonia and Fiji. In time a trade route was established, connecting northern coastal Malakula with Santo. Malo people purchased pandanus leaves from Tangoa Island, which they then traded for Malakulan shell money.

In 1768 Bougainville became the first European to set foot on Malo. By the early 20th century, European planters were established, and the ni-Vanuatu were dying in large numbers.

When European-introduced gonorrhoea began to spread, the disease caused a rapid drop in the population, which was compounded by blackbirding. Many died when their enemies fed them with rat poison stolen from the planters, who used it to protect their crops from damage.

Medical Services
There's a clinic at Avunatari.

Places to Stay & Eat
If you want to check accommodation possibilities on Malo in advance, contact the Sanma provincial government offices (☎ 36644) in Luganville. They'll know what's available at Avunatari and elsewhere on Malo.

Most villages have their own cooperative store where you can buy basic food items.

There's also a government *guest house* (☎ 36639) in Avunatari, with two bedrooms and cooking facilities for 1000VT per head. The *Presbyterian Mission* (teleradio YJT326) also has some rooms, charging the same price as the council.

Getting There & Away
The only access to Malo is by speedboat. There are regular crossings from Santo to Avunatari leaving from the mission just south of the Bougainville Resort. These cost about 400VT per person one way. You can charter a speedboat from Port Latour on Aore Island to Avunatari for about 2500VT.

Getting Around
Occasional trucks travel the island's main roads, especially the one around the island, and you may be lucky enough to hitch a ride.

AROUND MALO ISLAND
Avunatari
A long reef extends nine km off Malo's western coast from Avunatari to just beyond Nanuku. Although close inshore at Avunatari, it's usually about 800 metres offshore elsewhere. The reef offers excellent coral diving and snorkelling.

Off the coast west of here lies the sunken wreck of the WW II destroyer USS *Tucker*. It hit a US-laid mine, just like the SS *President Coolidge*, and now lies in two parts on the sea bed. Its easy accessibility has made it a popular dive site (for more information see the Activities section earlier in this chapter).

The following distances are from Avunatari, anticlockwise around the island.

Malo Peak (6 km) There's an easy footpath from Avunatari up this 326-metre mountain, from where you can see most of southern Santo. The summit was used as a US observation post during WW II.

Mt Mbwelinmbwevu (13 km) This peak is more difficult to climb than its taller neighbour, and the view isn't as good.

Amalo (21 km) This is an attractive sandy inlet with coral growth and good swimming.

Asamaranda (26 km) Take a canoe from here over to the extremely beautiful Malokilikili Island.

At low tide you can walk across the island's magnificent reef to some neighbouring islets, each of which is surrounded by sandy beaches and connected by a sandbar.

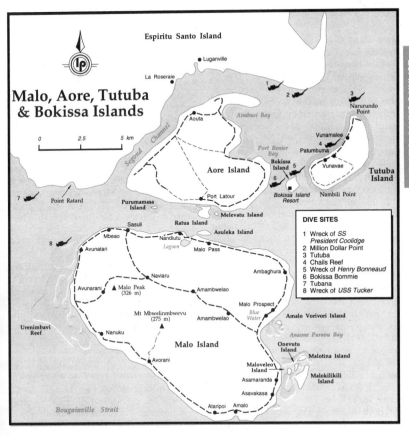

ESPIRITU SANTO ISLAND

Malo, Aore, Tutuba & Bokissa Islands

0   2.5   5 km

DIVE SITES
1 Wreck of *SS President Coolidge*
2 Million Dollar Point
3 Tutuba
4 Chails Reef
5 Wreck of *Henry Bonneaud*
6 Bokissa Bommie
7 Tubana
8 Wreck of *USS Tucker*

Malokilikili has a few residents, but the islets are uninhabited.

Anaone Paravu Bay (30 km) In the language of eastern Malo people, the name of this bay appropriately means 'long white beach'. It extends along the shore six km from the middle of the bay to beyond Malokilikili Island. Coral gardens abound throughout this area, making it an ideal place for scuba divers and snorkellers.

Malo Prospect (31.5 km) Ask the caretaker at the plantation for directions to Blue Water, a large freshwater spring that makes an excellent swimming hole.

Malo Pass (42.5 km) You can walk to Asuleka Island at low tide from Malo Pass. One km inland to the west is a small, brackish lagoon where there are many different wading birds. An eight-km white sand beach runs all the way from Malo Pass to Mbeao and offers good swimming in sheltered water.

Sasuli (48 km) The cross-island route to Malo Prospect starts here. Three km along it is a high point at Naviaru from where you'll get good views of Aore and Luganville.

In the 1940s, a 5.5-metre saltwater crocodile was found in a small lake near the village. Local people are still not willing to swim or wash in the water.

From Sasuli it's another four km back to Avunatari.

AORE ISLAND
Aore (pronounced 'ow-ree') is low, mainly flat and largely covered by cocoa and coconut plantations. It also has numerous caves containing thousands of bats, which makes it something of a magnet for bat enthusiasts. If you're interested in seeing hermaphrodite pigs, which have immense value in Santo's scale of social grading, ask Chief Takau if he'll show you his.

The island is 11 km long and nine km wide.

Medical Services
There's one clinic on the island, at Port Latour.

Beaches
Aore's east coast has intermittent stretches of coral shallows and white beaches. At the northern tip of Port Benier Bay is a profusion of beautiful coral growth in clear blue water. A white sand beach stretches all along the bay's south-eastern shore. There's another sandy inlet at Aimbuei Bay.

Aore's western coastline has several long sections of sand. Coral also grows abundantly on Aore's southern shore, where there are several good snorkelling spots.

Port Latour
This village has been named after a particularly obnoxious 19th-century settler called Georges de Latour, who was notorious for his insults towards the long-suffering people of Aore. Finally a Santo man decided he'd had enough and killed him.

Half a km west of the village and close to the shore is a whirlpool where flotsam is sucked down and disappears. Obviously, this is not a good place to swim.

There are two attractive, small islands close to Port Latour. Ratua and its much smaller neighbour, Melevatu Island, are surrounded by reefs and offer good coral viewing. You can walk across to both at low tide.

Places to Stay
At Port Latour, there's a Seventh-Day Adventist mission and village in a beautiful setting by the shore. You'll find a *guest house* at the mission, though it's often full with Adventists from other islands. Contact the mission school on ☎ 36414 for details.

Getting There & Away
To get to Aore, go down to the mouth of the Sarakata River in Luganville where you'll usually find speedboats for hire. A shared one-way ride costs about 400VT.

A chartered trip across the short stretch of water between Port Latour to Nandiutu on

Malo's northern coast is around 500VT. In contrast, a similar ride to Avunatari, further around Malo, costs about 2500VT.

TUTUBA ISLAND

The small population of Tutuba lives in villages along its north-western shore. Shaped rather like a sock, this island is seven km long and 2.5 km at its widest point. There are footpaths around its southern end.

Golden beaches line Tutuba's west coast, and there are colourful coral gardens located at Narurundo Point in the north. There are some excellent diving and snorkelling spots here.

BOKISSA ISLAND

Also known as Voisa or Abokisa Island, Bokissa is a very attractive, low-lying island covered with rainforest and coconut palms. A number of walking tracks cut across the 64-hectare island. There's also a lovely sandy beach along the south-western shore.

For details on the Bokissa Island Resort see Places to Stay in the Luganville section of this chapter.

ESPIRITU SANTO ISLAND

Pentecost Island

Pentecost gets its name because it was first seen by Europeans on Whitsunday. The island is famous for its land diving, which occurs in villages in the south. Every year, between April and June, males aged from seven or eight leap from specially built towers, some up to 27 metres high. With only two springy vines to break their fall, they plummet down to touch the ground with their hair. This dramatic, time-honoured ritual is believed to guarantee an abundant yam crop in the next season.

Pentecost is 63 km long, 12 km wide at its widest point, and covers 500 sq km. The island is flatter on the western side, its mountainous spine rising to 947 metres at Mt Vulmat.

About 11,500 people live on the island, mostly in the highland centre, along the north-west coast and in pockets around the southern coast. The rugged east coast, which is drenched with more than 4000 mm of rain annually, is largely uninhabited.

History

Pentecost emerged from the ocean about 18 million years ago. According to the local mythology, the first male children evolved from the fruit of a coconut tree. One day the eldest brother hurled a coconut at a younger one. The coconut stuck fast to his penis. With great effort the young boy pulled the coconut off. His male organs came away too, so he became a she!

Early European Contact On 22 May 1768, the French navigator Bougainville became the first European to see Pentecost. A strong breeze and treacherous reefs prevented him landing, so he sailed on.

Island legends tell of an unidentified group of White men who reached northern Pentecost many years before Europeans began to settle the island in the 1870s. They were so exhausted, and their ship such a wreck, that they survived for only a short time after their arrival.

Who were they? Perhaps they were survivors from the French expedition led by La Pérouse, which was lost in the south-eastern Solomons in 1788. Alternatively they might have been the crew of a 17th-century Dutch or Portuguese vessel, the details of whose journey and loss were kept secret at the time out of commercial shrewdness. Whoever

these seamen were, there were no Europeans officially recorded on Pentecost until the late 19th century.

John Higginson, the Francophile Irishman, visited the island in late 1882. He and his staff bought large tracts of the southwestern coastal strip for a song, leaving occasional markers on the shore as proof of his purchase.

The 20th Century French settlers brought Roman Catholicism to south and central Pentecost, while the DOM soon dominated the island's north. A breakaway DOM movement, called the Danielites, sprang up in 1931 when their leader, Daniel Tambe, began teaching a new brand of fundamentalism and called for the abandonment of traditional customs. In return, he prophesied islanders would rule over Europeans.

One of his followers foretold several events, including war. Huge numbers joined the Danielites when these events occurred, especially at the outbreak of WW II. During the war, civil strife broke out in northern Pentecost between the Danielites and orthodox DOM members. After a week the Danielites were beaten and the movement withered away.

Between 1945 and 1947, the Bula cargo cult spread around the Melsisi area. Its members, led by John Bula, said cargo would definitely appear. The movement slowly dissipated when the expected bounty failed to materialise.

Most people in the northern part of the island supported the government during the Santo Rebellion of mid-1980. About 100 people from southern and central Pentecost were later arrested for backing the rebels.

Land Diving

Melanesia's most remarkable custom is the *naghol*, as land diving is called by Pentecost people. Every year, as soon as the first yam crop begins to emerge in early April, islanders in the south begin building at least one huge wooden tower per village. These are usually 18 to 23 metres high, although they can reach to 27 metres.

On one or two chosen days from April to early June, men jump from these strongly built structures with only two long, springy *lianas*, or vines, to break their fall. Villagers believe that the ritual 'leap into oblivion' is required to guarantee a bountiful yam harvest the following year.

Legendary Origins Many centuries ago, the young wife of Tamalié, a legendary southern Pentecost tribesman, found him unbearable to live with. She tried many times to escape, but every time he managed to find her. Finally he pursued her up a huge banyan tree, where she threatened to leap to her death. She dared him to follow, saying that if they survived they must truly be meant for each other, and she would remain with him ever after.

Tamalié was either very foolish or very brave, or perhaps he truly loved his wife, because he accepted the challenge without a second thought. Too late, he saw she had tied vines to her ankles and had attached them to the tree. While Tamalié crashed to his death, she survived.

For some years after Tamalié's death, women re-enacted their courageous sister's jump. But whenever they did this, the wind whistled eerily through the trees. Taking this as a sign that Tamalié's spirit was distressed, the elders ruled that only men could perform the jump.

Construction of the Towers Before Europeans arrived, islanders used to jump from tall banyans once every five years. As modern tools became available, they began to build towers annually, constructing them around a tall tree stump used as an anchor.

Towers are built on gentle slopes close to flat ground where there can be dancing. The soil directly in front is cleared of rocks, then loosened to a depth of about 25 cm. This helps to reduce the chance of injury to the divers.

Each tower takes three to seven weeks to erect. All materials come from the surrounding bush, including more than a dozen large tree trunks and a multitude of saplings and

PENTECOST ISLAND

branches. These are all bound together with vines. To give the tower extra strength, other vines secure it to neighbouring trees.

A full-sized tower is vertical for its first 16 metres or so, then leans backwards. It makes a sighing sound as it bends in the wind, indicating that Tamalié's spirit has returned. People believe it will occupy the tower until the land diving is finished.

Each land diver makes his own diving base on the ground, carefully selecting his own vines so nobody else can be blamed if there is an accident. If they extend too far, he will crush his skull on the ground. If they are not long enough, he may well break some bones as he is jerked back against the tower. The vines need be only 10 cm too long or too short for this to occur.

Early Training Many boys learn land diving soon after they can walk. Fathers teach their sons to leap from their shoulders while they hold tight to their ankles. At about age four, boys begin jumping into the sea from large boulders. A year later, they practise using homemade towers over two metres tall. When they are seven or eight they are circumcised, and only then can they make their first real jump. A land diver is no longer considered to be a baby.

When a boy is land diving for the first time, his mother watches anxiously while holding an imitation cloth baby. Once he has completed the jump she tosses the 'baby' into the air, signifying to all that her son's childhood is over.

Who Dives? Only one European is definitely known to have land dived, and this was at Bunlap in the early 1970s. Some untrained Solomon Islanders have done so since. But most villages quite sensibly forbid it to outsiders because of the extreme dangers involved.

Some men from southern Pentecost freely admit they have never land dived, and never will! Others say that once was enough. Yet others, even some of middle age in important government positions, dive every year in complete confidence that there's no danger.

The Dive Between 20 and 60 males per village will dive on the chosen day. The youngest, some of them only seven or eight years old, go first, leaping from as high as nine metres. Each successive diver uses a progressively higher position depending on previous experience.

As each man prepares to dive, his friends tie the ends of his vines to his ankles and the tower. The stage is now his. As he raises his hands, the people below stop their singing, dancing and whistling.

Just before diving, he tells the crowd his most intimate thoughts, often about family or marital problems. Despite such breaches of domestic confidence, the women below remain silent regardless of the criticisms aired. After all, these could be his last words.

Finally he raises his arms, claps his hands, crosses his arms over his ribs and leans forward until he topples over the edge. As he

Land diving

falls, he keeps his back arched until the vines stop his downward rush. As he jerks to a stop, male relatives help him to his feet and untie his vines. Only his hair touches the soil below, but that's enough to fertilise the yam crop for another year. The crowd roars its appreciation for his courage, and dances in tribute.

The final dive from the tower's narrow pointed peak is the most difficult one. This is the responsibility of the 'chief of the tower', who has overseen its construction. It's his duty to go last. Instead of just falling forward, this diver must lunge far enough outwards to avoid hitting any parts of the tower jutting out below him. If he leaps too far out he will stretch the vines, causing them to pull him back against the tower.

Sometimes a land diver decides at the last minute not to jump. No problem. Another man may take his place, and there's no stigma attached to pulling out.

In custom-oriented Bunlap, men dive wearing red-dyed nambas only. Below the towers, their women dance in white grass skirts made from the sun-bleached fibres of *burao*, or wild hibiscus. Elsewhere, men may dive in shorts while female spectators wear their usual mission gowns. However, all jumps for visitors are done in traditional dress.

Safety Precautions To ensure there are no accidents, one of the most experienced of the village elders is put in charge of the vines. He checks every liana to see that they are strong and elastic enough to be used.

Age-old tabus prohibit women from seeing the tower being built. On land-dive day, they must remain at least 20 metres away until the naghol is complete.

Despite such precautions, accidents do sometimes occur. At times, one or both vines snap, although by then they will have checked the diver's fall enough to prevent serious harm. Only very occasionally have bones been broken; the commonest injury is a ruptured spleen.

Other than Tamalié, villagers say no one ever died while land diving until 1974, when an unseasonal naghol was laid on for Queen Elizabeth II. Unfortunately the vines were more springy than they would have been in April or May, and a man was killed in front of her. Islanders blamed the diver himself. Apparently he'd breached an important tabu by concealing a lucky charm under his shorts when he dived.

When & Where Land diving often occurs at a number of places in southern Pentecost, including Lonorore Airfield. Diving sites at Pangi and Rangususu are set aside mainly for the entertainment of tourists, with villagers from surrounding areas taking it in turns to perform there. At these places, diving usually occurs one day a week during the season. If possible, see if you can time your visit to coincide with Bunlap's turn as they put on the best, most spontaneous show.

In 1995, the government cancelled the land diving for a year because they said it had become too commercialised and wanted time to revive the ceremony's cultural value.

Frank King Tours, Tour Vanuatu and Tropical Adventure Tours, all in Vila, know the dates planned for land dives up to six months ahead. They will fly you to Pentecost in the morning in time to see some dives, and return you to Vila the same evening. However, these trips are very expensive – Tour Vanuatu charges around 40,000VT, which includes a 7500VT camera and entrance fee. There may be a high surcharge on video or movie cameras, so check this before you go.

Air Club Vila offers the cheapest option for one-day visits, charging about 30,000VT all inclusive (except the video surcharge) provided four of you can get together and hire the plane.

Alternatively, you can take a berth on one of the cruising yachts that operate from Vila. Four-to six-day land-dive yacht charters are available from Tour Vanuatu and Tropical Adventure Tours.

Other Local Customs
Dances Circumcisions in southern Pentecost are followed by the men's *taltabuan*

dance. Central Pentecost women dance the *sowahavim*, wearing red mats as skirts, called *tsips*.

Sand Drawing Pentecost shares several sand designs with Ambae and Maewo. Pentecost's specialities include an elegant roselike drawing of Vatangele Rock, where spirits of the newly dead are believed to go.

Nimangki Ceremonies Grade-taking is still followed in the more traditional parts of Pentecost, though it's an expensive business to become a chief in such areas. An aspirant to the top grades may need to slaughter over 100 pigs in a single day. In addition, he may have to provide sufficient taro and yams for all the guests at the subsequent feast, as well as enough red pandanus mats for everyone to sit on.

Descent & Lineage In northern Pentecost, people inherit land through their aunts, a unique form of matrilineal descent. The child's nearest male relative is the maternal uncle, not the natural father.

Ghosts Despite Christianity there's a strong belief in ghosts. These are considered to be people who have failed a basic test soon after death.

According to legend, the spirits of the newly dead must jump from two rocks at either end of Pentecost. Before the second jump, they have to do two sand drawings absolutely correctly. One of these depicts the legend of Vatangele Rock, onto which the spirits must leap. The other is a good-luck design. Islanders believe if the spirits fail these tests, they are condemned forever to wander the island as ghosts.

Handicrafts
Soft, red pandanus mats are mainly worn by central Pentecost women during ceremonies. However, they are also exchanged at nimangkis, births, marriages and deaths.

Once the mat is woven, it is rolled around a printing block fashioned from the bark of a banana tree. Then it's dipped in a tub of red plant dye. Nambas are also coloured this way.

Women weave decorated baskets from dried pandanus leaf and make delicately bound combs.

Men carve uncoloured masks to represent ancestral spirits. Some have round moon faces with long, sinister grins, some are more rectangular, while others have hooked noses and bulging eyes.

Language
There are three languages in northern Pentecost, although only one is spoken widely. In contrast, the south has 25 different tongues, often coexisting within a few km of each other.

The area from Melsisi south to Wali has many different languages, the main one being Atma. The Sao language covers the whole of southern Pentecost from Wali to Varsare with the exception of Bay Barrier, which has its own dialect called Skie (pronounced 'skee').

Medical Services
There's a hospital at Melsisi and clinics or aid posts at Abwatuntora, Renbura, Batnavne, Wutsunmel, Ranmawat, Pangi, Bay Barrier, Ranwas and Poinkros.

Places to Stay
The Roman Catholic mission in Melsisi has guest rooms, as does the Ranwadi school. There are guest houses in Abwatuntora, Loltong, Lonorore, Nazareth, Panas and Salap. For more details see the Places to Stay sections in Around Pentecost.

Getting There & Away
Air Pentecost has two airfields: Sara in the north and Lonorore in the south-west. Vanair has three return flights each week from Vila to Luganville via Lonorore, Sara and the three airfields on Ambae.

A one-way ticket from Sara costs 2800VT to Lonorore, 2500VT to Longana (on Ambae), 4800VT to Luganville and 9300VT to Vila.

From Lonorore it's 3700VT to Longana, 4900VT to Luganville and 8300VT to Vila.

Sea There are several ways to travel to/from Pentecost by sea.

Ship Each week or so, Ifira Shipping's MV *Saraika* visits ports along Pentecost's west coast on its return run between Vila and Luganville. It also calls in to Epi, Paama, Ambrym and Ambae en route. Aloara Coastal Shipping's MV *Aloara* has a similar service, but includes Tongoa, Maewo and Malakula as well as the islands visited by the *Saraika*.

Ifira charges 4000VT for a ticket between Vila and central Pentecost, while Toara's fare is 4500VT. Both charge 500 to 1000VT if you're just travelling between Pentecost and its immediate neighbours.

The launch MV *Mangaru* does a more or less weekly return service between Lakatoro in north-eastern Malakula and Pentecost, calling at Ambrym and Paama on both legs of the journey.

Yacht Pentecost's topography means good protection from the south-east trade winds right along the west coast. There are numerous anchorages and landing places, with Panas and Loltong being popular.

Speedboat A chartered speedboat ride across Patteson Strait between Laonai in north Pentecost and Asanvari or Annmari Bay in south Maewo is around 3000VT.

A one-way charter from south-west Pentecost to Olal Mission in northern Ambrym will cost about 4000VT, and an extra 2000VT if you want to go as far as Ranon.

Getting Around

Most tourists come on day trips by air to see the land diving. But if you want to experience the island as a whole, you'll find the west-coast road offers the best way to get around. The island has a number of taxis scattered about at various villages, and you can always try walking or hitching, which may not be an option if you are in a hurry.

Guides In the north, where there are relatively few tourists, the only payment your guide may ask for a day walk is a packet of cigarettes, a kg of rice or a tin of fish.

Panas is probably the best place to find a guide if you want to do walks in the southern mountains, including the trek across to Bunlap (see the following Footpath to Bunlap & Bay Barrier section).

AROUND PENTECOST
Central & Northern Pentecost

The island's central area is one of the few parts of Vanuatu with an appreciable inland population. The northern and central regions are the island's most heavily populated, with 85% of its people living there.

Until recently, the region to the east of the central divide was virtually uninhabited. However, people have begun to settle there as unused agricultural land in the north-west becomes scarce.

The following distances are from Melsisi.

Melsisi This village is attractively perched on a hillside overlooking a long sandy beach. Three km inland is striking **Melsisi Gorge**, while **Batnavne Gorge** is six km to the north. Both are accessible by paths.

Kava and cocoa are exported to other parts of Vanuatu from the Melsisi area. You can hire 4WD taxis in the village if you want to explore further afield into the nearby mountains – the one-lane road up the mountainside towards Hubiku has much to recommend it if you want an adrenaline rush. There are magnificent views along the way, but it's not advisable to look down.

Melsisi's large Roman Catholic mission has *guest rooms* where you may be able to stay for a small donation. You can contact the priest-in-charge by teleradio or by leaving a message at the wholesale store (☎ 38392).

Loltong (19 km) The road travels through inland villages from Melsisi to Batnavne, then goes inland to Nasa and on to Namaram where it follows the coast to Loltong, Pentecost's administrative centre. Loltong

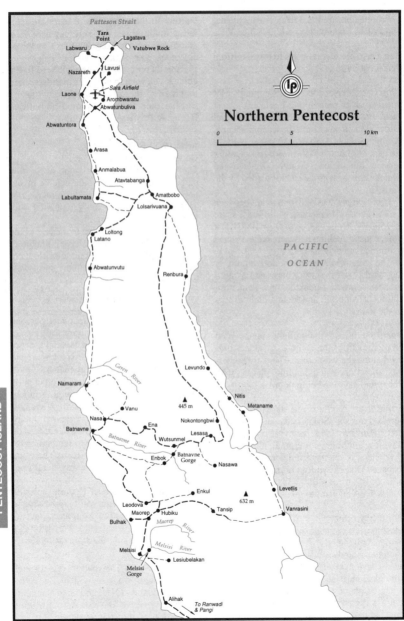

Northern Pentecost

has one of the best anchorages around Pentecost.

Loltong has a festival of music and dancing each year in mid-September. Traditional customs are still zealously preserved in the area, especially at **Labultamata**, two km north of Loltong. Nine km across the mountains at **Renbura**, there's a custom stone site where nimangki grades used to be taken.

The provincial government *guest house* (provincial office ☎ 38394) costs 1000VT per person and has basic cooking facilities. You can buy reasonably priced island-style meals at the nearby *Tiare Roundhouse Restaurant*, where kava and a number of handicrafts are also sold.

Abwatuntora (25 km) There's a government *guest house* (provincial office ☎ 38304) here, with two twin bedrooms costing 1000VT per person. It's quite a nice place and has a gas cooker, bedding and pit toilet, but no shower.

Laone (29 km) At Laone there's a pleasant white sand beach and a coral reef ideal for snorkelling. The local disco welcomes visitors and is open every Friday and Saturday night. Sara airfield is just one km to the east.

Nazareth (31 km) A store and a one-room *guest house* adjoin the high school, which services all of north Pentecost. The guest house has a cooker, but you must use the primitive washing and toilet facilities at the school. A bed costs 1000VT per person.

Tara Point (33 km) Poking out of the sea just to the east of this headland is **Vatubwe Rock**. Islanders believe the spirits of deceased people from north Pentecost must pass through a gap in the rock if they want to go to paradise.

South-Western Pentecost

You can get good views of Ambrym and its two active volcanoes from south-western Pentecost. On a clear day you can also see Lopevi in the distance.

A sandy beach extends 12 km from just before Lonorore airfield all the way south to Ranputor. Coconut plantations occupy the narrow plains between mountains and sea.

The highest peaks in the area are **Mt Vulmat** and **Mt Vetmar** (pronounced 'batmar'). They are immediately behind Baravet and Lonorore respectively, and are home to many wild pigs and cattle which are hunted by villagers.

The following distances are from Melsisi.

Ranwadi School (5 km) There's a taxi and teleradio here. You may be able to use the school's accommodation facility, which is very basic.

There are some large **caves** between here and Waterfall, 1.5 km to the south.

Waterfall (6.5 km) Boasting one of the island's best yacht anchorages, this village has a pleasant beach and a number of freshwater springs and streams in the immediate area. About 1.5 km inland, **Waterfall Falls** tumble down the mountain range in one long drop, then continue via several cascades to the sea. This spectacular spot is reached by a path along the creek. The area has some very nice walks, including one featuring a large cave and several leading to the top of the range.

Waterfall has a very basic *guest house* costing 500VT per person – you can leave a message by teleradio with the Ranwadi school. It's the local custom for visitors to join villagers for kava in the nakamal.

Lonorore Airfield (14 km) Each year the men of Bunlap supervise the building of a **land-dive tower** on a hill near the southern end of the runway.

Just to the south-west, in 12 metres of water, is a single-engine WW II US **fighter aircraft** with its canopy open. Both wings snapped off when it ditched, but otherwise it's in good condition.

Hotwata (17.5 km) There are two **hot springs** near this village. The first one is right on the shore, just beyond a cattle grid.

PENTECOST ISLAND

PENTECOST ISLAND

Southern Pentecost

The second is on the seaward side of a banyan tree 150 metres further south – villagers scald their chickens and pigs here before cooking them. Both springs give off a strong reek of sulphur.

Punmahava Falls (18 km) This waterfall is high up on the mountainside inland from the coast road. It usually only flows in the summer wet season.

Rangususu (18.5 km) Villagers build a **land-dive tower** here each year.

Panas (20 km) The large **crucifix** outside the village trade store commemorates a small boy who was taken by a shark in 1984. Since then villagers have refused to swim in the sea.

One or more **land-dive towers** are erected annually on the hills between here and nearby Wali.

The *Melten Women's Council Guest House* costs 1500VT per person including three meals. You can leave a message for the manager, Evelyn, by calling the provincial office in Pangi on ☎ 38301.

Wali (21 km) The two large creeks nearby are ideal for a cooling swim. Indeed, Wali means 'waters' in the local Sao language. This is one of the best spots to watch land diving.

After fording the second, deeper creek, the Lonpoa River, bear west off the main coastal road just beside the bank. A narrow track leads you 300 metres to a small round circle called **Greyn**. Chiefs used to meet here to decide on custom and land ownership matters.

Ateu Point (23 km) Continuing along the track for about 600 metres from Greyn, you come out at the sea beside several small coral caves. Standing on or close to the shore are five smallish rocks, the largest of which is called **Captain Cook's Rock**.

On the shore nearby you'll find 'ST5'

Captain Cook's Rock

marked on a concrete roundel. About 25 metres further along and two metres up on the coral cliff face is more writing. Sketched apparently with a finger on a small slab of cement is the inscription 'CNH TOAD STOOL 1888'. These are probably markers that indicated the boundary between early coconut plantations.

Pangi (24 km) The provincial office in Pangi (☎ 38301) has an unfurnished *guest room* which costs 500VT a night. This town is another land-diving site.

Salap (24.5 km) There's a small but pleasant white sand beach at Salap (pronounced 'sarap'), and also a river with cool, clear water. This is the jumping-off point for the trek to Bunlap.

The spartan *Bay Homo Guest House* has four beds, each costing 1500VT including meals.

Ranputor (26 km) This very attractive village is only a few metres from a white sand beach. Residents impose fines on anyone who makes the place untidy. There are some good views of nearby Ambrym and along Pentecost's west coast as far north as Melsisi.

One km beyond Ranputor is **Banmatmat**, where there's another fine beach. Two km further is **Wanuru**, with yet more sand.

There's a launch at Ranputor, the *Ivanhoe*, which travels around Point Taloas on to Ranwas, Bunlap and Bay Barrier. The charter cost is 8000 to 12,000VT per day.

Bay Martelli (31.5 km) You can charter a speedboat here to see the rugged coast from Poinkros to Ranwas or Bay Barrier. The cost is around 8000VT per day.

Point Taloas (32 km) Also known as Guhunon or Devil's Point, this is believed by locals to be where the spirits of newly deceased southern Pentecost people come. Two km to the east is **Vatangele Rock**.

Footpath to Bunlap & Bay Barrier

The cross-island route from Salap over the mountains to Bunlap is difficult and will take you at least five hours one way.

Unless you're very fit, pay your guide to be your bearer as well – he'll be more than happy to do this. He'll also need accommodation and food. A two-day round trip will cost perhaps 2000VT in bearer's fees, plus meals and accommodation.

The walking track starts half a km beyond the tiny hamlet of Salap. It's no more than a narrow path through the grass into the nearby hills, and is just as obscure most of the way along.

One km beyond Salap is the Warbot River, which you will need to cross. For the next 4.5 km you alternately climb steep hills and descend rapidly into deep valleys, before reaching the tiny, custom-oriented village of **Builaeut** (pronounced 'bull-ee-oh'). Here you turn north (left) to Bay Barrier or south to Bunlap.

If you take the Builaeut option you'll reach another small, traditional village called **Lonbwe** (pronounced 'lam-wee') two km of very winding path. Descending rapidly, you reach Sai and the sea one km later.

The following distances are from Salap.

Bay Barrier (9.5 km) This village is also called Ranon, which means 'white sand beach' in the local Sao language. Bay Barrier's people are still very traditional, many wearing nambas and grass skirts. The village has four nakamals and a Roman Catholic mission.

The south-east is largely unpopulated north of Bay Barrier. Five km along a twisting path via Ponov (pronounced 'fonop') is **Vasare** (pronounced 'batsari'). There's occasional land diving here also.

Bunlap (10 km) Turning south (right) at Builaeut, you're faced with a two-km climb up rugged mountain ridges, then a slow, two-km descent to Bunlap.

This rather large custom village lines both sides of a central path leading up a steep hillside. It has three large nakamals and two ceremonial dancing areas ringed with coral stones. All around are traditionally designed leaf houses, built so low their roofs just about touch the ground.

Traditions are strictly preserved in Bunlap and all attempts to introduce Christianity, as recently happened at neighbouring Bay Barrier, have failed. Here villagers wear nambas and grass skirts all the time. There are no schools because village elders can see no value in them, and the women are forbidden to speak Bislama.

Land Diving The men build four or five land-dive towers here each year. Although their neighbours from the south-western coast often dive dressed in shorts, Bunlap men have never deigned to do so. The only time they have made an exception to this was in 1974, in the presence of Queen Elizabeth.

Bunlap is not a commercial land-dive spot, so it will pay you to go first to the Cultural Centre in Vila and ask if it's possible to visit during the naghol season. As well, your presence there at the time of the land dive is no guarantee that you'll be invited to watch. If they like you, you will be – but it'll cost.

Places to Stay & Eat The village has a basic palm-leaf *guest house* with room for six people. It costs 2000VT per person per night, including food.

PENTECOST ISLAND

The province of Penama, which incorporates Ambae, Maewo and Pentecost islands, has its administrative headquarters at Saratamata on Ambae Island. Beterara is the main village in neighbouring Maewo.

The populations of both Ambae and Maewo islands exhibit some distinct Polynesian characteristics including language and physical features – for example, many have light-brown skin with straight, dark hair. Three indigenous languages, as well as Bislama, are spoken on each island.

Movement and trade along Ambae's coastline has traditionally been much easier than in Maewo, where villages are usually small and separated by rough terrain. A consequence of this isolation is Maewo's cultural diversity, whereas Ambae, despite its much greater population, is much more homogeneous.

In the past, people on both islands wore small pandanus mats as everyday wear. Nowadays, however, they are only used for barter, in ceremonial dances, and as currency. Like pigs, they are exchanged or presented at marriages, births, funerals and when grades are taken.

Ambae Island

Ambae is 39 km long, covers 405 sq km and rises to 1496 metres at Mt Lombenben, the highest point on the rim of a dormant volcano. There are three craters in the volcano, each occupied by a lake whose waters are heated by thermal springs.

Covered mainly by thick forest, the island is rugged everywhere except along the flattish coastal strip at its south-western end. Elsewhere the land rises steeply to an upland plateau containing the three lakes. Its upturned-boat shape gave James Michener his vision of what the mysterious island of Bali Hai looked like in his book *Tales of the South Pacific*.

Ambae is one of Vanuatu's heaviest rainfall regions. The south-eastern tip around Redcliff receives over 4000 mm (157 inches) per year, leaving the central crater lakes frequently shrouded in mist. The south-western corner is in a rain shadow, so is much drier than the rest of the island.

Ambae's population of about 8500 lives mainly along the south-western and north-eastern coasts, while the rugged central portion is uninhabited. A feature of populated areas is the many straight hedges and occasional dry-stone walls that separate the gardens.

Coastal waters off Ambae's western end are shark-infested, so the beaches here are definitely not recommended for swimming.

History

Ambae was the traditional home of Tagaro (known in the Cook Islands as Tagaroa), the cultural hero of both Ambae and Maewo. In

Ambae/Maewo Islands

the past, villagers from nearby islands, particularly south Malakula, used to make pilgrimages here to pay homage to him.

Local legend claims that Tagaro arrived in Ambae from Samoa in about 1400 AD. The island was probably already occupied, as carbon dating indicates that the early migratory peoples, such as the Lapita culture, reached this area before 500 BC.

Ambae's legends also tell of a chief called Vevineala who had risen to the top of his ceremonial grades. He was a man of great wealth, with many pigs and 10 wives but no children. One day, while on the way to Maewo to trade pigs, Vevineala accidentally let his clothes slip. This revealed that 'he' was really a woman! The wives all scattered, mortified.

European Arrival In 1606, Quiros reported seeing a large island in the distance to the east of Espiritu Santo, with two long promontories at either end. It seems he mistakenly thought the three islands of Ambae, Maewo and Pentecost were all one land.

In 1768, the French explorer Bougainville visited Ambae in search of food and water. While there he claimed the island for France, burying an oak plaque on shore to commemorate the event. He named it Lepers Island in the mistaken belief that the heavy tattoos he saw on many people were signs of leprosy. This dread disease did make its appearance in the mid-19th century – at one time there was a leprosarium near Lolowai – but thankfully is no longer present.

Missionaries & Settlers The first European settlers on Ambae were Anglican missionaries, who arrived in 1861. They established their headquarters for the Vanuatu chain at Lolowai and had the island all to themselves for the next 40 years.

Although the missionaries' lives were in no great danger here, sailors and traders had to be much more wary. In 1878, people from

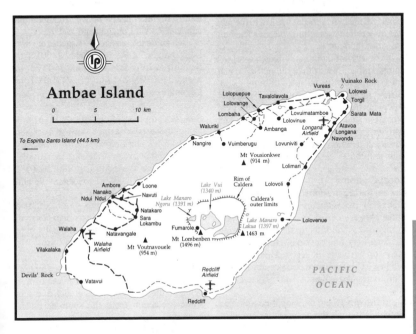

Longana, needing a human corpse for a grade ceremony, killed five crew of a blackbirding ship. As there was little official reaction, other people from north-eastern Ambae decided to do the same. In 1881 an English trader and two sailors were murdered as part of a funeral ceremony. This time a British warship put the offending village to the torch.

WW II & After The huge wartime US base in south-eastern Santo provided ready employment for villagers from western Ambae. In 1945 many were employed at Million Dollar Point. Here they helped the Americans dump surplus equipment into the sea by day, returning at night to recover what they could.

Inevitably a cargo cult developed. Adherents to the faith believed that aircraft, vehicles and weapons were being manufactured in underground workshops near the central crater lakes. Perhaps they thought subterranean rumblings from the volcanoes were the sound of equipment being assembled. When the cargo failed to arrive as expected, the believers put it down to the fact that they'd done something wrong. The cult has since died out.

In the 1970s Nagriamel villages sprouted up on Ambae, just as they did on Santo and most other nearby islands. In June 1980, during the turbulence following national independence, Ambae proclaimed its own secession and formed a government. The uprising collapsed three months later when 130 local people were arrested and charged with sedition.

Local Customs
Grade-Taking In Ambae, men only take four grades in the *nahunggwe* ceremonies, as nimangkis are called locally. Each aspirant to the next grade kills up to 25 pigs during the ceremony, and provides a feast for those men who have already reached that level. To become a chief, a man has to pass through all four grades and kill about 100 pigs in all.

Sand Drawing Sand drawing is common on Ambae, although the designs are less intricate than those of Ambrym. Nevertheless, the artists produce some beautiful work. One of the best is a roselike design which represents laplap made from breadfruit.

Medical Services
There is a hospital at Lolowai, and clinics at Ndui Ndui, Redcliff, Vilakalaka, Lolopuepue, Vuimberugu and Lolovange.

Places to Stay
There are guest houses in Lolowai, Nanako, Ambore and Saratamata, and at the Longana airstrip. See the following information about these places in the Around Ambae section.

Getting There & Away
Air Ambae's airfields are at Longana in the north, Redcliff in the south-east and Walaha in the west.

Vanair offers three return flights a week between Vila and Luganville – these visit all three of Ambae's airfields as well as Sara and Lonorore on Pentecost. There are also three return flights weekly between Luganville and Maewo via Longana and Walaha.

As a guide to costs, a one-way ticket from Longana is 2500VT to Walaha, 2400VT to Redcliff, 2700VT to Maewo, 2500VT to Sara, 3700VT to Lonorore, 4200VT to Luganville and 9800VT to Vila.

Sea Ifira Shipping's *Saraika* calls in to ports along the west coast of Ambae between Devils' Rock and Lolowai on its fortnightly return trips between Vila and Luganville. From Lolowai it's 4500VT to Vila, 1000VT to Devils' Rock, 2000VT to Luganville and 500VT across to Pentecost.

Toara Coastal Shipping's *Aloara* offers a similar service, but is a little more expensive. Unlike the *Saraika*, this ship also calls in to Maewo on its journeys back and forth.

Yacht There's a secure anchorage at Lolowai with a three-metre clearance beneath the average keel. Redcliff offers some protection from the south-east tade winds.

AMBAE ISLAND

immediate area comprise the commercial centre of west Ambae.

Nanako (11 km) The very basic, two-bedroom *Nanako Guest House* has cooking, washing and toilet facilities and costs 1500VT per person.

Ambore (12 km) The government *guest house* (teleradio YJT419) has two double bedrooms and charges 1000VT per head.

Loone (15 km) This village has an attractive black sand beach, where there is safe swimming close to shore. The path from here to Lolopuepue crosses rough, mountainous country, so expect hard walking.

Nangire (22 km) Taremulimuli, an important chief in Ambae's past, is buried overlooking the sea on the clifftop at Nangire. His 300-sq-metre **burial enclosure** is marked by several tall stones and has an inner section shaped like a boat.

Waluriki (25 km) You'll find a long black sand beach here and more safe swimming.

Lombaha (28.5 km) There are several **caves** and **dancing sites** at Lombaha. Some are associated with traditional gods, especially Tagaro, who is said to have lived close by. Villagers believe he still appears from time to time, and claim to see his footprints occasionally.

Another local god is Merabuto. He was one of Tagaro's rivals, and used to play tricks on him. Villagers will tell you more about these legends if you ask.

Lolopuepue (31 km) The *Roman Catholic mission school* here has dormitory-style accommodation that you may, in time of need, be allowed to use.

Tavalolavola (34 km) Villagers regularly bathe in the **hot springs** on the shoreline.

Vureas (40 km) This site is taken up by an Anglican junior-secondary school. The

Getting Around

Vehicle access on Ambae is limited to a reasonable network of tracks in the south-west and a short coastal route in the north-east. These are joined together by coastal walking tracks on both sides of the island.

Taxis invariably meet incoming aircraft at Walaha and Longana airfields. You can hire speedboats at most of the larger coastal villages.

AROUND AMBAE ISLAND
Western Ambae

The following distances are from Devils' Rock.

Devils' Rock The spirits of recently deceased persons are believed to come to this rock, where they leap into the sea and turn into sharks. This is the local explanation for the large number of shark attacks in the area.

Walaha (5 km) There's a large Apostolic mission and an airfield in Walaha, which is the main gateway to west Ambae.

Ndui Ndui (10.5 km) This village has a health clinic attached to the local Church of Christ mission. Friday night is usually dance night, with either a string band or rock group providing the music. The villages in this exceptional **black sand beach** just beyond the school is one of the best swimming spots on the island.

Eastern Ambae

The following distances are from Lolowai.

Lolowai The high rock just beyond the inlet here is called **Vuinako**, which Ambae people believe to be the female companion of Gwala, or Devils' Rock. Both originally lived together near Vureas. However, they fell out one day over a pig, and Gwala fled to the western tip of Ambae to escape Vuinako's wrath.

Lolowai contains Vanuatu's principal centre for the DOM. The village has a post office, hospital, wholesale store and National Bank of Vanuatu agency.

Behind the commercial centre there's a one-bed *guest house* which has a large open area where a group can sleep if they have mats. Ask about this at the store, or leave a message by ringing the post office on ☎ 38347.

Saratamata (3 km) This village has a four-bedroom provincial government *guest house* (provincial office ☎ 38348), which costs 1000VT per night. It has a gas stove, bedding, shower and flush toilet.

The *Tausala Guest House* (☎ 38348) at nearby Longana is basically a three-bedroom house with a store attached. Although it experiences problems with water it offers a reasonable standard of accommodation for 1000VT per person self-catering or 2500VT with meals. To make a booking, leave a message at the Saratamata provincial office for Gladys Bani, the guest-house manager. If you can't get through, ask Vanair in Vila or Luganville to pass on a message for you. Gladys can also arrange fishing excursions and walks to various places, including the lakes.

The taxi fare from Saratamata to Longana airstrip is 300VT.

Atavoa (3.5 km) This is considered the best beach on eastern Ambae.

Lolimari (7 km) To get from here to Redcliff you have to walk. Ask about guides at the provincial government office in Saratamata.

Lolovenue (17.5 km) The **thermal springs** in the school grounds are a popular swimming place in winter.

Redcliff (30 km) The village gets its name from the colour of the nearby cliffs. The airfield is behind the cliff, and close to a small harbour formed by a drowned volcanic crater.

Sorcerers are still active here, although their power has declined very considerably in recent years. These days they're usually content to show off their conjuring skills, although a few are equally ready to cast spells on their rivals.

The Crater Lakes

The three craters below Mt Lombenben contain freshwater lakes. Two of these – Lakes Manaro Lakua and Vui – are quite large, while the smallest, Lake Manaro Ngoru, is less than a km across.

There are some interesting aspects to the lakes, apart from the fact that they're full of prawns. First, Manaro Lakua is blue, while Vui is green. Second, Manaro Lakua is 57 metres lower than Vui, even though they're only about 300 metres apart. The waters of Lake Vui have healing qualities and locals afflicted with skin complaints go there to bathe.

Mt Lombenben probably hasn't erupted for more than 300 years, but during 1994 and into 1995 seismic activity caused increasing concern that the next event might be close at hand. When it last erupted, lava flowed west towards what is now Walaha and caused many casualties.

There are several legends about the mountain and its lakes. One tells how Tagaro removed the volcano from Mt Lombenben and planted it on Ambrym, then drowned the three main fiery vents by filling them with water. These are the present lakes, the largest of which are said to represent Lombenben's eyes.

Trekking to the Lakes Mt Lombenben's summit is considered to be sacred ground. In fact, the whole area is beset with tabus which can rather inhibit access.

The mountain is often blanketed by mist and rain, a fact that's helped create some of the finest cloud forest in Vanuatu. The craters are interesting, but the harsh contours are softened by jungle so don't expect anything dramatic. The views from the top are restricted by trees and clouds.

Water levels in the two larger lakes drop considerably in the dry season. This exposes a beach at Manaro Lakua which – if you can ignore the frogs – makes an excellent camping spot. The lakes are the only sources of drinking water on the mountain. Villagers sometimes make the trek up the mountain to catch prawns, but because of their fear of devils they don't like spending the night there.

The usual pathways to the top are from Redcliff in the south, Ambanga in the north and the Natakaro area in the west. Once on the mountain all routes are gruelling, with steep slopes climbing endlessly upwards through the damp, misty jungle. Allow three days for the return walk if trekking from Ambanga – it's about seven hours each way – and at least two from the other take-off points. Camp sites are extremely limited on top owing to the terrain and vegetation, so don't leave it too late before you start looking.

Maewo Island

This thin, rugged island is 56 km long but averages a mere five km across. It covers about 310 sq km.

Maewo receives well over 4500 mm (177 inches) of rainfall per year, and is Vanuatu's wettest island. Consequently there are numerous fast-running rivers and permanent springs. Because of the climate and inhospitable terrain, very few European settlers ever made their homes here.

The mountainous central spine and the

Maewo Island

south-eastern coast are good places to see Maewo's varied bird life. In addition, many wild pigs roam freely, so take care if you go bushwalking. Some feral bullocks run loose in Maewo's northern tip; it would be wise to watch out for them too.

Both coastlines in the island's north have long stretches of black sand beach. However, Maewo is very rocky south of Point Rokao and Kerembei. The island's south-eastern seaboard experiences almost continuously rough seas.

The north-eastern coastal waters are well stocked with fish, while the reefs are a good place to find lobsters. There are also plenty of freshwater crayfish in the rivers along the coast, and coconut crabs on the sandy shore.

History

Maewo was created in a sequence of volcanic eruptions 18 million years ago, about the same time as neighbouring Pentecost. It was the first island to be seen in the Vanuatu chain by Bougainville's expedition in 1768 and by Cook six years later, but neither explorer landed.

In the 1870s four of Maewo's villages were put to the torch and canoes smashed by French blackbirders after a number of clashes between them and local islanders. Yet only a short while later, the Anglican bishop Selwyn reported how Maewo people were the most pleasant and honest he had met in the archipelago.

Ultimately, this friendliness and generosity towards Europeans cost them dearly. Contact with foreigners introduced many previously unknown diseases which had almost wiped out the island's population by the end of the 19th century. Today, it stands at about 2500 – Maewo's population is thought to have been 20,000 or more in the time of Cook.

The move towards national independence in the late 1970s affected Maewo just as it did in the other northern islands. Several villages joined the Nagriamel movement and a number of local people actively supported the Santo rebellion. About 50 were arrested during the clean-up operations in September 1980.

Local Customs

The islanders still practise many different custom dances, though the churches have often tried to discourage them. A number of skilled sand drawers also live here.

Pig killing occurs, as elsewhere, when men take grades. On Maewo there are only a few stages to pass through, so this only happens once to each aspirant every few years.

Traditional Dances Local men perform several sacred dances which women may not see. Indeed, females must keep away from the dancing ground which remains tabu for a long period after the dance is over. Conversely, Maewo women have their own special dances which in return are forbidden to men. These restrictions naturally apply to visitors also.

The Mid-Year Hurters If you are in Maewo during the yam harvest from April to August you may be chased and injured by groups of masked men wearing sacks and banana leaves. They are armed with thorny sticks and are called 'hurters'.

The hurters shout as they come to a village. If you hear them, hide in a house. If you don't, you'll be struck by their sticks. Every year people are injured, sometimes seriously enough to require medical attention. Fortunately this ritual only occurs once a fortnight and in daylight.

It's thought that this strange tradition had its origins in the rites of a now-forgotten secret society. Such societies, which were commonplace in Maewo's past, were only open to adult men who had passed through a painful initiation. Women and children were executed if they went near the group's meeting ground.

Magic Some local sorcerers claim to be even more skilled than those in Ambrym. A few say they can make their rivals sick, or even make them die.

Most sorcerers are found on the central coasts, mainly in Gaiofo, Narovorovo and Kerembei on the west coast, and across the mountains at Naviso. Women also practise the black arts and some are very powerful.

Whenever there is a festival on the island, magic is part of the show. Children are taught from an early age to do conjuring tricks.

Medical Services

There are clinics at Kerembei, Nasawa, Marino, Narovorovo and Asanvari.

Places to Stay

There are guest houses in Betarara, Narovorovo and Nasawa. See the following information about these places in the Around Maewo section.

Getting There & Away

Air Maewo's only airfield is at Naone in the north.

Vanair offers return flights three times a week from Luganville to Maewo via Longana and Walaha on Ambae. One-way tickets from Maewo cost 2700VT to Longana, 3500VT to Walaha and 4800VT to Luganville.

Sea Toara Coastal Shipping's *Aloara* visits ports in western Maewo on its fortnightly return trips between Vila and Luganville. To get there from Vila costs 5000VT to the island's south, 6000VT to its central coast and 6500VT to the north. From Luganville its 2400VT to the south and centre, and 2800VT to the north. It costs 500 to 1000VT to get to or from the neighbouring islands of Pentecost and Ambae.

Speedboat You can get a speedboat to take you across Patteson Strait, between Asanvari and Laonai at the northern tip of Pentecost, for about 3000VT.

Getting Around

Walking is the main means of transport around Maewo. The island's only continuous stretch of road runs down the west coast from Lolarouk to beyond Nasawa. Taxis generally meet scheduled flights into the airfield. Otherwise you'll have to try and hitch a ride.

From the end of the road, a footpath hugs Maewo's western shore, passing through a few tiny, isolated hamlets all the way southwards to Asanvari and Annmari Bay. Another footpath, which forms a loop around Mt Woutkararo, links villages in the centre of the island.

AROUND MAEWO ISLAND

You'll see numerous remains of long-deserted dwellings in western Maewo, and hear places referred to which have long disappeared. You'll also find abandoned lines of stones built in the past either for defensive purposes or to act as pig enclosures. Huge banyans stand beside clearings that were clearly once used as natsaros.

Only a few people live in the island's interior and there are even fewer on the exposed eastern coast.

The following distances are from Lolarouk.

Lolarouk

Here you find a series of **white sand beaches** stretching halfway down the west coast from Lolarouk to Navenevene, with the occasional rocky section. A **hot spring** is located close to the shore 3.5 km north of Lolarouk.

Naone (9.5 km) The island's airfield is on the plateau above the village. In the nearby river, about 100 metres in from the coast, are some impressive **cascades**, with a waterfall a little further upstream. Several large, deep pools between the two make good spots for a swim.

There's a large **custom stone** one km south of the village, just to the east of the road. You may visit the area with permission but you mustn't touch the stone. As on the islands of north-east Malakula, monoliths such as this mark men's ceremonial areas. These are tabu to 'unqualified' men and all women and children.

Gaiofo (16 km) The small **hot spring** about one km south of Gaiofo is an excellent spot for a wash. There's a sandy **beach** here with good snorkelling.

Betarara (19 km) This village, which is beside an attractive bay, has a *guest house* (☎ provincial office 38305) with two bedrooms. The charge is 800VT per person.

The local Church of Christ also has a *guest house*, although its rooms are often occupied by visiting church members.

Kerembei (20.3 km) This is the largest village on the west coast and has a store selling limited food lines. The local women's group runs a two-bed *guest house* where you can stay for 1000VT. There are no cooking facilities.

Within the village are two small **coral monoliths** that represent people who were turned to stone. Ask the villagers and they'll be happy to tell you the story.

A hard two-hour walk along the **Naviso footpath** takes you through attractive rainforest, plantation and garden areas and small villages to the top of the central range. There are nice views from the track on the eastern side of the summit.

Allow at least 1½ days if you intend doing the loop walk from Kerembei to Naviso and back to Talise.

Talise (29 km) Close to the shore and just below the surface is the **wreck** of a 19th-century blackbirding ship. Just north of Talise is **Malangai Tufela**, a cave with two shapes in its ceiling said to represent two men who were killed and then hung up in the cave.

The **footpath** from Talise to Naviso is just as scenic but somewhat easier than the Kerembei to Naviso route (above).

Nasawa (32.5 km) This village was the first base in Vanuatu of the Nagriamel Federation movement. A **flagpole** with a concrete star at its base is a reminder of those turbulent times. It now forms a national historic site.

Just south of the village is a large coastal **cave** called the 'Hole of the Moon'. A large circular indentation in its roof shows where the god Tagaro tore out a piece of rock and hurled it into the sky, thus creating the moon. Near the cave mouth is a rock wall covered in petroglyphs.

Asanvari (53 km) There's a beautiful **waterfall** at the village, and nice sandy **beaches** offering good swimming. The government office (☎ 38346) can advise you on accommodation in the area.

Annmari Bay (55 km) The harbour entrance is between two tall rocky headlands, which make a most impressive sight.

Nine km up the east coast is **Nalolo Bay**, an inlet providing a very good refuge during cyclones.

MAEWO ISLAND

The Banks & Torres Islands

Forming the new province of Torba, the Banks and Torres groups are both administered from Sola on Vanua Lava. Within this region are 62 islands, 13 of which are inhabited. Most of the remainder are either sandy islets or jagged volcanic rocks poking out of the sea.

This area is one of Vanuatu's most humid, and has an average rainfall of 3900 mm (154 inches) per year.

As elsewhere, the islands suffered heavily from blackbirding and disease in the latter half of the 19th century. By the 1930s there were barely 2000 people left, but now the population is recovering and currently stands at about 6000.

Prior to the 1950s, the people of Tikopia, a Polynesian island in the Solomons chain, 180 km north-east of Mota Lava, made regular seasonal journeys by canoe to this part of Vanuatu, particularly the northern Banks. Both the Banks and Torres groups show signs of Polynesian influences, though they are more pronounced in the latter.

There are four airfields in the area, but little in the way of accommodation and motor transport. Despite its considerable beauty and fascinating culture, very few visitors make it to this part of Vanuatu. Most of those who do come are yachties. If you want to visit, come prepared for camping and a lot of walking.

The Banks Islands

Lying 65 km south-east of the Torres Islands, the Banks' nearest neighbour is Maewo, 47 km due south. This scattered, mainly volcanic chain is 144 km long and includes two largish islands, Gaua and Vanua Lava. Both are still volcanically active.

There are a number of Polynesian-sounding place names in the Banks chain, but the people are predominantly Melanesian.

History
Origins Archaeologists have found Lapita-style pottery on tiny Kwakea Island, just off Vanua Lava. These have been dated to about 1100 BC, with the site remaining in continuous use until about 400 BC. Kwakea appears to have been reoccupied in about 300 AD by a new people who probably stayed there some 800 years.

Whether these later settlers were Melanesians who lost the art of pottery, or another race who were slaughtered by ancestors of the present-day inhabitants, we may never know. However, it's unlikely they were cannibalised. Islanders say the eating of human flesh was never practised in this group.

Spanish Arrival In 1606, Quiros became the first European to lay eyes on the Banks Islands when he sailed past Mere Lava. He made his first Vanuatu landfall at Gaua, which he called Vergen Maria Island. The

THE TORRES ISLANDS
Hiu island
Tegua Island
Loh Island
Toga Island
Vot Tande Island
To Tikopia Island (Solomon Islands) (180 km from Mota Lava Island)
Ureparapara Island
THE BANKS ISLANDS
The Reef Islands
Mota Lava Island
Mota Island
Vanua Lava Island
Gaua Island
Merig Island
The Banks & Torres Islands
Mere Lava Island
0   25   50 km
PACIFIC OCEAN
To Espiritu Santo Island (73 km from Gaua Island)

267

local people welcomed his crew enthusiastically, as the foreigners were thought to be envoys of Qat, their mythical culture bringer.

One man, probably a chief, told the Spaniards of larger islands to the south. Regrettably, although the islanders were friendly, Quiros instructed his crew to take two hostages, but both escaped.

In a remarkable display of arrogance and insensitivity Quiros then seized the chief. Before releasing him, he ordered his prisoner's hair and beard to be shaved off, unwittingly breaking a local tabu. In the Banks Islands, men's hair and beards traditionally were deemed to be sacred. They were not to be touched, let alone shaved off by someone else. This affront led to immediate hostilities. The Spaniards withdrew, shielded by a volley of bullets.

During their stay, the Spaniards had noticed that Gaua was heavily cultivated and carried a huge abundance of pigs, chickens, coconuts and bananas. Quiros estimated there were 200,000 people living there, but this figure was probably deliberately exaggerated to impress his patron, the king of Spain. The more likely total was about 20,000.

Later Explorers In May 1768, Bougainville saw a tall pinnacle a long way off. It was Mere Lava, but before he could get there he saw Ambae and Maewo, and made for them instead.

Captain William Bligh sailed through the Banks in 1789 in his longboat while searching for the Portuguese island of Timor, in modern Indonesia. He had been cast adrift by his crew shortly before, following the famous mutiny on the *Bounty*. Bligh was the first navigator to log the Banks Islands' position accurately. He named the group after Joseph Banks, the botanist on Cook's 1774 expedition.

Recent Events The Banks group was one of the first areas in Vanuatu to be ravaged by blackbirders. Labour was recruited or kidnapped to work in New Caledonia, Fiji and Queensland. About 50% of the adult male population were taken overseas in the 1860s, which was the first decade of blackbirding. Many never returned.

The Anglican missionaries of the DOM tried hard to prevent such depredations, but without much success. Most Banks people took up the Anglican form of Christianity, but continued to practise it in tandem with their ancient traditions.

In the early 1920s, two islanders returned from Australia and claimed that they had been trained as Anglican priests. They prophesied another great flood, this time on Vanua Lava, and the imminent arrival of Americans to remove the British authorities and settlers. When neither prediction occurred, popular support for their movement waned.

Local Customs

Grade-taking is called *sukwe* in the Banks group. Though it still occurs on some islands, particularly Mota, its significance has declined considerably due to the influence of the DOM church.

Dances Banks Islands dancers are a regular attraction at Vila cultural shows. Their most popular dance is a humorous fertility rite from Mota, called the *ma*, or snake dance. This is performed by men striped with white paint, who hold a long, carved, decorated stick representing a snake. While they dance, the performers wear traditional boat or fish-shaped headdresses. A similarly dressed clown leaps about wearing a varied collection of nontraditional aids, such as diving glasses, or a mask and snorkel tube.

Another dance is the *mato*, in which everyone takes part – men, women and children. As on Malakula and other northern islands, when Banks people dance they often wear bunches of nuts around their ankles. By stamping vigorously with their feet they make a sharp rattling sound to accompany the drum beats.

Tattooing Until the end of the 19th century, European visitors to the Banks would find most women, and some men, tattooed all over their bodies with intricate designs. These showed either how far the person had progressed through their sukwe grades, or were representations of mythical heroes, particularly Qat. Tattooing disappeared with the spread of Christianity.

Handicrafts

Bark paintings are still produced in the Banks, traditionally by men. A strip of bark is outlined on a tree, then carefully peeled off and dried. The resulting board makes a hard surface for the artist to paint on. He usually chooses traditional subjects based around mythology or grade-taking rituals.

Other traditional handicrafts include the making of basketware, mats, bows and arrows, headdresses and pig-killing clubs. Small carved figurines called *tamates* represent spirits or mythical beings. These are also found in Vanikolo in the south-eastern Solomons, though tamates there are human-sized, devil-type characters.

Information

The provincial government office (☎ 38550) in Sola on Vanua Lava is the best place to ask about accommodation, speedboats, guides etc anywhere in the Banks group.

Medical Services

There are clinics at Lembot on Gaua, Lekwel on Mere Lava, Vureas Bay and Sola on Vanua Lava, Veverao on Mota, Ngerenigman on Mota Lava, and Lehali on Ureparapara.

Places to Stay

There are guest houses at Sola on Vanua Lava, and on Ra Island off the southern tip of Mota Lava Island.

Getting There & Away

Air There are airstrips at Sola on Vanua Lava, Lembot on Gaua and Ablow on Mota Lava. All are serviced by Vanair twice weekly from Luganville, with one flight calling in to the Torres group as well.

A one-way ticket from Luganville costs 6000VT to Gaua and 6900VT to both Sola

and Mota Lava. From Sola it's 2400VT to Mota Lava, 2900VT to Gaua and 5100VT to Linua in the Torres group.

Sea Several small trading vessels serve the area from Luganville. The best people to ask about this are at Dinh Shipping and the LCM Store, both in Luganville.

Yacht There are a number of good anchorages in the Banks group. These include Bushman's Bay, Losalava and Kaska Bay on Gaua, Port Patteson, Mosina and Vureas Bay on Vanua Lava, Mele Bay on Mota Lava, and the rather choppy and uneven Lorup Bay at Ureparapara.

Getting Around

There are only 30 km of public roads in the Banks group, with 14 of these being on Mota Lava – Gaua and Vanua Lava have eight km each. The only options for visiting most places are either by speedboats or walking.

As a guide to speedboat fares, the trip from Sola to Tasmate, on nearby Mota Island, is 4500VT each way, and to Var on Mota Lava is 6000VT. However, the seas are often too choppy for safe travel.

GAUA ISLAND

A rugged, forested island covering 330 sq km, Gaua is the second largest in the Banks group after Vanua Lava. Its highest point is 797-metre **Mt Garet**, whose peak rises 115 metres above the floor of a semiactive volcanic crater. Below the crater is seven-km-long, sulphur-tinted **Lake Letas**.

Gaua's north-eastern coast, where most of the total population of 1300 lives, is fringed by extensive coral gardens and has several white, sandy beaches. The southern and western coasts are only sparsely populated. The former is extremely rocky, with occasional beaches separated by dense bush. High cliffs fall straight into the sea on the rugged west coast.

History

Quiros estimated that there were up to as many as 200,000 people on Gaua in 1606, but only 15,000 remained by 1874. Large numbers were wiped out by a series of epidemics in the next 12 years. Finally, measles in 1928 and flu seven years later brought the population down to 700. It remained static until the late 1970s, when it slowly began to increase.

Following this drastic depopulation, a number of people from other, more crowded islands cast their eyes on its vast tracts of unused land. Polynesian canoeists from Futuna in the Tafea group landed on Gaua in the late 19th century. A few managed to

settle, but most were slaughtered by the Melanesian inhabitants. More recently the eastern part of the island has been settled, mainly from other islands in the Banks group.

Stone Relics Although most of inland Gaua is uninhabited, the evidence of more populous times is everywhere. Most obvious are long stretches of dry-stone walls, not to mention building foundations made of large rocks. It's said that stone foundations can even be seen in Lake Letas. Stone platforms

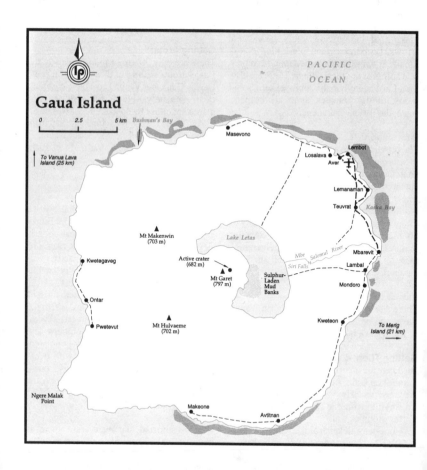

and obelisks litter the bush, while you'll often find stone bowls piled up at the bases of huge nabanga trees.

Stones about 1.5 metres high were occasionally carved, and these were treated as powerful gods. One of the island's more famous relics is that of a particularly large **monolith** about two metres across. Apart from its great size, the remarkable thing about it is the rich variety of petroglyphs that cover almost the entire surface. It's located in the south of the island, a three to four-hour walk from the airport.

Ancestor houses were once a special feature of Gaua. Dramatic carvings adorned

the
were
lar that
European a
such artefacts

Orientation & Infor
Most of Gaua's popu
Losalava, Aver, Teuvrat a
You should be able to hire a g
these places to take you up the st
trail to Lake Letas and Mt Garet.

Glen Russell, of Butterfly Tours in Lu
ville, is an excellent source of information o
Gaua. You can contact Glen through Espiritu

Gaua's Scenic Centre
Almost exactly in Gaua's centre, white smoke billows from a great rupture in the south-eastern flank of the Mt Garet volcano. Below the cleft, the mountain is stained by the orange-coloured sulphurous emissions that bubble out as thermal geysers and boiling mud.

Mt Garet erupted in mid-1965 and made loud rumbling noises in 1973, the latter causing a temporary evacuation of the whole island. It's considered the most dangerous volcano in Vanuatu as far as its potential for disaster is concerned. There is only a thin layer of rock between the magma chamber and the bottom of Lake Letas, so a major rupture could cause another Krakatoa.

Lake Letas
Sometimes called Lake Tes, this crescent-shaped mass of water is the largest freshwater lake in the South Pacific outside Papua New Guinea. It curves part way around Mt Garet, and the water on that side is stained by the orange-brown, sulphurous mud that continually oozes from the mountainside.

Beside the mountain Lake Letas is near to boiling point, but its ends are cooler and this is where you find eels and freshwater prawns. Villagers take their catches to the hotter parts and cook them in the simmering water.

Megapodes, or incubator birds, lay their eggs in the warm mud along the lake's western edge and leave them to hatch. The north-western end is a major duck-breeding site, with literally thousands of birds to be seen there during the breeding season.

Islanders often call Lake Letas 'Lake Reflection'. Somehow, ships and boats far offshore in the ocean are at times mirrored in the lake's still surface.

Siri Falls
This huge waterfall, which can be seen easily from the coast, is about two km from Lake Letas' eastern shore. The falls are fed by the lake's sulphur-tinged overflow and lie in a beautiful misty rainforest. Allow at least half a day to get there on the paths from Teuvrat and Lambal.

Trekking to the Lake & Volcano
It's a two-day return walk along the overgrown paths that lead up from Losalava and Lambal. Unfortunately, very steep terrain makes it difficult to visit Siri Falls from the Losalava track, but the one from Lambal allows you to see everything. Both routes are steep and strenuous.

Coming from Lambal, you arrive at Lake Letas just south of the overflow into the Mbe Salomul River, where there's good camping on the sandy shore. A dugout canoe is left here so your guide can paddle you across to the volcano – it'll take a maximum of five passengers and the return trip will cost 2500VT. It's a fairly easy climb from the lake up to the volcano. ■

entrances, while finely carved objects
...tored inside. These were so spectacu-
...they are said to have inspired
...ists such as Picasso. Sadly, all
...ave been sold to collectors.

...ation
...ation lives around
...nd Lemanaman.
...ide at any of
...ep, rugged

A road runs dow... ...
at Lembot to near the mouth of the Mos...
Salomul River at Mbarevit. The 14-km drive
costs 1500VT by taxi.

The island's best yacht anchorage is at
Losalava.

MERIG ISLAND

Formerly called St Claire, St Clarel or
'Gaua's Small Child', Merig is 21 km due
east of Gaua. About 50 people live in its
single village, **Levolvol**.

The island is only 800 metres across in any
direction, and 2.2 km around its perimeter.
You can easily walk round it in 40 minutes,
skirting its small central peak.

MERE LAVA ISLAND

Quiros sailed past this island in 1606 and
called it Nostra Señora de la Luz. Bougain-

...mpsing it from afar in 1768, instead
...it Star Peak. Meanwhile, islanders
...lled it Maralaba, Merlau and Mere-
...well as its current name of Mere Lava,
...means 'Big Child'.

...e Lava is only 4.5 km long and three
...ts widest point. The island is an extinct
...o which rises abruptly from the sea.
...ar-perfect central cone, **Mt Teu**, climbs
...y to a height of 883 metres.

...om the island's summit you can clearly
...Gaua 51.5 km away to the west, and
...wo 47 km due south. The main crater,
...d Durdurlav or 'Big Hole', contains a
...ller one named Durdurwirig or 'Small
...e'. Once on top you'll immediately
...ice the dangerously strong gusts of wind
...t occur whenever a cloud passes it. Make
...e you hang on tightly.

Many of the island's 800 people have built
their houses on stone platforms up the lower
sides of the island's central peak. Each
dwelling has several levels connected by
embankments and steps. As the water supply
is limited to a few springs, most households
have their own rainwater catchment tanks.

Despite the Anglican Church's considerable influence, most people on Mere Lava

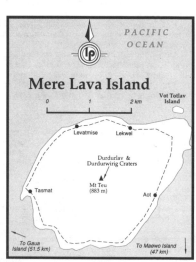

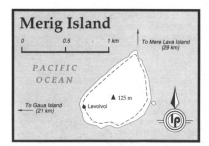

A: Copra drier (DO)
B: Hibiscus (DH)
C: Man from custom village, Tanna Island (MC)
D: Hibiscus (DH)
E: Typical village hut (DO)

A: Removing coconut from tree (AV)
B: Coconuts at Port Vila market (AV)
C: Basket weaving with pandanus (AV)
D: Woven items (AV)

still believe in spirits, claiming that certain places and practices are tabu. Medicine men are always called in when it's believed sickness has been caused by touching a tabu object or by going to a forbidden place.

VANUA LAVA ISLAND

Also called Varuka, Vanua Lava covers 331 sq km. The largest island in the Banks group by a mere one km, it's almost 28 km long by 19.5 km wide.

Vanua Lava's highest mountain is 946-metre **Mt Tola**, or Tow Lav. Only slightly

lower is the semiactive volcano **Mt Sere'ama**, or Suretimeat, which gives off clouds of steam that can be seen from Sola.

The island has several long stretches of beach. Vureas Bay in the south-western corner has black sand, while **Mosina** in the south-east has a white sandy shore. There are more beaches along the island's northern coast between the Pe Lav River outlet and Letelwut, and a long stretch of brownish sand at Port Patteson in the east.

One of Vanua Lava's most dramatic sights is **Waterfall Bay** on the west coast. Here, two

Vanua Lava Island

large, spectacular waterfalls, known collectively as **Sara Falls**, tumble over the cliffside straight into a large pool close by the sea.

People

Vanua Lava's population numbers about 1400, most of whom live along the south coast. A small number of recent arrivals from Mota Lava also live at Kwanglav, opposite their former home.

Fauna

Vanua Lava is one of the country's few islands where the Pacific boa is plentiful. Megapode birds breed in the warm sands of Port Patteson and up on Mt Sere'ama, while turtles lay their eggs in secluded spots along the east coast. Villagers regularly hunt the many wild pigs living on the sides of Mt Sere'ama.

Crocodiles More formidable are the now depleted saltwater crocodiles that live in the brown-coloured Selva, or Sulphur, River and its near neighbour, the dark-green Tahiti River. Once you could go crocodile hunting on Vanua Lava, but the 1972 cyclone devastated the population. Now only two remain. One is estimated to be six metres long, and the other two metres.

Islanders say the ancestors of these crocodiles were brought to Vanua Lava by Bishop Patteson in the 1860s. According to this tale he had two in a cage on his boat, but they escaped. Patteson then commanded them to refrain from eating humans, and so far they have obeyed his injunction – although there have been some close escapes. Instead, the crocs live on a diet of fish, wild pigs, bullocks and dogs.

A more scientific explanation for their presence is that they swam down from the Solomons after losing their bearings during a cyclone.

Sola

Sola is the administrative headquarters for the new Torba province. As such it has the government offices and a fishery base, as well as a trade store. It even has electricity, although for limited hours only.

The provincial government's self-catering *guest house* (provincial office ☎ 38550) has beds for 1000VT.

The nearby *restaurant* has a limited local menu, but it's cheap and sells kava in the evenings.

The following distances are from Sola.

Kerepua (1.5 km)

One km to Sola's east is a coconut grove full of bush crabs. Beyond it is the hillside site of the abandoned village of Kerepua. All that remains now is an assembly of large stones up a steep incline. This village was occupied in the early 1950s.

Mosina (4 km)

This friendly village – the island's largest – has a large, square next to the DOM church. It was relocated to its present spot after the original site was destroyed by a tidal wave. A beautiful **white sand beach** extends from Mosina back around the headland, past Kotonwul Island and three other small sandy islets, to a tiny island called **Leneu.**

Between Mosina and Mberiot is a large freshwater swamp where **Caledonian crabs** are caught. These creatures have nearly as much meat on them as coconut crabs, but have paddles instead of claws. Villagers use steel rods to pull them out of their mud holes.

Kwakea Island (6 km by boat)

Also called Qakea and Pakea, this small, lightly populated island was probably the earliest inhabited member of the Banks group. Artefacts found here are similar to material unearthed in Tikopia in the southeastern Solomons. In the early 1900s a canoe party from Tonga attempted to settle on Kwakea, but all were killed by Vanua Lavans and their Tikopian allies.

Kwakea is connected by a broad sandspit at low tide to its smaller unpopulated neighbour, **Nawila Island**. Both islets are surrounded by an extensive fringing coral reef, with the lagoon between the two being excellent for snorkelling.

Ravenga Island (10.5 km & 1 km by boat)
This low, sandy islet has a fringing reef on
its eastern side. Although inhabited on a
seasonal basis in the past, its only occupants
nowadays are sea birds.

Tikopians used to regularly sail to
Ravenga from their home island in the Solomons, 203 km to the north-east. Once there
they would trade items such as mats, betel
nuts, breadfruit, narli nuts, canoes, sennit
rope and tapa cloth with the peoples of Vanua
Lava and Mota Lava. As recently as 1891, an
Anglican missionary called Coddrington
reported seeing 11 large Tikopian trading
canoes at Port Patteson at the same time.

Mt Sere'ama (19 km)
Deep in the bush and 730 metres up on the
mountain's northern side, you'll find two
fumaroles regularly spurting steam. Nearby
are pools of boiling mud and two small lakes
whose water levels change from day to day.
Despite all this thermal activity, Mt
Sere'ama has not been genuinely threatening
since 1965 when it erupted in sympathy with
Mt Garet on Gaua.

On a clear day, when the fumaroles aren't
putting out too much steam, one or two
islands of the Solomons group can be seen
from the summit.

The ascent is hard going, climbing up
steep slopes and through dense vegetation,
so allow at least two days there and back. It's
wise to carry spare clothing and medical
supplies as you'll probably get torn about by
the forest. Ask at the provincial government
office in Sola about guides.

Getting Around
There are a number of simple ways of getting
around.

To/From the Airport Transport from Sola
meets each flight. The taxi ride in to the
government centre costs 400VT.

Around the Island The gravel road from the
airstrip, via Arep and Sola, continues over
the hills to Mosina. From there, the route

continues westwards as a footpath to
Kerembitia, and then to Vureas Bay. Another
track continues on to Wosaga. Another path
from the airstrip to Kwanglav, is the starting
point for the climb up Mt Sere'ama and the
canoe trip to Ravenga Island

MOTA ISLAND
Only 10.5 km from Vanua Lava, Mota is a
raised coral island with a central peak of 411
metres called **Mt Tawe**, and looks like a
high-crowned hat. The island is 4.5 km wide
and four km long. Its 550 people live in six
small, scattered, mainly coastal villages.

Mota has some short, narrow, white sand
beaches on its northern and western sides,
though they are fronted by dead coral at low
tide. There's some living coral on the island's
sheltered north-western corner.

In the late 19th century, Mota was the
main DOM centre where young ni-Vanuatu
from the northern islands were trained to be
missionaries. For a while, the Anglicans used
the local language as the lingua franca in
their teachings throughout the Solomons and
Vanuatu, as it was less complicated than
most other local tongues.

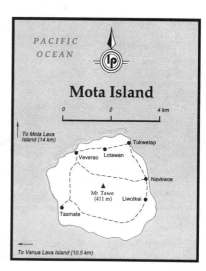

MOTA LAVA ISLAND

Sometimes also called Valua, Mota Lava measures 12 km long, is five km at its widest point, and covers 35 sq km.

It has two upland areas. The first is towards the eastern tip of the island and the other is in the narrow 'saddle' towards the western end.

There's a long stretch of white sand along the island's south-western shore. A sandbar connects Mota Lava with its tiny neighbour, Ra Island.

Most of the island's 1200 people live in the south-western corner or on Ra. In recent years there has been some migration to Vanua Lava, where more land is available.

Mota Lava is a strong centre for traditional activities, especially dancing. Despite their Christian beliefs, most islanders still invoke spirits.

Getting Around

A taxi meets each scheduled flight.

A footpath follows the north and west coastline, joining up with the main southern road at the airport. A round-island walk will take about seven hours.

RA ISLAND

Ra is a very scenic island covering just over one sq km. It has some huge rocks in the centre, the highest of which offer spectacular views. Down below there's an old 'devil cave', whose resident spirit was exorcised by an early missionary. Prior to that, anyone who entered the cave was doomed.

The idyllic *Harry Memorial Guest House* on Ra has seven attractive, traditional-style bungalows costing 900/1800VT for singles/doubles. It also has a bar and restaurant.

And who was Harry? He was the father-in-law of Father Luke Dini, owner of the guest house.

Getting There & Away

You can fly into Ablow and take a taxi for 1500VT to Ngerenigman, on the mainland opposite Ra. A dugout ride across to the guest house costs 100VT.

Alternatively, you can charter a speedboat from Sola to Ra for 6000VT one way.

THE REEF ISLANDS

Also called Rowa, the Reef Islands should not be confused with the small, highly pop-

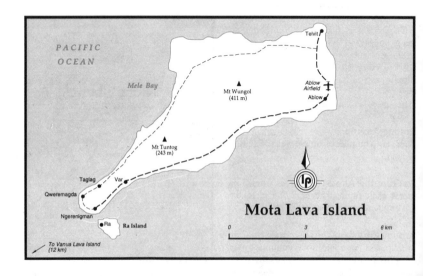

Mota Lava Island

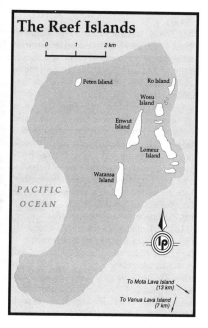

The Reef Islands

0   1   2 km

Peten Island   Ro Island

Wosu
Island

Enwut
Island

Lomeur
Island

Watansa
Island

PACIFIC
OCEAN

To Mota Lava Island
(13 km)

To Vanua Lava Island
(7 km)

William Bligh from his longboat in 1789. It's almost circular in shape and varies between seven and eight km in diameter.

Ureparapara is the top of an extinct volcano whose central crater was breached, letting the sea in to form a fine harbour about three km long. This is called **Lorup Bay**. To enter, you pass between the two immense headlands of **Ngeye Byo Point** and **Ngeye Vet Point**, both of which tower over 300 metres above the water. In front, 764-metre **Mt Tow Lap** dominates the scene. All in all Lorup Bay makes an awesome introduction to the island.

The people who live around the bay consider their home to be a paradise and, like the inhabitants of small remote islands elsewhere in Vanuatu, will be delighted to show you its attractions. A combination of heavy rainfall and fertile volcanic soil produces abundant fruit and vegetables. Even so, only about 300 people live on Ureparapara.

Yachts anchoring in Lorup Bay may find it to be an uncomfortable mooring, as strong ocean swells sometimes create surprising turbulence.

ulated archipelago of the same name in the south-eastern Solomons.

Vanuatu's Reefs group consists of 12 low-lying, coconut and scrub-covered islets with white sand beaches and dazzling coral. The two largest – **Lomeur** and **Enwut** – are just over one km long and barely 300 metres wide, while the six smallest are minute. These are the only true coral atolls in the country.

US forces blasted away part of the fringing reef in WW II for various military purposes. Since then, the central lagoon has attracted a large population of sharks and other pelagic fish. This makes the group an excellent game-fishing site and a popular destination for fishing trips from Vanua Lava and Mota Lava.

The islands are no longer populated due to the lack of drinking water.

UREPARAPARA ISLAND

This unusual landform was first sighted by

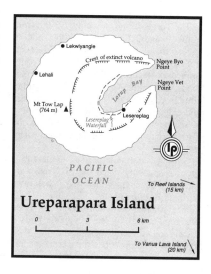

Lekwiyangle

Crest of extinct volcano

Ngeye Byo
Point

Lehali

Ngeye Vet
Point

Lorup Bay

Mt Tow Lap
(764 m) ▲

Lesereplag
Waterfall

Lesereplag

PACIFIC
OCEAN

To Reef Islands
(15 km)

Ureparapara Island

0   3   6 km

To Vanua Lava Island
(20 km)

VOT TANDE ISLAND

Vot Tande consists of two unpopulated, rocky islets which together cover a mere 700 sq metres. Their highest point is 64 metres above sea level.

Although it's 42 km north-east of Ureparapara, you can see Vot Tande from any high point there.

The Torres Islands

This small, isolated archipelago stretches for 42 km and has six main islands, four of which are populated. They are relatively low lying, with only five points exceeding 200 metres above sea level.

To the west of the Torres group, the extremely deep waters of the narrow Vanuatu Trench widen into the much broader Torres Trench. This huge ocean-floor chasm stretches from the Torres Islands northwards far into the Solomons.

The terrain in the Torres Islands is much less rugged than in the Banks, with the bush growing less thickly. Dazzling white sand beaches are the general rule.

The Torres Islands are only 173 km from Vanikolo and 215 km from Tikopia, both in the south-eastern Solomons. However, unlike Vanua Lava, this group had only limited contact with the Polynesian Tikopians. Even so, Torres Islanders display similar eastern-Pacific genetic, linguistic and cultural influences. Betel-nut chewing, a Solomons favourite, also occurs in the Torres group, the only part of Vanuatu where it does.

Surfing is particularly good in the Torres group, especially when the SE Trades are blowing. Islanders either make their own surfboards, or body-surf.

The islands, particularly Loh and Toga, are good places to see megapode birds – locally called 'scrub hens'. They lay their eggs 70 to 90 cm deep in the warm sand and leave them to incubate untended.

History

The Torres Islands are among Vanuatu's oldest, its highest hills having risen from the waves about 22 million years ago. Seven million years later there were more upheavals, causing the islands to expand to their present size.

The group gets its name from Luis Vaez de Torres, Quiros' second-in-command. However, there is no clear evidence to suggest that he actually saw these islands. Indeed, this group was among the last in the Pacific to be officially reported by European explorers. Captain Hunter possibly saw them from the freighter *Marshall Bennett* in 1835, though Captain Erskine in HMS *Havannah* was the first to record them in 1850.

Torres Islanders were never cannibals. This proved to be their disadvantage, as their more peaceful reputation meant it only took a decade for them to feel the scourge of relentless blackbirding, followed by devastating epidemics. By the 1880s, there were too few people left for recruiting ships to bother with.

As recently as the late 1930s, there were only about 150 people in the group. This number fell to a handful in 1942 following mass evacuations by the government, which was fearful of a Japanese invasion. Since then, the population has risen again to something approaching 450.

Medical Services

The Torres Islands' only clinic is at Lunaragi on Loh Island.

Places to Stay & Eat

There is a small, very basic provincial government *guest house* at the Linua airfield which costs 500VT per person.

Although fresh fruit, vegetables and seafood are plentiful, you should bring some extra supplies with you as stocks of canned and packaged foods are very limited. As elsewhere in remote areas, any gifts of tinned meat, fish, tobacco sticks or matches will always be greatly appreciated by your hosts.

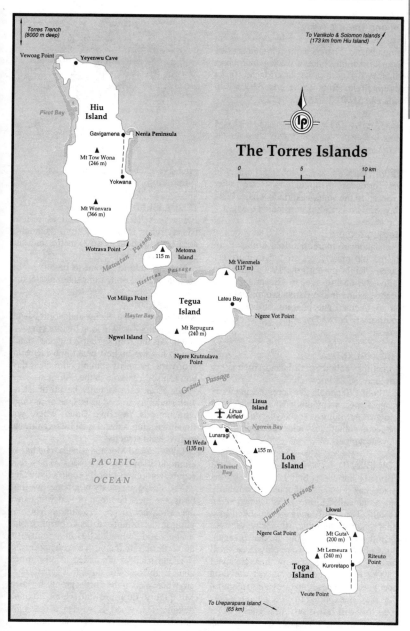

Torres Trench
(8000 m deep)

To Vanikolo & Solomon Islands
(173 km from Hiu Island)

Vewoag Point
Yeyenwu Cave

Hiu
Island

Picot Bay

Gavigamena
Nenia Peninsula

Mt Tow Wona
(246 m)

Yokwana

Mt Wonvara
(366 m)

The Torres Islands

0   5   10 km

Wotrava Point

Matwatan Passage

Metoma
Island
115 m

Hestreux Passage

Mt Vienmela
(117 m)

Vot Miliga Point

Tegua
Island

Lateu Bay

Hayter Bay

Ngere Vot Point

Ngwel Island

Mt Repugura
(240 m)

Ngere Krutnulava
Point

Grand Passage

Linua
Island

Linua
Airfield

Ngerein Bay

Lunaragi

Mt Weda
(135 m)

155 m

Loh
Island

PACIFIC

OCEAN

Tutumel
Bay

Dumanoir Passage

Likwal

Ngere Gat Point

Mt Guta
(200 m)

Mt Lemeura
(240 m)

Kuroretapo

Riteuto
Point

Toga
Island

Veute Point

To Ureparapara Island
(65 km)

Getting There & Away

Air The Torres group's only airfield is on Linua Island. There's a direct Vanair service from Luganville once a week which costs 10,300VT. If you're heading for the Banks group, flights from Linua cost 5100VT to Sola and 5500VT to Mota Lava.

Sea Check with Dinh Shipping and the LCM store in Luganville as they may have vessels in the area.

Yacht There are several good anchorages in the Torres group, though most are rather exposed to the south-east trade winds. Picot Bay, off Hiu Island, is considered the best.

Getting Around

No islands are more than four km apart, so the people mainly get around in outrigger canoes. Right up until the 1950s, islanders sailed the 65 km over to Ureparapara, the nearest island in the Banks group, and then on to Vanua Lava, 20 km further to the south-east. Nowadays they prefer speed-boats.

TOGA ISLAND

Sometimes called South Island, Toga is six km long by 4.5 km wide.

About 170 people live here, making it the group's most populous island. Local boys and girls as young as seven years old smoke tobacco, sometimes using a coconut-crab claw as a pipe.

LOH ISLAND

Formerly known as Salt Island or Lo, this island has a small, unpopulated, northerly neighbour called **Linua**, on which there is an airfield. The two islands are separated by a tidal sandbank less than 100 metres across.

In the 1950s, following the mass evacuations of WW II, there were only three small families living on Loh. Now there are about 130 residents who dine almost daily on coconut crab. These creatures are so plentiful that they're exported to Vila, although how long this will last is anyone's guess. Other seafood is also abundant, and there's an

Coconut crab

extensive and beautiful coral garden to view at **Lunaragi**.

TEGUA ISLAND

Formerly called Tuga as well as Middle Island, Tegua is separated from its smaller northern neighbour by a 600-metre, sand and coral-lined channel.

Metoma Island is said to be alive with coconut crabs despite rampant exploitation.

HIU ISLAND

Also known as Seu, Sieuw and North Island, Hiu measures 14.5 km long by five km wide and thus is the Torres group's biggest island. It also has the highest peak: 366-metre **Mt Wonvara**. From its summit on a clear day, you can see Vanikolo in the Solomons.

Hiu is an exceptionally beautiful island with smoothly shaped hills. One of its other attractions is **Yeyenwu Cave**, where you find interesting stalactites and stalagmites as well as hand stencils.

Like Loh and Metoma islands, Hiu has an abundance of coconut crabs. They're a regular part of most local people's daily diet.

You'll also see plenty of ground-dwelling birds, the most common of which is called the swamp hen, or purple gallinole. You may glimpse the bright-red beak, purplish-blue feathers and yellow feet as they scuttle off the footpath into the bush as you approach.

Island teak, as it's called locally, grows abundantly on Hiu, though it's not found anywhere else in the Torres group. It's ideal for quality furniture and is an artisan's delight. The wood is so dense that nails buckle when you try to hammer them in.

Glossary

Anglophone – English-speaking. Refers to ni-Vanuatu educated in English-language schools. Prior to independence, this term included islanders who preferred British culture to that of France.

Atoll – low-lying island built up from successive deposits of coral. The classic atoll is circular, enclosing a shallow lagoon. Atolls sit on submarine volcanic peaks, and the surrounding ocean is by definition deep.

Banyan – also called a *nabanga*. Tree of the fig genus, which can grow to immense size. Aerial roots reach down from the branches into the soil to become new trunks. The tree's maximum height is 30 metres, but its girth can increase throughout its lifetime.

Betel Nut – round, greenish-orange nut which is commonly chewed throughout South-East Asia and parts of northern Oceania as far south as the Solomon Islands. Most ni-Vanuatu prefer kava for its effect, except for a number of Torres Islanders who also have a taste for this nut.

Bigman – common Melanesian expression for chief.

Booby – gull-sized seabird with a brown or blackish body and white head. It usually lives in large colonies on tall, sea-girthed rocks.

Breadfruit – large, starchy fruit with a coarse green skin. It can be boiled or mashed, or fried like chips. Although a popular dish in Polynesian areas, the elegant breadfruit tree is uncommon in Vanuatu. The tree's sap is used as a traditional medicine: wrapped as an emollient over a sprain or bruise, the swelling quickly subsides.

Bush Knife – Pacific version of a machete or panga.

Caldera – a large crater formed by the explosion or subsidence of a volcano.

Cargo Cults – religious movements whose followers hope for the imminent and magical delivery of vast quantities of modern wealth (cargo), through the generosity of supernatural forces or the inhabitants of faraway countries, particularly the USA.

Cassava – edible, starch-yielding root of the tapioca plant. A popular food, but before it is eaten, poison in the root must be leached out by cooking.

Cay – a coral island on a shallow continental shelf.

CCNH – Compagnie Calédonienne des Nouvelles-Hébrides; French-owned company which acquired large tracts of land in Vanuatu in the late 19th century. On liquidation, the CCNH's activities were taken over by the SFNH.

Cicatrices – pattern on the human body caused by the deliberate practice of regularly raising sections of skin. Occurs in some parts of Vanuatu, as well as in Africa and Australia, as a particular style of tattooing.

Copra – dried coconut meat which is processed to make oil for margarine and soap.

Croton – decorative plant whose leaves are frequently used in traditional ceremonies. Crotons are often planted beside a house, as the plant's delicate perfume drives insects away.

Custom Ownership – traditionally acknowledged ownership of a piece of land, objects, or even stretches of reef. Such items can be owned by individuals, families, clans or tribes. Custom owners may refuse access to their property, and expect to be asked permission before anyone crosses their land or uses anything considered by tradition to be theirs.

DOM – Diocese of Melanesia; branch of the worldwide Anglican Church.

Expats – short for 'expatriates'. Often used as an alternative for 'European' to describe White foreigners who are resident in Vanuatu.

Francophone – French-speaking. Refers to ni-Vanuatu educated in French-language schools. Prior to independence, this term also included islanders who favoured French culture and language in Vanuatu. They initially opposed independence as they believed this was likely to produce an Anglophone supremacy, which in fact occurred.

Fumaroles – small volcanic or thermal fissures in the ground from which columns of steam, smoke or gas arise, or where naturally heated water bubbles up. Some gases emitted by fumaroles can be sulphurous and may cause choking.

Granadilla – passionfruit with a yellowish outer coating.

Groper – large, robust fish which can weigh more than 250 kg and grow up to 3.5 metres in length. It can be dangerous, and has attacked divers. It's mostly pelagic, but at times lives around coral caves and coastal inlets. Gropers, also called 'groupers', vary in colour with age. Adults are usually brown with yellowish fins, and young fish are yellow to golden with broad, brownish bands across their bodies.

Kumara – also known as sweet potato, this root vegetable is a favourite of people living in Pacific highlands. It's not clear when or how it was introduced to these areas from South America, but it is believed to have reached Melanesia, including Vanuatu, at least 400 years ago (ie before the first Europeans).

Laplap – Vanuatu's national dish, consisting of tightly wrapped packages of doughy mix filled with meat or fish, cooked in a ground oven.

Larfwood – very strong timber, sometimes called 'ironwood', particularly favoured in Vanuatu for making tamtams.

Leeside – side of a building, hill or island which points away from the prevailing wind.

Lycée – French-language secondary or high school.

Mal mal – a T-piece (see following defini-

tion) of cotton on tapa cloth worn by male dancers.

Manioc – another name for cassava.

Modérés – or 'Moderates'. Collection of small, Francophone political parties which grouped together in pre-independence Vanuatu to resist the Anglophone Vanua'aku Party. Called 'moderates' by French speakers because they were initially opposed to national independence.

Nabanga – pronounced 'nam-banga'; traditional ni-Vanuatu name for banyan tree (see Banyan).

Nagria – indigenous plant which characteristically stands up proudly and erectly. Traditionally associated with honour and masculinity.

Nakamal – clubhouse where men meet at the end of the day to talk and drink kava. May be a building, an open hut or simply a shelter beneath a large tree. Usually strictly tabu for women.

Namale – indigenous plant associated with femininity, which islanders use to proclaim ownership and territory. The namale bush is often called *tambutri* or 'sacred tree'.

Nambas – penis-wrappers or sheaths, worn by most traditionally minded ni-Vanuatu males during ceremonies. Some men from very custom-oriented villages wear them all the time. Nambas are made from dried pandanus or banana leaves and are red, purple or green depending on the vegetable dye used.

Natsaro – also called *nasara*. Traditional dancing ground, usually surrounded by bush, which has been cleared specifically to provide a place where ceremonies can be held. Some are no more than a plain circle, while others are surrounded by tamtams or tall stone obelisks.

Nimangki – status and power earned by taking a series of grades. Prestige flows to those aspirants who have publicly given away their wealth, and in the process, built a series of spectacular ceremonies which are always accompanied by traditional dancing and feasting.

Ni-Vanuatu – indigenous people of Vanuatu.

Pandanus – sometimes called 'screw pine' because of the coiled shape of its slender stems, the palm-like pandanus grows mainly in marshy ground. Its saw-edged leaves are used for a number of purposes including being woven into very strong floor mats.

Pareu – also spelt *pareo* and known in Bislama as a *parpar*; a length of material worn by men like a sarong. In some parts of the Pacific it is called a *sulu* or a *lava-lava*.

Pawpaw – also known in some parts of the Pacific as *papaya*, this fruit grows on a slender three to four-metre tree. A staple, sweet-tasting food in many parts of Oceania, it is called *meresinfrut*, or 'medicine fruit', by some ni-Vanuatu.

Pedalo – paddle-operated, two-person pleasure boat.

Pomelo – also called *pamplemousse*. Large, dry-tasting, sweet grapefruit which has a pink interior.

Quonset Hut – US WW II military shelter made of corrugated steel sheeting and with a rounded cross section. Some are still in everyday use, especially in Luganville.

Sago Palm – three to four-metre, palm-like tree which is topped with stiff, glossy fronds. Its slender trunk and leaves are often used as house-building materials, while sago (a starchy cereal) is extracted from the roots. During periods of drought, villagers drain starch from the stem and eat this as survival food.

SDA – Seventh-Day Adventist.

SFNH – Société Française des Nouvelles-Hébrides; a large, French-owned commercial organisation, established in the late 19th century out of the defunct CCNH.

South Pacific Forum – association of small, independent Pacific Island countries, plus Australia and New Zealand, which meets annually to discuss common regional matters.

Stockmen – Oceanic term for cowboys and other horse-riding workers in the cattle industry.

Tapa – cloth made from the bark of ebony, paper mulberry or breadfruit trees. Though mainly made and worn by Polynesians to denote high status, it's also used by a few Melanesian groups on ceremonial occasions. The bark is peeled off the trees, then beaten with wooden or stone mallets until white. Once it has dried in the sun, it's often decorated with various traditional, usually geometric, designs.

Taro – called *dalo* in Fiji and Papua New Guinea, this root crop is eaten as a staple food all over the Pacific. It can be boiled, crushed, roasted, baked, steamed or chopped up and fried like chips. Taro grows best in moist areas, though it can also be grown in upland terrain if rainfall is sufficient. Taro's large green leaves, often called 'elephant's-ears', taste like spinach. The leaves are not edible until they have been cooked.

T-piece – small piece of cloth which covers the groin area only, leaving the abdomen exposed (see Mal mal).

Trepang – another name for *bêche-de-mer* or sea cucumber. Lethargic, bottom-dwelling sea creature that can merge into the sand, taking the shape of a rock, yet out of the water it looks like a burnt black brick. Trepang is highly prized by Chinese chefs because it adds texture to Oriental cooking.

USP – University of the South Pacific. Its main campus is in Suva, Fiji, though there are annexes elsewhere, including in Vila.

Yam – starchy tuber; staple Melanesian food. Yams can range in length from 20 cm to over a metre, and weigh up to 45 kg. The texture can vary from tender to crisp, depending on the species. Yam plants have deep roots. Often the only proof of their subterranean presence is a mass of long, unruly, greenish vines growing freely over a thin triangular structure of two-metre garden stakes.

Index

LONELY PLANET PHRASEBOOKS

Nepali phrasebook

Ethiopian Amharic phrasebook

Latin American Spanish phrasebook

Ukrainian phrasebook

Greek phrasebook

Vietnamese phrasebook

Building bridges,
Breaking barriers,
Beyond babble-on

Listen for the gems

Speak your own words

Ask your own questions

Master of your own image

- handy pocket-sized books
- easy to understand Pronunciation chapter
- clear and comprehensive Grammar chapter
- romanisation alongside script to allow ease of pronunciation
- script throughout so users can point to phrases
- extensive vocabulary sections, words and phrases for every situation
- full of cultural information and tips for the traveller

'...vital for a real DIY spirit and attitude in language learning' – Backpacker

'the phrasebooks have good cultural backgrounders and offer solid advice for challenging situations in remote locations' – San Francisco Examiner

'...they are unbeatable for their coverage of the world's more obscure languages' – The Geographical Magazine

---

Arabic (Egyptian)
Arabic (Moroccan)
Australia
  Australian English, Aboriginal and Torres Strait languages
Baltic States
  Estonian, Latvian, Lithuanian
Bengali
Brazilian
Burmese
Cantonese
Central Asia
Central Europe
  Czech, French, German, Hungarian, Italian and Slovak
Eastern Europe
  Bulgarian, Czech, Hungarian, Polish, Romanian and Slovak
Ethiopian (Amharic)
Fijian
French
German
Greek

Hindi/Urdu
Indonesian
Italian
Japanese
Korean
Lao
Latin American Spanish
Malay
Mandarin
Mediterranean Europe
  Albanian, Croatian, Greek, Italian, Macedonian, Maltese, Serbian and Slovene
Mongolian
Nepali
Papua New Guinea
Pilipino (Tagalog)
Quechua
Russian
Scandinavian Europe
  Danish, Finnish, Icelandic, Norwegian and Swedish

South-East Asia
  Burmese, Indonesian, Khmer, Lao, Malay, Tagalog (Pilipino), Thai and Vietnamese
Spanish (Castilian)
  Basque, Catalan and Galician
Sri Lanka
Swahili
Thai
Thai Hill Tribes
Tibetan
Turkish
Ukrainian
USA
  US English, Vernacular, Native American languages and Hawaiian
Vietnamese
Western Europe
  Basque, Catalan, Dutch, French, German, Irish, Italian, Portuguese, Scottish Gaelic, Spanish (Castilian) and Welsh

LONELY PLANET JOURNEYS

JOURNEYS is a unique collection of travel writing – published by the company that understands travel better than anyone else. It is a series for anyone who has ever experienced – or dreamed of – the magical moment when they encountered a strange culture or saw a place for the first time. They are tales to read while you're planning a trip, while you're on the road or while you're in an armchair, in front of a fire.

JOURNEYS books catch the spirit of a place, illuminate a culture, recount a crazy adventure, or introduce a fascinating way of life. They always entertain, and always enrich the experience of travel.

ISLANDS IN THE CLOUDS
Travels in the Highlands of New Guinea
Isabella Tree

Isabella Tree's remarkable journey takes us to the heart of the remote and beautiful Highlands of Papua New Guinea and Irian Jaya – one of the most extraordinary and dangerous regions on earth. Funny and tragic by turns, *Islands in the Clouds* is her moving story of the Highland people and the changes transforming their world.

Isabella Tree, who lives in England, has worked as a freelance journalist on a variety of newspapers and magazines, including a stint as senior travel correspondent for the *Evening Standard*. A fellow of the Royal Geographical Society, she has also written a biography of the Victorian ornithologist John Gould.

'One of the most accomplished travel writers to appear on the horizon for many years . . . the dialogue is brilliant' – Eric Newby

---

SEAN & DAVID'S LONG DRIVE
Sean Condon

Sean Condon is young, urban and a connoisseur of hair wax. He can't drive, and he doesn't really travel well. So when Sean and his friend David set out to explore Australia in a 1966 Ford Falcon, the result is a decidedly offbeat look at life on the road. Over 14,000 death-defying kilometres, our heroes check out the re-runs on tv, get fabulously drunk, listen to Neil Young cassettes and wonder why they ever left home.

Sean Condon lives in Melbourne. He played drums in several mediocre bands until he found his way into advertising and an above-average band called Boilersuit. *Sean & David's Long Drive* is his first book.

'Funny, pithy, kitsch and surreal . . . This book will do for Australia what Chernobyl did for Kiev, but hey you'll laugh as the stereotypes go boom'
– Time Out

LONELY PLANET TRAVEL ATLASES

Lonely Planet has long been famous for the number and quality of its guidebook maps. Now we've gone one step further and in conjunction with Steinhart Katzir Publishers produced a handy companion series: Lonely Planet travel atlases – maps of a country produced in book form.

Unlike other maps, which look good but lead travellers astray, our travel atlases have been researched on the road by Lonely Planet's experienced team of writers. All details are carefully checked to ensure the atlas corresponds with the equivalent Lonely Planet guidebook.

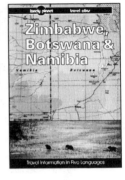

The handy atlas format means no holes, wrinkles, torn sections or constant folding and unfolding. These atlases can survive long periods on the road, unlike cumbersome fold-out maps. The comprehensive index ensures easy reference.

- full-colour throughout
- maps researched and checked by Lonely Planet authors
- place names correspond with Lonely Planet guidebooks
  – no confusing spelling differences
- legend and travelling information in English, French, German, Japanese and Spanish
- size: 230 x 160 mm

Available now:
Chile & Easter Island • Egypt • India & Bangladesh • Israel & the Palestinian Territories •Jordan, Syria & Lebanon • Kenya • Laos • Portugal • South Africa, Lesotho & Swaziland • Thailand • Turkey • Vietnam • Zimbabwe, Botswana & Namibia

---

LONELY PLANET TV SERIES & VIDEOS

Lonely Planet travel guides have been brought to life on television screens around the world. Like our guides, the programmes are based on the joy of independent travel, and look honestly at some of the most exciting, picturesque and frustrating places in the world. Each show is presented by one of three travellers from Australia, England or the USA and combines an innovative mixture of video, Super-8 film, atmospheric soundscapes and original music.

Videos of each episode – containing additional footage not shown on television – are available from good book and video shops, but the availability of individual videos varies with regional screening schedules.

Video destinations include: Alaska • American Rockies • Australia – The South-East • Baja California & the Copper Canyon • Brazil • Central Asia • Chile & Easter Island • Corsica, Sicily & Sardinia – The Mediterranean Islands • East Africa (Tanzania & Zanzibar) • Ecuador & the Galapagos Islands • Greenland & Iceland • Indonesia • Israel & the Sinai Desert • Jamaica • Japan • La Ruta Maya • Morocco • New York • North India • Pacific Islands (Fiji, Solomon Islands & Vanuatu) • South India • South West China • Turkey • Vietnam • West Africa • Zimbabwe, Botswana & Namibia

The Lonely Planet TV series is produced by:
Pilot Productions
The Old Studio
18 Middle Row
London W10 5AT UK

For video availability and ordering information contact your nearest Lonely Planet office.

Music from the TV series is available on CD & cassette.

PLANET TALK

Lonely Planet's FREE quarterly newsletter

We love hearing from you and think you'd like to hear from us.

When...is the right time to see reindeer in Finland?
Where...can you hear the best palm-wine music in Ghana?
How...do you get from Asunción to Areguá by steam train?
What...is the best way to see India?

For the answer to these and many other questions read PLANET TALK.

Every issue is packed with up-to-date travel news and advice including:

* a letter from Lonely Planet co-founders Tony and Maureen Wheeler
* go behind the scenes on the road with a Lonely Planet author
* feature article on an important and topical travel issue
* a selection of recent letters from travellers
* details on forthcoming Lonely Planet promotions
* complete list of Lonely Planet products

To join our mailing list contact any Lonely Planet office.

Also available: Lonely Planet T-shirts. 100% heavyweight cotton.

LONELY PLANET ONLINE

Get the latest travel information before you leave or while you're on the road

Whether you've just begun planning your next trip, or you're chasing down specific info on currency regulations or visa requirements, check out Lonely Planet Online for up-to-the minute travel information.

As well as travel profiles of your favourite destinations (including maps and photos), you'll find current reports from our researchers and other travellers, updates on health and visas, travel advisories, and discussion of the ecological and political issues you need to be aware of as you travel.

There's also an online travellers' forum where you can share your experience of life on the road, meet travel companions and ask other travellers for their recommendations and advice. We also have plenty of links to other online sites useful to independent travellers.

And of course we have a complete and up-to-date list of all Lonely Planet travel products including guides, phrasebooks, atlases, Journeys and videos and a simple online ordering facility if you can't find the book you want elsewhere.

www.lonelyplanet.com
or
AOL keyword: lp

LONELY PLANET PRODUCTS

Lonely Planet is known worldwide for publishing practical, reliable and no-nonsense travel information in our guides and on our web site. The Lonely Planet list covers just about every accessible part of the world. Currently there are nine series: travel guides, shoestring guides, walking guides, city guides, phrasebooks, audio packs, travel atlases, Journeys – a unique collection of travel writing and Pisces Books - diving and snorkeling guides.

EUROPE

Amsterdam • Austria • Baltic States phrasebook • Britain • Central Europe on a shoestring • Central Europe phrasebook • Czech & Slovak Republics • Denmark • Dublin • Eastern Europe on a shoestring • Eastern Europe phrasebook • Estonia, Latvia & Lithuania • Finland • France • French phrasebook • Germany • German phrasebook • Greece • Greek phrasebook • Hungary • Iceland, Greenland & the Faroe Islands • Ireland • Italian phrasebook • Italy • Lisbon • London • Mediterranean Europe on a shoestring • Mediterranean Europe phrasebook • Paris • Poland • Portugal • Portugal travel atlas • Prague • Romania & Moldova • Russia, Ukraine & Belarus • Russian phrasebook • Scandinavian & Baltic Europe on a shoestring • Scandinavian Europe phrasebook • Slovenia • Spain • Spanish phrasebook • St Petersburg • Switzerland • Trekking in Spain • Ukrainian phrasebook • Vienna • Walking in Britain • Walking in Switzerland • Western Europe on a shoestring • Western Europe phrasebook

Travel Literature: The Olive Grove: Travels in Greece

NORTH AMERICA

Alaska • Backpacking in Alaska • Baja California • California & Nevada • Canada • Chicago • Deep South• Florida • Hawaii • Honolulu • Los Angeles • Mexico • Mexico City • Miami • New England • New Orleans • New York City • New York, New Jersey & Pennsylvania • Pacific Northwest USA • Rocky Mountain States • San Francisco • Southwest USA • USA phrasebook • Washington, DC & the Capital Region

Travel Literature: Drive thru America

CENTRAL AMERICA & THE CARIBBEAN

• Bahamas and Turks & Caicos • Bermuda • Central America on a shoestring • Costa Rica • Cuba •Eastern Caribbean •Guatemala, Belize & Yucatán: La Ruta Maya • Jamaica

SOUTH AMERICA

Argentina, Uruguay & Paraguay • Bolivia • Brazil • Brazilian phrasebook • Buenos Aires • Chile & Easter Island • Chile & Easter Island travel atlas • Colombia Ecuador & the Galápagos Islands • Latin American Spanish phrasebook • Peru • Quechua phrasebook • Rio de Janeiro • South America on a shoestring • Trekking in the Patagonian Andes • Venezuela

Travel Literature: Full Circle: A South American Journey

ISLANDS OF THE INDIAN OCEAN

Madagascar & Comoros • Maldives• Mauritius, Réunion & Seychelles

AFRICA

Africa - the South • Africa on a shoestring • Arabic (Moroccan) phrasebook • Cairo • Cape Town • Central Africa • East Africa • Egypt • Egypt travel atlas• Ethiopian (Amharic) phrasebook • Kenya • Kenya travel atlas • Malawi, Mozambique & Zambia • Morocco • North Africa • South Africa, Lesotho & Swaziland • South Africa, Lesotho & Swaziland travel atlas • Swahili phrasebook • Tunisia Trekking in East Africa • West Africa • Zimbabwe, Botswana & Namibia • Zimbabwe, Botswana & Namibia travel atlas

Travel Literature: The Rainbird: A Central African Journey • Songs to an African Sunset: A Zimbabwean Story

MAIL ORDER

Lonely Planet products are distributed worldwide. They are also available by mail order from Lonely Planet, so if you have difficulty finding a title please write to us. North American and South American residents should write to Embarcadero West, 155 Filbert St, Suite 251, Oakland CA 94607, USA; European and African residents should write to 10a Spring Place, London NW5 3BH; and residents of other countries to PO Box 617, Hawthorn, Victoria 3122, Australia.

NORTH-EAST ASIA

Beijing • Cantonese phrasebook • China • Hong Kong • Hong Kong, Macau & Guangzhou • Japan • Japanese phrasebook • Japanese audio pack • Korea • Korean phrasebook • Mandarin phrasebook • Mongolia • Mongolian phrasebook • North-East Asia on a shoestring • Seoul • Taiwan • Tibet • Tibet phrasebook • Tokyo

Travel Literature: Lost Japan

MIDDLE EAST & CENTRAL ASIA

Arab Gulf States • Arabic (Egyptian) phrasebook • Central Asia • Central Asia phrasebook • Iran • Israel & the Palestinian Territories • Israel & the Palestinian Territories travel atlas • Istanbul • Jerusalem • Jordan & Syria • Jordan, Syria & Lebanon travel atlas • Lebanon • Middle East • Turkey • Turkish phrasebook • Turkey travel atlas • Yemen

Travel Literature: The Gates of Damascus • Kingdom of the Film Stars: Journey into Jordan

ALSO AVAILABLE:

Brief Encounters • Travel with Children • Traveller's Tales

INDIAN SUBCONTINENT

Bangladesh • Bengali phrasebook • Delhi • Goa • Hindi/Urdu phrasebook • India • India & Bangladesh travel atlas • Indian Himalaya • Karakoram Highway • Nepal • Nepali phrasebook • Pakistan • Rajasthan • Sri Lanka • Sri Lanka phrasebook • Trekking in the Indian Himalaya • Trekking in the Karakoram & Hindukush • Trekking in the Nepal Himalaya

Travel Literature: In Rajasthan • Shopping for Buddhas

SOUTH-EAST ASIA

Bali & Lombok • Bangkok • Burmese phrasebook • Cambodia • Ho Chi Minh City • Indonesia • Indonesian phrasebook • Indonesian audio pack • Jakarta • Java • Laos • Lao phrasebook • Laos travel atlas • Malay phrasebook • Malaysia, Singapore & Brunei • Myanmar (Burma) • Philippines • Pilipino phrasebook • Singapore • South-East Asia on a shoestring • South-East Asia phrasebook • Thailand • Thailand's Islands & Beaches • Thailand travel atlas • Thai phrasebook • Thai audio pack • Thai Hill Tribes phrasebook • Vietnam • Vietnamese phrasebook • Vietnam travel atlas

AUSTRALIA & THE PACIFIC

Australia • Australian phrasebook • Bushwalking in Australia • Bushwalking in Papua New Guinea • Fiji • Fijian phrasebook • Islands of Australia's Great Barrier Reef • Melbourne • Micronesia • New Caledonia • New South Wales • New Zealand • Northern Territory • Outback Australia • Papua New Guinea • Papua New Guinea phrasebook • Queensland • Rarotonga & the Cook Islands • Samoa • Solomon Islands • South Australia • Sydney • Tahiti & French Polynesia • Tasmania • Tonga • Tramping in New Zealand • Vanuatu • Victoria • Western Australia

Travel Literature: Islands in the Clouds • Sean & David's Long Drive

ANTARCTICA

Antarctica

THE LONELY PLANET STORY

Lonely Planet published its first book in 1973 in response to the numerous 'How did you do it?' questions Maureen and Tony Wheeler were asked after driving, bussing, hitching, sailing and railing their way from England to Australia.

Written at a kitchen table and hand collated, trimmed and stapled, *Across Asia on the Cheap* became an instant local bestseller, inspiring thoughts of another book.

Eighteen months in South-East Asia resulted in their second guide, *South-East Asia on a shoestring*, which they put together in a backstreet Chinese hotel in Singapore in 1975. The 'yellow bible', as it quickly became known to backpackers around the world, soon became *the* guide to the region. It has sold well over half a million copies and is now in its 9th edition, still retaining its familiar yellow cover.

Today there are over 240 titles, including travel guides, walking guides, language kits & phrasebooks, travel atlases and travel literature. The company is the largest independent travel publisher in the world. Although Lonely Planet initially specialised in guides to Asia, today there are few corners of the globe that have not been covered.

The emphasis continues to be on travel for independent travellers. Tony and Maureen still travel for several months of each year and play an active part in the writing, updating and quality control of Lonely Planet's guides.

They have been joined by over 70 authors and 170 staff at our offices in Melbourne (Australia), Oakland (USA), London (UK) and Paris (France). Travellers themselves also make a valuable contribution to the guides through the feedback we receive in thousands of letters each year and on our web site.

The people at Lonely Planet strongly believe that travellers can make a positive contribution to the countries they visit, both through their appreciation of the countries' culture, wildlife and natural features, and through the money they spend. In addition, the company makes a direct contribution to the countries and regions it covers. Since 1986 a percentage of the income from each book has been donated to ventures such as famine relief in Africa; aid projects in India; agricultural projects in Central America; Greenpeace's efforts to halt French nuclear testing in the Pacific; and Amnesty International.

'I hope we send people out with the right attitude about travel. You realise when you travel that there are so many different perspectives about the world, so we hope these books will make people more interested in what they see. Guidebooks can't really guide people. All you can do is point them in the right direction.'

– Tony Wheeler

LONELY PLANET PUBLICATIONS

Australia
PO Box 617, Hawthorn 3122, Victoria
tel: (03) 9819 1877 fax: (03) 9819 6459
e-mail: talk2us@lonelyplanet.com.au

USA
Embarcadero West, 155 Filbert St, Suite 251,
Oakland, CA 94607
tel: (510) 893 8555 TOLL FREE: 800 275-8555
fax: (510) 893 8563
e-mail: info@lonelyplanet.com

UK
10a Spring Place,
London NW5 3BH
tel: (0171) 428 4800 fax: (0171) 428 4828
e-mail: go@lonelyplanet.co.uk

France:
71 bis rue du Cardinal Lemoine, 75005 Paris
tel: 01 44 32 06 20 fax: 01 46 34 72 55
e-mail: bip@lonelyplanet.fr

World Wide Web: http://www.lonelyplanet.com
or *AOL keyword: lp*